WOMAN SUFFRAGE IN AUSTRALIA

Studies in Australian History

Series editors:
Alan Gilbert, Patricia Grimshaw and Peter Spearritt

Steven Nicholas (ed.), *Convict workers*
Pamela Statham (ed.), *The origins of Australia's capital cities*
Jeffrey Grey, *A military history of Australia*
Alastair Davidson, *The invisible state*
James A. Gillespie, *The price of health*
David Neal, *The rule of law in a penal colony*
Sharon Morgan, *Land settlement in early Tasmania*
Paula-Jane Byrne, *Criminal law and colonial subject*

WOMAN SUFFRAGE IN AUSTRALIA

A GIFT OR A STRUGGLE?

Audrey Oldfield

Published by the Press Syndicate of the University of Cambridge
The Pitt Building, Trumpington Street, Cambridge CB2 1RP, UK
40 West 20th Street, New York, NY 10011-4211, USA
10 Stamford Road, Oakleigh, Melbourne, Victoria 3166, Australia

© Audrey Oldfield 1992
First published 1992

Printed in Hong Kong by Colorcraft

National Library of Australia cataloguing in publication data
Oldfield, Audrey, 1925- .
Woman suffrage in Australia: a gift or a struggle?
Bibliography.
Includes index.
ISBN 0 521 40380 4. ISBN 0 521 43611 7 (pbk).
1. Women – Suffrage – Australia – History. I. Title. (Series: Studies in Australian history) (Cambridge, England).
324.6230994

Library of Congress cataloguing in publication data
Oldfield, Audrey.
Woman suffrage in Australia: a gift or a struggle? Audrey Oldfield.
– (Studies in Australian history)
Includes bibliographial references and index.
ISBN 0 521 40380 4. ISBN 0 521 43611 7 (pbk).
1. Women–suffrage–Australia–History. I. Title. II Series.
JQ089.043 1992
324.6′23′0994–dc20   91-37328
                                                                  CIP
A catalogue record for this book is available from the British Library.

ISBN 0 521 40380 4 hardback
ISBN 0 521 43611 7 paperback

*For Katherine, Elizabeth, Joel, Mitchell and Amy.
A generation which will learn that their mothers, as well
as their fathers, made Australian history.*

'Power is the ballot, the symbol of freedom and equality, without which no citizen is sure of keeping even that which he hath, much less of getting that which he hath not.'

SUSAN B. ANTHONY, 1871

'What is a vote? It is a certain factor in the system of our government. Does Miss Badham suppose that we are merely fighting for this piece of machinery, which may be here today and gone tomorrow? No, we are battling for the liberty, the freedom of women.'

ROSE SCOTT, 1896

'The history of men's opposition to women's emancipation is more interesting than the story of that emancipation itself.'.

VIRGINIA WOOLF, 1929

Contents

Illustrations ix
Abbreviations xi
Preface xiii

Part I: The Campaigns

1 Introduction 3
2 South Australia, 1894 22
3 Western Australia, 1899 45
4 The Commonwealth Vote, 1902 59
5 New South Wales, 1902 68
6 Tasmania, 1903 103
7 Queensland, 1904 112
8 Victoria, 1908 131

Part II: Synthesis and Beyond

9 The Politicians and the Women 172
10 The Arguments and the Issues 186

11	'The Knife without the Blade': The Gift Theory and the Legacy	212
12	Australian Suffragists and Suffragettes in Britain and America	231

Bibliography 244
Index 257

Illustrations

In mid-1900 the Queensland Premier promised to introduce a woman suffrage bill	xii
In 1893 a woman suffrage bill was rejected by the the South Australian Parliament	37
The *Bulletin*'s view of early moves for woman suffrage in the New South Wales Parliament	73
The *Bulletin*'s view of a Woman's Christian Temperance Union deputation, 1894	91
The Queensland Premier, Robert Philp, prepares to kill moves for woman suffrage	115
Premier Arthur Morgan forces the Queensland Legislative Council to reconvene	124
How *Melbourne Punch* saw the Victorian women's threat to take militant action, 1908	158
A Woman's Christian Temperance Union leaflet	188
How *Melbourne Punch* saw women on the hustings	193
How *Melbourne Punch* saw the threat of women in Parliament	197
Melbourne Punch's view of Vida Goldstein	202
Women were pictured as unable to understand political issues	205

Plates following page 82

Mary Lee
Elizabeth Nicholls
Jessie Ackermann
Catherine Helen Spence
Dr James Stirling
Sir John Forrest
Christine Clark
The *Western Mail* summed up the debate
Walter James
Frederick Holder
Charles Kingston
Dora Montefiore
Elizabeth Ward
Annie Golding
Rose Scott
Louisa Lawson
Emma Miller

Plates following page 162

The Celebration Meeting of the Womanhood Suffrage League of New South Wales, 1902
Jessie Rooke
Elizabeth Brentnall
Mary Love
Annie Lowe
Brettena Smyth
Henrietta Dugdale
Marie Kirk
Annette Bear-Crawford
Vida Goldstein
Dr William Maloney
Lilian Locke
Sir Thomas Bent
A Victorian voter's right
Alice Henry and Miles Franklin
Margaret Fisher, Emily McGowan and Vida Goldstein

Abbreviations

Libraries
BL:WA	Battye Library, Western Australia.
JOL:Q	John Oxley Library, Queensland.
LTL:V	La Trobe Library, Victoria.
ML:NSW	Mitchell Library, New South Wales.
ML:SA	Mortlock Library, South Australia.
SL:NSW	State Library, New South Wales.
SL:Q	State Library, Queensland.
SL:SA	State Library, South Australia.
SL:T	State Library, Tasmania.
SL:V	State Library, Victoria.
SL:WA	State Library, Western Australia.

Parliamentary Debates
CAPD	*Commonwealth of Australia, Parliamentary Debates.*
NSWPD	*New South Wales, Parliamentary Debates.*
QPD	*Queensland, Parliamentary Debates.*
SAPD	*South Australia, Parliamentary Debates.*
VPD	*Victoria, Parliamentary Debates.*
WAPD	*Western Australia, Parliamentary Debates.*

Organisations
WCTU	Woman's Christian Temperance Union.

In mid-1900 the Queensland Premier, Robert Philp, promised a delegation of the three suffrage groups that he would introduce a woman suffrage bill, but did not fulfil his promise.
Worker (Brisbane), 17 November 1900. Mitchell Library, State Library of New South Wales.

Preface

In the early 1980s, during an election campaign which generated much discussion as to whether women's issues might determine the outcome, I went to the New South Wales State Library to research an article on the granting of the vote to Australian women. I found only a few pieces in academic magazines, but they said little about the women themselves. Driven to contemporary newspapers and to the Mitchell Library's stock of documents, I soon realised that this could be no article. The stories of the campaigns have had to be pieced together like a giant jigsaw, using parliamentary debates, press reports, surviving records of societies, Louisa Lawson's *Dawn*, Vida Goldstein's *Woman's Sphere*, and the records of the Woman's Christian Temperance Union. Rose Scott's meticulous preservation of letters gave me references to what was happening at the time in other states, and when I visited their Australiana collections I sometimes augmented my knowledge of the New South Wales movement. I am left with some sadness at the end of my years of research, however; there are some gaps in the jigsaw because so many quite prominent women did not think their experiences important enough to commit to paper, and much of what the others left has been destroyed.

The New South Wales suffragists held what they termed a 'joy meeting' in late 1902 to celebrate the granting of the Commonwealth and New South Wales votes. The platform of the Sydney School of Arts was crowded with politicians, all of whom were eager to accept the credit, and in the process woo the new electorate. Rose Scott told the men that their names would live 'not only in the history of Australia, but in that of the world', while the names of the women would be forgotten. Her words have been true for the best part of a century. I hope that this book will reverse the situation.

Being so heavily dependent on original sources, I have relied very much on the aid of librarians. I cannot speak too highly of the help given to me in the Mitchell Library, but I must also thank those in the Tasmanian Archives, the La Trobe Library in Victoria, the Mortlock in South Australia, the John Oxley in Brisbane, and the Battye in Perth. In all capital cities I was received warmly and courteously at the offices of the Woman's Christian Temperance Union and was given access to their material. They have my thanks. I also express my appreciation to those of the above institutions which gave me permission to publish material from their collections.

Every effort has been made to obtain permission to use copyright material; the publishers trust that their apologies will be accepted for any errors or omissions.

Audrey Oldfield

PART I

THE
CAMPAIGNS

1

INTRODUCTION

Terminology

Any writer on the woman suffrage movement of the nineteenth and twentieth centuries must also be a chronicler of the development of the wider women's movement, for the struggle for the vote brought together disparate groups of activists demanding a political weapon with which to storm the huge edifice of related laws and customs which kept the nineteenth-century woman in a state of legal and economic subservience. For a time the women's battle for freedom became one with the suffrage movement, but the groups which coalesced to achieve this particular objective always retained their individual identity beneath the surface of unity. In every country after the vote was won the suffrage movement disbanded, each group to continue to do battle with that aspect of oppression which it considered to be most burdensome. There is a dilemma for the writer who wishes to record this unity *and* diversity in the woman suffrage movement and it centres on terminology, particularly on the words 'feminism' and 'feminist'.

The terms did not exist in the lexicon of the nineteenth-century women's movement in America, Britain and Australia; *feministe* was a term coined in France in the late nineteenth-century to describe the French woman who was fighting for improvements in the status of her sex. The word travelled to England where feminist and feminism were in common use by the second decade of this century. Historians have, however, not limited the terms to the years after 1910; they have found them useful for all periods. Yet one need only ask, 'What is, or what was, a feminist?' to realise that feminism and feminist are slippery terms for slippery concepts. The feminism of the Woman's Christian Temperance Union of the nineteenth century fighting for liquor control in order that the woman and her children might be fed and clothed by, and freed from the drunken rages of, the male wage earner has little in common with the feminism of the 1980s and 1990s demonstrating for the right to abortion and the woman's control over her own body. Yet both are feminisms of their time. There was also, as we shall see, a great deal of difference between the feminism of Henrietta Dugdale of Victoria and that of Elizabeth Nicholls of South Australia. Yet both worked to gain the vote for Australian women.

It has been suggested that the terms feminism and feminist might more validly be used for the late-twentieth-century analysis of society's attitudes and assumptions—an analysis which has resulted in demands for profound cultural and economic changes which can accommodate both women's equality with men and differences from men.[1] I have not followed this suggestion, for I feel that by doing so I would not be allowing for the unity and continuity of women's demands for reform over two centuries, nor would I be allowing for the fact that, for instance, Louisa Lawson's analysis and protest would have been more at home in the 1970s in Australia than in the 1890s. I have therefore decided to use feminism and feminist for all stages of the women's movement, qualifying them by borrowing phrases coined by other writers in the field: 'public sphere' and 'private sphere' feminism, 'domestic' feminism, 'expediency' feminism, 'social' feminism ... Where necessary I have coined my own qualifications to describe individuals or groups of women.

The terms radical, moderate and conservative also raise problems when applied to feminists and suffragists. There are those who would maintain that a conservative feminist is a contradiction in terms, and they have a point. In the mid-nineteenth century, for instance, any woman anywhere who wanted change might be termed radical, and in the 1880s in Australia any woman who wanted the vote might also be termed radical. Yet I contend that the terms can validly be used to compare types of feminism within a certain time span, and I have done so in this book. A feminist/suffragist in the nineteenth century could be radical as compared to other women in two ways: in the degree of change required in society to accommodate the new image of the woman and her special needs, and in the methods used to agitate for change. So Louisa Lawson's analysis of cultural attitudes was radical in the context of her time, although she never resorted to militant tactics. The suffragettes in Britain from 1906 to 1914 were radical in their methods of agitation, but were as moderate in their demands as the main body of women led by Millicent Garrett Fawcett. Feminism in the nineteenth century had, as it has now, many faces, and all must be recognised.

Antecedents and Influences—Britain and America

The Australian suffrage movement cannot be fruitfully explored in a vacuum. Australian workers drew both their inspiration and their ideology from the women's movements in Britain and North America. These in turn had common roots in the eighteenth-century Enlightenment and the Age of Reason, which emphasised the inherent rights of all male citizens to equality and freedom. As these subversive ideas swept over Britain, Europe and America in the 1700s, some women dared to suggest that they too should be considered as citizens of the State, but their voices were drowned in the clamour of men demanding release from tyranny. John Adams was in Philadelphia in 1776 helping to draft the American Declaration of Independence, one of the most significant documents to emerge from the eighteenth century's ferment of democratic thought. His wife Abigail, left to manage the farm and care for the children, wrote requesting that consideration should be given to 'the ladies' who, if their rights were not written into the document, would not hold themselves bound by laws in which they had 'no voice or representation'. The future President replied that he could not but laugh at her suggestion.[2] Thirteen years after Abigail's fruitless request, the paroxysms of the French Revolution not only gave birth to the Declaration of the Rights of Man and of the Citizen; it launched upon the world the struggle for the rights of the individual woman. On behalf of French women demanding that they be considered in the early freedoms of the Revolution, Olympe de Gouges (who was to be guillotined during the terror) produced a parallel Declaration of the Rights of Women and in 1792 the English writer Mary Wollstonecraft, who had been living in France the better to observe the Revolution, published *A Vindication of the Rights of Woman*.

In the first part of what was intended to be a three-volume work, Wollstonecraft attacked the conditioning and training of middle- and upper-class girls which concentrated only on fitting them for a life of submission and humility in marriage. Some of her most withering comments were directed against the educational theories of Jean-Jacques Rousseau, which, she said, denied girls any 'vigour of intellect' or healthy physical exercise, and she pleaded for 'a proper education' for a woman, leading to 'a well-stored mind'.[3] The work was denounced and its importance undermined by vicious attacks on Wollstonecraft's unconventional life-style—she had borne one child out of wedlock and refused on principle to marry her lover, the philosopher William Godwin, until she was carrying their child. In spite of attacks on its author, the book's indignation must have struck a responsive chord in female readers, for it went to four American and six English editions in the nineteenth century. Occasional references by Australian suffragists indicate that the *Vindication* spread its influence as far as the colonies. Wollstonecraft did not develop an argument for women's political participation in this first volume, and in 1796 died after childbirth before writing a second.

Early-nineteenth-century women read Wollstonecraft's words in a climate of repressive laws which, although a loved daughter or a woman in a happy marriage might not realise it, took away rights exercised (if not codified) in previous centuries and made them little more than slaves. British women, including those in the colonies, were constrained by English common law, as were women in America even after it had severed its British ties. In many European countries the 1804 Civil Code of Napoleon formally ended the brief flowering of feminist thought which had taken place before the terror overtook the French Revolution. Under both systems the single woman was under her father's control and the woman who married lost her legal identity. As Sir William Blackstone wrote: 'they [the husband and wife] are one person in law, so that the very being and existence of the woman is suspended during the coverture, or entirely merged or incorporated in that of the husband'.[4] The French expression for this absorption of the woman in her husband's identity was *femme couverte*. Its anglicised form, 'a woman under coverture', was often used by Australian politicians when they argued that even if single women and widows needed the vote, their married sisters did not.

The absorption, or legal non-existence, of the nineteenth-century woman in marriage meant that she could not lay claim to any rights in law. Unless a contrary settlement were drawn up, the property she might bring to the marriage, and any money she might earn after it, passed to her husband. She could not make a will, enter a contract or sue. She could not give evidence in a court of law except under special circumstances, but she could be put on trial and sentenced to death or imprisonment. Her person was completely under her husband's control and he was legally obliged only to provide her with the minimum of food and clothing when he was alive and was not forced to make any provision for her in his will. If she absconded, a writ of habeas corpus could be served against anyone who sheltered her and she could be brought back and cohabitation forced upon her. She had legally no share in her children: her husband could take them from her and give them into the care of another, refusing her access. If he died, his will could appoint others as their guardians. Divorce in England was obtainable only by an Act of Parliament until 1857 and when this was rectified the man could secure a divorce on the grounds of one act of adultery, while the woman had to plead aggravated adultery: repeated offences, adultery with cruelty or desertion, sodomy, bestiality or incest. Male and female Liberal reformers battled to remove the most blatant of these injustices in the nineteenth century, the most significant of their victories being the laws (passed in the 1880s in England and the Australasian colonies) which established the woman's right to her own property and earnings. At the end of the century, however, a great body of discriminatory laws still existed.

For almost fifty years after Wollstonecraft's *Vindication*, feminism was kept at bay in Europe, Britain and North America. Wollstonecraft's spiritual successors, Frances Wright and Harriet Martineau, were subjected to the same ridicule as she had been. When the British male franchise was extended in the First Reform Act of 1832, legislators made it quite clear that women were excluded by using for the first time the term 'male persons' for eligible voters. Mary Smith, a Yorkshire woman, protested (unsuccessfully) by presenting the first woman suffrage petition to the British Parliament on behalf of those with the necessary property qualifications. There were some articles supporting votes for women in the 1830s and 1840s, and in 1847 Anne Knight wrote an advocatory leaflet. The British Chartists at first included women when in the 1840s they demanded the reform of the electoral system with universal suffrage, but dropped this demand when they thought it might jeopardise their other demands.

The United States, too, had its isolated voices, but in the 1840s the first women's movement as such appeared there. Its forcing ground was the anti-slavery campaign which brought significant numbers of women into public life in the northern states. Many were from well-to-do families and had been educated at home or in private schools for girls. Some were Quaker women who shared the general repugnance of Quakers towards slavery. Quakers educated their girls, although not usually to the same standard as the boys, and women were already accepted as ministers and lay preachers in their pulpits. As long as the anti-slavery women confined their activities to working supportively within the established societies they were viewed with approval, but when they joined the movement's public-speaking circuit they were much criticised. In response to a pastoral letter of condemnation read in Congregational churches in 1837 a

Quaker woman, Sarah Grimké, published *Letters on the Equality of the Sexes and the Condition of Woman*, in which she maintained that it was a woman's duty as well as a man's to protest against the ills of society. She attacked both the conditioning which made a woman feel inferior, and the literature specially written for her, 'which destroyed her character as a rational creature'. She protested against the 'enormous evil' of poor wages and conditions for the female worker, and the laws which gave men complete control over women, thus condoning domestic violence. She drew a graphic picture of the plight of the female slave, subject to the same evils as the man but to sexual exploitation at the hands of her owner as well.[5]

It was inevitable that a close analysis of slavery should lead anti-slavery women to compare their own legal situation with that of the Negro, and they began to weave the two causes together in their public speeches. Lucy Stone, to be one of the great leaders in the woman suffrage movement, wrote that she 'was so possessed by the women's rights idea that I scattered it in every speech'.[6]

In 1840 Elizabeth Cady Stanton and Lucretia Mott (another Quaker woman) travelled with male and female workers to London to attend the British and Foreign Anti-Slavery Convention. They were astounded to be told that no woman was allowed to take part; the only concession they could gain was permission to sit in the gallery and listen to the proceedings. When she returned to America, Stanton's already existing feminism grew, fuelled by her readings and by 'the general discontent I felt with woman's portion as wife, mother, housekeeper, physician and spiritual guide'.[7] She was eventually to have seven children for whom to perform these offices. In 1848 she and Mott called a public meeting to discuss 'the social, civil and religious conditions and rights of women'. Mott's husband chaired the meeting of three hundred men and women, and a Declaration of Sentiments and Resolutions was presented. It was modelled on the American Declaration of Independence in much the same way as Olympe de Gouges had in 1891 modelled her document on the French Declaration of the Rights of Man and of the Citizen.

The first half of the Seneca Falls Declaration echoed the sonorous excerpt from the Declaration of Independence, but with two vital words included:

> We hold these truths to be self-evident; that all men *and women* are created equal; that they are endowed by their Creator with certain inalienable rights; that among these are life, liberty and the pursuit of happiness; that to secure these rights governments are instituted, deriving their just powers from the consent of the governed;[8]

The Seneca Falls Declaration accused the male of having established 'an absolute tyranny' over the woman and spelt out how this had been done. Twelve resolutions were adopted by which the status of the woman could be changed. Only one of these—'That it is the duty of the women of this country to secure for themselves the sacred right of the elective franchise'—was not passed unanimously. Many anti-slavery workers were not willing at this stage to divert their energies to a campaign for votes for women. The movement launched at Seneca Falls spread rapidly, drawing in women who had begun to agitate about specific educational, legal and social disabilities of women, and Women's Rights Conventions were held yearly till the 1860s in focal centres in North America.

These early American feminists were drawn from generally prosperous backgrounds: some were sharing public life with sympathetic husbands; some earned their own living in the narrow range of occupations open to them (teaching and journalism were two of these); some were daughters of well-to-do and sympathetic families or were independent because their fathers had settled money on them. They were intellectual women who were demanding release from the boredom of domesticity, and the opportunity to operate as they saw fit in the world outside the home, but they were also demanding improvements in the lives of all women.

No wide-ranging campaign for female suffrage was waged in the United States before the 1860s, although votelessness was condemned at Women's Rights Conventions. The women believed that the Republican party, which they supported, would include them when the vote was extended to Negroes after the civil war. The proposed constitutional amendment, however, stipulated that votes should be given only to Negro males. Anthony, Stanton and others protested vigorously, but the abolitionists persuaded a majority of those who had worked against slavery that it was 'the Negro's hour'. The woman's vote would have to wait.

The women, angry and disappointed with this and with the slow pace of legal and economic reforms for women in the 1850s and 1860s, formed the National Woman Suffrage Association in New York. The new association, as well as lobbying for the vote, set itself the task of arousing in American women a consciousness of the legal and economic ills which beset them. The vision of women's rights rapidly permeated American society, seeping down through the middle classes. The movement by the 1870s found itself with a large membership of women to whom the vision of combining marriage and a career was quite impractical. They could not afford servants to shoulder the responsibility and the work involved in running their households, and they saw women's rights as not so much a moving out of the home as a legal redefinition of their place within it. They wanted recognition of the work they were doing to rear the citizens of the future society, and reform of the laws which did not recognise them in that role as full citizens of the State. The changing membership and emphasis caused tensions in the new suffrage association. The more conservative women were not prepared to tolerate radicals, particularly those like Victoria Woodhull and her sister Tennessee Claflin who edited a magazine which advocated 'free love'—and practised what they preached. In 1870 the more conservative women under Lucretia Mott and Lucy Stone broke away to form the American Woman Suffrage Association. In the 1870s and 1880s the radical organisation declined and the less radical had a dramatic growth, and in this period the Woman's Christian Temperance Union, to figure so prominently in Australia's suffrage campaign, added its voice to the debate.

The split between the two suffrage associations lasted for twenty years, but by 1890 the views of the two leaders of the more radical organisation had begun to diverge. Stanton was increasingly convinced that the women's movement should move on to a critique of the economic and social bases of marriage and society, and Anthony was finding more common ground with the benevolent and family reformers in the sister society. Under Anthony's influence the National merged with the American in 1890. The composite organisation, the National American Woman Suffrage Association, did not expel radicals like Stanton from its ranks, although in 1896 they denied identification with Stanton's critique of religious discrimination, *The Woman's Bible*. By the early 1900s labouring women were finding their own voice through trade unions and the settlement movement and were demanding the vote on their own behalf. Black women were building up their own network of clubs and societies for, although they had been freely admitted to early Women's Rights Conventions, they had been frozen out of the suffrage organisations which were formed after the civil war. The black women not only protested against the backlash of hatred and violence unleashed upon all Negroes in the period after the civil war, but demanded that the Negro man should not be prevented from claiming his legal right to the vote by menacing state regulations or the threat of violence, and that the right to vote should be given to the Negro female. The movement produced its own outstanding women like the Reverend Olympia Brown and Josephine St Pierre Ruffin.

By the turn of the century in America an enormous number of women were involved in a very active and visible woman suffrage movement, but little headway was being made in the state or the federal systems. Only four states had the vote, and two of those had gained it while they were still territories, when a majority vote in each legislature could grant it. After a territory was admitted to the Union, a referendum of male voters was required for any extension of the franchise. The motives for granting the vote in the two territories, Utah and Wyoming, will be discussed in this work when it explores the reasons why Australian women gained their votes before those American and British women who had been agitating for so much longer.

The American feminists who emerged in mid-century have been labelled variously as equal-rights feminists because they based their beliefs firmly on the premise that a woman had an innate right to self-development and did not exist to meet the needs of others, and public-sphere in that they demanded an equal right to share in the professions and in the public life of the State, society and church. The less radical feminism which developed by the 1890s in America, however, has been labelled as social or reformist in that it did not challenge the existing ordering of society, and private-sphere or domestic feminism in that it took for granted that the married woman would be fully occupied for a long period of her life in bearing and rearing children, and that she would only take part in public life, as most of the philanthropists did, from a home base. Some feminists and historians have lamented the decline of the more radical feminism and deplored the emphasis of that which grew from it. The lament has concentrated on the differences between the earlier and later women and has not given enough attention to their complementary nature. The later woman did not deny the claim that male and female were equal; she affirmed it in a different context. The later woman as well as the earlier claimed that she was an autonomous individual either inside or outside marriage. Both demanded a widening of opportunities and better wages and conditions for the woman who earned her own living. Both demanded reform of the laws which gave the husband complete control over his wife and children, and both wanted an escape route (on the same terms as those for the man) for the woman who was tied to an unfaithful, violent and improvident partner. But the feminist who emerged in the 1890s was more pragmatic; she recognised the then intractable boundaries within which all but the wealthy married woman, who could afford servants, operated. She knew that the existing domestic technology and lack of reliable birth control meant that her life was circumscribed. Within that circumscription she wanted both the equality of the Seneca Falls Declaration plus special consideration for the unique circumstances of her life. The later feminists saw not so much the injustice which kept their more wealthy sisters tied to the home, but the injustice which condemned thousands of widows, deserted wives, and wives of improvident men to labour for diminished wages and in wretched conditions outside as well as in the home.

The first stirrings of the movement for female suffrage in Australia took place in the early 1880s, when the difference in emphasis of the two groups of American suffragists was expressed by two separate suffrage societies; and the Australian movement was gaining vigour and momentum in 1890, when the American amalgamation took place which, although it tolerated some who were more revolutionary in their approach, wanted changes which would bring improvements in the lot of most women in society.

In Britain in the 1840s no major cause such as the anti-slavery movement propelled women in large numbers onto the public speaking platform or led them to develop an ideological base comparable to the Seneca Falls Declaration, but ideas moved freely between America and Britain and the yeast of feminist thought was fermenting in British intellectual society. Some families went against the current trend in giving their daughters a wide-ranging education at home, and many of these women moved into public life through the philanthropic movement and male reform causes such as Chartism and the repeal of the Corn Laws. The British Liberal reform movement which fought these battles on behalf of men, however, showed little sympathy until after mid-century for the legal disabilities under which women laboured, even when some of these were highlighted by experiences of women like Anna Wheeler, who had been married at fifteen and forced to flee a drunken husband. To publicise her legal predicament, William Thompson published in 1825 the pamphlet *An Appeal of One Half the Human Race, Women, against the Pretensions of the Other Half, Men, to Retain them in Political and thence in Civil and Domestic Slavery*. In 1855 the publicity given to Caroline Norton's case, however, may have had some influence on the passing of the Marriage and Divorce Act of 1857 which made divorce possible, but harder for the woman to obtain than the man. Norton had left a husband who ill-treated her, and she was then denied all access to her children. When she tried to earn her living by writing, she found that all moneys earned by her belonged to him.

Even though little reform of the legal situation was taking place in the first sixty years after Wollstonecraft, progress was being made for women of the middle and upper classes on another front. That progress was triggered by a problem which did not exist in America and in the British colonies: Britain had a large 'surplus' of single women who were obliged to earn their own living. The Victorian middle-class woman who did not marry (and whose family was unable or unwilling to maintain her indefinitely) had two choices: she could live out her life in the home of a relative, receiving food, board and lodging in return for help with the house and the children, or she could seek employment in the narrow range of ill-paid but approved occupations open to her.

Dressmaking, millinery and governessing were three such. Although the wage was small, governessing was a respectable occupation and it provided food and lodging, so there was intense competition for the positions available: 810 women applied for one such position in 1862.[9]

The educational movement had its genesis in lectures which aimed to give governesses, or would-be governesses, a basic grounding in grammar, arithmetic and the sciences. From this grew the great nineteenth-century British educational movement for girls to which many talented women devoted their lives. Girls' schools with high academic standards were established, and university colleges were opened, carefully located at some distance from male colleges so that fathers would not be discouraged from allowing their daughters to live there. The women were given lectures by university tutors and allowed to sit for examinations, but not until late in the nineteenth century were they allowed to take degrees at any British universities. Oxford University did not allow women to graduate until 1920 and Cambridge held out until 1948. Australia's educational movement for women roughly paralleled the British, but Australian universities were less resistant to female graduates than their British counterparts.

The British educational movement soon produced women who spoke and wrote about the contradiction between the concern shown by the British reform movement for the liberties of British men and its lack of concern about the laws which oppressed women, and they combined their assertions with the demand for female suffrage. The women had support from some of the democratic philosophers—Jeremy Bentham, Richard Cobden, Joseph Hume and Jacob Bright—but it was theoretical support, and only Jacob Bright was to use any energy on their behalf in the later campaign. The Liberal reformers had drawn freely on the energies of their women to fight their battles but would not take up the cause of women, either because they did not believe that women should have parallel freedoms or because they thought that such agitation would jeopardise further advances for males. Barbara Bodichon (who was born Barbara Leigh Smith and was a cousin of Florence Nightingale) is credited with beginning the British women's movement in the mid-1860s, but Bodichon merely acted as a catalyst. Women by then were frustrated, disenchanted with their men, and ready for battle on their own behalf.

Bodichon came from a radical reformist family and was given a good education. Her parents were involved with the anti-slavery movement and when she was in her early teens had welcomed to their home Lucretia Mott and Elizabeth Cady Stanton, then in London for the Anti-Slavery Convention at which women were refused the right to speak. In her late teens she worked with Cobden and Bright in their campaign against the Corn Laws. In 1854, when she was twenty-seven years old, she began collecting material for a pamphlet on the laws which affected women's lives and this resulted in a petition of 26,000 signatures from the Law Amendment Society, requesting that women should be granted the right to own property and make wills. The petition was received with hostility by the Parliament and an 1857 bill along these lines was defeated. In 1866 Bodichon published *Reasons for the Enfranchisement of Women* and in 1867 *Women and Work*, thus firmly linking woman suffrage with conditions for women in the labour market.

In 1865, the year before Bodichon published *Reasons for the Enfranchisement of Women*, John Stuart Mill, one of the most important of the women's advocates, was elected to

Parliament. In 1867 he presented a women suffrage petition and unsuccessfully moved an amendment to include women in a bill which that year widened the franchise for men. Mill had, in 1861, supported the franchise for women in one of his essays on political philosophy, *Considerations on Representative Government*. He acknowledged that his opinions on the participation of women in the State, and indeed all his philosophical views, had been influenced by Harriet Taylor, his intellectual companion for twenty years and then, after the death of her husband, his wife for seven years until her death in 1858. Mill was defeated in the election of 1868, and in 1869 published *The Subjection of Women*, which he had written eight years before. It was the most important work on behalf of women to appear in Britain since Mary Wollstonecraft's protest.

In this work Mill's basic premise, as Wollstonecraft's had been, was that existing marriage was tantamount to slavery.[10] Mill added that this was 'a monstrous contradiction to all the principles' which lay behind the reform movement of the nineteenth-century. Now that the Negro had been freed, there remained 'no legal slaves, except the mistress of every house'. The unfitness of men for unlimited power in the political sphere was recognised by the democratic reforms which had taken place, and yet the law gave unlimited power to the man over the woman. It was useless to argue that some men did not misuse their power, for others physically abused their wives under the impression that 'the law has delivered her to them as their thing'. Mill did not accept that it was the 'nature' of the man to govern and the 'nature' of the woman to be governed, and contended that male and female were conditioned into their roles. He denied the current contention that women accepted their inferior position and cited the suffrage petitions already presented and the demands for education and access to the professions in England, the movement for women's rights in America, and agitation for legal reforms in France, Italy, Switzerland and Russia. Many more women would speak out if they could, he contended, but the married woman was 'in a chronic state of bribery and intimidation combined', as her very survival depended on her accepting her 'tightly riveted yoke' with good grace. Mill's work was read widely in England and the colonies, as his earlier works on representative government had been, and taken together they gave British and colonial women a theoretical framework in which to operate. Mill died in 1873, four years after he published the *The Subjection of Women*.

Once begun, the suffrage movement spread rapidly, its adherents travelling all over England addressing groups and forming new societies of both middle-class and working-class women. The large group in Manchester was one such which spoke for women in the mills. When the 1867 Reform Bill was passed, the women were angry that no consideration had been given to their claim to the franchise and in Manchester 5346 applied to have their names put on the rolls. The matter was taken to court and the court ruled that every woman was personally incapable of casting a vote. The ruling referred not to intelligence or physical capacity but to the woman's standing in law.

Suffragists pinned their hopes on the Liberal party which had been responsible for widening the franchise for men. Liberal leader William Gladstone was hostile, however, and Benjamin Disraeli was unenthusiastic, both of them fearing that the women who would be enfranchised on the property basis which applied to men would vote for the Tory party. Both were probably influenced, too, by the opposition of Queen Victoria, who announced in 1879: 'The Queen is most anxious to enlist anyone who can speak or write or join in checking this mad, wicked folly of "Woman's Rights", with all its attendant horrors'.[11] In vain the women petitioned the House: in the 1870s approximately three million signatures were submitted. Sympathetic parliamentarians introduced many private bills, but all were aborted. In 1885 the Liberal government lost office to the Tories and did not regain it until 1906; suffrage agitation did not cease but it must have been apparent to all suffragists that a Tory Government would obstruct all moves on their behalf.

Because of the imbalance of the sexes, the struggle of factory women for work opportunities in the male marketplace was even more intense in Britain than it was in Australia. Women jealously guarded jobs which from the beginning had been regarded as women's work, and when new processes developed were eager to move into areas which were created. Employers preferred to put women in the new areas because the women were willing to accept lower wages. There was much hostility between the men and the women in industry as not only young single women, but those who faced a lifetime in the labour force, fought to maintain their gains. Because the women's trade union movement which developed in the 1880s vowed that its women would use the vote to bolster their demands, woman suffrage received little backing from the male union movement. In 1884 the Trade Union Congress voted to support it, but did nothing until after the turn of the century, and even then spoke up only intermittently. Some parallels with Australia will become apparent in this work.

When British Labour made its first attempts to enter Parliament in the 1890s, a levy was imposed on all trade union members to support parliamentary candidates. The women were incensed that they had to contribute to the campaigns of candidates for whom they could not vote, and they pressured the Labour party to include woman suffrage in its programme. The party replied that, although it approved in principle, there were more important battles to be fought first. The battles referred to were two: the vote for every man, and abolition of the plural vote. Manhood suffrage as it was defined in Australia, a basic vote for every male in the Lower House of the Parliament, did not yet exist in Britain. Qualifications for male electors had been relaxed in stages throughout the century, but a voter still had to own property or pay a certain minimum amount for the home he and his family occupied. The plural vote in Britain gave an extra vote to the man who operated a business in an electorate (which had particular impact upon election results in the large cities), and gave university graduates a vote for special university seats. Labour's reluctance to give support to votes for women, however, was not just because it wanted to abolish both the household qualification and the plural vote before considering the women; it was aware that if women gained the vote on the same terms as men, few from the working class would be enfranchised. The women who owned property or leased it on their own behalf would, they thought, be unlikely to vote for Labour representatives. Individual Labour men supported votes for women on the same grounds as men (to be followed then, they said, by a parallel development of rights for both sexes), but the Labour movement itself refused to back the women's claims. Since Australian governing institutions grew out of those in Britain, it is only to be expected that many points of correspondence will be found when the party politics facet of the Australian suffrage movement is explored.

The British women themselves, like the Australian, were not of one mind as to the qualifications their suffrage should have. Some, like Lydia Becker and her followers, wanted it initially only for single women or widows with the necessary qualifications. Some, like the Pankhursts, wanted it for all women on the same grounds as men (although the household franchise would usually mean that only the husband would have the vote under that qualification). By 1897, however, most suffrage societies had been brought under the umbrella of the National Union of Women's Suffrage Societies to fight for the vote on the same grounds as men had, or might have, it. Only Socialist women who were demanding adult suffrage with no property qualifications were left outside the fold. The vital Millicent Garrett Fawcett took over the leadership of the national organisation and directed the continuing campaign. In spite of its unremitting efforts and good financial support (in 1900 its budget was £45,000) the movement could make no headway. There was no interest shown in Parliament by the Tory Government, by the Liberals in opposition (in spite of the fact that their own party women were pressuring them), or by the small Labour group. As in America, the British woman suffrage movement was stalled as the century turned.

The Australian Background

New Zealand was the first country to give its women the vote, in 1893.[12] Australia was the second when, in 1902, its first Commonwealth Parliament used the powers it was given in its 1901 Constitution to proclaim adult suffrage for all future federal elections.

The prevailing wisdom in Australia, until the resurgence of feminism in the 1960s and 1970s and the consequent exploration of women's history, was that the vote was 'gracefully laid at the feet' of Australian women. Having obtained it so easily, it was contended that they did not appreciate it enough to make any significant use of it. This view is simplistic, both as regards the gaining of the vote and the subsequent use which was made of it.

The first generalisation, that the vote was given as a gift, has in part arisen because the gift referred to has always been the right to vote for the Commonwealth legislature. Those who have made this generalisation have ignored the fact that from the 1850s Australia had five legislatures and from 1870, when Western Australia's advisory Legislative Council became partly elected, six. In every colony, beginning in the 1880s, campaigns for female suffrage were fought. Each colony had its suffrage society, or societies, and all issued a great variety of propaganda leaflets. Debates and public meetings were organised and the speakers, male and female, were not only in demand in capital cities, but travelled extensively, usually by rail, addressing meetings in the open air or in halls owned by town councils, by the School of Arts movement, and by churches and temperance organisations. Branches of suffrage societies were active in many country towns. The suffragists who were letter-writers kept the debate alive in city and country newspapers. Deputations waited on Parliaments, petitions were presented, and there was intense lobbying of candidates before elections and of members of Parliament before suffrage bills were presented in the Lower or Upper Houses of the states.

The open suffrage organisations were supported in the fray by the Woman's Christian Temperance Union, which was brought to Australia from America by the Union's 'missionaries' in the 1880s. It, and the existing male temperance organisations, aimed to impose liquor trade restrictions (if not outright prohibition) on Australian society. The debate in two states generated anti-suffrage societies, claimed by the WCTU to be the mouthpieces of the liquor interests. The temperance question affected the debate in ironic ways, bedding down conservative feminists with those who were on the far left of the movement. Members of the WCTU came for the most part from the nonconformist churches and by supporting votes for women they sometimes, but not always, found themselves at odds with the spokesmen of their churches. This book will examine the role of the churches and the WCTU in individual colonies, and will assess the importance of the WCTU in the overall Australian movement.

In 1894 the women of South Australia were enfranchised after a campaign which in many ways paralleled that of New Zealand (where the vote was given the year before), and in 1899 the women of Western Australia were granted their franchise by a Premier who hoped to use it to his own advantage. With each of these successes the suffragists in other states increased their agitation for women to vote in their own state elections. Conventions (of males) were held throughout the 1890s to draft the Constitution for the federation of the six colonies. The coming of federation at this stage in the suffrage campaign gave Australian women a unique opportunity to influence the drafting of the Constitution under which the new nation would operate. In each colony, whether that colony had woman suffrage or not, pressure was brought to bear on delegates to have adult suffrage, with no sex qualification, written into the Constitution itself. When they failed in this, the suffragists exerted themselves yet again to have the first Commonwealth Parliament use the powers it was given in its Constitution to grant women the national vote. When news of the victory came through in 1902, celebrations were held to honour prominent suffragists—and in some cases to honour quite undeserving politicians who claimed credit for the measure but who had jumped on the band wagon only at the last minute.

The fact that all Australian women (except Aboriginal women in Queensland and Western Australia) were given the Commonwealth vote in 1902 did not oblige the four states without woman suffrage automatically to confer it for their own Parliaments. As part of the gift theory, however, a further generalisation has been that after federation the other four states, their women now having the vote in the federal sphere, capitulated with good grace. This, again, is simplistic, and in Victoria's case quite erroneous. New South Wales and Tasmanian women, it is true, gained their state franchises in 1902 and 1903 respectively, but Queensland held out until 1905 and in Victoria it was not given until 1908, after angry confrontation and after Victorian women had voted in two Commonwealth elections. The organised struggle, taking all states into account, had thus extended over at least twenty-eight years.

The gift theory, then, needs to be qualified, although the Australian struggle was certainly shorter than the more than sixty years of agitation in Britain and more than seventy years in America. The contention that Australian suffragists did not work hard is no doubt due in part to a comparison of the three time spans, but it also arises because they were generally very conventional in their forms of agitation. They were not driven to militant tactics by frustration as their British and, to a lesser extent, American sisters were after the turn of the century. There were no suffragettes in the Australian campaigns; suffragette was a label first given in 1906 by the London *Daily Mail* to those British women who had become disillusioned with the normal channels of agitation and were moving to more spectacular forms of protest. It is interesting to conjecture, though, whether more militant tactics might have been adopted in Australia if efforts had been blocked for as long as they were in the other two countries—in Britain until 1918 and in America until 1920. At least two Australian suffragists, Dora Montefiore and Nellie Martel, joined the militant wing of the British movement when they returned to England early in the century, and Vida Goldstein expressed support for militant tactics when she visited London in 1911.

The other claim, that women have made little use of their vote until recently, will also be examined in the course of this work. Those who have made the claim have usually measured the use of the vote by the numbers of women who have stood for, or been elected to, state or federal legislatures. Australia's record of female members of Parliament, at either level, has been very poor when compared with countries in which women were enfranchised much later in the century. No woman sat in an Australian Parliament until 1921 and by 1929 when, for instance, there were forty-one female members of the German legislature, only four had been successful in Australia, none of them for a seat in the Commonwealth Parliament. Women in other parts of the world, to whom Australia's early gaining of the franchise was an inspiration to continue their struggle, have queried the situation, as have Australian women themselves. This problem will be considered when all the campaigns have been chronicled. An analysis of the arguments used by the Australian suffragists should contribute, as should a review of some limiting factors peculiar to Australia.

As everywhere, the battle for votes for women was fought on two fronts, political and ideological. Any extension of its franchise has important implications for a country's political status quo, and central to the woman suffrage struggle in any country was its Constitution and electoral system. Settled in the aftermath of the French Revolution and the Declaration of the Rights of Man and of the Citizen, Australian colonies gained self-determination at a time of Liberal ascendancy in the Western world. Australian Liberals were, on the whole, enthusiastic about the Chartist concept of manhood suffrage, but fearful of how it might work out in practice. Like John Stuart Mill, they believed that in government 'though everyone ought to have a voice, that everyone should have an equal voice is a totally different proposition.'[13]

This philosophical concern with brakes on democracy was reflected in colonial Constitutions. All had bicameral legislatures with Upper Houses either appointed or elected on a high property franchise (with higher property qualifications for candidates). Each Upper House was, in theory, to provide a review of hasty legislation. In practice, as the nineteenth century progressed, colonial Legislative Assemblies found themselves locked in combat with Legislative Councils over change, the degree of antagonism varying from colony to colony and depending on the radicalism of the Assembly and the conservatism of the Council. Australian women had first to win victory in their particular House of Assembly. Once the battle was won there, however, they usually found themselves opposed by an Upper House which was not only more ideologically conservative on the question of votes for women, but which viewed with suspicion *any* change in the electoral system proposed by its Lower House.

Manhood suffrage for its Assembly was written into South Australia's Constitution, and achieved by the 1860s in New South Wales, Victoria and Queensland. Tasmania's property qualifications for the Assembly were lowered gradually and the suffrage did not apply to all men until 1900. Western Australia gave manhood suffrage, but with limiting residential qualifications, in 1893, two years after its first fully elected Parliament assembled. The effect of this democratisation of the Lower Houses, however, was checked by the plural vote. In every colony except South Australia a man was entitled to a vote for each electorate in which he held property. Technically then, he could have as many votes as there were electorates in his colony. From the first this emphasis on the representation of property was rationalised not only by reasoning that property which paid taxes deserved its own representation but by equating its possession with personal qualities valuable to the State; and therefore with superior political acumen. The *Brisbane Courier* wrote at the height of the interwoven Queensland campaign to abolish the plural vote and give the state franchise to women:

> The general rule, especially in new countries, is that men are possessed of property because they are possessed of the industry, and enterprise, and foresight and thrift which are valuable to the State, and which in an eminent degree qualify a man to vote helpfully to his country. Even when property has come apart from any personal quality of the possessor, as by inheritance, the very possession confers an interest in public affairs which by itself is valuable as a qualification to vote.[14]

The battle to abolish the plural vote was to be one of the main concerns of the working-class movement in Australia, and in all colonies except South Australia was to complicate the suffrage campaign. Even when sympathetic to the claims of women, the Labor movement invariably refused to give its support until one-man-one-vote had been achieved for colonial Assemblies. To make the issue more complex, the suffragists themselves were divided on the question of the plural vote. Some, but not many, thought that women should have their suffrage only if plural voting were retained; some thought they should have it on whatever grounds applied to males at the time; and some thought that it should only be granted if plural voting were abolished. In Queensland, where the Labor party claimed that the plural vote was being manipulated by the creation of bogus or nominal holdings, differences were to lead to a schism in the woman suffrage movement from the beginning. Two suffrage societies were formed, one demanding the vote 'on the same grounds as it is, or shall be, granted to men', and the other declining to work for any but full adult suffrage. In other colonies the different points of view were to cause tensions in the ranks of the women and of their supporters. With some variations these Australian disjunctions paralleled those in the British suffrage movement, but not the American, where one-man-one-vote had been achieved before any significant woman suffrage agitation.

Concerted action by Australian women dates from the comparatively stable 1880s. By the time the agitation intensified, however, a severe economic depression had hit the colonies, rudely shattering the dream of an Australian Utopia in the southern seas and forcing a dramatic reappraisal of the relationship between capital and the labour force. Not only was it the period of the rise of the political wing of Labor, but factions along the whole line of the political spectrum were coalescing and the future party system taking shape. How women might vote in this volatile electoral situation became a matter of serious concern for the still flexible political groupings. A party's attitudes, although couched in ideological language about the 'proper sphere' of women, could depend very much on whether that party thought that women would support it. So the vote became a matter of political expediency as well as ideological commitment and response to agitation. There were cases of striking conversions when it seemed that such conversions might serve a political purpose. The most spectacular was that of Sir John Forrest, Premier of Western Australia. He changed from stubborn opposition to enthusiastic support in 1899 when he decided that the woman's vote would balance the radical voice of the goldfields and return him to office in the coming state election. He was correct in the first assumption but wrong in the second.

The suffrage period was also one in which the movement of Australian women out of domestic service into industry, retailing and clerical work was accelerating. They were being joined by middle-class daughters seeking independence. In the marketplace male and female work was clearly defined; conditions of employment for females, especially in industry, were poor; and in some cases wages could be as low as one-third of that of the male. With the exception of specialised areas, such as tailoring, the women had little political muscle. The suffragists openly avowed that the system must be changed. Women needed higher wages to support themselves. They considered the high rate of prostitution in the capital cities to be due entirely to such low wages, and with their British and American sisters thought that it would completely disappear if women could support themselves in other ways. They pointed out that large numbers of women were not supported by husbands and fathers, and that the parlous predicament of widows and deserted wives was a major problem in Australia. They vowed that women, when they gained the vote, would address themselves to 'women's issues' and these included access to education at every level, better working conditions, higher wages (a surprising number went so far as to claim equal pay) and new opportunities for employment.

Male unionists, as in other industrial societies, found themselves in a quandary. They had always feared the cheap labour of women, as they feared cheap Asian labour, for in times of depression both could deprive them of their jobs. But improving women's working conditions, increasing their wages and opening up new areas of work could make employment outside the home more attractive to women. An increased female labour force might well pose more of a threat than the existing cheaper one. The result in the Australian as in the British union movement was a general paralysis of will, and male unions gave female suffrage little support, even if they did not directly oppose it.

As in Britain and America in the 1880s and 1890s, the concept of votes for women—allied to the wider question of women's rights—had filtered down through the social structure and involved women from widely disparate backgrounds. Because there have been claims that the world suffrage movement was essentially middle-class, this book must address itself, both in the individual campaigns and in their synthesis, to the class structure of the Australian movement. It must also address the wider question of the ideology of the Australian movement as compared to that in Britain and America. Because most Australian women married after a short period in the paid work force, Australian suffragists were concerned not only with conditions and remuneration for working women, but they put particular emphasis on the legal, economic and social position of women within marriage. In Britain and America women were being ideologically defined as radical, moderate or conservative feminists largely by the degree of change they were demanding in this area, for at stake was the role which the woman should play in the broad social structure. In exploring the attitude of the Australian suffragists to their role in society, certain related factors peculiar to Australia must be taken into account: Australia was a sparsely populated Anglo-Saxon society adjacent to densely populated Asian states. A preoccupation with defence and with increasing the population put pressure on the woman to see herself primarily as a childbearer, and a preoccupation with rearing healthy units of population put pressure on her to devote herself solely to the nurture of the children she produced. The tension produced by the need to reconcile the rights of the individual woman with the needs of society was therefore particularly pronounced in Australia. As will be seen, most propaganda of the Australian movement produced two distinct sets of arguments: one claiming the vote on the grounds of justice and the right of the individual to a share in the government of the State and, increasingly so as the campaigns progressed, another pointing out the advantages which would accrue to the nation from woman suffrage.

It is the contention of this book that the course of the Australian suffrage movement overall was intricately related to the prevailing customs, beliefs and laws which then dictated the place of women in society everywhere, and to economic, technological and political movements taking place in the Western world. Certain factors peculiar to Australia, however, also influenced its overall development. Each colonial movement, too, had its own distinctive characteristics. These depended on the degree of sophistication and cosmopolitanism from which that colony's suffragists were drawn, and on the colony's form of government and the political struggles taking place within its legislature.

Notes on Parliamentary Procedure

The Constitutions of all Australian colonies allowed their legislatures to vary their franchises with Constitutional amendment bills or electoral bills—such bills requiring a statutory majority vote of both Upper and Lower Houses. No referendum was required to ratify the decision in any colony. Readers not familiar with the political process will find this explanation helpful when following the political manoeuvring in each colony's legislature.

There were three ways in which a debate on votes for women could be initiated in any colonial Parliament:

1. *The Motion*. Any member of the House could propose a motion which would simply test the opinion of the Parliament on a particular subject. Wordings could vary, but a typical one on woman suffrage would be that moved by Walter James in Western

Australia's Assembly in 1897: 'That in the opinion of this House the best interests of the colony require the extension of the franchise to women.' Even if a motion were passed by a large majority, it did not commit the Government to any action.

2. *The Bill*. A bill to give votes to women could be introduced in either the Upper or Lower House, and if it then passed through all stages in both Houses it became law. The first reading of a bill was a formality which gave notice that a debate would take place on a date to be fixed. The interim allowed members to form their opinions, parties to assess whether they had enough support to either pass or defeat the bill, and woman suffrage organisations to lobby individuals or the Government. There was no debate at this first reading. Many bills proposed by individual supporters of votes for women (private members' bills) went no further than a first reading, for the Premier and his Cabinet, if they disapproved, could block the bill by not timetabling it for debate. If the bill were a Government-sponsored one, however, it was assured of a timeslot for a second reading.

The second reading, which could be days, weeks or months later, initiated a full-scale debate on the floor of the House. With adjournments, such a debate could itself range over days, weeks or months before a division was taken. The bill died if the numbers went against it at the division. During the second reading of a bill an elaborate game could be acted out on the floor of the House by opponents and supporters, with one side playing for adjournment of the debate if it estimated that the vote might go against it, and the other trying to force a decision on the bill if it estimated that it had a majority. This happened in the South Australian Upper House in 1894. After several nights of manoeuvring the bill which eventually gave South Australian women the vote was passed with a majority of only one. Stonewalling was one tactic a member could use to delay the taking of a vote until a more favourable time. During the passage of the New South Wales woman suffrage bill through the Assembly in 1901, a Wilfred Spruson talked until after five o'clock in the morning, but supporters refused to agree to an adjournment and the second reading of the bill affirming votes for women passed as dawn was breaking.

If a bill survived its second reading, the House resolved itself into a committee and the measure was examined clause by clause. As bills could be altered in spectacular ways by amendments in committee, the battle continued even at this stage, as we shall see. If a bill survived its second reading and its committee stage, its third reading was a formality affirming what had already been decided, but the bill then had to pass through the same processes in the other House. A great number of woman suffrage bills which passed through colonial Legislative Assemblies were negated by Legislative Councils.

3. *The Amendment*. Many woman suffrage supporters initiated discussion by moving amendments to bills which dealt with other electoral matters. None of these moves eventually gave women votes, but they did help to keep the question alive in the Parliament and in the community.

Notes

1. This problem of terminology has been discussed in three recent works by Nancy Cott: 'Feminist theory and feminist movements' (1986); *The Grounding of Modern Feminism* (1987); 'What's in a name? The limits of "social feminism": or, Expanding the vocabulary of women's history' (1989).

2. Abigail Adams to John Adams, 31 March 1776, and John Adams to Abigail Adams, 14 April 1776, quoted in Miriam Schneir (ed.), *Feminism: the Essential Historical Writings*, p. 3.
3. Mary Wollstonecraft, *A Vindication of the Rights of Woman*, pp. 67, 81.
4. William Blackstone, *Commentaries on the Laws of England*, vol. 1, p. 441.
5. Sara M. Grimké, quoted in Miriam Schneir (ed.), *Feminism*, pp. 44-5.
6. Lucy Stone, quoted in Miriam Scheir (ed.), *Feminism*, p. 103.
7. Dale Spender, *Women of Ideas: and what men have done to them*, p. 205.
8. 'Declaration of Sentiments and Resolutions, Seneca Falls, 1848', in Miriam Schneir (ed.) *Feminism*, pp. 77-82.
9. Ray Strachey, *The Cause: a short history of the women's movement in Great Britain*, p. 97.
10. The following quotes are from pp. 439, 467, 521, and 522, in John Stuart Mill, *The Subjection of Women*.
11. Roger Fulford, *Votes for Women: the Story of a Struggle*, p. 75.
12. In 1893 New Zealand had the status of one of the British colonies of Australasia. If it had decided to federate with the other Australasian colonies, as was at first envisaged, Australia would have been able to claim the honour of being the first nation in the world to enfranchise its women.
13. John Stuart Mill, *Representative Government*, p. 282.
14. *Brisbane Courier*, 22 July 1896.

South Australia, 1894

South Australia, the first Australian colony to give its women the vote, was officially settled in 1836, forty-eight years after Governor Arthur Phillip brought his convoy of convict outcasts to the forbidding eastern seaboard of Australia. South Australian immigrants—men and women in roughly the same proportions—came to the new colony under the Wakefield Scheme, a plan for systematic development which was to forestall the problems of the first fifty years of settlement in the east. No convicts were to drag down South Australian society, and no very wealthy upper class was to be created by the granting of large tracts of free land. Allotments were to be sold and the proceeds used to finance the immigration of a moral, industrious workforce. A capitalist, Liberal and comparatively egalitarian Utopia was to be planted in a new world. Serpents were to appear almost immediately in this Eden, but nevertheless the ideological underpinnings of the new colony were to attract reformers committed to the British Liberal theories of justice, and of social and political equality.

The South Australian Constitution of 1856 was the fruit of this reformist Liberal ideology: from the first the Assembly had manhood suffrage, secret ballot, no plural voting and no property limitation on candidature. Although the Legislative Council was elected on a property qualification and had a property qualification for candidates, these were lower than for other Australian Upper Houses. Before the mid-1880s, when agitation for woman suffrage began, no major dichotomy existed between Liberals and Conservatives in the Lower House; politics were largely factional, with Governments forming and reforming in response to internal alliances. This created instability—there were twenty-eight Governments in the first twenty years—but nevertheless by the 1880s South Australia was proud of the social legislation which had been passed by the mutual consent of the kaleidoscopic factions in the Lower House and confirmed by an Upper House which was less confrontational than others in Australia.

There was discussion about woman suffrage from the earliest days of settlement. Robert Caldwell said in an 1888 Assembly debate: 'fifty years ago it was said that if manhood suffrage was conceded the enfranchisement of women must follow. The battle had been fought and won, but the victors in the field refused to divide the spoil with those who remained at home'.[1] Nothing was heard of votes for women in the legislature until 1883, when the Married Women's Property Bill was before the Assembly. Before then the property of South Australian women had, unless a contrary marriage settlement were drawn up, passed to the husband on marriage. The man could also claim as his own any money earned by his wife after marriage. There had been several notorious cases in South Australia of a husband deserting his wife and returning after a period legally to claim and squander assets the woman had built up in his absence. The South Australian bill, like others passed in the Australian colonies in the 1880s, allowed the woman to retain the possessions she either brought to the marriage or acquired afterwards. Alexander Hay, speaking to the bill, warned the Assembly of the possible dire consequences if it went any further in this matter of women's rights: '[He] should be sorry to see women vote . . . imagine a female brigade going into the House of Parliament when some great question was under discussion, such as whether we should declare war against Russia or some other power'.[2]

The remark did not initiate a discussion. Two years passed before Dr Edward Stirling, a new member of the Assembly, made a move to test the opinion of the Parliament on the subject. Stirling was Professor of Medicine at Adelaide University and had successfully championed the admission of women to degrees. Women had been able to attend lectures since 1876, but not to graduate. Like many others who were to take a leading part in the Australian suffrage movement, he had been greatly influenced by John Stuart Mill's *The Subjection of Women*, published in 1869. In July 1885 he introduced a motion, as distinct from a bill: 'That in the opinion of this House, women, except under coverture, who fulfil the conditions and possess the qualifications on which the Parliamentary franchise for the Legislative Council is granted to men, shall, like them, be admitted to the franchise for both Houses of Parliament.'[3]

Stirling's speech was lengthy and his exposition as to why women should have the vote was masterful and eminently quotable. It was to provide refrains for all the Australian campaigns.

> So long as half the human race was unrepresented our boasted representative government was a hollow mockery of an ideal which it did not even approach.
>
> By what right did half the community set itself up as the judge of what was the proper sphere for the other half?

Stirling demolished the common arguments: that women did not ask for the vote (they had been trained to be servile and not to expect political freedom); that they had sufficient indirect influence ('the influence of the boudoir or the back stairs was unsound in its consequences'); that they were not as intelligent as men (his own students had proved otherwise); that they were emotional (he knew of many emotional men who were members of Parliament) ... He argued that women needed the vote to improve their wages and conditions of employment, and that they should be having a say in the late-nineteenth-century legislation which would affect their position in the family and society.

There was a basic contradiction between Stirling's exposition and the limited vote he was submitting for approval. If followed to their logical conclusion, his arguments proved that the vote should be given to all women. He made no rationale for excluding women without property, other than to say that if the Parliament wanted the vote for all women it could decide on that later—as it could also decide whether women should be allowed to enter Parliament. He did, however, explain at length why he did not include married women in his proposal. If he had followed his own inclinations he would have done so, but prior canvassing of members had convinced him that he would lose many supporters if he did; these members objected strongly to their wives having votes, for 'it raised horrible visions of households politically divided, and of a strong and factious opposition not to be tolerated anywhere outside of a Legislative Assembly.' There was, too, Stirling said, some justification for excluding the propertied married woman; her property could be said to be represented by her husband, but that of the single woman had no representation.

Members of the Legislative Assembly pointed to the contradiction between Stirling's arguments and his request that it approve only a limited suffrage. Whether one supported a limited franchise or votes for all women, however, one could still vote for the motion. It did not commit a member to any concrete action. The motion was passed without a division and with enthusiastic cheering.

Stirling's move brought the whole question into the public arena. The press debated the property franchise versus votes for all women, and some newspapers came out strongly against votes for women under any circumstances: '[it] conflicts with time-honored views as to the true relation of woman to the other sex and to the State',[4] and 'This is not the country of the strong-minded, or even the unprotected female.'[5]

In June 1886 Stirling gave notice of a bill which was substantially the same as his motion of the year before: it would give a vote to unmarried women with property. The Trades and Labor Council, formed in 1884, decided it was time to let its voice be heard. South Australia had never had a property franchise for its Assembly, and it seemed no coincidence that one was being introduced at a time when Labor in Australia was considering the creation of political bases in the Lower Houses of colonial legislatures. A petition was signed by the President of the Trades and Labor Council and by the twenty-eight delegates representing trade societies. Johann Scherk presented the petition to Parliament and claimed that it represented 3000 artisans and mechanics in the colony.[6] It asked that 'the property qualification of the Bill ... should be amended, and that the franchise should be extended to women irrespective of property or wealth.'[7]

When Stirling introduced his bill for debate at the end of July, he defended its property qualifications.[8] He did not have any sinister design in thus limiting it, he said. Not all women were 'fitted for the duties and responsibilities' of voting; in general it was those with property who were most likely to possess 'that independent judgment, that intellect and ability' required. Stirling seems to have honestly believed that his motion in 1885 and his bill in 1886 should not have been attacked for their exclusiveness. In this he was being incredibly naive for such a well-educated and intelligent man, for it was Liberalism, before Labor developed a voice, which had insisted that all property representation be kept out of the Assembly when the colony's Constitution was drawn up.

The bill had a long and straggling debate, fitted into short periods on separated nights. Thomas Playford, to be Premier the following year, spoke against it, and Charles Kingston, to be Premier in the final years of the campaign, also opposed it. Kingston challenged supporters, wanting to know whether they would go so far as to allow women to sit in Parliament. John Downer replied that 'he did not say that the time might not come when they would be entitled to a seat'.[9] Downer, the Attorney-General and a supporter, was constantly heckled by opponents who made flippant remarks about the 'absurdity', not of women voting, but of women in the legislature. Patrick Coglin's was typical. 'If he had one or two alongside him, he could not legislate',[10] he said. There were thirty-six present and the bill received nineteen votes, but as it was a bill to amend the Constitution it needed twenty-seven for a statutory majority of the whole Assembly. No conclusions can be drawn from the voting about attitudes to woman suffrage per se: some voted for the proposal as the thin end of the wedge; some approved it because it would hinder Labor's attempts to gain influence in the Assembly; and some voted against it because of its élitist qualification.

In the 1887 elections Labor, licking its wounds after its defeat in the Adelaide maritime strike, made its first move for parliamentary influence by backing nine Liberal candidates who were sympathetic to many of its aims.[11] It is possible, in the light of the 1886 petition from the Trades and Labor Council, that one of the pledges required from each candidate was that he should not support votes for women on a property basis. Seven of the nine were returned. Stirling lost his seat after his short spell of three years and never returned to Parliament. His support for woman suffrage henceforth was to be from outside the legislature. Thomas Playford, an opponent of votes for women, became the new Premier.

Shortly after the new Parliament assembled, Robert Caldwell, a country member and Stirling's supporter in 1885 and 1886, introduced a bill which gave votes to all women over twenty-five for both Houses. He had omitted the property qualification because of the outcry against it, he said, but he had raised the age because women 'had been in the past somewhat handicapped in intellectual progress and were a few years behind their male associates in matters political'.[12] Alfred Catt opposed the bill on behalf of the Government and did little more than sentimentalise. 'The true woman, virtuous, modest and shunning publicity', he said, would not be interested in voting. She would be content to have as her mission in life 'the welfare of her husband and children'.[13] Caldwell's bill gained only eighteen votes on its second reading.[14] Its defeat was greeted with cheers in a House which three years before had unanimously applauded Stirling's proposal to give votes to a few propertied women. Since then the Assembly had begun to dichotomise into Liberals and Conservatives after thirty years of factional politics, and Labor had developed as a considerable lobbying force, although there was no Labor party. Woman suffrage, and the form it should take, would from now on be caught up in the practicalities of South Australian party politics.

The forerunner of the Women's Suffrage League of South Australia was the Women's Committee of the Society for the Promotion of Social Purity. The main aim of the society was to raise the age of consent for girls from thirteen to sixteen years and so prevent those under sixteen from soliciting on the streets or being recruited into brothels. The society itself was predominantly male. It was initiated by Joseph Kirby, a Congregational minister, and had in its membership John Colton (a past Premier), Charles Kingston (a future one), parliamentarians, other prominent ministers of religion, and some leading citizens. Many, but not all, members of the society were to be strong supporters of the suffragists. Mary Colton (wife of John) was President of the Women's Committee, and Mary Lee, Rosetta Birks and Hannah Chewings were members. The society ran an aggressive campaign which succeeded in pressuring the Government to pass the 1885 Criminal Law Consolidation Act which raised the age of consent to sixteen years.[15]

The Women's Committee, calling itself the Ladies' Social Purity Society, now championed other issues involving the rights and welfare of women and children. By the time Caldwell's 1887 bill was introduced, the women had decided that they needed the vote to reinforce their agitation on specific issues. A meeting was called of interested men and women at which

> it was resolved that as woman's political enfranchisement is deemed by this Society absolutely necessary to the right fulfilment of her duties as a citizen, and to her moral, social and industrial interests, this Society pledges itself to urge by every legitimate means the cause of woman's suffrage in this Colony.[16]

Stirling presided over the 'large and enthusiastic meeting' which was called publicly to constitute the Women's Suffrage League on 21 July 1888. There were 'ministers of religion, members of Parliament, but principally ladies' in the audience.[17] Stirling gave a rousing speech, echoing his parliamentary oratory, but as far as we know he made no mention of the property qualifications which had figured in his two parliamentary moves. Kirby followed Stirling, and then a 'very nervous' Mary Lee, who made a timid disclaimer she would probably have scorned in her fiery speeches of the later campaign: 'The women of South Australia were no shrieking sisterhood demanding women's rights. They simply asked a modicum of power to assist in obtaining what were the rights of women.'[18] The proposal brought to the meeting was that the league should adopt the qualification Caldwell was putting forward in Parliament, and agitate for votes for women over twenty-five. There was considerable opposition to this from the audience, and the platform which emerged was

1. That the women of this Colony should have a voice in the choice of representatives to the Houses of Legislature.
2. That the qualifications entitling women to vote should be the same as those which apply to men.
3. That while Woman's Suffrage is desired no claim is sought for any right to act as representatives.[19]

It was a significant platform in the light of moves which had gone before and which were still to come. The women rejected any limitations of age or property on their suffrage and, no doubt influenced by the antipathy shown to women as representatives, decided not to press for the right of candidature. Stirling was elected President of the league, and Mary Lee Co-Secretary with Hector McLennan. Rosetta Birks was Treasurer. 'An influential committee' of thirteen women and fifteen men was appointed.

Three women present at the league's inauguration deserve attention in the light of the work they were to do in the six to seven years of its existence. The most fascinating of the three is Mary Lee. Lee had come to South Australia from Ireland as recently as 1879.[20] She was then a 58-year-old widow of a cathedral organist. She had borne seven children, and she came with one daughter to nurse a son who was dying. She never returned to Ireland; indeed, she could not afford to do so. Instead, at an age when she could have been forgiven for contemplating a rocking chair, she threw her prodigious energy into causes which would benefit women and children. Her first major commitment after her son's death seems to have been to the Social Purity Society, and then she moved on to the Women's Suffrage League. She was a tiny, plump woman ('five feet nothing') with a keen intellect, practical egalitarian values and a professed Christian faith. The league's secretarial duties fell entirely to Lee when her Co-Secretary resigned at the end of the first year. Although her first speeches show some trepidation, her volatile nature soon asserted itself and she became a fiery and devastatingly logical orator and letter writer, and the best-known apologist for woman suffrage in the South Australian campaign.

Lee's impassioned nature was in contrast to the more placid temperaments of the two women with whom she worked so closely and harmoniously in the league. Rosetta Birks was the league's Treasurer for the whole campaign. She was the wife of Charles Birks, the prosperous proprietor of Adelaide's largest grocery establishment (who is said to have sustained the league financially for its six years). She had married Birks after her sister, his first wife, died, and was stepmother to his six children. Mary (Lady) Colton, wife of a former Premier, who became President in 1891 when Stirling resigned to go on a trans-Australian exploring expedition, had five children. Both Rosetta Birks and Mary Colton were involved in other social work committees, and they were both committed church members, Colton a Methodist and Birks a Baptist.

The new league extended its network through drawing-room meetings, the formation of branches, and the gathering of signatures to petitions. It is not surprising, given the number of clergymen at its inauguration and the number of committed church members involved, that it early sought the cooperation of the churches. There is no record that the Anglicans replied, but Congregationalists, Wesleyans, Baptists and Bible Christians gave their support to the league's platform.[21] The Society of Friends said that it endorsed the league only 'insofar as it seeks to extend the vote to women who have qualifications as property holders equal to the one required for electors to the Legislative Council, but [we] do not at present support the policy of ... universal suffrage to women'.[22]

Among those invited to attend the preliminary meeting to discuss the formation of the league were members of the Adelaide Woman's Christian Temperance Union, a small band of women which had been limping along in the temperance cause since 1886. The Union had seventy-five nominal members, but less than a dozen active ones. The women reported back to their fellow members and recommended that they should support votes for women.[23]

The Woman's Christian Temperance Union was founded in America in 1873 by a group of women concerned about the effect drunkenness was having on the social and economic position of other women and their children. Women were being deprived of the basics of life not only by their own intemperance but by the intemperance of their supporting spouses. The Union spread and in the late 1870s and 1880s, with the dedicated Frances Willard at its national helm, it became a considerable lobbying force in federal and state legislatures, agitating on all aspects of the liquor question and on other matters affecting the lives of women and children. Convinced that only the vote would give women control over legislation vital to them and help to impose prohibition in America, it adopted woman suffrage as a fundamental objective.

Fired with proselytising zeal because of its success at home, the American Union began to see its mission in global terms. In 1884 it dispatched its first world missionary, Mrs Mary Leavitt. Leavitt travelled via the Sandwich Islands to New Zealand and Australia, trusting to gather financial backing en route. In the sixteen months she was in Australasia she established Unions in all colonies except Western Australia (New Zealand, eleven; Tasmania, three; Queensland, five; New South Wales, one; Victoria, one; and South Australia, one). In New Zealand, Queensland and Victoria the movement grew after Leavitt's departure, but it languished in other states until the vital and charismatic Jessie Ackermann arrived in 1889.

Ackermann, who was thirty-two when she arrived in Australia, was met at Adelaide railway station in June 1889 by the WCTU women, who were impressed by her 'bright and winning personality'.[24] Under the aegis of the WCTU and the male temperance societies, she held a ten-day temperance mission in Adelaide town hall. Then, ignoring the gloomy prognostications of those who told her that 'temperance sentiment is dead in the country',[25] she departed for a tour of the colony, lecturing and forming WCTU branches. She returned after nine weeks, with all her expenses met along the way and able to flourish the credentials of twenty-four new branches.[26]

With characteristic enthusiasm Ackermann organised delegates from all branches into a Convention in August 1889, and there began the regulatory work she was to continue all over Australia. She made the South Australian WCTU into a tight, cohesive unit run along strict organisational lines. Convention officers were nominated and then elected by secret ballot, and all business was conducted according to parliamentary rules. These officers, with district Presidents, were to form a Colonial Executive to voice the official opinions of the Unions in the periods between future yearly Conventions. At this gathering Ackermann also validated the distinctive structure which the American Union had developed to enable it to work along several different fronts at once. Every local Union divided its work into the number of departments it considered it could handle—legal, 'moral purity', educational, suffrage, and so on—and each of these had a Superintendent who was responsible for its activities. There were Colonial Superintendents of each cause who coordinated the work of departments within individual branches. In practice this meant that when woman suffrage was adopted as Union policy, a Colonial Superintendent of Suffrage was appointed and delegates went home to their branches to organise suffrage departments at the local level. The WCTU network of departments provided an extraordinarily efficient system of working for woman suffrage in every colony. Political lobbying, publicity and educational work were both localised and centralised, and could be carried out efficiently even when, as often happened, there were members in the individual branch who did not approve of votes for women. Dissenters were able to channel their energies into other Union causes.

Ackermann moved on from South Australia to begin the work in Western Australia and to organise and inspire Leavitt's embryonic movements in other colonies.[27] By 1891 she had the Union functioning on a national level, with triennial Australasian Conventions planned. She herself became the first Australasian President. In this position she travelled widely, and by the force of her personality reinvigorated the WCTU wherever she went. Everywhere she emphasised how necessary the vote was to women if they were to establish either prohibition or controls on the liquor industry, and if they were to change the laws which discriminated against them. Ackermann, although an American, must be considered a major voice in the Australian suffrage movement. The WCTU came to regard their 'dear sister' as an honorary Australian, and indeed she saw more of Australia on this visit (which ended in 1894) and subsequent visits than many Australian women did in the whole of their lives. Among other things she rode horseback through the bush to the Jenolan Caves and went underground to explore them; she and the obligatory chaperone travelled in a covered wagon with an outback missionary; and she defied convention by going down a coal-mine. In these activities she was setting the pattern for the unconventional things she was to do in Japan, China, Burma, India, Africa, and Alaska. On her last visit to Australia, in 1912, she wrote a remarkably perceptive book, *Australia from a Woman's Point of View*, in which she commented on, and sometimes trenchantly criticised, the country's ethos, its politics, and particularly its attitude to the education of girls and to the participation of women in public life. Although ostensibly motivated only by her commitment to temperance, Ackermann's writings reveal a woman of wide interests who belongs in the company of nineteenth-century 'lady explorers'. WCTU records report her establishing the work in Iceland between 1894 and 1897, and camping in 1898 in the Yosemite valley in America to regain her strength for more travel.

In 1889 Ackermann left the work in South Australia in the hands of Elizabeth Nicholls (who was to be Colonial President for the whole of the campaign) and Serena Lake, the first and most vital of its three Colonial Suffrage Superintendents. Details of Lake's background are scarce, but we do know that she was a Primitive Methodist missionary before she married the Reverend Octavius Lake. She was a fiery speaker on the suffrage *or* evangelical platform and a caustic and incisive letter writer. Elizabeth Nicholls was born to one of Australia's early settler families, and she and her supportive husband were both working members of an Adelaide Wesleyan church. They had four sons and a daughter. In 1889, when she became South Australian President, Elizabeth was thirty-nine years old, her child-bearing and most onerous child-rearing years behind her, and a long and distinguished career in public life before her. She was to be South Australian President for twenty-one years, and Australasian President for nine. Her years as Australasian President coincided with the suffrage struggle in other colonies and she travelled extensively, taking the place of Jessie Ackermann in enthusing each colonial organisation and particularly in hammering the necessity for votes for women. Many qualities are attributed to her—earnestness, tact and wisdom, determination, calmness, self-possession, dignity—but perhaps the most evocative description is her nickname, 'The Chieftain'.[28]

Under Nicholls' and Lake's guidance the 1889 WCTU Convention moved 'That as the franchise is the symbol of freedom, and half the members of our nation are deprived of that right, we petition our Legislature to enfranchise the women of South Australia.'[29] The 1889 WCTU report then went on to assure the Government, as it did in all other colonies, that 'the majority of women may be confidently expected to vote on the side of morality and good order.'[30] A Mrs Eake was appointed Colonial Organiser and by August 1890 she was to report twenty-six new Unions, making a total of fifty-two in the colony. Lake then did the follow-up work, urging each new Union to establish its Suffrage Department. The total membership did not grow as rapidly as the number of Unions—from approximately 1000 members in 1889 to 1565 in 1892—but each branch had, in 1892, an average of thirty members.

In mid-1889 there was a change of ministry and Dr John Cockburn became Premier. He was a progressive Liberal and both the league and the WCTU hoped that he might introduce a bill giving all women the vote, but the only parliamentary move that year was by Robert Caldwell, who had in 1887 proposed votes for all women over twenty-five. In October Caldwell introduced a bill which gave propertied women over twenty-one a vote for the Upper House only. He explained why his bill was only for propertied women.[31] He had come to realise after the moves of the last few years, he said, that it was unwise to expect too much. Talking with other members had convinced him that he could get a property vote for the Upper House through, but not a vote for all women for the Lower House. The Assembly applauded him when he said this. The bill did not exclude the married woman with property; she could vote 'unless she were willing to delegate the responsibility' to her husband'.[32] There was much support for the bill. Alfred Catt said: 'There was a House specially constituted for the representation of property, and it seemed to him that property should be represented there whether it stood in the name of a man or a woman.'[33] The bill gained twenty-five votes, not enough to amend the Constitution.

In 1890 the Trades and Labor Council formed its political wing, the United Labor Party of South Australia. It ran no candidates on its own for the 1890 Lower House elections but, as the Trades and Labor Council had done in 1887, endorsed Liberals who were sympathetic to its aims. It doubled its influence in the Assembly when Liberal sympathisers increased from seven to fourteen.[34] On the hustings practically every candidate had been forced by the Women's Suffrage League and the WCTU to declare himself on the subject of woman suffrage. There were three groups of answers: those who opposed it on principle, those who favoured it for all, and those who would support it only for women with property.

Before the subject was raised in the new Parliament, another group appeared which was pledged to working for votes for women. Under the guidance of the Trades and Labor Council, a Working Women's Trade Union was formed to lobby for better conditions for women in the clothing industry. Mary Lee, already Secretary of the Women's Suffrage League, became Secretary of the new trade union. Augusta Zadow, a

German woman married to an Adelaide tailor, became its President. Zadow was to speak at many League and WCTU suffrage meetings, always linking the woman's vote to the achievement of better wages and conditions for women in the paid work force.

At the same time the Women's Suffrage League was steadily expanding its branches and influence. In March 1890 its annual report showed that not only had it been holding meetings in Adelaide and suburbs, but throughout the colony. Serena Lake continued to travel and lecture to WCTU branches and distributed copious amounts of literature with her enthusiastic circulars. Both Nicholls and Lake were now members of the Women's Suffrage League, and petitions common to both were circulated for the rest of the campaign. During March 1890 Mary Lee, in the *Register*, published 'Letters to Women' in which she presented all the major arguments for women having the vote.[35] Influenced, no doubt, by her new position as Secretary of the Working Women's Trade Union, she emphasised the woman's vote as an industrial weapon. This would have done nothing to allay the fears of those who were watching with alarm the incursion of the Labor party's influence into the Assembly.

In mid-1890 Caldwell reintroduced his 1889 bill giving votes to female property holders (married or unmarried) for the Upper House only.[36] He had the support of the Premier, Dr John Cockburn, and the rest of the ministry. Kingston, not in the Cabinet, warned the House that the bill would increase the power of the Upper House at the expense of the democratic chamber.[37] Caldwell excused this bill too by claiming that it would be the first step in enfranchising all women.[38] Why not, then, said Scherk cynically, start with the Lower House and leave the Upper House till later?[39] An amendment to give all women the vote was defeated; the bill reached its statutory majority, and it became the first to be sent to 'the other place'. Of the Legislative Council's twenty-four voting members, only thirteen were present for the debate. John Warren, when introducing the bill, pointed out that propertied women voters would give the Upper House more power in dealing with the Lower, and 'if they did not take this opportunity perhaps they would not have it again'.[40] Only one member stood out against the property franchise and because of his lone vote the bill did not reach its statutory majority and pass into law.

In spite of Mary Lee's early 1890 published letters which made clear her belief that working women desperately needed the vote to improve their conditions, both the Suffrage League and the WCTU supported Caldwell's bill. They were seduced by the fact that it would at least give some women the vote, and they believed Caldwell when he claimed that votes for all women would follow. The WCTU rationalised its support: 'Of course the Bill does not satisfy Mr Caldwell or us insofar as it was more a recognition of property than womankind. But it is a larger advance than at first appears, since the House of Assembly has for the first time by formal enactment declared women to possess individual political rights and powers.'[41]

When the Women's Suffrage League gathered for its annual meeting in March 1891, however, it decided that it would not again support any bill which gave limited suffrage. The Trades and Labor Council had approached the league and let it be known that it would throw its full support only behind adult suffrage,[42] and the women had been made aware that several Liberal members of Parliament had refused to support

Caldwell's bill because it did not give all women the vote.[43] In April the Women's Suffrage League's council had a meeting with Caldwell, who tried to re-enlist their support for a limited franchise which he would submit later in the year, but the women were adamant: all women must have a vote.[44]

This hardening of the league's attitude to the propertied vote could have been influenced by the visit to Adelaide in early 1891 of the 79-year-old 'autocratic democrat', Sir George Grey. Grey, sent by the Colonial Office to impose some financial order on the young improvident colony, had served as Governor of South Australia from 1841 to 1845. He moved on to New Zealand (1845–53), to the Cape Colony (1853–61), and back to New Zealand (1861–7). After a soujourn in England Grey returned privately to New Zealand where, in 1874, he entered politics and was Prime Minister from 1877 to 1879. Grey's political beliefs had become more radical with the years and during his short ministry he drafted a bill to give the New Zealand Parliament one-man-one-vote for its Assembly, a measure achieved by his successor in office in 1889. In 1891 he came to Australia as delegate to the Convention which was considering the first draft of a Constitution to unite the Australasian colonies, and eloquently urged that one-man-one-vote be written into the document. Then he went on a tour of the eastern colonies, lionised by Labor and radical Liberalism. In Adelaide at a banquet and an enthusiastic public meeting he heaped praise on the South Australian Constitution, the only one, apart from New Zealand, which had one-man-one-vote, and he unfavourably compared the nominated New Zealand Upper House with South Australia's, which was elected on an uncommonly low property qualification.[45] The Women's Suffrage League could hardly have been unaffected by the democratic fervour gripping the city during his visit. Grey used the term 'adult suffrage' in his oratory; he did not canvass for woman suffrage, although he was to support it in New Zealand for the next three years. While in Sydney he had a profound influence on the young widow Dora Montefiore, who attended his public meeting and met him socially. 'He spoke to me of the enfranchisement of women in the colonies, where things moved more rapidly than in the older countries',[46] she wrote. Grey urged Montefiore to emulate the women of New Zealand and form a suffrage organisation. Montefiore began to put out feelers in the upper-class social milieu in which she moved, and the responses led to the Womanhood Suffrage League of New South Wales.

In 1891 Catherine Helen Spence decided to give her support to the Women's Suffrage League and was elected as one of its Vice-Presidents. Spence, at sixty-six, was probably the best-known woman in public affairs in South Australia. Her life, since she arrived in 1839, aged fourteen, had spanned South Australian history. Her fiction books, her book *The Laws we Live Under* (which was used in schools), and her literary and journalistic comment had earned her the respect of the colony, but she also had its affection. Although single, she was the maternal figure who had brought up three families of orphans, cared for her aged mother, and still found time to mother the abandoned and neglected children of South Australia through the Boarding Out Society and the Destitute Board. Spence had delayed giving her support to votes for women because she considered that the electoral system should be reformed first; that only under proportional representation could the will of the electorate be reflected in its government. Since the 1860s she had been travelling, lecturing and writing in the cause of 'effective voting', and was to do so until the end of her life. She wrote later in her autobiography:

> For myself, I considered electoral reform on the Hare system of more value than the enfranchisement of women ... I was accounted a weak-kneed sister by those who worked primarily for woman suffrage, although I was as much convinced as they were that I was entitled to a vote, and hoped that I would be able to exercise it before I was too feeble to hobble to the poll ... it was not until the movement ... grew too strong to be neglected that I took hold of it at all; and I do not claim any credit for its success.[47]

Weak-kneed sister she may have been, but Spence's support, even though she was out of the colony for one of the four years she was associated with the league, would have increased the credibility of the movement considerably.

Although the league was now at odds with Caldwell over the form of suffrage which women should be given, it was foolish enough to ask him to introduce a deputation to the next Premier, Thomas Playford, on 2 August 1891. Caldwell had been asked to introduce the delegation 'according to the principles of the League',[48] but his opening words were: 'They confined the measure to the representation of property, and he was not aware whether the deputation would ask the Government to go further just now.'[49] The women did intend to ask the Government to go further, as succeeding speakers, particularly Lee and Spence, were at pains to point out. Lee spoke plainly: 'We are not asking for the vote', she said. 'We are demanding it.'[50] Playford's response to their assertiveness was hostility. If Caldwell cared to reintroduce his bill giving votes to propertied women he would support it, he said, but he was against votes for all women. He launched into a tirade against the principle, using quotes from opponents all over the world.[51]

As a result of Caldwell's ambiguous introduction of the deputation, newspaper and journal reports were confusing. Mary Lee clarified the situation for the Trades and Labor Council[52] and the council then attacked Caldwell for his duplicity. Caldwell counter-attacked, claiming that he was free to say what he liked, and accusing the Trades and Labor Council (and, by inference, the league) of being unrealistic in their expectations. The league's attitude, he said, was 'If you cannot get all you want, have nothing.'[53]

In 1891, in accordance with the South Australian Constitution, one-third of the Legislative Council members vacated their seats, and the eight outgoing Councillors were obliged to retire or contest an election. The United Labor Party for the first time stood three endorsed candidates in its own name. It was unusual in Australia for a Labor party to make its first foray into colonial politics via the Upper House, and was made possible by the low property qualification for candidacy, and by the payment of members. The three men, all pledged to full suffrage for women, were elected.[54] Progressive Liberalism also made gains in the Council, and the stage was set for discord in a chamber with a record of harmony.

Caldwell made no move in the Assembly in 1891, but shortly after the deputation to Playford which had caused such a furore John Warren, a strong supporter of Caldwell, introduced an almost identical property suffrage bill in the now liberalised Upper

House.⁵⁵ There was a minimum of ideological contention (centred on the sentimentality of keeping women separated from the hurly-burly of politics and up on the pedestal) and the rest of the heated debate concerned the form of the bill. Andrew Kirkpatrick, one of the new Labor members, attacked Warren for introducing a measure which was designed to disadvantage the democratic Lower House, and which went against the expressed wishes of the Women's Suffrage League.⁵⁶ An amendment was carried which completely changed the form of the bill. It gave votes to all women on the same basis as men. The new bill passed, but not with a statutory majority. The WCTU, slow to grasp the political implications of increasing the propertied vote in the Legislative Council, had presented petitions to support Warren's bill, but the Women's Suffrage League withheld theirs 'lest such action should be regarded by the signatories as supporting a measure which was generally regarded with disgust, if not with absolute aversion'.⁵⁷

In early 1892, in one of the periodic upheavals in the Legislative Assembly, Frederick Holder became Premier. Holder had opposed propertied bills and his daughter and wife Jane were members of the WCTU. All the women were optimistic now about their prospects, and sent a combined deputation.⁵⁸ They did not make the mistake this time of asking Caldwell to introduce them; they were introduced by the Legislative Council member, Sylvanus Magarey, also a member of the Council of the WCTU. Speaker after speaker made clear that the deputation would have nothing to do with a propertied franchise. Mary Lee said that all agreement with Caldwell had ended last year.⁵⁹ The WCTU speakers showed that at last the Union was becoming aware of the political manipulation which lay behind the propertied vote. She was glad, Elizabeth Nicholls said, that the suffrage 'had not been given in a partial manner'.⁶⁰ Catherine Helen Spence reminded Holder that he had supported votes for all women in previous suffrage debates, and told him that the women 'earnestly hoped that the Government would take up the matter'.⁶¹ Holder said he was completely in accord with the wishes of the women; he would consult his colleagues, and if they did not see their way clear to introducing a bill sponsored by the Government in the present session, the Liberals would make it an issue at the coming elections.⁶² The women's hopes were dashed when he wrote ten days later that his Cabinet had decreed that there would be no bill in 1892.⁶³ As it happened, however, Holder's Government did not last for the session; it tumbled to one led by John Downer, a firm supporter of propertied votes only. When the women sent a deputation to Downer his reply was curt: he 'declined to grant the prayer of the delegation'.⁶⁴

Caldwell did not give up easily. In the confusion of the session there was no room for another bill, but in a bill to clear up misconceptions about male eligibility for candidacy to the Legislative Council he tried again by amendment to give propertied women the vote for the Upper House. The chamber refused to accept the amendment because it did not have a close enough relationship to the original bill.⁶⁵

If there had been any doubts remaining about the basis on which the suffragists would accept the vote, they must have been dispelled by a large public meeting in March 1893. The three arms of the movement were represented: the league, the WCTU, and the Working Women's Trades Union. All emphasised that votes should be for all women. Elizabeth Nicholls demonstrated the full conversion of the WCTU: 'To pass a property suffrage would mean putting a power into the hands of the propertied classes which would afterwards be bitterly regretted. (hear, hear).'[66] Augusta Zadow, for working women, put the claim as 'woman suffrage irrespective of property or position'.[67] Catherine Helen Spence's motion, for woman suffrage on the same conditions as for men, was enthusiastically carried. This was to be the last blow for the cause Spence was to strike; she left soon afterwards for the United States and England and did not return until the eve of the granting of the woman's vote.

In early 1893 South Australian politicians were on the hustings for an Assembly election, and the women's combined meeting was a way of ensuring that their vote became an election issue. The elections marked an important turning point in South Australian politics. The Labor party carved out a place for itself in the Assembly when eight members (supported by two Independents with Labor sympathies) moved in to support the three Labor members in the Upper House.[68] But more than that: for the first time a strong Liberal leader, Charles Kingston, united the progressive Liberal factions behind him in what could be called a party. The resulting Government was to last for a record nine years. Labor supported Kingston, and was crucial in giving him the numbers to defend himself against a strong Conservative opposition, forged in response to the rise of Labor. There were three former Premiers in the ministry which Kingston formed: Cockburn, Playford and Holder, and the first question the women asked themselves was: 'Does it augur well for votes for women?' Kingston had opposed woman suffrage as such in the debates, Cockburn had supported propertied votes (although he seemed to do this as a step on the road to votes for all women), and Playford, when Premier for a short time, had refused to give the women a hearing. Only Holder had been unequivocally in support of their aims.

In the light of Kingston's former opposition, the women must have been rather surprised when he assured their deputation that there would be an adult suffrage bill in the coming session. On 15 August Dr Cockburn, now Minister for Education, introduced it for its second reading and explained its provisions.[69] The early clauses were simple enough; they gave women the vote for both Houses on the same conditions as men, and excluded women from sitting in Parliament. But this suffrage, even if both Houses passed the bill, was to be provisional on two referenda. One would record the opinions of all males eligible to vote for the Assembly, and the other of all females in the colony over twenty-one. A further complexity was introduced: the voters would not be asked simply whether they approved of votes for women on the same grounds as men; they would answer two questions:

(1) Do you wish the franchise for the Legislative Council to be extended to women?
(2) Do you wish the franchise for the House of Assembly to be extended to women?

The implications of the referenda were themselves complex. In either the male or the female referendum voters could decide to give women the vote for one House, or the other, or both, or neither. Furthermore, any suffrage at all had to pass both referenda!

There was an outcry from the suffragists. The league protested that no referendum should be held,[70] and Mary Lee called the Labor party members 'a lot of nincompoops'[71] for allowing such a bill to be brought forward. She spoke at at least one meeting presided over by a Labor member, which demanded that woman suffrage be treated as any other amendment to the Constitution had been treated,[72] and she wrote to the *Advertiser* pointing out that there had been no referendum when manhood suffrage had been granted.[73] Her fiery speeches at this period earned her a couplet.

> Mary had a temper hot that used to boil and bubble,
> And e'er the suffrage she had got it landed her in trouble.[74]

The WCTU was in Convention during the passage of the bill and passed a resolution: 'That we earnestly protest against the proposal to peril the safety of the measure by submitting it to a referendum vote ... [which] will give thoughtless men and women, and women who would not value a vote, the power to deprive others of a right.'[75]

There was much discussion outside Parliament, and woman suffrage per se was usually smothered by debate about the referenda. In Parliament an attempt to inject some ideological content into the debate in the form of what the Norwood WCTU called 'sickly sentimentality'[76] was soon overtaken by accusations as to why the Government had included the referenda in the bill in the first place. Some said that it wanted to strengthen the Upper House by not giving the vote for the Lower; and some said that it wanted to strengthen the Lower House by not giving it for the Upper! But emerging was one strong inference: Kingston's Government was making a token gesture to placate Labor and its most radical Liberals, and the referenda were included to ensure that the bill was wrecked, if not in the Lower House, then in the Upper. In the debate there were those for the referenda, those against, and those who thought that only one question should have been posed. The bill emerged from committee with the referenda clauses intact. It gained twenty-four votes but required twenty-eight for a statutory majority. All the Labor members voted for the referenda to be held; Mary Lee's opinion of them as 'nincompoops' was confirmed. Adding to the women's frustration with the Government's handling of their franchise bill was the feeling that they had been robbed of the opportunity to lead the Australasian colonies in this reform, for in late 1893 New Zealand women gained their vote.

On 13 November Dr Magarey introduced a large combined deputation to the Premier. It asked the Government to reintroduce the bill, but this time with the referenda clauses eliminated.[77] The Premier was noncommittal. To support their demands, the league and the WCTU began circulating a petition. Mary Lee went on a campaign tour, addressing large audiences in Port Augusta, Port Pirie and other towns.[78] The WCTU printed ten thousand copies of each of four leaflets for distribution, and held meetings 'public and private' in various centres.[79] Elizabeth Nicholls, after the resignation of her second Colonial Suffrage Superintendent since Serena Lake, who had left Australia in 1891, now held that position, as well as those of Colonial and Australasian President.

In early 1894 there were elections again for one-third of the members of the Legislative Council. The result of these elections was critical for woman suffrage. Labor increased its membership in the Upper House; there were now six men in the Council who were Labor or who would support Labor. This gave it one-quarter of the voting power.[80] With the increased Liberal representation in the Upper House, South Australia now had that most unusual situation in nineteenth-century Australian politics: an Upper

SOUTH AUSTRALIA, 1894   37

In 1893 the Premier, Charles Kingston, introduced a woman suffrage bill into the South Australian Parliament, but because its implementation was made conditional on complex referenda, the Legislative Assembly refused to pass it.
Quiz, 6 October 1893. Mortlock Library, State Library of South Australia.

House with a non-Conservative majority. But in both Houses there were what the *Advertiser* called 'powerful and vigorous' Conservative oppositions.[81]

Responding perhaps to Labor pressure and to the representations of the women, the 1894 bill which was introduced in the liberalised Legislative Council had only two clauses: it gave women the vote for both Houses on the same basis as men, and it excluded them from sitting in Parliament.[82] In the Legislative Council debates, which were to last over two months and involve eleven sittings, there were long and ponderous speeches, especially from opponents, extolling the moral virtues of woman and quoting the opinions of wise men and poets on her and her place in the world; little was heard of the woman's opinion of herself. But leaving out the obsession with the woman as 'the angel of the house', and the usual arguments against women in public life, the struggle was essentially the continuing South Australian one between Labor and those Liberals who wanted all women to vote, and Conservatives who wanted a limited property vote or none at all. An amendment to give only property holders the vote for the Legislative Council was defeated,[83] as was one to raise the age to twenty-five years.[84] Then Ebenezer Ward moved that the clause forbidding women to sit in Parliament should be struck out.[85] Magarey accused him and his supporters of trying to wreck the bill: 'It was refreshing to see the new-born zeal of members who kept on moving amendments to a Bill which they opposed . . . It was to alter the measure into such a form that it would not prove acceptable to the other branch of the Legislature.'[86] The amendment was carried. The right of candidature had been given to South Australian women by its opponents!

The women spent much time in the parliamentary gallery during the debate and commented tartly later on 'the pedestal lady' with whom the male sentimentalists were obsessed. On 23 August, as the third reading of the bill was beginning, the women judged it opportune to present their petition of 11,600 names. There were to be larger petitions in other colonies, but this was impressive enough; a great roll tied with gold ribbon, it would have opened out to 400 feet, and it contained more names than any petition in South Australia's history up to that time.[87] The petition repeated the first part of the 1888 Constitution of the Women's Suffrage League, which demanded woman suffrage on the same conditions as for men, but it omitted the last clause, which denied any ambition to enter Parliament. The 1888 pioneers may not have desired that right, but the opinion of women who had come into the movement since was divided. The bill went to its final vote the same day, and was carried thirteen to six, the bare statutory majority required for an amendment of the Constitution.[88] The bill had survived the pitfalls of the Upper House and even emerged with more privileges than originally intended. Now it had the Lower House to contend with.

The Premier made no move to introduce the bill in the Lower House for nearly three months. One account of the South Australian movement says that this was because the Government had to wait until it was sure it had the twenty-eight votes required for a statutory majority in the Assembly.[89] Cockburn eventually introduced the second reading debate on 8 November, confident that the bill had thirty-one supporters.[90] But to the consternation of the Government, three supporters paired, so leaving it with only the minimum twenty-eight votes. There was one elderly member of the House who always left at ten o'clock at night. (One source calls him 'practically the father of the House'[91] and the other names him as 'Jimmy' Howe.)[92] For several nights the Opposition stonewalled until his seat was empty, and each time the Government avoided a vote being taken by adjourning the debate. On 11 December the stonewaller, seeing the empty seat, sat down. But Howe had been detained outside. The Government agreed to the vote being taken, Howe was hustled in again, and the bill had its twenty-eight votes![93] It now went to committee, where unsuccessful attempts were made to limit the franchise[94] and add a referendum clause.[95] An amendment was successfully put to allow women to vote by post—supporters of the move were concerned that a woman could be detained at home by her 'duties' or because she was in 'a certain condition'.

The bill was to pass its third reading in the Assembly on 17 December. Although traditionally the third reading of a bill only confirmed the decisions made in committee, the women attended the House in the afternoon to have the satisfaction of seeing it pass. When it was delayed most chose to go that night to a Welcome Home to Catherine Helen Spence. After the appropriate speeches the President suggested that all repair to the parliamentary galleries 'to await the ultimate decision, even if they had to wait all night'.[96] They arrived during the adjournment for dinner. The *Advertiser* described the scene.

> Ladies poured into the cushioned benches to the left of the Speaker, and relentlessly usurped the seats of gentlemen who had been comfortably seated there before. They filled the aisles and overflowed into the gallery to the right, while some of the bolder spirits climbed the stairs and invaded the rougher forms behind the clock. So there was a wall of beauty at the southern end of the building.[97]

The women went home when the debate adjourned soon after midnight. When Elizabeth Nicholls arrived for the next day's proceedings she heard the division bells ringing for the final vote. It was thirty-one to fourteen, three more than the required majority; the three who had endangered the second reading by pairing were in their seats. Caldwell did not register his vote.

The Women's Suffrage League would surely have held a thanksgiving demonstration of some kind, but I have been unable to find any details of it in the press, and the league's papers have been destroyed. The WCTU delayed its official celebration until its September 1895 Colonial Convention, when delegates from all branches were in Adelaide.[98] John Gordon, who had introduced the 1894 bill in the Council, addressed a large audience, and was followed by Spence and Nicholls. Congratulations were the order of the day and the Union gave due acknowledgement of the work of the league and those within it, while still reserving much of the credit for itself.

On the surface the WCTU and the league worked amicably together during the campaign, but this does not mean that there was accord on aims other than the gaining of the vote. Mary Lee, evidently in response to a complaint by Rose Scott about the discourtesy of one of the WCTU women, wrote in 1897, 'we know the plane on which they live move and have their being and I am not in sympathy with them.[99]

There was, too, some jostling for credit after the vote was won, but not so much by the women themselves. The *Bulletin* lauded Mary Lee's contribution at the expense of the temperance women,[100] and Cornelius Proud in his account of the movement was eager to claim greater glory for the WCTU—and in the process magnify his own contribution as a member of the Union's council.[101] This is unfortunate. Although the WCTU was more politically naive, and slower to realise that it was being used for Caldwell's conservative purposes, both organisations laboured hard for votes for all women, and both had their outstanding workers.

Elizabeth Nicholls' work for female suffrage did not finish in 1894; as Australasian President she visited other colonies when the triennial WCTU Conventions rotated, and invariably invigorated the franchise work there, and she went as a representative to the WCTU World Convention in Boston in 1906, no doubt enthusing temperance women from other countries who were still struggling for their franchise. Outside the WCTU she joined the group advocating proportional representation in Australian Parliaments and, firmly non-party in her agitation for women's rights, helped to form the Australian Federation of Women Voters, which she represented at the International Alliance of Women for Suffrage and Equal Citizenship in Geneva in 1920. Nicholls' funeral in 1943 defied custom in that it was conducted, not by men, but by women from the South Australian and Australian Union.[102]

Mary Lee, Nicholls' counterpart in the Women's Suffrage League, was seventy-three when the South Australian vote was won. In February 1896, on her seventy-fifth birthday, Kingston presented her with a testimonial acknowledging the work she had done for the women's franchise, and with a purse of sovereigns which had been gathered by public subscription. The fund had been launched by two Labor Party members to alleviate the poverty of Lee's last years. Lee must have considered the gaining of the vote to have been the major achievement of her life, for when she died in 1909 her tombstone bore the words 'Secretary of the Women's Suffrage League'. Catherine Helen Spence, the 'weak-kneed sister' in the campaign, who was in her last years affectionately referred to as 'The Grand Old Woman of Australia', was to continue in public life till her death in 1910, aged eighty-five.

Several factors contributed to the gaining of the women's vote in 1894. The most important was the confluence of Liberal and Labor forces in the Upper and Lower Houses after the 1894 election. The suffrage was granted, but only just, on the crest of this convergence. In the Legislative Council elections in 1897 the Conservatives gained ground and the bill would probably not have gone through the Upper House, while in 1899 the increased Conservative party membership of the Assembly, and the parting of the ways for Liberalism and Labor, would have posed difficulties for it in the Lower.

With political forces so precariously balanced in 1894, other factors were crucial: the fact that the South Australian Labor Party did not have to choose between the abolition of the plural vote and votes for women; the cumulative effect of nearly seven years of agitation by the women and their insistence since 1891 on woman suffrage on the same grounds as for men; the aura of 'respectability' around most of the women which persuaded politicians that the women's vote would enhance the image of South Australia as a 'moral society'; the linking of the vote to reformist Christianity which was then so strong in the colony; and, not least, the vision that South Australia had of itself as a leader in progressive legislation.

The South Australian movement did not grow out of the one in New Zealand, as has sometimes been claimed. The two movements ran independently, and there was some rivalry about who should be first. South Australian women were very disappointed when Kingston's referenda provisions in the 1893 suffrage bill robbed them of any chance they had of leading the way. The New Zealand movement has been well-covered by Patricia Grimshaw, but as the two finales were so close and as New Zealand at the time had the same colonial status as South Australia, it is worth noting some parallels. New Zealand women gained their vote by a very narrow margin and in a period of political change, for the 1890 election had brought in the first New Zealand Government which had some freedom from factional alliances; the Government was a progressive Liberal one which had the support of the growing Labour movement, and it embarked on a series of radical government intervention measures, of which woman suffrage was one; and the New Zealand campaign, as that in South Australia, was not hampered by the struggle for one-man-one-vote, for this had been achieved in 1889. Moreover, the members of the New Zealand Franchise Leagues (which existed in all the main centres) and the Woman's Christian Temperance Union (which spread its tentacles all over the islands) came generally from families which were highly respected, and the two organisations (with considerable cross-membership) worked amicably together; and many of the prominent members of both were held in high regard because of the work they were doing in philanthropic organisations.

New Zealand women, however, did not gain the right to sit in Parliament until 1919. South Australian women were as surprised as everyone else when they were given this privilege (theoretical as it turned out to be), for the rhetoric of the politicians had been so strongly against it. Signals given out by the movement had been conflicting: Mary Lee, in a deputation to Holder in 1892, had gone out of her way to emphasise that women did not want candidature, but the 1893 WCTU Convention passed a resolution: 'That we consider the clause to debar women from becoming Members of Parliament unnecessary and offensive, for while we believe that few women would accept such a responsibility, even if sufficient votes could be secured to return them, we do not see why a law should be made to prevent it.'[103]

Both Catherine Helen Spence (then seventy-one) and Mary Lee (then seventy-five) were urged to stand for the South Australian 1896 elections, but declined, Spence because of her commitment to the gospel of proportional representation, and Mary Lee (who had been nominated by the trade unions) because she preferred not to pledge herself to any party. Spence did, however, stand unsuccessfully for election to the 1897 Commonwealth Convention which was to finalise the Constitution for the new Commonwealth. She had hoped not only to have voting rights for all Australian women written into the Constitution, but to persuade the Convention to adopt proportional voting for both Houses of the Commonwealth. It was adopted for the Senate, but not for the House of Representatives.

The women enrolled quickly and in large numbers, and by 1896 the political parties—Labor, Liberal, and the National Defence League for the Conservative party—were working to harness their votes. In 1895 a non-party organisation was founded by Spence's niece, Lucy Spence Morice (aided by Spence herself) which urged women to 'stand together as women apart from all considerations of class and party'. When it went out of existence in 1897 the WCTU held the non-party fort, urging women to vote for righteous men, against the liquor trade, and in women's interests. Only in 1909 did Spence's Non-party Political Association make the next effort to organise women along non-party lines.

Notes

There are no volume numbers for South Australian parliamentary debates until the session which began in August 1893. Each page in the record of debates has two numbered columns, so references are to these.

As far as we know, the Women's Suffrage League of South Australia printed only two reports, so references to those reports often indicate events which occurred several years before.

1. *SAPD*, 7 November 1888, c. 1636.
2. *SAPD*, 24 July 1883, c. 536.
3. This reference and the following quotes are all from *SAPD*, 22 July 1885, cc. 319-331.
4. *Observer*, 25 July 1885.
5. *The Lantern*, quoted in Helen Jones, *In Her Own Name: women in South Australian history*, p. 87.
6. *SAPD*, 18 August 1886, c. 761.
7. *SAPD*, 20 July 1886, c. 429.
8. This and the two following quotes are from *SAPD*, 20 July 1886, c. 475.
9. *SAPD*, 8 September 1886, c. 944.
10. ibid.
11. Norman J. Makin, *The Labor Party in South Australia: 1882–1956*, p. 9.
12. *SAPD*, 8 August 1888, c. 530.
13. *SAPD*, 10 September 1888, c. 1065.
14. *SAPD*, 7 November 1888, c. 1636.
15. Helen Jones, *In Her Own Name*, pp. 25-8.
16. Women's Suffrage League of South Australia, Report, 1891.
17. *Observer*, 28 July 1888.
18. *Advertiser*, 21 July 1888.
19. Women's Suffrage League of South Australia, Report, 1891; *Observer*, 28 July 1888.
20. The material for this sketch of Mary Lee has been largely drawn from Helen Jones, *In Her Own Name*.
21. *Dawn*, June and November 1889.
22. *Dawn*, October 1889.
23. WCTU of South Australia, Annual Report, 1888.
24. Isabel McCorkindale, *Torch-Bearers: the Woman's Christian Temperance Union of South Australia, 1886–1948*, p. 14.
25. ibid.
26. ibid.
27. The following sketch of Ackermann is drawn from Elizabeth Riddell's introduction to the 1981 edition of Jessie Ackermann, *Australia from a Woman's Point of View*, and from Ackermann's own writings.
28. Isabel McCorkindale, *Torch-Bearers*, p. 2.
29. ibid., p. 38.
30. WCTU of South Australia, Annual Report, 1889.
31. *SAPD*, 30 October 1889, c. 1382.
32. *SAPD*, 13 November 1889, c. 1553.
33. ibid., c. 1154.

34. Norman J. Makin, *The Labor Party in South Australia*, p. 10.
35. *South Australian Register*, 21 March, 14 April 1890.
36. *SAPD*, 2 July 1890, c. 329.
37. ibid.
38. *SAPD*, 6 August 1890, c. 766.
39. *SAPD*, 1 October 1890, c. 1169.
40. *SAPD*, 12 December 1890, c. 2388.
41. WCTU of South Australia, Annual Report, 1891.
42. *Dawn*, June 1891.
43. WCTU of South Australia, Annual Report, 1890.
44. Women's Suffrage League of South Australia, Report, 1891.
45. *Observer*, 18 April 1891.
46. Dora Montefiore, *From a Victorian to a Modern*, pp. 31-2.
47. *Catherine Helen Spence: an autobiography*, p. 77.
48. Women's Suffrage League of South Australia, Report, 1891.
49. *Advertiser*, 3 June 1891.
50. *Dawn*, June 1891.
51. *Advertiser*, 3 June 1891.
52. Helen Jones, *In Her Own Name*, p. 96.
53. *Advertiser*, 9 June 1891.
54. E. L. Batchelor, *The Labor Party and its Progress*, pamphlet held by the Mortlock Library, Adelaide.
55. *SAPD*, 22 July 1891, c. 458.
56. *SAPD*, 5 August 1891, c. 609.
57. Women's Suffrage League of South Australia, Report, 1891.
58. ibid., 1894.
59. *Advertiser*, 9 July 1892.
60. ibid.
61. ibid.
62. Women's Suffrage League of South Australia, Report, 1894.
63. ibid.
64. ibid.
65. *SAPD*, 9 August 1892, c. 547.
66. *Advertiser*, 15 March 1893.
67. ibid.
68. Jim Moss, *Sound of Trumpets: a history of the labour movement in South Australia*, p. 174.
69. *SAPD*, vol. 1, 15 August 1893, c. 927.
70. Women's Suffrage League of South Australia, Report, 1894.
71. *Quiz and the Lantern*, 24 November 1893.
72. *Observer*, 22 July 1893.
73. *Advertiser*, 12 July 1893.
74. *Quiz and the Lantern*, 24 November 1893.
75. *Advertiser*, 8 September 1893.
76. *Advertiser*, 26 September 1893.
77. WCTU of South Australia, Annual Report, 1894.
78. *Voice*, 25 May 1894.
79. WCTU of South Australia, Annual Report, 1894.
80. E. L. Batchelor, *The Labor Party and its Progress*.
81. *Advertiser*, 7 June 1894.
82. John Gordon, *SAPD*, vol. 1, 10 July 1894, c. 434.

83. John Warren, ibid., 14 August, c. 894.
84. James Martin, ibid., c. 897.
85. Ebenezer Ward, ibid., 16 August 1894, c. 963.
86. Sylvanus Margerey, ibid., c. 964.
87. Isabel McCorkindale, *Torch-Bearers*, p. 38; WCTU of South Australia, Annual Report, 1894.
88. *SAPD*, vol. 1, 23 August 1894, c. 1083.
89. Cornelius Proud, 'How woman's suffrage was won in South Australia', p. 34.
90. *SAPD*, vol. 2, 8 November 1894, c. 2236.
91. Cornelius Proud, 'How woman's suffrage was won in South Australia', p. 36.
92. W. G. Spence, *Australia's Awakening: thirty years in the life of an Australian agitator*, p. 423.
93. *SAPD*, vol. 2, 11 December 1884, c. 2801.
94. Clement Giles, *SAPD*, vol. 2, 17 December 1894, c. 2908.
95. Henry Grainger, ibid., c. 2913.
96. *South Australian Register*, 18 December 1894.
97. *Advertiser*, 18 December 1894.
98. WCTU of South Australia, Annual Report, 1895.
99. Mary Lee to Rose Scott, 25 March 1897, in Woman Suffrage Correspondence, 1887–1899, ML:NSW, MSS A2271, item 261.
100. *Bulletin* (New South Wales), 3 August 1895.
101. Cornelius Proud, 'How woman's suffrage was won in South Australia'.
102. Isabel McCorkindale, *Torch-Bearers*, p. 22.
103. WCTU of South Australia, Annual Report, 1893.

3

Western Australia, 1899

It was not until 1887, when the white population reached 40,000 in Western Australia, an area of approximately one million square miles, that the British Colonial Office would agree to the drafting of a Constitution. The Constitution gave a fully elected Legislative Assembly, but a Legislative Council which was to be nominated for the first six years or until the population reached 60,000. For the Assembly there were property qualifications for electors and elected, with plural voting and no payment of members. With only 5900 males eligible to vote, the first legislators were drawn from the wealthy and influential in a society more rigidly stratified than in the other more populous colonies. The first Assembly of thirty members met in January 1891. All candidates stood as individuals, for there were no parties and no leaders. The 44-year-old John Forrest became Premier over the conglomerate body, and was to remain so until 1900, the year after the woman's vote was granted.

Votes for women had been discussed in Western Australia seventeen years before. In 1874, when a municipal franchise was proposed by the partly elective Legislative Council which advised the Governor, it included votes for women who owned property. There was some comment in the colony's small press on whether the woman's vote would be desirable when eventually a colonial Constitution was granted. Press opinion was against it. No justification for the opinion was given, although the *Inquirer* did say that it thought a voting woman would 'disturb domestic peace'.[1] There were some challenging letters supporting female suffrage,[2] but then the subject died. It was not until 1892, the second year of the new Government, that the subject again raised its head when the Woman's Christian Temperance Union was founded in the west.

Mary Leavitt, the first American WCTU missionary, did not visit Western Australia on her mid-1880s tour, so it was left to the second, Jessie Ackermann, to establish the Union there. She formed six branches in early 1892 and the first Colonial Convention was held in August. Within three years there would be eleven branches. A central Suffrage Department was established at this first Convention, with Janetta Foulkes as Colonial Superintendent, so votes for women was the policy from the Union's inception. Shortly after the Convention, a deputation of fifty-five Union members waited on Sir John Forrest with a rather vague petition: 'that the moral welfare of the country should receive the same consideration as its material welfare'.[3] Different members of the delegation translated this in different ways, but Jessie Ackermann, the leader, told Forrest that votes should be given to women 'for the protection of the home'. Forrest was noncommittal.

The key to the Union's wide-ranging demand lay in Forrest's early concentration on the material development of the colony. Social legislation which was being passed in other colonies would, in his opinion, have to wait on much needed roads, bridges and harbour facilities. Forrest had probably been chosen as Premier because of his expertise in these matters. He had risen to his prominent place in Western Australian society from humble origins. One of ten children born to Scottish parents who came out as servants in 1842, he had studied surveying, made a name for himself in exploration, and become Surveyor-General and a member of the pre-1890s Colonial Executive. His position was consolidated when he married into one of Perth's wealthy and influential families and his childless wife devoted herself to extending his sphere of influence, and so his career, with her hostessing. The women's inflexible opponent till 1899, he was an imposing man, even intimidating; he weighed over sixteen stone, and had a formidable presence and energy.

Although the Constitution had stipulated property qualifications for electors of the Lower House, it had the power to alter its own franchise. In 1892 Forrest introduced a bill which would have given the vote to all adult males who could fulfil strict residential qualifications.[4] There was cursory mention of woman suffrage, but no debate about it. Manhood suffrage passed the Assembly by only one vote, but was rejected by the appointed Legislative Council.

In 1893, to quell growing unrest about the Assembly franchise among those who were streaming into Western Australia from other more democratic Australasian colonies in response to the great gold discoveries, Forrest tried again. He introduced a bill to amend the Constitution which would fix the qualifications for electors and elected to the new Legislative Council (the white population had reached the stipulated 60,000 earlier than expected) and, as in the 1892 bill, would give the vote to all males with the stipulated residential qualifications.[5] It was time, the Premier said, that Western Australia brought its institutions into line with those of other colonies. J. Cookworthy moved an amendment to the proposed qualification for electors of the new Legislative Council to allow single, widowed or divorced women with the same property qualifications as men to have a vote.[6] He admitted that his motive was to offset the democratisation of the Assembly. R. Sholl, another Conservative member, supported him.[7] Speakers for the amendment contended that there was no need to include married women with property in the new privilege as they were 'merged in their husbands'. All supporters were enthusiastic that the votes of women ('the most conservative class in the world as regards politics')[8] would bolster the Council's ability 'to protect the sacred rights of property'.[9]

The debate then moved into the wider ideological area. The Premier was against votes for any women: 'he did not believe in ladies mixing up in politics. He thought the proper place for a woman, whether she were a widow or a spinster, was to look after her home, and not to be running about all over the place.'[10] Timothy Quinlan made a comment which must have angered the WCTU women *and* those who voted at municipal elections. 'His experience of ladies at municipal and other elections', he said, 'had been that they were somewhat weak in mind ... His own opinion was that ladies, like cats, were best at home.'[11]

This Conservative move to counteract the democratisation of the Assembly by increasing the propertied vote in the Council was defeated by only one vote. Nothing daunted, Sholl waited until the qualification for electors to the Lower House came up for discussion, and moved that 'every spinster, widow or femme sole' with property should vote in the Assembly.[12] The proposal lacked the logic of Cookworthy's move, for it meant that the voting qualifications for a woman in the Assembly would not be the same as those for a man. Forrest accused Sholl of trying to defeat manhood suffrage by altering the bill in such a way as to make it unacceptable to the Upper House.[13] Sholl's amendment was defeated 13–10. When the bill passed through all stages it gave what was referred to as 'manhood suffrage', but the qualification was so limited by residential restrictions that radicals in the 1890s were to argue that it gave no such thing. Cookworthy and Sholl were often referred to in later years as pioneers of woman suffrage in Western Australia, but they do not deserve the honour. The suffrage proposed had little to do with equal political rights for men and women, and everything to do with the preservation of the power of the Conservatives in the legislature.

Elizabeth Nicholls, President of the South Australian WCTU, accepted an invitation to visit the Western Australian Convention in October 1893. It involved her in a journey of several days by ship. When she left Adelaide the bill giving votes to women in that colony had just been defeated because of its referenda provisions, and the feelings of South Australian suffragists were running high. Probably because of Nicholls' indignation about the situation in her own colony, the 1893 Western Australian Convention was permeated with discussion of woman suffrage.[14] A supporter in the Assembly, George Throssel, gave an enthusiastic address to the women, and papers were presented in support. Nicholls presided over and was chief speaker at a public meeting which demanded votes for women, and another Assembly member, W. Traylen, supported her. The Union decided to circulate a petition requesting the right 'on the same terms as men', and a deputation waited on Forrest. He dismissed their request because, he said, votes for any women would 'upset the electoral machinery'.[15]

When Parliament assembled after the 1894 election Forrest was still able to conscript enough supporters to form a new Government. Candidates stood as individuals, but a rudimentary Opposition was taking shape as some members defined themselves as opposed to the Premier and his Cabinet. The opposition group had, however, no united policies, organisation or leader. Labor as yet had no representation, but the Trades and Labor Council of Perth had given support to some Liberal candidates in the election, and representatives from the goldfields reflected the radical leanings of the miners. In the last three years there had been dramatic demographic changes in Western Australia as miners poured onto the rich goldfields at Kalgoorlie and Coolgardie. Great pressure was put on the Government to provide the infrastructure to support the fields, and Forrest stepped up his development of railways and harbour facilities. At the 1894 Convention of the WCTU Janetta Foulkes, working hard as Colonial Suffrage Superintendent, was pessimistic about Forrest ever taking up the cause; she said she thought his priorities were elsewhere—that the women would have to wait for a change of government.[16] The following year the Union again considered the question of the Government's priorities and Foulkes told members that although railways, roads and harbours were needed 'to make it possible to exist' in Western Australia, it was essential that the Government should also pay attention to social questions—'and that includes woman suffrage'.[17]

In 1895 the Government introduced a bill into the Assembly which relaxed the machinery for the registration of new voters. The bill had nothing to do with the qualifications of electors, but opponents of the existing qualifications used it to air their discontent. Frederick Illingworth, a member from the goldfields, claimed that large numbers of miners could not get their names on the roll because they rarely stayed at one address for six months.[18] Another goldfields member, Charles Moran, maintained that the miner's right should be sufficient qualification for voting for the Lower House.[19] Both were overruled on the grounds that a bill to amend the Constitution was needed to alter qualifications. Then Walter James, a Liberal who was to become Premier after Forrest in 1900, announced that he 'should like to introduce in this bill a provision for the extension of the franchise to women'.[20] Septimus Burt said that he would be out of order in doing so. James replied tartly that he could not understand why Burt should oppose the move, as he was a supporter of the Government, and everyone knew that women would vote conservatively. There was little discussion of rights and wrongs of woman suffrage and the Speaker supported Burt in ruling the clause out of order. The 1896 WCTU Convention sent a note of thanks to James for his support.[21]

In 1896 the Government introduced a bill to increase the number of members in both Houses in response to the great increase in population. Illingworth, who had the year before criticised the residency provisions for voters, now attacked the Government on the non-payment of members.[22] More seats for the goldfields were commendable, he said, but there was little hope that miners would be represented by men sympathetic to their needs if only those with independent incomes could stand for seats. Walter James strongly supported Illingworth on the payment of members, but when James indicated that he would move to have woman suffrage included in the bill,[23] the two men parted company. Illingworth told the Parliament: 'I want to declare—finally, absolutely and forever—my distinct and positive opposition to woman suffrage . . . the whole experience is that the women and men vote together, and you get two votes instead of one.'[24]

The key to understanding the opposition of Illingworth—unusual in a radical Liberal or a Labor politician—is that there were few women on the goldfields, and Illingworth's aim was to gain greater representation for these electorates. The vote for all women would substantially increase the number of voters in the settled areas of the colony, making it necessary to increase the representation of these areas in the Assembly, while it would make little difference in the number of voters on the goldfields. James found little support for votes for all women and neither this measure nor payment of members was inserted into the bill.

There was still no Labor party in Western Australia when the 1897 elections took place, and in spite of the heavy influx of men to the goldfields, no Trades and Labor Council there, although there was a Trades and Labor Council in Perth. The eight representatives from the goldfields cannot be termed Labor party members in the full sense, but they were elected by the radical voice of the miners and they were to fight for the interests of their electorates (and this meant opposing woman suffrage) in the 1897–1900 Parliament.

Forrest was still able to govern when the new Parliament assembled, but his factional mode of retaining his position was becoming increasingly difficult to sustain. The 1894 elections had brought some men into Parliament who did not belong to the old social and political élite within which such factional manoeuvring took place, and their numbers increased in 1897. In December 1897, only two years before women gained the vote, Walter James made the first move for female suffrage which was not entangled with other parliamentary moves. Women, he said, needed the vote to improve their position in Western Australian society. He moved: 'That in the opinion of this House the best interests of the Colony require the extension of the franchise to women.'[25]

James, a powerful and eloquent logician, claimed that although married women could now retain their property when they married, Western Australia (in 1892) had been the last colony to allow them to do so. They still had no rights of guardianship over their children, and their rights in divorce were not equal to those of men. There had been no Factory Act passed in Western Australia to protect the working conditions of either women or men. The Premier repeatedly interjected when James was speaking, until the usually unflappable lawyer retorted, referring, no doubt, to the popularity of Forrest's development measures, 'There are questions of social legislation in this Colony which are more important even than the continued existence of the Premier in office.'[26]

Opponents of woman suffrage took up popular arguments against the franchise, among them that women should provide a comfort and solace for men by remaining at home. James replied: 'I look on my easy chair as one of the comforts and a solace in my home. That is part of the furniture of the home—and my wife is not. The duty rests upon me as much as upon my wife to make the home the comfort and solace to both of us.'[27] Forrest opposed the motion vigorously even though, he said, 'there are organizations in Perth which take a great deal of interest in this question . . . at the present time many meetings are being held on this question by women'.[28]

Illingworth was again the main opponent and he referred to James's argument that women needed the vote to improve their working conditions. Women should not be in the work force, he said, because their competition was destroying 'the family wage' of the man.[29] Charles Moran, a member for Coolgardie, warned other goldfields members that they would be 'cutting their own throats' if they voted for the motion—that they would be giving the coastal districts extra voting power at the expense of the goldfields electorates. Moran claimed that the matter had come up at every one of his meetings in the last election, and that the feeling against the woman's vote was ten to one.[30] He indicated however, that he was not, like Illingworth, against woman suffrage as such: 'I do not oppose the motion on ethical grounds, but on the ground that it is inexpedient and bad policy on the part of goldfields members.'[31]

When the 1897 WCTU Convention was held, Janetta Foulkes analysed the position on the fields: 'On the goldfields, where owing to the floating population one would hardly have expected much sympathy with it, I am glad to hear that the mining element is as a whole in favour of it.'[32] Members from the fields, she said, were not voting according 'to the courage of their convictions'. If they did the vote would be carried at least in the Assembly.

Elizabeth Nicholls came again to Western Australia for the 1897 WCTU Convention, this time in her official capacity as Australasian President. For some unknown reason the Convention asked a Cabinet member, Frederick Piesse, to chair the special franchise meeting. He did not approve of votes for women and 'expressed his opinion that woman's sphere was at home, and not in politics'.[33] Nicholls enthusiastically took him to task. There was no way that women's wrongs would be redressed, she said, until women had a voice in the election of representatives. At the Convention Mrs Christine Clark took over from Janetta Foulkes as Suffrage Superintendent.[34] Goldstein described Clark as 'a broad-minded woman, intensely interested in all social and industrial problems, a good speaker, and of charming personality'.[35] Clark was to be an enthusiastic and energetic successor and to carry the weight of the suffrage campaign until it was won in 1899. Although there were suffrage sympathisers in the Karrakatta Club, the only other women's organisation in Perth, no official support came from the club itself.

In late 1894 a group of women from leading families in the city had formed the Karrakatta Club as a forum for discussing social issues, particularly those which affected women and children. (The name was a corruption of the Aboriginal designation of the land upon which Perth was built.) Technically any woman of 'good moral character' could belong. The *West Australian* commented:

> it is in no sense intended to be a class institution ... It is open, so it is stated, to all women who desire to secure its benefits. Within its precincts there will appear to be nothing to prevent mistress and maid joining in friendly discussion on the everlasting 'servant-girl' question and kindred topics.[36]

The writer was probably being facetious; no servant girl could have felt comfortable in the Karrakatta. The first President was Madeline (Margaret) Onslow, wife of the Chief Justice (she was to become Lady Onslow in 1895, when her husband was knighted). Lady Forrest, wife of the Premier, was a member, as was Eleanora, the wife of Walter James, the Assembly member who championed the woman's cause. Edith Cowan, who would in 1920 become the first woman in Parliament in Western Australia, was the first recording Secretary. Not only would a woman from a lower social level have felt uncomfortable in the Karrakatta; she would probably have been 'blackballed'. There were thirty-eight foundation members and the Constitution provided that thereafter each new member must be nominated and approved by the existing membership—one black ball in seven rejected the candidate.[37]

The club provided activities for its members: socials, annual picnics, occasional entertainments at Government House. Yet the Karrakatta was more than a social club. In one of her reports Lady Onslow spoke of it interesting itself in divorce laws, the guardianship of children, intestate estates, and equality of pay for teachers. Possibly taking the WCTU as their model, the members distributed their interests over 'departments'—legal and educational matters, current events, public speaking, literature. It was inevitable that discussions should soon come round to woman suffrage, and in August and September 1896 a debate was held which spread over two nights, probably triggered by the August debate in Parliament in connection with the Constitution Amendment Bill.[38] Janetta Foulkes, from the WCTU, was one of the debaters. She may have been invited to speak or she may have been a member of both organisations. The verdict of the club was in favour of the vote, with two dissenting voices. There is no way of knowing whether members were voting for a full suffrage or a limited one, but it is likely that they supported the vote for women on the same conditions as men. In July 1897 the subject was raised again: a paper was read and a long discussion followed.[39] The tenor of the discussion was that women needed the vote if they were going to do battle with laws which discriminated against them. Yet for all the interest shown, the Karrakatta stopped short of agitation. Edith Cowan wrote to Rose Scott in New South Wales that votes for women had recently been discussed by the Karrakatta Club, and that most members were in favour of it. It had not, however, been thought 'expedient' to actively join the agitation, and the campaign was being left to the WCTU. 'For obvious reasons', she said, 'it would not be advisable to turn the Club into an institution for the furtherance of political ends.'[40]

The reasons certainly were obvious. Many of the men to whom the women were attached were involved in politics and these men were not necessarily in agreement as to whether, or what kind of, female suffrage should be granted. In 1898 the club continued its interest but members who wanted to do more joined in WCTU meetings. Dr Roberta Jull, the club's historian, wrote of 1898 that 'The question of the franchise was much debated and many public meetings held, some of which members attended in numbers.'[41]

Clark's enthusiasm as WCTU Suffrage Superintendent triggered a series of regional public meetings in 1898, in the period before the opening of Parliament in July. One such was held at Northcote in June. The secretary was Ada Throssell. George Throssell, the member of the Legislative Assembly for Northcote, was Minister for Crown Lands in the Forrest ministry, and he had been a supporter of the franchise to the extent of voting against the rest of the Cabinet. Ada Throssell conveyed not only the resolution of the meeting to the Premier, but some advice: 'The addition of women to the electoral roll', she wrote, 'would go far to minimize the extravagant demands likely to result from a large unsettled male population possessed of political powers.'[42] The letter shows the disquiet felt by the settled population of the colony as the flood of immigrants to its fabulous goldfields showed no signs of abating. There was no contradiction between this concern and the contention of the WCTU since its inception that women were entitled to the vote on grounds of natural justice. The Premier's reply to the Northcote WCTU showed some ambiguity; he did not categorically reject their petition, as he had others which had come from the Union, but said that 'he did not think the matter was one of urgency'.[43]

In July and August 1898 the *West Australian* came out strongly in support of woman suffrage. The question should not be based on expediency, it said, but justice. The *West Australian* too was disturbed at the invasion of the colony by unattached males in search of quick wealth. Woman suffrage might, the editor wrote, 'prove an inducement to men to bring their wives and families here', and it might 'strengthen the voice of the family rather than the individual'.[44] The editor pointed out in another editorial that the Divorce Bill which was before Parliament demonstrated the anomaly of a Parliament elected by men deciding issues which vitally affected the lives of women.[45] The editor's discussion led to a spate of letters both defending and condemning votes for women.

On 10 August 1898 Walter James tried once more to have the Assembly affirm the principle. He moved again 'That, in the opinion of this House, the best interests of the Colony justify the extension of the franchise to women.'[46] James once more gave a logical exposition of his case, but then concentrated on arguing that social legislation affecting women was coming increasingly before the Assembly, and women should have a share in electing the men who dealt with it. He was not impressed with the colony's record thus far. Not long before, in spite of representation from the WCTU and the Karrakatta Club, the Legislative Council had rejected a measure obliging employers to provide seating for their female shop assistants. 'It is humiliating and degrading', he said, 'to think that there is a body of men at the end of the nineteenth-century who can commit themselves to such inhumanity.'[47] James may have been referring to the bill providing for easier divorce for women ill-treated by their husbands when he went on: 'Legislation designed to protect women from insult, cruelty and wrong, ten thousand times worse than that inflicted on a dog is cast out with contumely and insult.'[48]

James was taunted and ridiculed. Forrest accused him of wanting to ingratiate himself in the women's eyes: 'He is a hero among them, a sort of cock-bird.'[49] Moran, an opponent from the goldfields, took up the analogy, accusing him of joining 'the tea and cackle union' and pluming himself before the 'hen-conventions'.[50] James answered attacks with assurance and civility. When a member asserted that women did not want the vote, James replied, 'Why not run a risk, and give them the chance?' 'Rubbish,' he said, when one member claimed that women were weak and had to rely on men for protection,[51] and when Forrest said, opposing the motion, 'We all know, as the member for East Perth has told us time after time, what a charm and solace woman is to man in his home.' James interjected quietly, 'I do not patronise them in this fashion.'[52] Illingworth was again the most vocal opponent. He told the women that if they wanted to use their influence to improve social conditions they should join the WCTU, teach Sunday school or dispense charity. He gave his own version of women's rights.

> The rights of woman, what are they?
> The right to labour and to pray;
> The right to watch while others sleep;
> The right o'er others' woes to weep.[53]

This poetic flight was greeted with general applause from the floor of the House; Alfred Morgans claimed that it brought tears to the eyes of some members.[54] No-one knows what the women in the gallery thought about it. During the debate several references were made to a letter written by Christine Clark which was being circulated in Parliament. One member referred slightingly to it as being written by the 'reverend' Mrs Clark.[55] He was called to order and excused himself by saying that he really meant to say 'revered'.

The political content of the 1898 debate was more significant than the ideological. Not only goldfields members opposed woman suffrage because it would give increased representation to the towns. Walter Kingsmill voiced the fears of the large country electorates: 'I would ask honorary members for the remoter districts whether they are not likely to be acting against their own interests, and not only their own interests, but the interests of the Colony, in advocating the extension of the franchise to women, and thereby doubling the voting power of the metropolis.'[56] Forrest's statements during the debate are important in the light of 1899 developments. 'I have not changed my opinions during the last eight or ten months,'[57] he said. He then made a long speech opposing the vote, but it was full of ambiguities. 'I am inclined to think', he said, 'that as time goes along woman's suffrage will be granted.'[58] James was fully alert to the signals from Forrest's speech. 'I feel almost inclined to give a sigh, and say that on the next occasion the Premier will be found voting for it', he said. 'On each occasion his opposition has become less and less.'[59] The motion was defeated eighteen to eleven, and Forrest and his Cabinet in opposing it found themselves in the curious position of voting against the urban representatives and in league with an almost solid block of pastoral and goldfields members.

The great problem facing Forrest's Government in 1899 was the growing power of organised labour on the goldfields. The first Western Australian Trades Union and Labor Congress was held at Coolgardie from 11 to 15 April 1899. The Congress forcefully affirmed that there should be a redistribution of seats on the basis of population. The goldfields, with 36 per cent of the population, currently had only ten of the fifty seats. The second demand was for payment of members of Parliament, which would make it possible for Labor to have direct political representation.[60] Forrest knew that the Government would eventually have to accede to these demands and that nothing could prevent Labor emerging with the new century as a strong political force which would challenge his hegemony. In this context woman suffrage, which would give increased representation to the older settled areas, was an attractive political option.

Against this background the WCTU continued its agitation through letters to the press and in public meetings. In April it decided to form a Woman's Franchise League which would bring into the movement those who were not sympathetic to the Union's total abstinence stand.[61] A meeting of interested parties was convened for 27 April. The league's Constitution stipulated that it would agitate for the vote 'on the same conditions as those which apply to men'.[62] A public meeting on 11 May elected officers and Council.[63] Prominent among office holders were WCTU women, Karrakatta Club members, and men who were either prominent public citizens or politicians sympathetic to the league's aims. Mrs Emily Hensman (WCTU) was President, Lady Madeline Onslow (Karrakatta Club) and Mrs Ferguson (WCTU) were among the Vice-Presidents, Christine Clark (WCTU) was Secretary and Mrs Eleanora James (wife of Walter and member of the Karrakatta Club) was Treasurer.

Soon there were several branches of the league, and the branches launched an aggressive campaign of public meetings.[64] One of these meetings, at York on 16 June, forwarded its resolution to the Premier and received the reply that woman suffrage had been discussed in Cabinet and it was proposed to introduce a bill.[65] This was the first public indication that the Government would do an about-face. Then, on 27 June in his office, Forrest announced the fact to a meeting of his ministers and supporters: 'As the proposed alteration in the boundaries and electorates of the Colony will necessitate the amendment of the Constitution, the Premier will propose for adoption when introducing the Constitution Amendment Bill, that the franchise shall be extended to women.'[66] Before Forrest was ready with his bill, Walter James moved in the Assembly for the third time: 'That in the opinion of this House early provision should be made for conferring the suffrage on women.'[67] It is possible that James's move was at the request of the Premier to clear the decks for the inclusion of woman suffrage in the coming bill. It is more likely that James wanted the satisfaction, after his previous rejections, of seeing a motion of his affirmed by both Houses—a satisfaction which, in the light of his unswerving and principled support, he richly deserved. He could not resist a flash of sardonic humour when speaking to his motion. It appeared, he said, that he had been engaged in missionary activity in the last few years, for 'there has been a sudden conversion of a great number of members of the House'.[68] Although James, a sophisticated politician, was well aware of the reasons for the Government's change of mind, he chose not to confront those who, for whatever reason, were now willing to give justice to women. It was left to Illingworth, that seasoned opponent of women's rights, to put his finger precisely on the reason for the Government's change of mind.

> it is no secret that honorary members have declared themselves in favour of voting for this question not because . . . they have reversed their opinions . . . but because they think it desirable to give some kind of balancing weight to the increased representation of the fields . . . Honorary members smile, but we know that if the motion is carried in this House it will not be carried on the conviction of honorary members.[69]

Forrest, imperturbable politician that he was, calmly parried accusations of inconsistency by replying that the Government had changed its mind because it was convinced the country was now in favour of woman suffrage.[70] While the motion was still before the House on 24 July, his brother Alexander Forrest, Mayor of Perth and also a member of the Assembly, called a public meeting of support, and there the Premier painted the Government as a paternalistic parent responding to calls for justice from its women.[71] The motion passed the Assembly by a majority of eleven votes—it had been defeated the year before by seven. On 26 July, when it was waiting to be dealt with by the Upper House, James presented a petition,[72] the first of any consequence to reach the legislature in Western Australia. In the Upper House, where woman suffrage was debated for the first time, James's affirmation passed by only two votes. Some members spoke against it and then left the chamber. One can only assume that they did not wish to record a vote against the Government.

It was clear from the voting on James's motion that the Government had the numbers to pass the Constitution Act Amendment Bill by the required statutory majority when it came before each House. It was the first and only Western Australian bill dealing only with woman suffrage; debates to this point had been on amendments to electoral bills or on motions for approval. A companion measure gave five new seats to the settled areas (because woman suffrage would add so many to the electoral rolls there) and five new seats to the goldfields (because of the continued increase in male electors). Forrest was angrily attacked for not abolishing plural voting at the same time as he introduced woman suffrage. He was accused of gaining further advantage for his party because the plural votes of propertied women would swell his support in the towns and pastoral areas. The Government weathered the storm of accusations beating about its ears, contending that those who owned property, be they male or female, deserved extra voting rights because they had a greater stake in the country's future than those who wished only to wrest riches from the colony and then move on. Western Australia, when it abolished the plural vote for its Assembly in 1907, was the last state to do so.

It has been claimed that Forrest's Government gave women their suffrage so that the women's votes would keep Western Australia out of the Commonwealth. The debates in Parliament do not support this. There is no doubt, however, that it yielded on votes for women because this was a way of balancing the rise of radicalism on the goldfields. Walter James's championship, the campaign waged by the WCTU and, for the last few months of the campaign, that waged by the Woman's Franchise League, should not be belittled because of this expediency, however. The WCTU kept the question before the eyes of the public from 1892 to 1899, and the honours in the Union go to Janetta Foulkes and Christine Clark. Foulkes and Clark were given support by the Union's two Presidents for the period, Mrs Emily Hensman (wife of Justice Hensman) and Mrs Ferguson. If political expediency had not intervened in 1899, the women who came from the Karrakatta Club to the Woman's Franchise League would undoubtedly have notched up more honours for themselves. Two of them were to achieve post-suffrage prominence. Edith Cowan stood successfully for the Western Australian election in 1921, a year after women were granted the right to be candidates in that state, and became the first female member of any Australian Parliament. The gentle and cultured musician, Lady Madeline Onslow, went with her husband to live in England in 1901 and was to figure in the British woman suffrage campaign.

As in all Australian colonies, the argument that women would want to sit in Parliament if they were granted the vote was raised by their opponents. The women did not deny it, but neither did they claim the right. Although several politicians, including James, said in the course of the debates that they did not see why women should not occupy political *or* judicial office, the question never became an issue, and when a male supporter proposed at the last public meeting that the women should insist on it, they themselves were unwilling to risk their franchise.

No credit for woman suffrage can be given to the Labor party, as it did not exist as a political entity until 1901. Although some goldfields representatives spoke and voted against it, they cannot be said to have been against it on principle—with the exception perhaps of Illingworth, who seemed genuine in his ideological, as well as his political, opposition. The question of opposing female suffrage until one-man-one-vote was achieved was sometimes mentioned, as in other colonies, but the main concern of the burgeoning Labor influence on the goldfields was the electoral redistribution which would validly follow from votes for women. There were no Labor women among the female suffragists; the women in the WCTU and those who came from the Karrakatta Club were middle- and upper-class, who nevertheless did show some concern for working women's conditions.

Western Australian women voted in the federal referendum in July 1900 which decided in the affirmative the vexed question of whether the colony should join the Australian Commonwealth, and then joined their South Australian sisters in voting for the first Commonwealth Parliament. In 1901 they voted in their first state election at which Forrest's Government, after he had signalled his intention of going into the Commonwealth Parliament, was defeated. Walter James, at the head of a Liberal Government, became Premier. It seemed a fitting reward for James, and a fitting defeat for a Government which had acted only for reasons of expediency.

Forrest was elected to the first Commonwealth Parliament in 1901, where he served intermittently as a Cabinet member over a seventeen-year period. In 1918 he became Baron Forrest—the first Australian so honoured—but his ambition to take his seat in the House of Lords was never fulfilled, for he died en route to England later that year.

Christine Clark, who energised the WCTU in the last two years and was a force behind the formation of the Woman's Franchise League in 1899, moved to New South Wales in 1901. There she did organisational work for the Temperance Alliance, fitting in a trip to New Zealand later that year to take part in their local option campaign.[73] In 1903 she became Secretary of the Alliance, but resigned three years later when four male members of the committee refused to work with her.[74] After becoming Secretary of the Sydney Rescue Society in 1906, she fades out of the official records.

Notes

1. *Inquirer*, 18 March 1874.
2. *Perth Gazette*, 6 March 1874; *Herald*, 31 March 1875.
3. *West Australian*, 17 August 1892.
4. *WAPD*, vol. 3, 21 November 1892, p. 105.
5. *WAPD*, vol. 4, 17 July 1893, p. 89.
6. ibid., p. 96.
7. ibid., p. 99.
8. George Simpson, ibid., 24 July 1893, p. 150.
9. ibid.
10. Sir John Forrest, ibid., p. 149.
11. Timothy Quinlan, ibid., p. 154.
12. R. Sholl, ibid., 27 July 1893, p. 195.
13. Sir John Forrest, ibid., p. 199.
14. WCTU of Western Australia, Annual Report, 1893.
15. *Daily News*, 31 October 1893.
16. WCTU of Western Australia, Annual Report, 1894.
17. ibid., 1895.
18. *WAPD*, vol. 8, 28 September 1895, p. 1111.
19. Charles Moran, ibid.

20. ibid., p. 1112.
21. WCTU of Western Australia, Annual Report, 1896.
22. *WAPD*, vol. 9, 29 July 1896, p. 200.
23. Walter James, ibid., p. 194.
24. Frederick Illingworth, ibid., p. 201.
25. Walter James, *WAPD*, vol. 11, 1 December 1897, p. 796.
26. ibid., p. 742.
27. ibid., p. 767.
28. Sir John Forrest, ibid., p. 761.
29. Frederick Illingworth, ibid., p. 748.
30. Charles Moran, ibid., p. 760.
31. ibid.
32. WCTU of Western Australia, Annual Report, 1897.
33. ibid.
34. ibid.
35. *Woman's Sphere*, June 1903.
36. *West Australian*, 29 November 1894.
37. Karrakatta Club: Constitution, BL:WA, MSS 863, 3049A/1.
38. Karrakatta Club: Meetings of the Legal and Educational Department, 1894–1897, BL:WA, MSS 863, 3049A/33.
39. ibid.
40. Edith Cowan, a handwritten account of the woman suffrage movement in Western Australia, in Woman Suffrage: Miscellaneous papers on Australian and Overseas movements 1888–1920, ML:NSW, MSS 38/38, item 471.
41. Dr Roberta Jull, History of the Karrakatta Club, 1894–1944, BL:WA, MSS 863, 3049A/12, p. 5.
42. Letter from Ada Throssell, Secretary of the Northcote WCTU, to Sir John Forrest, 27 June 1898, Premiers' File, Western Australia, BL:WA, MSS 863, 686/1898.
43. Letter from Sir John Forrest to Ada Throssell, 18 July 1898, ibid.
44. *West Australian*, 6 July 1898.
45. ibid., 22 July 1898.
46. Walter James, *WAPD*, vol. 12, 10 August 1898, p. 911.
47. ibid., p. 914.
48. ibid.
49. Sir John Forrest, ibid., 17 August 1898, p. 1038.
50. Charles Moran, ibid., p. 1043.
51. Walter James, ibid., p. 1035.
52. ibid.
53. Frederick Illingworth, ibid., 10 August 1898, p. 922.
54. Alfred Morgans, ibid., 17 August, p. 1053.
55. Charles Moran, ibid., p. 1040.
56. Walter Kingsmill, ibid., 24 August, p. 1025.
57. Sir John Forrest, ibid., 17 August, p. 1034.
58. ibid.
59. Walter James, ibid., 10 August, p. 916.
60. Trades Union and Labor Council of Western Australia: minutes and proceedings of the first congress at Coolgardie, April 11–15 1899, ML:NSW, 331.8806/53.
61. WCTU of Australasia, Fourth Triennial Convention Report, 1900.
62. Woman's Franchise League of Western Australia, Annual Report, 1900.
63. *West Australian*, 12 May 1899.

64. Woman's Franchise League of Western Australia, Annual Report, 1900.
65. Premier's File, Western Australia, BL:WA, MSS 863, 2017/99.
66. *West Australian*, 28 June 1899.
67. Walter James, *WAPD*, vol. 14, 12 July 1899, p. 298.
68. ibid., p. 298.
69. Frederick Illingworth, ibid., p. 299.
70. Sir John Forrest, ibid., p. 312.
71. *West Australian*, 22 July 1899.
72. *WAPD*, vol. 14, 26 July 1899, p. 531.
73. *Woman's Sphere*, June 1903.
74. Gar Dillon, *A Delusion of the Australian Culture*, p. 80.

4

THE COMMONWEALTH VOTE, 1902

The campaign for the federation of the Australian colonies ran concurrently with the woman suffrage movement. It emerged in the 1880s (although there had been some sporadic agitation before that) and in 1891 the first Convention to draft a Constitution was held. All colonial legislatures, including that of New Zealand, sent representatives. New Zealand was to attend all major conferences until 1901, not enthusiastic about entering the Commonwealth, but at the same time unwilling to surrender its options. If New Zealand had not become an independent nation, Australia would have the honour of being the first in the world, not the second, to give its women the national vote.

The committee appointed in 1891 to consider the suffrage for the Commonwealth Parliament recommended to the Convention that 'The qualification of electors of members of the House of Representatives shall be in each State . . . the qualification for electors of the more numerous House of the Parliament of the State.'[1] Delegates then debated the clause. Would it be advisable to adopt manhood suffrage instead, or would those colonies which did not have it boycott the union? What about plural voting? Should the Commonwealth Parliament have the power to vary its own franchise? Although no colony yet had female suffrage, James Munro of Victoria and Andrew Inglis Clark of Tasmania both thought that it should be considered by the Convention, and a petition was presented from the Victorian Woman's Christian Temperance Union which read, in part: 'May they hope that in this enlightened age the last-born nation of the world may have embodied in its Constitution universal suffrage without regard of sex.'[2] The Convention decided that it had enough problems on its hands trying to reconcile the existing colonial suffrages without introducing this 'new element'. It left the clause unaltered, but rejected plural voting.

From 1891 to 1897, when the next major Convention was to be held, the details of the proposed Constitution were debated passionately in Australia. When New Zealand granted its women votes in 1893 and South Australia did the same in 1894, woman suffrage ceased to be a 'new element'; henceforth all discussions of the collective franchise were obliged to take into account that some Australian women had the right to a state vote. A few examples suffice to show that woman suffrage for the Commonwealth was a crucial public issue from 1894 onwards: the Australian Natives' Association, a patriotic organisation founded in 1871 to which many prominent Liberals belonged, decided at their 1894 Convention that 'the time has arrived when the parliamentary franchise should be given to females over twenty-one years of age';[3] at a public meeting in Melbourne the same year the audience voted 71–70 against the inclusion of women;[4] the United Liberal and Labor Conference in Victoria that year decided by 67–17 to insert adult suffrage for the Commonwealth Parliament into its platform instead of manhood suffrage;[5] and the Intercolonial Temperance Convention which met in Hobart in 1895 urged not only the adoption of federal female suffrage but that all Australian women should have a voice in any referendum which might vote on the proposed Constitution.[6] Elizabeth Nicholls, as President of the Australasian WCTU, made sure that the franchise for women was not ignored at any official meetings between the colonies. For instance, in the lead-up to the Premiers' Conference in Hobart in 1895 to plan details of the critical 1897 Convention, she upbraided Charles Kingston of South Australia for speaking only of manhood suffrage for the Commonwealth Parliament and asked him to make sure that womanhood suffrage was discussed at the Hobart meeting.[7]

Queensland, where feeling against federation was very strong, stayed away from the 1897 Convention. Western Australia's delegates were appointed by their Parliament, but in other colonies elections were held to choose representatives. Catherine Helen Spence, in spite of predictions that she would not be able to take her seat if elected,[8] decided to stand as a South Australian delegate. She hoped to advance the cause of votes for women and that of proportional voting for both Houses. The press felt free to comment: 'For the average woman, no matter how good her mental gifts might be, the strain of political life would be too severe.'[9]

With women voting in South Australia, Spence polled 7000 votes and was twenty-second in a field of thirty-three. The WCTU blamed her defeat on the fact that she did not have the backing of any political group,[10] but the Tasmanian *Mercury* thought that she had identified herself too closely with the hyperbole of the WCTU, which was advocating that prohibition of alcohol should be written into the Constitution.[11] For all that, Spence's candidature was an important milestone; she was the first woman to submit herself to the judgment of the electors in Australia, and there was much talk of her 'courage' in so doing.[12]

The suffrage societies in New South Wales and Victoria—and the WCTU in all colonies—made an issue of woman suffrage when the candidates for the 1897 Convention went onto the hustings. The Womanhood Suffrage League of New South Wales published in the press an appeal to electors to choose men who favoured the cause,[13] and it and the United Council for Woman Suffrage in Victoria sent circulars to all candidates asking them to support the writing into the Constitution of a vote for every man and every woman.[14] Replies received indicated that even supporters of woman suffrage were divided about whether this should be done. In order to avoid the accusation of interfering in the affairs of individual colonies, many favoured using the suffrage of the Lower House of each to elect the first Commonwealth Parliament, and then allowing the new body to determine its own franchise. Labor, campaigning on the platform of one-adult-one-vote, was critical of this stance. W. G. Spence, founder and Secretary of the Australian Workers' Union, told Rose Scott that Labor would fight for woman suffrage at the Convention, and if they failed they would campaign against the adoption of the draft Constitution in the coming referenda.[15] Arthur Rae, who had been one of the first Labor members in the New South Wales Parliament, wrote that leaving the suffrage to be decided by the first Commonwealth Parliament had grave dangers, for it put adult suffrage 'on the same footing as any trumpery law which may be passed this session and repealed the next'.[16]

The New South Wales suffragists took their campaign to the hustings in the 1897 Convention elections, and the Sydney *Daily Telegraph* gives a glimpse of how they worked. Edmund Barton, who was to be Australia's first Prime Minister, addressed a street meeting from the balcony of the Newtown Town Hall because his audience was too numerous to fit inside. When Annie Golding and her 'valorous female contingent' in the crowd below challenged him on female suffrage in the Constitution, he said that he was personally against votes for women, 'but if the voice of the representatives of federal Australia demanded it ... he would bow to their decision'.[17]

When the Convention met in Adelaide in April 1897, petitions were sent from suffrage societies and from the Australasian WCTU and its colonial branches. The women argued that they would have to pay taxes to the Commonwealth and obey its laws, and that their work in education and philanthropy was helping to form the new nation. They pointed out the anomaly of South Australian women voting while other Australian women did not, and made much of the fact that Australia had the opportunity in a new century of giving birth to a Commonwealth which could from the beginning have a franchise 'without any distinction or disqualification on the ground of sex'.[18]

The franchise came up for discussion at the first session of the 1897 Convention on 15 April. The Drafting Committee submitted that the franchise for the first federal election should remain that which each colony had for its Lower House and there should be no plural voting, but that the future Commonwealth Parliament should be given the power to impose its own uniform franchise if it wished to do so. The South Australian delegates, most of whom had been elected on a platform of adult suffrage, attacked the Drafting Committee's proposal. Charles Kingston, supported by Frederick Holder, proposed that a vote 'for every man and woman of the full age of twenty-one years' should be written into the Constitution.[19] Kingston was attacked by delegates from other colonies. They contended that each colony should have the right to decide what its own federal franchise should be and that if woman suffrage were decreed for the Commonwealth they would be forced to give it in their own states. Kingston maintained that they could have whatever franchise they wished for their own Parliaments; that he was only concerned with a uniform franchise for the Commonwealth. He attacked those who were in favour of the principle but would not have it written into the Constitution. 'I have no sympathy with those who say they are in favor of it, but when they have an opportunity of extending it throughout Australia they will have nothing to do with it.'[20]

It was a long debate with a minimum of ideological content, but full of dire predictions that other colonies would refuse to join the Commonwealth if Kingston's proposal to write votes for women into the Constitution were carried. It was lost 23–12. Kingston and Holder had evidently mapped out a plan of campaign, for Holder immediately rose to his feet and proposed 'that no elector now possessing the right to vote should be deprived of that right'.[21] This meant that the Commonwealth could not deprive South Australian women of their vote and so would have to give it to all Australian women if it wanted uniformity. Barton and others angrily attacked Holder for trying to 'bind the hands'[22] of the Commonwealth Parliament in this way. Holder calmly replied that South Australia would probably vote against joining the Commonwealth in the forthcoming referendum if there were any possibility of its women being deprived of their federal vote at any time in the future. The threat worked and the Convention accepted Holder's proposal, but only by a majority of 18–15. The suffrage clause which was finally approved for the referenda now had the provision that

> no elector who has at the establishment of the Commonwealth, or who afterwards acquires a right to vote at the elections for the more numerous Houses of the Parliament of a State shall, while the right continues, be prevented by any law of the Commonwealth from exercising such a right at the elections for either House of the Parliament of the Commonwealth.[23]

Holder made another attempt to insert one-adult-one-vote into the Constitution at the second session of the 1897 Convention held in Sydney later that year, but was unsuccessful; South Australian delegates had to be content with having ensured that their own women could not be federally disenfranchised.

Referenda to approve or disapprove of the proposed Constitution were held in June 1898 in South Australia, Victoria, New South Wales and Tasmania, and the women in the last three colonies were angry about their exclusion from the decision-making process. May Evans wrote to Rose Scott: 'It is manifestly unjust that this great national question of Federation should be decided by only half the adult population of New South Wales.'[24] Not all suffragists would have voted for a Commonwealth. Rose Scott, Vida Goldstein and Leontine Cooper were all against it, but they took care to emphasise that they spoke as individuals, not on behalf of their suffrage organisations. All referenda achieved a majority in favour, but in New South Wales the majority was 8045 short of what had been stipulated. The Premiers met in early 1899 to consider amendments, and by July all four colonies had given their approval to these amendments. Queensland consented in a referendum in September 1899 and Western Australia in July 1900.

Defeated in attempts to have woman suffrage written into the Constitution, the women now had to ensure that men favourable to their cause would be elected to the first Commonwealth Parliament. Circulars were sent out to candidates in Queensland, New South Wales and Victoria. The tenor of the circulars was that of the one from the Queensland Woman's Equal Franchise Association, which read 'Are you in favour of the Federal Parliament at once dealing with the Federal franchise so as to make it uniform in all the States?'[25] Only entrenched opponents of the Commonwealth vote for women returned negative replies. Waverers, like Barton, surrendered in the face of the clause in the Constitution forbidding the cancellation of the votes of the South Australian women. As one candidate wrote to Rose Scott: 'The politicians think it is the proper card to play.'[26] New South Wales returned only five opponents out of thirty-two members, and Vida Goldstein estimated that four in every five of the new Parliament overall were supporters.[27]

Even now the women did not relax their efforts. They prepared petitions for the new legislature. There were many from individual groups; there was one from the Victorian United Council for Woman Suffrage which had been circulated interstate to be signed by office-bearers of suffrage and other societies;[28] and there was one from the Australian WCTU which had been sent to male temperance societies as well as to the Union's branches.[29]

The first Commonwealth Parliament was opened in Melbourne with histrionic ceremony on 9 May 1901 by the Duke of York. The following day the first Governor-General, Lord Hopetoun, announced to Parliament that a measure was in preparation 'for the grant of an uniform suffrage in all Federal elections by the adoption of adult suffrage'.[30] It was almost twelve months, however, before the Commonwealth Franchise Bill was presented in the Senate for its first hearing—ostensibly because of the pressure of so much legislation requiring the attention of the Lower House. The Prime Minister, Edmund Barton, who had never been enthusiastic about female suffrage when a member of the New South Wales legislature, was able to avoid the passage of the bill because he had left Melbourne the week before to attend the coronation of Edward VII. Sir William Lyne, a former Premier of New South Wales and now an unequivocal supporter, was Acting Prime Minister.

On 9 April 1902 Senator Richard O'Connor introduced the bill giving a vote to all adult British subjects in Australia, whether they had a state vote or not.[31] There were two major implications in the bill: women in the four eastern States could now join their sisters in South Australia and Western Australia (where women had gained the vote in 1899) at the Commonwealth ballot-box; and all Aboriginal men and women would have the Commonwealth vote. The two issues were interwoven in the debate, but in the interests of clarity it is better to examine them separately.

Woman suffrage, as it had been at the 1897 Convention, was attacked by representatives of those states without it on the grounds that the Commonwealth was insidiously putting pressure on them to give their women state votes. O'Connor denied this, as Kingston had done in 1897. The state franchise, he said, was completely outside the jurisdiction of the Commonwealth. Opponents of woman suffrage per se trotted out the whole gamut of objections. Edward Harney (Western Australia) forecast the 'Americanization' of Australian women; it would be 'the thin end of the wedge', he said, which would lead women to 'forsake their homes' and 'despise their position as housewives',[32] Simon Fraser (Victoria) thought that if he were a woman 'he should infinitely prefer the position of looking up to man as my director, my guide and adviser.'[33] He denied that women needed the vote to protect their interests. 'In a British country', he said 'women have only to let their position be known to be rescued from their troubles.'

Edward Pulsford was sure that it would affect 'the strength of the State' because it would 'lessen the great solemnity and earnestness attaching to women in social and domestic life'.[34] All ideological adversaries except Pulsford, however, indicated that they would vote for woman suffrage in the interests of uniformity. All knew that it would win the day but could not, it seems, resist the temptation to register their mournful lamentations. Pulsford, in the committee stages of the bill, tried to amend 'all adult persons' to 'all adult male persons' because, he said, if the Commonwealth Government held out, South Australia and Western Australia might be persuaded to drop woman suffrage, and so a common franchise would be achieved.[35] He was ruled out of order because the Constitution expressly stated that the Commonwealth could not disenfranchise those who had a state vote. The bill was passed in the Senate without a division.

Sir William Lyne took charge of the measure in the House of Representatives, where it had much the same reception; there were those who opposed it but reluctantly consented to vote for it, and there were a couple of bitter dissenters like Henry Higgins (Victoria) who 'could not see that the Committee is forced into the position of conceding a franchise for the mere reason that in some States it has been conferred'.[36] The bill went through all stages and by 12 June 1902 it had received royal assent and all white Australian women could vote for the Commonwealth Parliament and stand as candidates for either the Senate or the House of Representatives.

In 1902 Aboriginal males could vote in all states except Western Australia and Queensland,[37] and Aboriginal females could vote in South Australia. The privilege was for the most part academic. During the debate on the Commonwealth Franchise Bill Thomas Playford said that in South Australia there were on the roll 'only one or two who have been civilized and are settled on the land';[38] Sir William Lyne said he could recall seeing some vote once in New South Wales;[39] and it was claimed that there were no Aborigines left in Tasmania to claim the vote[40]—a statement tragically very close to the mark.

The Commonwealth Franchise Bill, by giving all adult British subjects in Australia a vote, would have enfranchised all Australian Aborigines, male and female. Delegates from Western Australia and Queensland, which had the greatest numbers of Aborigines, heatedly attacked this aspect of the bill. It must be admitted that their objections had validity in one respect: tribal Aborigines living in and around the cattle stations—few, if any, of whom could read or write—might be brought together by the station owner (who would probably be the returning officer, and perhaps even the candidate) and instructed to put their mark against the name approved by him. This, however, was only part of the debate. Members from these two states, supported by some others, attacked the assumption that Aborigines were worthy of the franchise. Phrases like 'the most degraded people in the world'[41] and 'these savages'[42] were used without compunction. The most vehement invective, however, was saved for the Aboriginal women who under the bill would have been given the same privilege as 'our wives and daughters'.

> If anything could tend to make the concession of female suffrage worse that it is in the minds of some people, it would be the giving of it to any of the numerous gins of the blackfellow. It cannot be claimed ... that the Aboriginal native is a person of very high intelligence, who would cast his vote with a proper sense of the responsibility that rests upon him. And it can even less be claimed that the gins would give a vote which would be intelligible.[43]

To its credit the Senate held firm to the provisions for the vote for all Aboriginal men and women, but when the bill went to the Lower House opponents renewed their attack and the Senate's decision was reversed. The press commented:

> While Senator O'Connor was appealing to the one Chamber for the vote on the grounds of humanity and generosity to a dying race, Sir William Lyne, in the other, was drawing grotesque pictures of the high-toned members with a black gin or two sitting next to them.[44]

When the House of Representatives refused to treat Aborigines as it had treated women a special disqualification was added to the bill: 'No Aboriginal native of Australia, Africa or the Islands of the Pacific except New Zealand shall be entitled to have his name placed on an Electoral Roll unless so entitled under section forty-one of the Constitution.'[45] Section forty-one of the Constitution was that which stipulated that the Commonwealth must give a vote to any adult having a state vote. As New South Wales (1902), Tasmania (1903), and Victoria (1908) enfranchised its women for state legislatures so black women in these states gained Commonwealth privileges also. Aborigines in Queensland and Western Australia could not vote until an Act in 1962 gave them the Commonwealth vote, and Queensland and Western Australia then followed with state rights.[46] The proud boast that Australia was the second nation in the world to federally enfranchise its women ignores the fact that black women and their men in two states had to wait until 1962 to gain access to the ballot-box.

The first Commonwealth Government was obliged to give all white Australian women their franchise in order to retain the balance of representation between the states. It knew, too, that it would be under great pressure from proliferating women's organisations in the unenfranchised states if it did not do so. The rights of Aborigines, male and female, could be denied in Queensland and Western Australia because there was nothing to fear in the way of protest from a black population with little education and either isolated from or pushed to the fringes of white settlements. There was no reaction from the women about the special exclusion of Aboriginal women who did not have votes in their own state, just as there had been no concern shown during the campaigns for the voting rights, or plight, of Aboriginal women in any colony. As far as we know, there was not one Aboriginal woman in any of the suffrage societies, and it is unlikely that they would have been welcome. Only one organisation, however, spelt out their exclusion: the Secretary of the Woman's Equal Franchise Association of Queensland told its annual meeting in 1896 that 'we are always prepared to accept the hand of all white women in membership, irrespective of wealth or standing'.[47] The possibility of black women in their societies would not have occurred to most suffragists; they shared the prevailing belief that the Aboriginal race was dying out. Louisa Lawson in the *Dawn* pleaded for Aboriginal women to be treated with kindness for this very reason.[48] The suffragists, moreover, shared the Anglo-Saxon feelings of superiority over all coloured races, and more than one petition from the women protested that they should not be excluded from a vote which was given 'to aliens and even to blackfellows'. Insulated in their urban areas, most suffragists knew little about, or preferred to turn their eyes away from, the cruelties and sexual degradation being visited upon black women by white men in the period. It was only in the 1930s that women's organisations in Australia began to show any great concern for the plight, and rights, of their Aboriginal sisters.

Although suffrage for women, black or white, is still not written into the Australian Commonwealth Constitution, it is secure in that it has been given in the states by amendments to their Constitutions, and the vote which the state has given the Commonwealth must also give.

Notes

1. *National Australasian Convention Debates, Sydney 1891*, p. 613.
2. ibid., p. 633.
3. *Woman's Voice* (New South Wales), 15 June 1895.
4. ibid.
5. ibid.
6. WCTU of Western Australia, Annual Report, 1895.
7. WCTU of Australasia, Report of the Third Triennial Convention, Brisbane, 1897.
8. ibid.; WCTU of New South Wales, Annual Report, 1897.
9. Undated, unsourced newspaper clipping, in Womanhood Suffrage League of New South Wales: note-books of the Secretary, and newspaper clippings, ML:NSW, MSS 38/35, item 4:206.
10. WCTU of Australasia, Report of the Third Triennial Convention, Brisbane, 1897.
11. *Mercury*, 10 March 1897.
12. ibid.; Womanhood Suffrage League of New South Wales, Annual Report, 1897.
13. Womanhood Suffrage League of New South Wales, Annual Report, 1897.
14. WCTU of Victoria, Annual Report, 1897.
15. W. Spence to Rose Scott, 25 February 1895, in Woman Suffrage Correspondence, 1887–1899, ML:NSW, MSS A2271, item 253.
16. Arthur Rae to Rose Scott, 20 February 1895, in ibid., item 254.
17. *Daily Telegraph*, 16 February 1897.
18. *National Australasian Convention Debates, First Session, Adelaide, 1897*, p. 637.
19. ibid., p. 715.
20. ibid., p. 723.
21. ibid., p. 725.
22. ibid., p. 725.
23. ibid., p. 731.
24. May Evans to Rose Scott, 4 June 1898, Woman Suffrage Correspondence, 1887–1899 ML:NSW, MSS A2271, item 307.
25. *Worker* (Brisbane), 28 February 1901.
26. Undated letter to Rose Scott, signature indecipherable, Woman Suffrage Correspondence, 1900–1902, ML:NSW, MSS A2272, item 618.
27. *Woman's Sphere*, December 1901.
28. Womanhood Suffrage League of New South Wales, Annual Report, 1901.
29. WCTU of Australasia, Report of the Fifth Triennial Convention, Melbourne, 1903.
30. *CAPD*, vol. 7, 10 May 1901, p. 29.
31. ibid., vol. 9, 9 April 1902, p. 11450.
32. ibid., p. 11488.
33. ibid., p. 11558.
34. ibid., 10 April 1902, p. 11466.
35. ibid., pp. 11570, 11571.

36. ibid., 24 April 1902, p. 11977.
37. In Queensland there was a provision that an Aboriginal male could vote under a £100 freehold qualification. This right was withdrawn in 1905.
38. *CAPD*, vol. 9, 10 April 1902, p. 11580.
39. ibid., 24 April 1902, p. 11975.
40. Alexander Matheson, ibid., 10 April 1902, p. 11582; Richard O'Connor, p. 11584.
41. Sir William Zeal, ibid., p. 11584.
42. John Watson, ibid., 24 April 1902, p. 1197.
43. Sir Edward Braddon, ibid.
44. Unidentified, undated newspaper clipping, in Womanhood Suffrage League of New South Wales: note-books of the Secretary, and newspaper clippings, ML:NSW, MSS 38/35, item 3.
45. An Act to provide for a Uniform Federal Franchise for the Commonwealth of Australia, Clause 4, in *Commonwealth Acts of Australia*, vol. 1, 1902, p. 289.
46. Murray Goot, 'Electoral Systems', p. 189. From 1944 in Western Australia it was possible for anyone classed as an Aboriginal to apply for citizenship rights if that person were self-supporting and leading a settled existence.
47. *Worker* (Brisbane), 4 April 1896.
48. *Dawn*, November 1987.

5

NEW SOUTH WALES, 1902

In 1842, when South Australia and Western Australia were small struggling settlements, eastern Australia had a white population of more than 200,000 and was given its first electoral representation by the British Colonial Office. Under a high property qualification for electors and elected, approximately one-quarter of the combined male population of New South Wales and Van Diemen's Land became eligible to elect two-thirds of the members of the Legislative Council, which until then had been a nominated and advisory body. The territories which were later to become Victoria and Queensland were still part of New South Wales.

What is almost certainly the first published demand for female suffrage in Australia came soon after the 1842 act.

> WHY THE LADIES SHOULD HAVE VOTES.
>
> This argument on the convenience of cutting off half the claimants to votes at a blow, is really the only one of reasonable appearance the opponents have; for on every other ground the admission of women to vote would be a great addition of security for the general welfare. Among other reasons why it would be good, are two special ones—women in general are not such fools as men are; and secondly, they are not such knaves . . . Women, in fact, are vastly further advanced in civilization than men are; vastly more removed from the instincts and passions of savage life; more accustomed to calculate consequences, because it is on them that they have always fallen in their bitterness, and above all less deteriorated by that wear and tear with the meanness and villainy of the world.[1]

The article indicates that from the beginnings of electoral representation in Australia there was debate about whether women should have the vote, for it speaks of arguments and opponents. The journal in which it appeared was an organ of the early nineteenth-century temperance movement, which originated in England and gained support in Australia in the 1830s and 1840s. It is significant, considering the part played by the

Woman's Christian Temperance Union in the later campaigns, that the first Australian advocacy should have been made by a temperance publication.

In 1850 the Australian Colonies Government Act made Port Phillip, plus an area to be determined, into Victoria. It conferred on it and Van Diemen's Land, to be renamed Tasmania, Legislative Councils modelled upon that of New South Wales. Queensland was not to exist as a separate entity until 1859. The Act gave all Legislative Councils the power to frame Constitutions and fix their own franchises. It was therefore only from the year 1850 that any Australian body had power to confer votes on men *or* women.

The public debate about the suffrage which should be embodied in the New South Wales Constitution began in the late 1840s. At a large meeting in Sydney in 1849, the young Henry Parkes made his first public speech, in which he urged that New South Wales should have universal suffrage.[2] He used the term as it was then understood, a vote for every male, not for every person. The *Sydney Morning Herald* attacked Parkes and the other speakers. It deplored the concept of universal suffrage, but went on:

> If, as was philosophically observed at the meeting, we are to set aside that idle chimera called the British Constitution, and to start for ourselves on the broad basis of reason and commonsense, let us make a bold push and go the whole animal. And let us begin by doing justice to that gem of Creation, the Fair Sex. Spurning the example of our ungallant forefathers, let us assert the Rights of Woman. There can be no universal suffrage until these rights shall have been completely established. Let the women be as free to vote as the men, for the women as well as the men pay taxes; the women as well as the men have a deep stake in the prosperity of the country; the women as well as the men can distinguish between right and wrong; the women as well as the men know the preciousness of liberty, and the sacredness of the rights of property. By all means then, let the women have the franchise as well as the men, and not the franchise only, but, if they choose, a seat in the legislature too.[3]

If one did not know otherwise, one would think that the editor was earnestly urging votes for women.

In the debate ranging over several years no-one with influence seems to have seriously suggested that women should be included in the New South Wales franchise. The Constitution which emerged gave an Upper House of proprietied males appointed for life, retaining the name of Legislative Council, which all colonies were to do for their Upper Houses. The Assembly was to be elected on a male property vote, but was then allowed to set its own franchise. The first Assembly sat in 1856, and two years later a bill giving manhood suffrage with plural voting was passed. While it was before the Assembly, William Piddington attacked the new franchise. It would, he said

> transfer the entire political power from the hands of those who had something into the hands of those who had nothing ... [and] transfer political power from the hands of the middle class, destroy their influence in the country and make the franchise so cheap and common as to deprive it of the character of a privilege ... If the suffrage were a sacred human right, on what ground did they exclude half the human race? Did not women belong to the human race; were they therefore justified on this principle in excluding them from voting, and by so doing, classing women with lunatics and felons? If the suffrage were a sacred, inalienable, indefeasible right common to human nature, how dared they to deprive the fairer half of creation of their indefeasible privilege? He asked were not women as industrious, and often far more intelligent, than men? And yet they were excluded, although to a drunken pauper they intended to give a vote. Did not women possess property and pay taxes, as well as men; are they not also liable to the penalties of your criminal law; why therefore, if they carried out the principle to its logical conclusion, should they be excluded from the Electoral Roll?[4]

Piddington, like the *Sydney Morning Herald* nine years before, was not seriously advocating the franchise for women, although he managed, ironically, to present some very cogent arguments in favour of it.

No other parliamentary speaker raised the question of woman suffrage, but outside Parliament the women themselves spoke out. Letters appeared in the *Sydney Morning Herald*, followed by an editorial.

> Several letters from lady correspondents have appeared in this journal, asserting the claims of their sex to political enfranchisement. Is their claim reasonable and just?
> We understand that they ask for the rights of electors only—the power to choose representatives to make laws for them. They allege that this exclusion is not simply unnecessary—it is unrighteous.[5]

The editor analysed the arguments of the letter writers and gave what he called 'a consideration of their claims, if not with favor, yet with candour'. He admitted the arguments put forward: that they should be represented if they owned property and paid taxes; that women were capable of forming independent and sound political opinions; that it would give them dignity in society; and that they were unlikely to choose candidates who were 'frothy, hoary and brutal'. A woman, he said, would not vote for 'a brute—for a man who beat or has deserted his wife—for a selfish, miserly wretch', but he concluded: 'We fear the time has not come to take these subjects out of the regions of "gallantry" and therefore of ridicule, and obtain for them a fair consideration.'[6] This argument, that the time was not yet ripe, was not laid to rest in any state until the vote was granted.

Although the subject was not raised again in the legislature until 1887, twenty-nine years later, there is evidence that it was being discussed in the intervening years. In 1875 Premier John Robertson and members of his Cabinet (with their wives) were entertained at a picnic on the shores of Sydney Harbour. Ferries transported more than six hundred guests and lunch was served under a huge marquee. The speeches reflect the jovial holiday mood. When it was Robertson's turn to reply to the heady compliments paid him, he said how pleased he was to see

> so many ladies assembled to do them honour (cheers) and it would be for his colleagues to consider whether, in the preparation of any new electoral law, the franchise should not be extended to the ladies of the colony. He had always taken the part of the ladies in parliament, and he should be quite prepared to do battle for them in this matter also.[7]

There is no evidence that Robertson backed up his ingratiating words with action.

A letter written to Rose Scott in the 1890s gives another glimpse of the subterranean debate in these years. May Evans replied to an invitation by Scott to stand for office in the Womanhood Suffrage League: 'I believe I was the first, or at least one of the first woman suffragists in Australia and when it was mentioned in whispers twenty-eight years ago, and confess to a wish to be in at the death.'[8]

In 1887, thirty-eight years after he had made his plea for 'universal' suffrage for the Constitution, Sir Henry Parkes gave his first support for woman suffrage in the Assembly. All but five of the intervening years had been spent in the legislature. He had just entered his fourth period as Premier and had behind him an impressive list of

Liberal reform achievements, especially in education. Now seventy-two, but still with eight more years to go in politics, he was an impressive paternalistic bearded figure, proud (some said excessively so) of his ten-year-old knighthood. An Assembly member asked if his Government intended to introduce a bill to amend the electoral laws. The questioner had in mind electoral redistribution and the abolition of plural voting. Parkes replied that the Government did intend electoral reform in several areas and

> another question which I think deserves consideration, especially of the intelligent men I see opposite, is a provision to enable the ladies of the country to vote. I say myself that I would admit them to the right of the suffrage tomorrow . . . I think we need not hesitate much if, indeed, we are the democratic country which gentlemen sometimes represent us to be. One thing I am quite sure of, and that is that on many questions—on questions of a social character—the vote of the women would be safer than that of the men.[9]

Parkes spoke again on the subject later in the year. Opposing a bill to extend the suffrage to the then excluded members of the police force and 'the permanent artillery', on the grounds that they might have to maintain order at election meetings and polling booths, he went on:

> the honorary member has not proposed, in the extreme liberality which seems to guide him, to extend the franchise to half of the human family . . . he extends his favours to the male population only. Well, I should have thought that a liberal man like the honorary member for Redfern would have required the Electoral Act to be amended in favour of half the human family who have to obey the laws, and to bear all the obligations imposed by society, and who are in many instances as well able to form a judgement as their brothers.[10]

In the next two years Parkes gave support outside Parliament. A letter to the *Sydney Morning Herald* attacked him for wanting women to enter 'the notorious political imbecility, dishonesty and corruption of public life' and went on: 'Sir Henry Parkes in his old age, seems to be the victim of strange delusions and somewhat grotesque notions and ideas . . . his oft-repeated and evidently serious intention to try and confer the franchise on women is the worst attack he has had yet of his present malady.'[11]

After the 1890 election which returned Parkes as Premier, the Governor's speech announced that a bill would be introduced to abolish plural voting and give women the vote. Labor, which had an uneasy coalition with the Liberals, was angry, and defiantly tried with an unsuccessful private member's bill for one-man-one-vote only. Labor members claimed that the Government was not serious about the abolition of plural voting if it was considering introducing 'countervailing provisions which would operate to negative the force of this principle of one-man-one-vote . . . does anyone believe that a bill containing . . . the principle of woman suffrage . . . has any chance of passing through the house?'[12] Labor was right. When Parkes introduced his double bill there were many who refused to support one-man-one-vote because they did not approve of woman suffrage. Thomas Waddell, to be a bitter opponent, claimed that 'to his mind a more insane proposal was never brought before the House'.[13]

The following year Parkes tried a different approach and moved: 'That in the opinion of this House, the franchise for the election of members of the Legislative Assembly should be extended to women on the same conditions and subject to the same disqualifications, as those imposed by law upon male electors.'[14] Parkes said his move was to allow woman suffrage to be debated as a special issue, but then muddied the waters by announcing that if the resolution were passed he would graft woman suffrage onto a bill to abolish plural voting. Nevertheless the discussion, which went from early in the night until an exhausted Parliament adjourned at 4.30 the next morning, did significantly air opinions about votes for women. Parkes used arguments based on both justice and expediency. Most of the opinions about 'woman's sphere' and arguments for and against her vote which were to be voiced in the Parliament in the next eleven years were put forward, and opponents were pinpointed. George Dibbs, a rival Liberal Premier waiting in the wings, maintained that 'the bulk of women throughout the world are utterly incapable of performing the duties of men'.[15] The vote against was 57–34, but as Parkes had linked the question indirectly with plural voting it was still not clear just what the Assembly thought of woman suffrage per se. This was to be Parkes's last move on votes for women. Later that year his Government fell to one led by George Dibbs, and in the 1895 elections he lost his seat. He was to die in 1896, revered by the New South Wales suffragists as their first political champion. Yet one must question his commitment to both the abolition of plural voting and the introduction of female suffrage. If he had been serious about either, he could have introduced two separate bills. He seems to have honestly come to believe that, although the woman's place was in the home, her vote would be a force for good, but his moves were desultory. By them he was, however, able to ingratiate himself with the body of influential women outside Parliament who were emerging to advocate female suffrage. This, to an old social lion like Sir Henry, would have been important.

Sydney in the 1880s, when the public debate emerged, was a thriving commercial city with an expanding industrial sector. It had generated a large proletariat work force and a significant middle class. Above these was a small close-knit upper society of influential and wealthy families whose men were in administration, law, commerce and politics. Louisa Macdonald, who came from England to Australia in 1887 and became principal of the new Sydney University Women's College in 1892, described this upper stratum.

> The Sydney we first knew was a small and delightful society where everybody knew everybody else. There was Government House at the top—the Navy . . . with the Admiral at Admiralty House across the Harbour, the Army with a Commanding Officer from Home, the Bench, the Bar, the University—the old aristocracy of the Colony with the tales and relics of old days, and the squatters, or big landowners who came up to Sydney at stated intervals.[16]

The wives and daughters of these influential families who moved onto boards and committees of worthy causes in the late 1880s knew each other and indeed were often related by blood or marriage. They were well-dressed and, as their code of respectability demanded, 'womanly' and 'ladylike' at all times. Although they had servants to back them in well-run households, they were energetic and hard-working in support of their chosen causes. The middle-class women who worked in charities linked generally to church and temperance organisations only occasionally overlapped with their wealthier sisters. We know from their writings that they, too, were very mindful of their 'ladylike' behaviour at all times. Concerned women from both groups, some Labor women,

Sir Henry Parkes introduced the first measure for votes for women into the New South Wales Parliament in 1890. This is how the *Bulletin* saw the reaction of the Woman's Christian Temperance Union to his early moves.
Bulletin, 16 July 1892. State Library of New South Wales.

and the odd maverick like Louisa Lawson were, in the 1880s and 1890s, to find their way into organisations agitating for better working conditions for women in industry and commerce, and for legal reforms in laws affecting women and children. The same cross-section was to find its way into the two organisations which worked so hard for woman suffrage.

The first evidence for women's agitation is in 1887, but a voice which was possibly raised earlier is that of Miss Helen Hart. George Black in 1917 claimed that Hart, 'an angular but kindly man-hater' was 'the pioneer advocate of woman suffrage in Australia'.[17] Rose Scott later said in a newspaper interview that Hart was one of the early advocates.[18] There is also an undated card among Scott's papers advertising a lecture by 'Helen Hart, Founder of the Woman Suffrage Movement in New Zealand and Australia'.[19] In early 1901 Emily Steel wrote to Scott that she had seen

> a notice in Queen's Hall that Miss Helen Hart is to give a lecture, claiming her as 'the founder of the Woman's Suffrage League of New South Wales' ... Was she and could she be assisted in some way in her aim of raising her fare to England to live with relatives? I have never spoken to her, but I have *seen* her, old and lonely and poorly dressed.[20]

The kindly man-hater remains obscure, and one hopes that she made it back to her relatives in England.

The Woman's Christian Temperance Union was the first to adopt the cause. The Sydney Union, Australia's first, was formed in 1882 by an American temperance lecturer, Mr Eli Johnson. It was a sickly infant, but was given an injection of strength in 1885 by Mrs Leavitt. By then the three women who were to be the motivating forces behind its suffrage work were members. They were Eliza Pottie, Euphemia Bowes and Elizabeth Ward.

Mrs Eliza Pottie came from a Quaker family and was married to a Congregationalist clergyman. Her brother, a temperance worker and member of the Legislative Assembly, was to be a strong supporter of female suffrage. Pottie was to be the WCTU representative at the first public meeting called by the embryonic Womanhood Suffrage League in 1891 and joined its first council, so for a time she worked through both organisations. She gained a reputation for clear logical speaking and was to be always in demand for delegations to Parliament in the 1890s. Mrs Euphemia Bowes was the wife of a Methodist minister. In 1885, then seventy years old, she stepped into the presidency which she was to occupy until 1892. She remained active in the Union until her death aged eighty-five. In spite of her age she is described at this stage as a powerful speaker in the cause of temperance, always ready with repartee.[21] She was to have plenty of opportunity to use this expertise in the cause of suffrage. The most notable suffragist within Union ranks, however, was to be Mrs Elizabeth Ward. A profile gives some insight into the middle-class background from which most WCTU women came. Her father had a Sydney veterinary business and was prosperous enough to send her to an Anglican girls' school. At fifteen she went to work as a milliner at a large department store where she rose to head position. She married and had seven sons, but still found time to work for Anglican church organisations. She brought to the Union a pleasant and persuasive personality which she was to need to overcome opposition to female suffrage within the

WCTU itself. The suffrage campaign revealed her talent for logical disputation and organisation which she used for arranging petitions and delegations to Parliament, writing propaganda leaflets, arguing for suffrage in letters to editors and addressing meetings in Sydney and country towns. The New South Wales Union was to throw up other capable suffragists. There was Sara Nolan, again a clergyman's wife, who juggled public work and a large family and who in middle life 'disclosed a gift for public speaking which surprised even the friends who knew her best'.[22] Sara was to travel the whole of the state lecturing on votes for women. There was Mrs Harrison Lee, later to become Mrs Lee-Cowie of New Zealand, also a great traveller and speaker, who was said to have 'delighted the audience with her quick repartee' at the first public meeting of the Womanhood Suffrage League.[23] Anglican Archdeacon F. B. Boyce, an honorary member, helped to give female suffrage a responsible public image and was a great help to Elizabeth Ward in her struggle against internal resistance.

Although the Union claimed in its annual report of 1892 that it first took up the work in 1882, there is no mention of any public utterances by the women until 1887. Early that year Euphemia Bowes is reported as having 'spoken on the subject at various public meetings' and she supported it in her addresses as Union President in 1888 and 1889, each time as a way of putting pressure on Parliament for amendments to the liquor laws. In 1889 there was a 'local option festival' in Sydney and Elizabeth Ward wrote to the *Sydney Morning Herald*:

> I was pleased to notice at the local option festival, and also at the public meeting . . . that several of the speakers were in favour of woman's suffrage. Mr Abigail, in fact, said that he would do his best to get it for us, and we know a great many other members of Parliament who are prepared to help us in this matter. I think, therefore, that the time has arrived when we should agitate for woman suffrage.[24]

At a Union meeting in March 1890 Eliza Pottie read a paper on the subject, and at her urging the Union decided to form a Woman's Suffrage League. A public meeting called by advertisement was held in the temperance hall. About twenty women attended, some not Union members. The WCTU had envisaged the proposed society as having a temperance base, but non-members at the meeting 'declined to work under the auspices of the Woman's Christian Temperance Union',[25] and the matter lapsed.

In 1891 Jessie Ackermann visited Sydney, and with her encouragement the Union expanded its branch network throughout the colony and appointed Elizabeth Ward as Colonial Superintendent of Suffrage. Ward wrote to all suburban and country branches asking them to establish suffrage departments, and by the time the 1892 Convention met nine had done so (two in Sydney and seven in the country). Ward was to work fervently during her eight years as Superintendent to enthuse the suffrage departments in the branches.

While the temperance women had been gathering their forces, the strongly individualistic Louisa Lawson had entered the debate. Her feminism had been forged in a different furnace to that of the WCTU women. Her father was a first-generation Australian, a builder and timber-cutter, and her mother a migrant domestic worker from Devon. She had a primary-school education in the country town of Mudgee and when she was fifteen moved to the Gulgong goldfields where the family ran a hotel and store and she helped serve the customers. She was a tall, well-built girl with a love of reading and writing, both of which were discouraged by a strong-willed father. When barely eighteen, 'as a wild act of protest after losing a battle of wills with her father'[26] she married Peter Larsen (later changed to Lawson), a 31-year-old Norwegian sailor who had deserted his ship for the goldfields. Lawson was to find that the marriage into which she had so thoughtlessly entered was to provide no escape from poverty, unhappiness, and intellectual starvation. Her husband was a gentle drifter and for seventeen years they moved from goldfield to goldfield or eked out a living on small unproductive plots of land. Peter often spent long periods away from home on carpentering jobs and she was left to care for the farm and children. Often out of reach of schools, she taught the children to read by the light of kerosene lamps and strove, with few books, to implant in them a love of literature. The long years of hardship and cultural deprivation seared her soul. Her later writings show that she felt that she had been trapped by a romanticised view of marriage and had been condemned from birth to have no control over her life because she was female.

In 1883, after seventeen years of marriage, she and Peter separated and she came to Sydney with three of their four surviving children, Henry (sixteen), Peter (ten), and Gertrude (six)—another son was with his grandparents. There she opened a boarding house and began to broaden her life. She and Henry became interested in the Labor movement; she found that the poet Henry Kendall's grave was unkempt and canvassed to have a tombstone erected over it; and, disenchanted from a young girl with the organised religion of her day, she attended the Spiritualist Association of Sydney. Here she met and was influenced by Susannah Gale, of the Windeyer family, who was strongly in favour of votes for women.

In May 1888, having failed to make a reasonable living by keeping boarders or by taking in sewing, Lawson began what was to be her vocation and her memorial, a magazine for women. She had bought a printing press from the short-lived *Republican* in 1887; now she canvassed for advertisements for her own paper, the *Dawn*, which was, after a short period with male typesetters, to be 'edited, printed and published by women'. Because of this policy she fought a war of attrition with the male typesetters' union, which objected to her use of non-union labour, but would not allow women to join their union. The *Dawn* was to run for seventeen years and was wound up only because Lawson was in poor health and would not trust anyone to publish it with the same slant on women's issues as she had.

In her first editorial Lawson wrote: 'Here we will give publicity to women's wrongs, will fight their battles, assist to report what evils we can, and give advice to the best of our ability ... This most potent constituency we seek to represent, and for their suffrages we sue.'[27] She kept her word for the life of the journal, putting her finger on overt and covert areas of discrimination. She claimed that wives, unable to work for themselves, should be entitled to a share in their husband's earnings, and deplored the cult of the self-sacrificing woman who must always put her husband's and children's interests before her own. She contended that many women married because they had no economic alternative, and pleaded for a wage that would allow a woman to remain single if she wished. She claimed that women would not be so ill-treated within marriage if escape by divorce were easier, and she publicised child abuse. The *Dawn* advocated social legislation which would give support to widows left destitute with young children, and spoke out against the labelling of single pregnant women as 'fallen'. A recurrent theme was the inequality of education given to boys and girls. Many articles protested against women's unsuitable clothing, and she attacked cruel mother-in-law and stepmother jokes and jokes about women's reputed loquacity and inability to keep secrets. When, at the time her son Henry was achieving prominence with his poetry, the *Bulletin* published an article about her with the title 'A Poet's Mother', she wrote, 'I hope some day to be able to look the public in the face as Louisa Lawson, not as the mother of a man.'[28] The best of Lawson's writing is elegant, logical and fervent dialectic. The worst is trite and sentimental, or full of bitter invective. In between stands a solid body of professional journalism which enabled her to keep her paper afloat when most small journals sank soon after publication.

The *Dawn* was the vehicle for Lawson's great passion, votes for women. From 1888 till 1905 it was suffrage, suffrage, suffrage—what she thought about it, what others said and wrote about it, and what was being done about it in other states and all over the world. Although many in the community were shocked by her iconoclastic ideas, large numbers of women voted approval by taking out subscriptions. She claimed to have two thousand subscribers in 1890, and for these subscribers the suffrage would seem to have been the corollary of an advanced feminism.

In 1889 Lawson formed the Dawn Club. In May she sent out invitations to a group of women to meet 'to endeavour to start a club or association for women'.[29] The women agreed that the club should exist 'for mutual development, mutual aid and for consideration of various questions of importance to the sex'.[30] Lawson's daughter wrote that 'the association was to have mother and the paper at the head of affairs.'[31] Membership information is sketchy but Margaret Windeyer gave a paper at the first meeting, and Lawson delivered an impassioned speech of 3000 words in favour of woman suffrage: 'Here in New South Wales every man may vote, let his character be bad, his judgment purchasable, and his intellect of the weakest; but an honourable, thoughtful and good woman may be laughed at by such men, they can carry what laws they please in spite of her.'[32]

It is not clear whether the Dawn Club was designated a suffrage society, but among Lawson's papers there is a copy of a tract, 'The Curse of a Bad Example', a piece of her more execrable writings: 'published by the Woman's Franchise Association, 26 Jamieson St. Sydney. Funds devoted to the dissemination of suffrage literature. Every woman interested in the emancipation of her sex should at once join.'[33] The address given is the publishing office of the *Dawn*. A year after the formation of the Dawn Club and a year before the formation of the Womanhood Suffrage League, the *Dawn* refers to Lawson as 'the president of the woman's suffrage society of Sydney',[34] and when Lawson reviewed the by then successful campaign in the *Dawn* in 1902 she wrote that the suffrage 'was not given any serious thought until 'the little pioneer band' took it up and circulated quantities of literature bearing on the subject. This was handed on from one to another and posted in parcels free to inquirers for information'.[35] 'The little pioneer band', the

Woman's Franchise Association with its address at Lawson's office, and the Dawn Club seem to have been one and the same.

Independent and forthright when such women were ridiculed as a 'shrieking sisterhood', Lawson defies categorisation in the spectrum of suffragists. She was to fit very uneasily into the ranks of the later Womanhood Suffrage League whose reins were held so firmly by Rose Scott for the whole of its life. She was, after the vote was won, very jealous of her claim to be 'the mother of woman suffrage in New South Wales', and certainly her *Dawn* articles and public speeches predated the abortive WCTU attempt to form a suffrage association, but they came after Euphemia Bowes' first independent speeches in favour of the vote as a means of liquor reform.

The Sydney Women's Literary Society, formed in August 1890 at the instigation of Mrs Matilda Curnow (wife of the editor of the *Sydney Morning Herald*) contained several women from influential families who were to be the nucleus of the New South Wales Womanhood Suffrage League: Rose Scott, Dora Montefiore, Maybanke Wolstenholme (an educationalist who was later to marry Professor Francis Anderson) and Lizzie Ashton (wife of the Sydney artist, Julian Ashton). Maybanke Anderson recalled in 1925 that at an early meeting she and Rose Scott spoke a few words on woman suffrage, and suggested that the society should take up the matter, 'one or two members began to give a guarded assent, when an energetic and much esteemed member rose and said with much heat, that she hoped that we would never discuss such a disgraceful matter'.[36]

Dora Montefiore would have been one of those who supported Scott and Anderson at the Literary Society meeting. A gently reared girl from a large and wealthy English family, who had come to Sydney eleven years before for a visit and married into Sydney society, she had been left a widow in 1889 with a daughter of five and a son of two years. She then had to interview trustees about her husband's will.

> One lawyer remarked to me, when explaining the terms of the will: 'As your late husband says nothing about the guardianship of the children, they will remain under your care'. I restrained my anger at what appeared to me to be an officious and unnecessary remark and replied, 'Naturally, my husband would never have thought of leaving anyone else as their guardian'. 'As there is a difference in your religions', he continued grimly, 'he might very well have left someone of his own religion as their guardian'. 'What! *my* children, the children *I* bore, left to the guardianship of someone else! The idea would never have entered his mind, and what's more, I don't believe he could have done it, for children belong even more to a mother than to a father!' 'Not in law', the men around the table interjected; while the lawyer who had at first undertaken my enlightenment added dryly: 'In law, the child of the married woman has only one parent, and that is the father'. I suppose he saw symptoms of my rising anger, for he appeared to enjoy putting what he thought was a final extinguisher on my independence of thought; but I could hardly believe my ears, when this infamous statement of fact was made, and blazing with anger, I replied: 'If that is the state of the law, a woman is much better off as a man's mistress than as his wife, as far as her children are concerned'. 'Hush', a more friendly man's voice near me remarked. 'You must not say such things'. 'I must and I shall say them', I retorted. 'You don't know how your horrible law is insulting to all womanhood'. From that moment I was a suffragist (though I did not realize it at the time) and determined to alter the law.[37]

Montefiore was showing the spirit which would later make her into a suffragette in the British suffrage movement. Converted by her experience and encouraged by Parkes's moves in Parliament, she sent out invitations to friends to meet at her home on 24 March

1891 to discuss a possible suffrage league. Present were Maybanke Wolstenholme and Rose Scott, the two who had offended the Literary Society; Miss May Manning, daughter of and secretary to Sir William Manning, erstwhile Supreme Court Judge and member of the Legislative Council and now Chancellor of Sydney University, who had secured full rights for women in the university in 1881; Margaret Windeyer, a foundation member of the Dawn Club and daughter of Sir William Windeyer, who in 1891 was appointed New South Wales Supreme Court Judge; and a Dr and Mrs Ellis.

On 4 April there was a second, expanded meeting, the most important additions being Lady Mary Windeyer (Margaret's mother) and Mr L. J. Brient, then editor of the *Daily Telegraph*. (The paper was to give a copious, accurate and sympathetic coverage to the whole campaign.) It was decided that a Womanhood Suffrage League should be formed at yet a third meeting on 6 May, of invited guests only. Much thought went into who should be invited to attend: 'I don't think that any meeting should be held till after Easter, when people come to town again . . . It will want very careful doing and much wisdom to steer the meeting through rocks and quicksands.'[38] The emphasis was on influential men, and on women who were capable of and would be willing to undertake responsibility. A Mr J. Simpson replied:

> I strongly recommend that you add to your committee the name of Mrs Lawson, who has for years been working in the 'Woman's Cause' and who has published in her journal 'The Dawn', many articles in favour of suffrage.
>
> I have assisted in a small way in her work and I would not care to join a League unless she had first been invited. In addition to her experiences she would bring you some schemes in this work already partly thought out. For instance, I believe she has Suffrage pamphlets on the way from America . . . The scheme has also been considered of publishing a Suffrage Journal, as this is the cheapest method of spreading literature on the subject . . .
>
> I have not mentioned the matter of the League to Mrs Lawson and if you decide to co-operate with her you will of course keep private the part of my having suggested her name. I should not like the woman who has done so much for women to be left in the rear of one who has done less.[39]

Rose Scott, either on her own initiative or with this prompting, went to see Lawson. Pointing out that the League was going to enlist influential people who would be able to bring influence to bear in the right quarters, she persuaded Lawson to wind up the Dawn Club and transfer its allegiances to the new organisation.[40]

Wolstenholme, Eliza Pottie, Lawson and several men addressed the fifty invited guests on 6 May, and it was decided to hold an open meeting on 4 June to constitute the Womanhood Suffrage League. The Sydney press, including the *Dawn*, gave advance publicity and reported the speeches. At the meeting Lady Mary Windeyer was installed as President, Maybanke Wolstenholme and Mr W. H. Suttor, a member of the Legislative Council, as Vice-Presidents, Rose Scott as Secretary, Dora Montefiore as Corresponding Secretary and May Manning as Treasurer. Lawson was one of the eighteen elected to the council, which included two professors, two doctors, and one reverend. The backgrounds of the office-bearers and most of the council were impeccable. It was impossible to dismiss the new organisation as a 'shrieking sisterhood'. Although individual members were to be criticised in the eleven years of the League's existence, it was always to retain its aura of respectability. This was to a large extent due to the profile of Rose Scott. Other office-bearers and members of the council came and went but Scott remained as Secretary for the life of the league, rejecting a suggestion in 1894 that she become President. Scott became so well-known through her public speeches, letters, and statements to the press that to a great extent she was the league, and her image was its image.

Scott had come to Sydney to live in 1879. She was thirty-three years old and unmarried, and her experience of country life had been far removed from that of Louisa Lawson. She was born at Glendon, a property near Singleton, on the Hunter River, into a wealthy family of the old squattocracy. She had a happy, but isolated, childhood; she said she saw a shop only once before she was ten years old and that was a travelling pedlar's cart. A trip to the then small country town of Grafton when she was ten astounded and delighted her. Rose's mother Sarah, the daughter of Canon Rusden, of the well-connected Rusden family, taught her to read when she was three. Books were plentiful and were an integral part of the family's life; at seven Rose was listening to Shakespeare's *The Taming of the Shrew* read aloud by her mother. In her later speeches and writings Scott was to show herself familiar with the great thinkers of the day and well-grounded in history and literature. She was far better educated and more widely read than many of the politicians she wooed so assiduously for the vote.

In the bank crashes of the 1840s Scott's father's fortunes suffered a severe setback. The family was far from poverty-stricken on the scale which Louisa Lawson would have used to measure her experiences, but her father was forced to accept various government posts and eventually to leave the land and move to Newcastle. When he died Scott and her mother moved to Lynton, a gracious two-storey home surrounded by a large garden, in Edgecliff, Sydney. Scott herself now had an income of £500 per year and the home was staffed with a cook and servants. Shortly after the move her brother was left a widower and she took upon herself the responsibility of rearing her baby nephew, whose mother had died.[41] Her connections through her father's and mother's families gave her immediate entry into Sydney society, and these and marriage alliances of her uncles and aunts and her three siblings provided her with a wide range of acquaintances. Following the family's tradition of hospitality, Scott's Friday night salons and Saturday afternoon gatherings at Lynton became a part of Sydney life. Politicians of all persuasions, society figures, clergymen of all denominations, scholars, artists, scientists, writers, country and interstate visitors and overseas celebrities were among her guests. All the vital concerns of the day must have been discussed at these gatherings.

Scott claimed that from a child she had been conscious of woman's inferior position. At seven *The Taming of the Shrew* had aroused her indignation that Katherine should submit to her husband's tyranny, and as she grew she became convinced that poverty could not be solved by charity; that root causes had to be tackled. When she came to Sydney she involved herself in specific causes, and in 1889 was on a committee pressing for the age of consent to be raised from fourteen to eighteen years; the committee was concerned that under the existing law girls could be pressed into prostitution at fourteen, or servant girls seduced, without redress, by members of their employer's family. When a bill to remedy the situation was introduced into the Legislative Assembly in 1890, it was greeted with loud laughter. Scott, already offended by the existing legislation, was further affronted by this 'insulting behaviour', and began to consider seriously the option of votes for women. She read all she could find about women's rights and was eventually made 'a convert and enthusiast' to woman suffrage by Mill's *Subjection of Women*.[42]

In the thirty years of crammed public life which followed her conversion, many comments were made about Scott's appearance and personality. All emphasise that she was a nineteenth-century 'lady' to her fingertips. Miles Franklin, a personal friend, wrote:

> Rose Scott had beauty and charm. She was the personification of all that was most desirable and commendable in femininity ... She was always sensibly and graciously dressed for time and occasion, and her bonnets were the delight of Sydney. It was claimed by wags that her complexion and her bonnets did more than her arguments to win the vote.[43]

The Brisbane *Worker*, when she visited Queensland in 1903 to speak on votes for women, not yet gained there, commented: 'Miss Rose Scott, whatever else she does here, will not set the fashion for wearing old clothes!'[44]

Those who underestimated Scott because of her femininity were soon disillusioned; the well-dressed and gracious exterior was the casing for a steely determination to carry her chosen causes to completion. Almost all were concerned with the welfare of women and children. She was involved with the Sydney University Women's College, the Prisoners' Aid Society, the Early Closing Act, the appointment of gaol matrons, the establishment of children's courts, the Sydney Women's Club, the National Council of Women, the Ladies' Swimming Club, the Peace Society (which she helped to found), the Cremation Society, agitation for equal treatment of female medical graduates, the Wattle Club (to foster national sentiment), raising money to help Indian child brides (the Little Wives of India Fund), agitation for public toilets for women, and protest about the lack of seats for shop assistants. The gaining of votes for women, though, was Scott's passion, for she saw it not only as the woman's birthright, but as the gateway to all the other reforms in the legal and economic position of women.

The first project of the Womanhood Suffrage League was to hold a public meeting on 13 June 1891, eleven days after the election of officers, to enlist support for Parkes's proposed motion in the Assembly. Its Vice-President, William Suttor, took the chair, and the first of a long line of resolutions was passed in favour of woman suffrage, and the first of a long line of petitions signed to be presented to Parliament. The league quickly put its house in order. General meetings were held once a month at which someone from inside or outside the league spoke on a political or social question affecting women. Council meetings were held once a month. For two years Lawson lent her office for these meetings and until the late 1890s did free printing for the league. Mr J. Simpson, a member of the league's council and the one who had reminded Scott of Lawson's pre-league activity, 'published at his own trouble, risk and expense the *Woman's Suffrage Journal*'.[45] It had eight small pages and sold for a penny, although many of the 40,000 copies were distributed free. It evidently ceased in 1892 because its sponsor could not afford to keep it going, but the publicity gave the league a good start. In her first annual report Scott wrote: 'Demands for information and literature on the subject have been received from all parts of the country, particularly from women ... Several gentlemen belonging to debating societies have applied for information and literature.'[46]

Individual members used their contacts and the first branches were formed in the suburbs, with members of the council visiting each new branch to lecture and encourage. As they gained confidence, individual branches began to hold their own public meetings, inviting their own speakers. At the end of the first year an estimate was given of five hundred members. There was an upsurge of interest in the press, with letters for and against, and two cartoons in the Sydney *Bulletin* in quick succession,[47] always a sign that a subject had captured the public interest.

Scott now began to canvass individuals and organisations, political and non-political. In spite of the fact that in April 1891 the Seventh Intercolonial Trades and Labor Congress of Australasia had voted against woman suffrage as a plank in its platform, claiming that it would jeopardise other electoral reforms,[48] and even though Labor members of Parliament in New South Wales had just opposed its inclusion in the electoral bill, Scott, on behalf of the league, wrote to the New South Wales Trades and Labor Council. Their reply was predictable: one-man-one-vote first.[49] She wrote to the Australian Socialist League, which had woman suffrage as part of its avowed programme. The Secretary wrote back admitting that indeed female suffrage was a plank, but they were considering its removal because they feared the women's vote would be conservative: 'Political power should be the means of bringing about a better social state, and therefore if we have reason to believe that women would use voting power to keep us in our economic Slough of Despond, it is better to withhold the principle.'[50] For all that, the Socialist League invited speakers, and when she and Dr Vandeleur Kelly accepted they found a sympathetic audience.

Individual Socialists, like individual Labor members, were supporters. Scott and Arthur Rae, a self-styled 'wicked republican', an official of the shearers' union and co-author of the *Hummer*, which later became the *Worker*, began a spirited exchange of letters. The correspondence must have considerably broadened Scott's understanding of the point of view of the workers. Rae assured her of his support and in subsequent letters they discussed one-man-one-vote, of which Scott appears not to have been convinced in the beginning. Rae thought that the league should be more militant. 'Your women's movement will never be successful while you preach "law and order" . . . I predict that some day you'll just march to the polls armed with brooms and other weapons and record your votes.'[51]

Scott retained her confidence in the power of persuasion and imposed her philosophy on the league for the whole of its life. On a public level the league worked through petitions, public meetings, addresses to any organisation which would hear them, and letters to the press. Scott, on behalf of the league, consistently solicited support rather than wait for it to come to her, and she tackled opponents who in speeches or in the press expressed opposition, either by writing her own letters to editors refuting their claims or by approaching the offender and offering to discuss the matter. Her letter-writing capacity on behalf of this and her other causes was prodigious. Miles Franklin wrote that the postal department had to install a special letter box outside her home and it was not unusual for her nephew to post fifty to a hundred letters for her at the end of the day.[52] Except when the recipient was someone like Sir Henry Parkes or Lady Mary Windeyer, who preserved correspondence, her own letters have been lost, but her meticulous

Mary Lee, Secretary and forceful chief spokeswoman for the South Australian Women's Suffrage League from 1888 to 1894.
State Library of New South Wales.

Elizabeth Nicholls, President of the South Australian Woman's Christian Temperance Union for the duration of that colony's suffrage campaign, and Australasian President from 1894, in which position she influenced the Union's campaigns for the federal vote and all other state votes.
Mitchell Library, State Library of New South Wales.

Jessie Ackermann, the American Woman's Christian Temperance Union missionary, who galvanised the Union's South Australian campaign in 1889, and spent five years in Australia doing the same for Union campaigns in other states.
State Library of New South Wales.

Catherine Helen Spence, the self-styled 'weak-kneed sister' who helped in the South Australian struggle for votes for women, but who contended that women would not gain very much without a system of proportional representation.
Mitchell Library, State Library of New South Wales.

Dr James Stirling, who introduced the first proposal for woman suffrage into the South Australian Parliament in 1885.
Mitchell Library, State Library of New South Wales.

Sir John Forrest, Premier for the whole period of the Western Australian campaign, and inflexible opponent until he thought that the women's votes would balance the radical voice of the goldfields.
Mitchell Library, State Library of New South Wales.

Christine Clark, who succeeded Janetta Foulkes as Suffrage Superintendent of the Western Australian Woman's Christian Temperance Union in 1897, and in 1899 became a Vice-President of the newly formed Woman's Franchise League in that State.
Mitchell Library, State Library of New South Wales.

Master Gold Fields: "I think I shall want all the remaining accommodation."
Sir John: "There's plenty of room for you both."

The *Western Mail* summed up Sir John Forrest's reasons for granting the vote to women, and the opposition to the move from the goldfields representatives.
Western Mail, 25 August 1899. State Library of New South Wales.

Walter James, the women's unwavering champion in the Western Australian Parliament. He became Premier in 1901, after the first state election in which women were allowed to vote.
Mitchell Library, State Library of New South Wales.

Above left: Frederick Holder who, with Charles Kingston, carried a clause at the 1897 Commonwealth Constitutional Convention which made it impossible to disenfranchise women for the Commonwealth Parliament if they had the right to vote in their state Parliament.
Mitchell Library, State Library of New South Wales.

Above right: Charles Kingston, the reluctant supporter of woman suffrage in the South Australian Parliament, but its champion at the 1897 Convention which debated the Constitution for the Commonwealth of Australia.
Mitchell Library, State Library of New South Wales.

Dora Montefiore, who called the first meeting to discuss the formation of the New South Wales Womanhood Suffrage League, and who later took part in the British suffragette movement.
Mitchell Library, State Library of New South Wales.

Above left: Elizabeth Ward, the most notable apologist for woman suffrage in the New South Wales Woman's Christian Temperance Union.
State Library of New South Wales.

Above right: Annie Golding, one of the three Golding sisters who were the chief Labor women in the New South Wales campaign.
Mitchell Library, State Library of New South Wales.

Rose Scott, the dynamic Secretary of the New South Wales Womanhood Suffrage League from its formation in 1891 till the gaining of the vote in 1902.
Mitchell Library, State Library of New South Wales.

Louisa Lawson, who made woman suffrage the main concern of her journal, the *Dawn*, from its establishment in 1888 to the granting of the New South Wales vote in 1902. The Dawn Club, which she formed in 1889, had as its prime aim the gaining of votes for women.
Mitchell Library, State Library of New South Wales.

Emma Miller, the redoubtable Labor adherent, who was President of the Queensland Woman's Equal Franchise Association from its formation in 1894 till the gaining of the vote in 1905.
By courtesy of Pamela Young.

collection of replies gives a unique picture of the way she worked and the efforts she had to make to keep the Womanhood Suffrage League, with its diverse membership, functioning smoothly. It also gives a detailed view, not available in any other state, of the manoeuvring of the women and the politicians as the initiative in the suffrage struggle shifted from one to the other.

By 1892 George Dibbs was Premier of New South Wales. He was a known opponent, but the suffragists nevertheless decided to storm the citadel. In October six women from the league visited Parliament House. It was their first delegation and the women were understandably nervous. Scott wrote in her report:

> [we] were courteously received by Sir George Dibbs, who, while expressing himself unfavourable to women having votes, promised to bring the request before the Cabinet. Sir George played to the press, telling them to give publicity to women's arguments but the press reported the arguments of Dibbs.[53]

Privately she wrote to Parkes, who had introduced the delegation.

> Sir George had nothing to say except that his wife and daughters did not agree and then made himself the mouthpiece of the Creator to dictate to women their sphere of life . . . If Lady Dibbs takes our side I am sure Sir George will be sufficiently punished.[54]

During this interview Louisa Lawson must have stepped beyond the bounds of Scott's code of decorous behaviour. Perhaps she reacted angrily when Dibbs attempted to 'dictate to women their sphere of life', for Scott also wrote to Sir Henry Parkes: 'We rejected Mrs Lawson's speech, thinking it unwise—but of course it is sure to be the thing the papers seize upon.'[55] Arthur Rae criticised the delegation's claim that the women's votes would change the morals of society: 'Your statements seemed to me to be beside the mark and calculated to excite ridicule. What, for instance, do you think you would *do* to abolish . . . drunkenness, streetwalking and seduction . . . evidently believed to be due to bad laws made by wicked men . . . a Vice-Suppression Bill?'[56]

Knowing that they had little hope of change while Dibbs remained in office, the women concentrated on educating public opinion and on spreading their net outside the capital. Wolstenholme stayed with Dean Selwyn (Scott's uncle) in Newcastle while she addressed meetings which 'all the influential people of the town' attended. She wrote, and the emphasis is hers: 'the Dean is with us to some extent but thinks in accordance with Paul to the Corinthians that *every married woman should give her vote to her husband* [sic].'[57] Wolstenholme, if not entirely successful with the Dean, had some influence on his timid and devout wife Rose, who, like so many women of the period, had been nurtured on Paul's biblical strictures to women. In her diary she wrote: 'When we bear all these things in mind, we shall be constrained to believe that many apostolic counsels are counsels of prudence under existing conditions rather than universal laws binding upon all women in all walks of life.'[58]

By now the Womanhood Suffrage League had several accomplished public speakers. As well as developing skills in straight speech delivery, these women were obliged to master the art of debating; every major city in Australia had its sprinkling of debating clubs, and public debates were a popular form of entertainment. Wolstenholme told an interviewer after the vote was won:

we spoke at drawing-room and public meetings wherever we were invited. I did so sometimes two or three times a week. Miss Dickie, Miss Golding and I were a debating team, and we never lost a debate. I remember only one fight. It was in Newtown Town Hall, and only a few chairs were broken.[59]

Arthur Rae, who had been a consistent champion when he addressed Labor party gatherings throughout the state, raised the spirits of the wilting league a little in November of 1893 when he introduced a motion in favour of woman suffrage in the Assembly. Although the league supported him with a public meeting—Sir Henry Parkes again in the chair—members knew that Rae's motion was a token gesture only. Scott wrote: 'The motion was crowded out by other business, as he fully expected, and his action in this matter was chiefly educational.'[60] One piece of news cheered the suffragists as 1893 drew to its close—New Zealand women were to have the vote. Louisa Lawson retorted tartly, however, that in New South Wales there was 'a great deal of doubtful wit at the expense of the women of New Zealand'.[61]

The WCTU held its Second Triennial Australasian Convention in Sydney in May 1894. There were visitors from America and around Australia, and the Convention received copious newspaper coverage. Lady Windeyer held a garden party for the delegates, giving the Convention a high social image. Under the guidance of Jessie Ackermann, Australasian President, suffrage was high on the agenda. There was a special suffrage rally, with Lady Windeyer and visiting delegates giving addresses. Fired with new enthusiasm, the New South Wales Union organised a deputation to the inflexible Dibbs the following month.[62] Dibbs received them condescendingly. The women appear to have put their case clearly and succinctly and to have replied with dignity to Dibbs' attempts to trivialise them. Temperance rhetoric was notably absent; they wanted the vote, they said, both because it was their right and with it they could 'assist in placing capable and honest men in Parliament'. When Dibbs asked if they themselves wanted to enter Parliament, Elizabeth Ward replied categorically that they did not, but her answer was modified somewhat by Mrs Dickie's interjection that they could ask for candidature later. Dibbs's speech in reply to the women's submissions was the classic short-circuit of reasoned argument.

> they seemed to assume that he was opposed to them, but he would like to say that for the very best of all reasons there was no man in the country who had greater experience of the value of womanhood than he had. Indeed for the very position he held that day he was indebted to the fact that he had a good mother. Therefore, as long as women lasted on this earth, there could be no more ardent admirer of them than himself.[63]

The only assurance the women gained from this plethora of words was that he would discuss the matter with his Cabinet. With an election looming, however, it is doubtful whether he even did that.

While both organisations were knocking vainly at the political door, the league was tackling internal ideological tensions which the temperance women did not have. At the November meeting in 1891 the speaker was Lizzie Ashton. The *Sydney Morning Herald* reported her as saying that

> the suffrage once fairly attained for women, their first work must be to amend the marriage laws, or, blasphemous as the words might sound, do away with them altogether ... They had grown to regard the marriage ceremony as a Christian ordinance ... It was purely a social custom. What was moral in one country stood for nothing in another.[64]

The speech was reported and ridiculed by the press. The Brisbane *Worker* interpreted Ashton as advocating 'lease marriages' which would be renewed after an agreed period; The *Bulletin* in Sydney commented:

> There is one incurably weak point about the advanced female; she always wants to abolish marriage, but she seldom has the courage to recommend anything as a substitute. If free-love is to be the substitute, then the average male will throw out his partner by superior brute force as soon as she becomes old and ugly, and leave her to maintain the family, and the navigation of our harbours and rivers will be hampered by the remains of lost, deserted women.[65]

The Governor's wife, Lady (Elizabeth) Jersey, wrote to Lady Windeyer that she thought the sentiments were 'atrocious' and she hoped the league would dissociate itself from them.[66] The speech confirmed the resolution of the temperance women to work separately, and Eliza Pottie resigned from the league's council. Elizabeth Ward told a WCTU committee meeting: 'it would seem desirable that members of our Union did not occupy a place on the platform of the above League while Mrs Ashton remained under the shelter of it.'[67]

Although what Ashton said was sensationalised, much serious discussion followed in the press of the marriage laws, the plight of deserted wives and of widows, and the current divorce laws which imprisoned men and women in wretched partnerships. The incident forced the Womanhood Suffrage League to take stock of what it stood for. The women openly contended that they needed the vote to change existing laws which discriminated against them, but Ashton's speech showed that cultural change meant different things to different people. Scott wrote to the *Sydney Morning Herald* distancing the league from Ashton's views or from 'any other irresponsible opinions which may be attributed now or hereafter to any individual member of its body'[68] and in her 1892 report Scott wrote that 'the League itself can only be held responsible for the object which alone unites its members, namely, the enfranchisement of women.'[69] In spite of this distancing, however, Scott and Ashton remained friends until the death of the latter in 1899.

Before the end of 1891 the league lost the member who had been primarily responsible for its formation; Dora Montefiore took her fatherless children back to England to live, where she was to ally herself with the militancy which erupted in the British movement in 1906.

Another league dispute at the end of 1893 culminated in Lady Windeyer's resignation. Windeyer, on a committee drafting a new set of rules, objected to several clauses, but most vehemently to one which allowed branches to hear addresses on any topic which concerned women and their vote.[70] She claimed that Scott had been a party to drafting the rules at her own home. To no avail Scott bombarded 'my dear Lady Windeyer' with conciliatory letters. The league eventually had to accept the resignation and Windeyer transferred to the WCTU, with whose emphasis she evidently felt more at home. She was to superintend the Suffrage Department from 1895 to 1897 when Elizabeth Ward withdrew for health reasons, and to be associated with the Union until her death in 1911. Others resigned, among them Dr Vandeleur Kelly, a prominent speaker. Wolstenholme replaced Windeyer as President and Dr Grace Robinson, the first woman to practise at

Sydney Hospital (with much opposition from male medical staff), joined the council. The dispute was a manifestation of the same problem which had surfaced a year before with Lizzie Ashton's speech, and the one which all Australian suffrage societies were to experience in varying degrees: that the suffragists were only fully united on one point—the gaining of the vote. On other aspects of 'the woman question' there was a wide variety of views.

Before the end of 1893 Lawson resigned from the council of the league and 'no longer found it convenient' to lend the *Dawn* office for meetings.[71] The reasons are not clear—she certainly would not have opposed, as Windeyer did, the free discussion of issues—but she was very busy earning her own living. She continued to give the League good publicity, but the fact that she was immediately to support a rival society formed in 1901 suggests that she may have found her own temperament incompatible with the image which the League was at such pains to project.

Internal problems plagued the league into the third year of Dibbs' premiership. Its most conservative members had resigned; now a radical group within the Surry Hills branch showed its disaffection by launching a magazine, the *Australian Woman*, which claimed to be 'The Official Organ of the Womanhood Suffrage League of N.S.W.'. The editorial of the first issue, in March 1894, attacked the central league for daring to call itself radical. The league, it claimed, had too narrow a base and was not truly representing the rights of women. Although the *Australian Woman* contended in its June issue that both Scott and Wolstenholme had wished it well, there was a flurry of correspondence and concern within the central branch, which ended with the league's denial in its 1894 annual report that it was 'connected with this paper in any way'. The *Australian Woman* now changed its wording; it claimed in April to be the official organ of only the Surry Hills branch, which it now called the Equal Suffrage League of New South Wales. The standard of writing in the paper was poor, and the sentiments expressed often so convoluted as to be almost incomprehensible. By the end of the year it had ceased publication, but before it did so it attacked a new paper, the *Woman's Voice*, which Maybanke Wolstenholme, with the blessing of friends within the league, was publishing. The *Woman's Voice* did not claim to be the official organ of any group. It dealt incisively and logically with women's issues and was refreshingly free from sentimental dissertations, but it could not maintain itself financially. By December 1895 it, too, was defunct. The truth was that Louisa Lawson's successful paper, the *Dawn*, was already reporting the suffrage campaign and all aspects of the women's movement; there was no room on the market for another. A clue as to why Wolstenholme and her friends felt that another journal was needed for suffrage propaganda can be found in the *Bulletin's* review of the first issue. The reviewer, probably taking a side swipe at the *Dawn*, wrote that the magazine aimed 'to be democratic but not revolutionary, womanly but not weak, fearless without effrontery, liberal without license ... a not unnecessary precaution, perhaps, in these days of reckless and thoughtless agitation ... [it] is free from that spitefulness which often mars similar productions.'[72]

In late 1894 there was an Assembly election, and both the league and the Union sent questionnaires to each candidate. Plural voting had been abolished in 1893, so candidates could not hide behind that issue. Some replies were for and against on principle;

some evaded comment by saying that they were waiting to see how the vote worked in New Zealand; and quite a few gave approval conditional on women not entering Parliament. One reply, however, suggested a way in which they might do so, in words which probably brought a frown to Scott's face and would, if she had seen them, have enraged Lawson: 'I see a hope for your sex yet, and that is an upper house for Ladies, for the present one is considered to be a nest full of old women, why not turn them out and have an upper house of young ones for a change.'[73]

The election reduced Dibbs' following and George Reid, ostensibly a supporter, became the new Liberal Premier, again with the support of Labor. With the old enemy gone, prospects seemed brighter. The league sent a deputation to the wily Reid, a man of immense physical proportions and a master of the witty riposte and the crushing retort. Reid was evasive; he was in favour, but he 'could make no definite promise, as he had many other obligations to fulfil'.[74] Reid was living up to his label of 'Yes-No Reid', given because of his reluctance to take a firm stand on issues, notably federation. In no area was the label to prove more appropriate: Scott said that for the five years of his two premierships he played with the league 'like a cat with a mouse'.[75]

There were several moves in Parliament during Reid's term in office, but the Government allowed only two debates. A motion by Dowell O'Reilly in 1894, 'That in the opinion of this House the time has arrived when the franchise should be extended to women', was passed 58–13[76] but in the course of the debate the words 'the time has arrived when' had been withdrawn. The motion as it emerged did not commit the Government to any action. Private member's bills introduced by William Willis in 1895[77] and 1896[78] and by Fegan in 1897[79] were aborted because the Government would not allow them 'a message from the Crown' authorising the expenditure which would be incurred in drawing up new rolls. Fegan's second bill was passed in 1898 on its first reading by the massive majorityof 61–5,[80] but it was still waiting to be allowed a second reading twelve months later when Reid lost office.

Reid was just as obstructive in his dealings with the women. On the few occasions when he consented to receive deputations he was either evasive, or curt to the point of rudeness. Shortly after the debate on O'Reilly's motion in 1894 which had generated so much discussion in the press and the community, Scott organised a large delegation of women and sympathetic members of Parliament. Reid told them that he believed in the cause so heartily that he would be willing to go to an election on it, but it *was* a major step to take, and not all members of the Cabinet agreed with him . . .[81] In 1895 Scott and O'Reilly interviewed him in an attempt to organise another delegation. A letter from O'Reilly to Scott immediately after the interview shows both Reid's rudeness and Scott's indignation. Scott set herself a high standard of courtesy and expected to receive it in return.

> you should aquit him of any desire to treat your League as tools in his hand . . . I say nothing in defence of him taking up and scanning the newspaper while you were having your interview with him . . . he had no intention whatever to offer you any insult . . . it was rather due to one of those lapses that come over the most polite and kind of men when their minds are preoccupied.[82]

In 1897 when Scott sent a letter requesting that Reid receive the women, he replied that a deputation would do them no good and that they should 'make themselves a power at the next election'.[83] On behalf of the league Scott attacked him in a long public letter which was sent to every member of Parliament and to city and country newspapers.

> The Council of the League emphatically protest against the inference contained in this reply, viz, that the present Parliament would do nothing to secure the Franchise for Women ... women, so many of them helpless to fight for themselves, were constantly having their just claims put on one side for less important measures ... the League had been constantly informed during the various Parliaments of the last six years, that the last session was the session for which to await patiently, and we have waited, only too patiently ... the Council of the Womanhood Suffrage League ... solemnly protests against any apathy or procrastination on a question of such burning injustice, and respectfully requests the Government and Members of Parliament to pass a woman suffrage Bill before the close of the next Parliament.[84]

Just before the mid-1898 election the Premier did consent to receive a delegation. He told more than fifty women and the large number of Assembly members that in all probability' the question would be placed upon the next ministerial programme. Encouraged, the league and the WCTU brought all their guns to bear on the election campaign, using the same tactics as in the two previous elections: circulars to candidates, approaches to every political organisation, however insignificant, and letters to the press. Scott contacted newspapers in country towns and interviewed editors of those in Sydney. Members of the Newtown branch of the league, with the Golding sisters to the fore, headed the hustings agitation by attending twenty-five meetings. They reported only three rebuffs from candidates.[85] The agitation had little effect, and Reid was returned to office.

In spite of the stalemate in Parliament, the women were not idle. When the subject was before Parliament public meetings were held by both the league and the WCTU and petitions presented. In 1896 a Citizens' Committee organised an outdoor demonstration in the Sydney Domain;[86] it was not instigated by the league, although Wolstenholme was Secretary of the Committee and members took part. Temperance organisations featured prominently. The rally drew spectators, but not in any great numbers, and the experiment was not repeated. All Australian women were to gain their vote before the period of great outdoor demonstrations in Britain and America.

In August 1895 the league approached the Labor party again for official support. A deputation waited on the Labor Electoral League and asked them to support woman suffrage as a plank in the Labor party platform at the coming Australasian conference. Arthur Rae sent circulars to all branches, and in 1896 female suffrage became part of the official policy of the Australasian Labor party.[87] Although no Labor member voted against woman suffrage in the Assembly after the plural vote was abolished in 1893, the New South Wales Labor party itself did not put pressure on the Liberal Governments until 1900; other measures took priority in its parliamentary negotiations.

Members of the police force were given the vote in 1897 and Scott commented angrily in her annual report:

> We noticed that Mr Hogue declared, and that with praise, that not one member of the Force had approached him on the subject ... and he said that it showed that the police of this country were not disposed to be agitators or discontented with their lot—and yet we poor women are constantly

blamed for not agitating *enough*! and told to make ourselves a power at election time! One would think that the police were better calculated to do that than ourselves, many of us having homes, children, men and aged people to look after, besides needlework and numberless household duties, even if we are not in the position that so many women are in, of being compelled to earn our own living.[88]

In early 1898 women who owned property were required to pay land tax. The organisations coordinated their protest, drafting a letter for women to send with their payment. Lawson published a copy of it in the *Dawn*: 'I pay this tax under strong protest, because I object to being taxed when I have no vote.'[89] As far as we know no Australian woman refused to pay her tax, as some English and American women were doing.

When Reid was toppled by a no-confidence motion moved by John Fegan in late 1899, William Lyne became Premier and Fegan Minister for Mines and Agriculture. Lyne had shown resistance to the idea of woman suffrage when it was first introduced by Sir Henry Parkes, but since then had become a firm supporter, so Scott wrote asking for an audience. Lyne replied that a deputation was not required, that he was with them 'heart and soul', but that he had his problems when it came to introducing a Government bill.[90] It must have seemed like Reid's procrastination all over again, but Lyne showed his sincerity when he backed Fegan in a new private member's bill. On 1 December Fegan gave notice of its introduction and five days later delivered the vital message from the Crown required for expenses incurred in implementing the measure.[91] The jubilant suffragists had no doubt that Fegan's Bill would pass when it was given time in the next session, to begin early the following year. Women in New South Wales might be able to join those in South Australia and Western Australia in voting for Australia's first Federal Parliament. But in January 1900, from one of the foreign ships berthed in the harbour, rats scurried down the ropes to the docks to mingle with rats in the foetid conditions of Sydney's worst slum area, and the bubonic plague burst upon the city. Within days thousands of the more prosperous fled the city and the suburbs, among them politicians and their families. The parliamentary recess was extended for six months and the Legislative Assembly did not reassemble until June 1900.

In May, some weeks before the sitting, the Labor party at last moved to bring pressure to bear. A deputation requested that in view of the fact that adult suffrage would almost certainly be adopted for the Commonwealth Parliament, Lyne should make it a Government measure as soon as possible.[92] On 4 June, two days before the Governor's speech, the league held 'a great public meeting',[93] the largest ever. Lyne was to have spoken, but was called to Tasmania'. Fegan took the chair and Edward O'Sullivan headed a long list of speakers which included James McGowan, leader of the Labor party. Catherine Helen Spence, in Sydney to speak on 'effective voting' and now eighty years old, added her voice. There were messages of encouragement from other colonies, and even Reid sent his support! Lyne, when he returned the following week, received a large delegation from the WCTU, the league, the Labor party and other organisations.[94] On 12 June the Governor's speech announced that the Government would 'be asked to consider the expediency' of giving women the vote.[95] Scott was displeased with 'expediency'; in a newspaper interview she claimed that either 'justice' or 'necessity' should have been used.[96]

Thomas Rose, a fervent opponent, made a move to block the proposed introduction of the Government bill. On 17 July he moved 'That, in the opinion of this House, the franchise should not be imposed upon the women of New South Wales until a majority of adult females voting at a referendum had approved of woman suffrage.'[97] The motion was lost 17–10, the supporters in the House scornfully maintaining that no referendum had been held to test whether men wanted to vote. In spite of frantic efforts by the speaker to make him confine himself to the question of the referendum, Rose in his speech launched into a full-blown attack on votes for women and the suffragists themselves. The WCTU, indignant at his insinuation that the moral and religious women of New South Wales did not want the vote, held a protest meeting on 17 September 1900.[98] The following day they waited on Lyne, pointing out, as the league had done, that time was running out to enfranchise them for the coming Commonwealth election.

Lyne seemed to stall; he gave notice of a bill for 25 September, but the women in the gallery watched impotently—and no doubt angrily—as other business crowded it out. When he announced it again for the beginning of November, the league sent a circular to all members of Parliament:

> we earnestly implore you not to allow the prorogation of Parliament to take place, leaving the interests of women without that political protection which you yourself value and have long since accorded to aliens and even to Blackfellows . . . [the measure] is more urgent than ever when it is remembered that under the Commonwealth Act our want of parliamentary franchise in New South Wales disqualifies us from voting at the election of representatives and of senators, thus working us a treble injustice.[99]

On 2 November 'women in large numbers' turned up at the House unannounced and demanded an interview.[100] Lyne, no doubt surprised at the spontaneity of this protest, granted them a hearing, and on 9 November he at long last introduced his promised bill, only two weeks before Parliament was to be prorogued.[101] Two days later it went to its second reading and debate, and the debate was taken up again at 2.35 p.m. twelve days later. Opponents stonewalled and delayed the vote in favour (52–20) until 5.41 the next morning. Scott wrote that the last speaker, a Mr Spruson, continued reading 'page after page of Ruskin . . . till he tired out even himself!'[102] Scott didn't say whether she herself stayed until the end of the debate, but her account makes one suspect so. The last reading passed with no fuss on 26 November 1900. For the first time a bill in favour of votes for women had been passed in the New South Wales Legislative Assembly. The clause in the bill which excluded women from candidacy had been debated, but retained. Scott wrote: 'Needless to say, we are of opinion that no restriction should be placed here as in South Australia upon women standing for election. It should be a matter, not for the House, but for the electors, to decide, whether they can be better represented by a woman or a man.'[103] In a private letter she was more acidic, perhaps referring to Spruson's stonewalling: 'Under the present scheme of party government, with no time limit to speeches, it is not likely that any woman could afford time, even if there were no other reason, to enter parliament.'[104]

The women's jubilation was short-lived; two days after the bill was passed in the Assembly, it was rejected in the Upper House by 22–19. Women in New South

The New South Wales *Bulletin's* depiction of the large Woman's Christian Temperance Union deputation to Premier Sir George Dibbs in 1894.
Bulletin, 23 June 1894. State Library of New South Wales.

Wales were thus deprived of a vote at the first Commonwealth election. The suffragists were particularly angered that the bill was not given serious consideration in the Upper House. A known opponent, Bernard Wise, introduced it, and there were only two speakers.

In response to the parliamentary activity of the 1900s a small counter-movement appeared. The New South Wales Anti-Suffrage League seems to have been formed about July of that year by a Mr P. J. Gandon, who claimed to be its Secretary. Its only address was a post office number. Gandon wrote numerous letters to the press quoting prominent overseas opponents and challenging the women to prove their case, drawing replies from Scott, Elizabeth Ward and others. In his propaganda leaflets and at some public meetings he launched into long expositions of scripture, trying to prove that women must always remain subservient to men.[105] No organisational structure can be discerned for the Anti-Suffrage League; some even cast doubts on whether this 'shadowy League with a Post Office Address' existed at all,[106] and challenged Gandon to produce a list of officers and members. There were claims, but no evidence, that the league was promoted by liquor interests fearful of the women's votes.[107] Whatever its composition, its canvassers, some paid, collected signatures in Sydney and Newcastle for petitions to be presented to the Assembly in 1900, and the Council in 1900 and 1902. True to her philosophy that the most confirmed opponent could be converted by reasoning, Scott wrote to Gandon and offered to discuss the matter with him. Her invitation drew a rather coy reply:

> I very much fear that you will withdraw the opinion you have so graciously formed of me—viz:—that I am open to reason, after you have seen me. As, however, I am willing to risk even that for the pleasure of an interview with you, I await your invitation.[108]

Scott evidently failed to convince, for the campaign continued.

By far the most interesting relic of the Anti-Suffrage League is the petulant letter Gandon wrote to Scott in October 1900.

> you are not aware of the kind of people for whom you are battling. As you probably know, we have a few ladies out with petitions against the suffrage ... We have had no reason to complain of results, but we have much reason to complain of the downright rudeness of the suffragists at whose houses we have accidentally called ... one case admits of no excuse ... As soon as she [the canvasser] announced her business she was invited in, the door closed and immediately subjected to the coarsest abuse. With her back to the door this person threatened and stormed and even made slanderous statements and appeared as if she was actually going to strike the unfortunate lady petitioner. Nor did this amiable person spare 'that fellow Gandon' ... She refused to let the lady leave the house until she had not only exhausted herself but positively frightened her victim. A mild request for her name was met with the oratorical reply that 'it would live when hers (the victim's) was forgotten'. Of course you have guessed that the person referred to is Mrs Dickie, and although the whole business is grotesque from an outside point of view I have felt compelled to instruct a solicitor to take immediate action so that the first fruits of our league may be in the direction of better manners and more womanly conduct.[109]

The Anti-Suffrage League was never a threat to the suffragists. Gandon's leaflets were rambling and vacuous, and in his speeches he made claims that were patently false: that the women were 'a little body of permanent and invariable agitators'[110] and that the suffrage movement was a 'socialistic and labour party movement'.[111] After the New South Wales vote was won he tried to interfere in the Victorian movement, but was bested in a debate with Vida Goldstein in October 1902.[112]

For six years the Womanhood Suffrage League had been free of apparent internal problems, but tension which had been building during 1900 came to a head in early 1901 when Annie and Belle Golding (Newtown branch) and Nellie Martel (central branch) challenged what they saw as a concentration of power within the central branch. From March 1901 there was a flurry of motions and counter-motions, with amendments and counter-amendments, aiming to redefine the rules of the league. Feelings ran high on both sides; uninvited branch delegates turned up at two of the council meetings and refused to leave; the Golding sisters made an appearance at a special meeting for central members only and insisted on being heard; and there were spirited exchanges between Scott and Nellie Martel, one in which Scott tried to censure Martel for a speech made during a deputation in 1900, and another in which she criticised her for leading (without the permission of the central office-bearers), a deputation of eighty women from inner-city branches. Martel vigorously defended her right to speak as she wished, and the right of branches to act independently. By August 1901 Scott and her supporters had succeeded in redefining the rules of the league in such a way that decision-making remained firmly concentrated in the central branch.[113]

Dissatisfaction on the part of many suffragists with the league's methods of agitation probably lay behind this demand that the branches should have a greater say in its affairs. Martel and the Golding sisters were more aggressive than Scott, and did not waste words on sentimentalising women's moral superiority. They did not belong either to the élite of Sydney or to the WCTU and were impatient with the genteel image which these suffragists cultivated so assiduously. Their roots lay firmly in the lower middle or working classes and their sympathies were openly with the Labor end of the political spectrum. Defeated in their efforts to change the emphasis of the league, the dissidents in September 1901 founded the Women's Progressive Association, with Martel as President and Annie Golding as Secretary.[114] Although the Goldings and Martel remained members of the league, the Women's Progressive Association must, until the vote was gained a year later, be regarded as a parallel society. It was to wage a vigorous campaign for the vote through public meetings, petitions and deputations, and to combine these with forceful demands for municipal, political and legal reforms in areas affecting women. Louisa Lawson immediately fell in behind the association,[115] becoming a member and giving it good coverage in the *Dawn*.

The women who formed the Progressive Association deserve some space, for they worked hard for the vote in both organisations. There were three Golding sisters: Annie, Belle and Kate (Dwyer).[116] They were born on the Tambaroora goldfields into a family in which politics, especially the politics of Labor, was an everyday topic of conversation. Their father was at times a mine owner and mine manager. Annie and Kate became teachers and as they moved around the working-class districts gained a knowledge of working conditions for both men and women. All had experience of the great mining strikes, which confirmed their Labor sympathies. In the 1880s Annie began to write under pen names about the social and legal disabilities of women. By the early 1890s the sisters, Kate married and Belle just out of her teens, were in Sydney. Annie and Belle were founding members of the Newtown debating society, and all three became enthusiastic members of the Womanhood Suffrage League. Annie and Belle were credited with starting several inner-city branches and all were competent speakers and debaters. Outside the league they were indefatigable workers against discriminatory laws. Belle was particularly concerned with factory conditions, and at one time brought girls from 'sweating shops' to Parliament to dramatise their intolerable working conditions. She was appointed a factory inspector in 1896 to police the Act which forbade night work (often unpaid) for women, and her appointment was extended to cover the Early Closing Act of 1899. Annie helped to form the Teachers' Federation and worked within it to improve prospects for women teachers, and she assisted the Trades Hall in the formation of women's unions. She campaigned against co-education because she saw it as abolishing the opportunity for women to rise to the top of the teaching profession, and she supported public schools instead of private schools because they had no class barrier. In the Women's Progressive Association she held various offices in which she emphasised sanitary and municipal reforms, agitated for women doctors to be given residencies in Sydney hospitals, worked for the woman's right to the guardianship of her children and to a share in the assets of the marriage partnership. She was a staunch campaigner over a long period for women to be admitted to juries and the legal profession, for she believed that women were at a disadvantage if on trial in an all-male courtroom.

Hardly less impressive is the third sister, Kate Dwyer. She was an able speaker and debater for the suffrage movement but, no doubt because of her children, her most active public life came after the suffrage campaign. She worked in the Women's Progressive Association, held office in the Political Labor League, was a delegate to the Labor Council, and was President of the Women Workers' Union. She was first President of the Labor Women's Committee formed in 1904 and travelled the state enrolling members. Underlying all her party work were efforts to change the discriminatory laws against which her sisters were protesting.

Nellie Martel, the other leading figure in the 1901 disaffection, was a native of Cornwall who had been converted to the cause after seeing the evils of sweated labour in London workhouses. She arrived in Sydney in the early 1890s and soon found her way into the Womanhood Suffrage League. She styled herself in her *Dawn* advertisements as a Professor of Elocution and conducted a school on the subject; she and her pupils gave regular recitals in the Sydney Town Hall. She was a colourful and forthright personality: the *Worker* of Brisbane described her in its malicious way as a walking pawnshop flashing with unredeemed jewels'.[117] An active and capable member of the league, she appeared on its council for the first time in 1894, and held positions as Recording Secretary, Secretary for Petitions, and delegate to the National Council of Women. With her professional platform presence she was much in demand as a speaker, and her arguments were said to be 'pungent, telling and convincing'.[118] Her brother, David Charleston, was a member of the South Australian Upper House and in 1903 Nellie, with Mrs Mary Ann Moore, was to stand unsuccessfully as a New South Wales candidate for the Senate.

The high publicity profile which Scott and those within her social milieu were able to command, and the copious amount of written material which they left, can obscure the importance of women like the Golding sisters and Martel. The instant strength and vigorous agitation of the Women's Progressive Association in the last year of the campaign indicates that there was by then a significant group of New South Wales suffragists who were Labor oriented and prepared to be more discordant in their demand for political privileges.

In March 1901 both Lyne and Reid resigned to enter Commonwealth politics, and the three political groups marshalled for the coming New South Wales elections. The electoral manifesto of John See (Lyne's successor in the Progressive party, which was roughly left-wing Liberal) included woman suffrage on the grounds that New South Wales should not have a narrower franchise than that expected for the new Commonwealth, thus for the first time making the vote an electoral issue. Charles Lee (leader of the Liberal party, which was further to the right than the Progressives) declared himself an opponent, although he did allow that Liberals should vote as they thought best. Rose Scott commented: 'Surely we could have expected more than this from a party calling itself Liberal.'[119]

Concerned to counter a repeat of allegations in the Legislative Council that the matter had not been before the public, the league and the WCTU lobbied energetically, canvassing candidates and attending meetings. Both precariously maintained a non-party stance by concentrating on individuals. A league notice carefully omitted any reference to parties.

WOMANHOOD SUFFRAGE LEAGUE
ELECTORS OF NEW SOUTH WALES
VOTE FOR NO MAN
who is AGAINST THE
ENFRANCHISEMENT OF WOMEN

The interests of Women and Children
cannot be looked after by men alone
any more than one class can look after
the interests of another class.[120]

On 4 September 1901 a bill sponsored by the Progressive party Premier, John See, reached the Legislative Council. Francis Suttor, Vice-President of the Executive Council, introduced it, emphasising that the Government now had a mandate for the measure. This time the Council considered the subject worthy of a full debate. John Want did his best to trivialise the bill, dismissing the New Zealand, South Australian and Western Australian votes as for 'three small villages' only,[121] and contended that 'the only reason ... the question was brought up at the last election was to enable honorary members to tickle the fancy of the wives of certain voters, and so secure the votes of their husbands.'[122] There was a prolonged debate about whether a clause should be inserted to allow women to sit in Parliament. Want and other opponents supported the inclusion of such a clause, claiming unashamedly 'that if we insert a provision of that kind in the Bill in this Chamber, they will throw it out in the other'.[123] Some friends of woman suffrage, including Labor members, however, supported the insertion because they believed it was consistent with women having the vote. The bill went to its third reading allowing women to be elected to the Legislative Assembly (the Legislative Council was nominated), and was defeated by 26–21. William Lyne wrote to Scott from Melbourne, then the seat of the Commonwealth Parliament, that he thought the Labor members had made a mistake in voting for candidature.[124] See made no attempt to reintroduce the bill, countering all approaches by the women with procrastinations.

In June 1902 the Womanhood Suffrage League further fragmented. Although many league members had defected when they joined the Women's Progressive Association in late 1900, Martel and the Goldings continued to work within both organisations. Now the five branches in the inner-city working-class area of Sydney from which the disaffection had sprung, still smarting under rules which denied them representation, banded together under the name of the United Branches of the Womanhood Suffrage League[125] and decided

> to withhold the annual reports and capitation fees from the honorary general secretary of the Womanhood Suffrage of New South Wales until the Central League allows branch delegates to represent them on the Womanhood Suffrage League Council, as the branches consider that taxing them and giving no representation on the Council is opposed to the principles laid down by the Womanhood Suffrage League, viz, no taxation without representation.[126]

The league countered by excommunicating the offenders. A public notice was sent to the *Sydney Morning Herald* stating that 'we have no other choice but to inform you, and to inform the public, that you have no longer any right to describe your associations as branches of this League'.[127] Nellie Martel resigned from the central branch in protest, and the Goldings were included in the rump which had been cut off. On the eve of the granting of the women's vote in New South Wales, the league which had worked since 1891 was disintegrating.

When See (now Sir John) eventually reintroduced his bill in July, he pointed out that women now had a vote for the Commonwealth Parliament.[128] The bill quickly passed through the Assembly, its opponents still fighting a rearguard action to have the right for women to sit in Parliament written into it. The *Dawn* commented:

> The proposal to add the amendment was rejected 52–14, Sir John See declaring that if carried, it would have the effect of destroying the measure. The transparent attempt to jeopardize the Bill was effectively prevented thanks to the firmness of the Premier and the good sense of the House generally.[129]

In their eagerness to have the vote, the New South Wales women were oblivious to warnings like the one to Scott from a New Zealand suffragist:

> Tonight's telegrams report that your House proposes to grant the right to vote without the right to be a candidate. That was the mistake in New Zealand. That, as Bebel says, "is the knife without the blade". For the sake of other countries as well as your own, fight for the whole loaf.[130]

In early August 1902 the bill went to the Upper House. When introducing it Francis Suttor, as See had done, pointed to the federal vote, and supporters warned the nominated Council against rejecting a bill which had been sent to it a third time by an elected chamber.[131] The bill passed its third reading quietly on 14 August 1902, with galleries crowded with suffragists from all three organisations.

The different groups now began organising their celebrations. Before the end of August the Women's Progressive Association, taking advantage of Sir William Lyne's presence in Sydney, held a meeting in the 'uncomfortably crowded' School of Arts, to thank him for his earlier efforts in New South Wales and for his success in guiding through the recent Commonwealth bill.[132] Scott, angry that the Womanhood Suffrage League was being pre-empted and that the Progressive Association was claiming credit which she considered belonged to the league, sent a telegram to Lyne which was delivered during the meeting. It contained a protest which she asked Lyne to read aloud when he made his speech. Lyne conferred with Annie Golding, who told him that if he did so she would be forced to make a speech 'in defence of their position'.[133] Lyne decided not to read it. The Progressive Association held a second meeting in September to honour Sir John See.

The league in September advertised its 'joy meeting' on large posters around the city.[134] On the crowded platform were Lyne and See and other politicians who had actively worked for the cause, with representatives of sympathetic organisations.[135] All politicians, with 320,000 new voters to woo, were eager to claim as much credit as possible. Two of the major figures in the Victorian movement, Annie Lowe and Lilian Locke, were among the scheduled speakers, who were all women. Lyne and See were given a chance to reply when presentations were made to them. Louisa Lawson, handicapped in her movements because of a recent tram accident, was there, although she had not been asked to sit on the platform; she was, after all, now a member of the Progressive Association, a rival organisation. Margaret Windeyer, at the back of the hall with Lawson, was not pleased, and amid loud applause she is said to have led Lawson forward to the platform where a place was made for her and Scott presented her with one of her own bouquets of flowers.[136] Although Scott gave Lawson due recognition in her speech when she briefly outlined the New South Wales campaign, there is no doubt that Lawson felt slighted at being excluded from the official invitations. A few days later Scott sent her a mollifying letter, again giving her credit for her early efforts, and Lawson published it in the *Dawn*.[137]

The WCTU held its celebration during its Annual Convention in October.[138] Being an ongoing organisation, it now only had to disband its suffrage departments. The Women's Progressive Association denied being a party organisation,[139] as did similar Women's Progressive Leagues in Victoria, but its leading figures were prominent in Labor party affairs, and its lobbying emphasised, although not exclusively, the improvement of conditions for working women.

After the vote was won, Scott received congratulations from all parts of Australia and from overseas; a great many writers gave her personal credit for the victory and requested photos and materials for articles. There were numerous requests from city and country for her to address meetings on women's political responsibilities. From within her own organisation the question being asked was: 'But what are we going to do now?'[140] The answer came when on 7 October, after discussion about how women should use their vote (which the *Sydney Morning Herald* called 'all very speculatory'),[141] the Womanhood Suffrage League disbanded itself and announced that the Woman's Electoral and Political Educational League would be formed. It would eschew loyalty to any party and would aim:

to educate women in the use of the franchise and generally to promote the interests of women and children; to organize deputations, public meetings, lectures, and to take any other steps which might be deemed desirable in order to obtain reforms and legislation whereby the interests of the whole community might be conserved ... it should not be aggressive ... and it would deal with the problems of all women.[142]

It is clear that from the beginning the New South Wales suffragists were not a homogenous group. The WCTU, suspicious of the diversity of opinion which the Womanhood Suffrage League tolerated, kept its distance from the open organisation, and the league did not want to identify itself with the Union's temperance objectives. In 1887, when the WCTU had tried to form an affiliated suffrage society, the attempt had failed when the women who came to the public meeting refused to work with the Union. The league had members from the whole range of the middle class, with many women from the lower stratum having affinity with the Labor party. Considering the rising strength of the inner-city branches in the late 1890s, it is reasonable to assume that the working-class segment increased as the period progressed. The diverse membership meant that the league was subject to considerable pressures, for, although there was agreement among the women about basic economic and legal changes (guardianship of children, property rights, raising of the age of consent, improving women's working conditions), there was much diversity of opinion when it came to cultural change. There were many women who were impatient with the league's ladylike image and decorous avenues of protest and, as the period progressed and party lines hardened, different party affiliations threatened unity. By the force of her personality and by her skilful manoeuvring, Scott kept the popping lid on these pressures until the vote was almost won. In the immediate post-suffrage period the women, as they did in all states, separated into political and apolitical groups, working in different ways to eliminate legal and economic discrimination. The most important figures in the early political lobbying were Scott, the Golding sisters, and Hilma Molyneux Parkes, who formed and was first President of the Women's Liberal League of New South Wales. Dora Montefiore and Nellie Martel were to carve names for themselves in the British movement.

Notes

1. *The Teetotaller*, quoted in Elizabeth Windschuttle, 'Women, Class and Temperance: Moral Reform in Eastern Australia 1832–1857', p. 20.
2. *Sydney Morning Herald*, 29 January 1849.
3. ibid.
4. W. A. Piddington was so proud of this speech that he had it printed as a pamphlet titled *Manhood Suffrage*.
5. *Sydney Morning Herald*, 14 August 1858.
6. ibid.
7. ibid., 19 August 1875.
8. May Evans to Rose Scott, 23 May 1894, Woman Suffrage Correspondence, 1887–1899, ML:NSW, MSS A2271, item 80.
9. *NSWPD*, vol. 25, 18 March 1887, p. 267.
10. ibid., vol. 28, 27 September 1887, p. 126.
11. David Buchanan to the *Sydney Morning Herald*, 17 January 1888.

12. *NSWPD*, vol. 45, 8 July 1890, p. 1888.
13. ibid., vol. 49, 7 November 1890, p. 5040.
14. ibid., vol. 52, 30 July 1891, p. 482.
15. ibid., p. 486.
16. Louisa MacDonald, *The Women's College Within the University of Sydney*, p. 11.
17. George Black, *The Labor Party in New South Wales: a history from its formation in 1891 until 1894*, p. 24.
18. Undated, unsourced newspaper clipping, in Woman Suffrage: Miscellaneous papers on Australian and overseas movements, 1888–1920, ML:NSW, MSS 38/38, item 5.
19. Undated, unsourced card in ibid., item 30.
20. Emily Steel to Rose Scott, 22 May 1901, Woman Suffrage Correspondence, 1900–1902, ML:NSW, MSS A2272, item 618.
21. Mrs M. J. Williams and Mrs A. Holliday, *Golden Records: Pathfinders of the Woman's Christian Temperance Union in New South Wales*, p. 81.
22. *White Ribbon Signal*, 1 November 1890.
23. Mrs M. J. Williams and Mrs A. Holliday, *Golden Records*, p. 57.
24. Elizabeth Ward, *Out of Weakness Made Strong*, p. 75.
25. ibid., p. 50.
26. Sylvia Lawson, 'Edited, Printed and Published by Women', *Nation*, 25 October 1958, p. 16.
27. *Dawn*, 15 May 1888.
28. Quoted by Sylvia Lawson in 'Edited, Printed and Published by Women', p. 15.
29. *Dawn*, 1 July 1889.
30. ibid.
31. Gertrude O'Connor, 'Woman Suffrage' in 'Louisa Lawson, her life and work', ML:NSW, MSS A1897, p. 6.
32. *Dawn*, July 1889.
33. Louisa Lawson: Papers and news cuttings, ML:NSW, MSS 4937, item 19.
34. *Dawn*, 5 July 1890.
35. *Dawn*, 1 May 1902.
36. Maybanke Anderson, *Sydney Morning Herald*, 2 May 1925.
37. Dora Montefiore, *From a Victorian to a Modern*, pp. 30–1.
38. Dora Montefiore to May Manning, undated letter, Woman Suffrage Correspondence, 1887–1899, ML:NSW, MSS A2271, item 1.
39. J. H. Simpson to Rose Scott, 15 April 1891, ibid., item 3.
40. Gertrude O'Connor, 'Woman Suffrage' in 'Louisa Lawson, her life and work', ML:NSW, MSS 1897, p. 1.
41. Miles Franklin, 'Rose Scott: some aspects of her personality and work', p. 107.
42. Rose Scott, 'Address to the Feminist Club', 12 April 1921, Feminist Club: Papers, ML:NSW, MSS AS75/2.
43. Miles Franklin, 'Rose Scott', p. 107.
44. *Worker* (Brisbane), 17 October 1903.
45. Womanhood Suffrage League of New South Wales, Annual Report, 1892. There are now no copies of the *Woman's Suffrage Journal* in the Mitchell Library. The few which were held have disappeared.
46. Womanhood Suffrage League of New South Wales, Annual Report, 1894.
47. *Bulletin*, 16, 23 May 1891.
48. Intercolonial Trades and Labor Unions Council of Australasia, official report of the seventh congress at Ballarat, 1891, ML:NSW, FM3/211, pp. 99–101.
49. Secretary of the New South Wales Trades and Labor Council to Rose Scott, 29 February 1892, Woman Suffrage Correspondence 1887–1899, ML:NSW, MSS A2271, item 16.

50. Secretary of the Socialist League to Rose Scott, 18 September 1891, ibid., item 9.
51. Arthur Rae to Rose Scott, 18 August 1892, ibid., item 53.
52. Miles Franklin, 'Rose Scott', p. 96.
53. Womanhood Suffrage League of New South Wales, Annual Report, 1893.
54. Rose Scott to Sir Henry Parkes, 17 October 1892, Parkes, Henry: Correspondence, vol. 58, ML:NSW, MSS A928, p. 680.
55. ibid.
56. Arthur Rae to Rose Scott, 17 November 1892, Woman Suffrage Correspondence, 1887–1899, ML:NSW, MSS A2271, item 63.
57. Maybanke Wolstenholme to Rose Scott, no date, ibid., item 75.
58. Selwyn, Rose: Papers, 1890–1897, ML:NSW, MSS 301/3, p. 3.
59. *Daily Telegraph* (Sydney), 21 April 1915.
60. Womanhood Suffrage League of New South Wales, Annual Report, 1894.
61. *Dawn*, November 1893.
62. Elizabeth Ward, *Out of Weakness Made Strong*, pp. 100–4.
63. ibid., p. 103.
64. *Sydney Morning Herald*, 11 November 1891.
65. *Bulletin*, 25 November 1891.
66. Lady Mary Jersey to Lady Mary Windeyer, 15 November 1891, Mary Windeyer Papers, ML:NSW, MSS 186/14, item 455.
67. WCTU of New South Wales. Minutes of Committee Meeting of the central branch, May 1892, Woman's Christian Temperance Union of New South Wales: Papers, 1882–1978, ML:NSW, MSS 3641.
68. *Sydney Morning Herald*, 16 November 1891.
69. Womanhood Suffrage League of New South Wales, Annual Report, 1892.
70. Lady Mary Windeyer to Miss Walsh, Windeyer, Mary: Papers, 1854–1911, ML:NSW, MSS 186/14, item 141.
71. Womanhood Suffrage League of New South Wales, Annual Report, 1894.
72. *Bulletin*, 19 August 1894.
73. Letter to Rose Scott, 12 July 1894, Woman Suffrage Correspondence, 1887–1899, ML:NSW, MSS A2271, item 92.
74. Womanhood Suffrage League of New South Wales, Annual Report, 1895.
75. Alec Chisholm, 'The lady of the treasure house', p. 9.
76. Dowell O'Reilly, *NSWPD*, vol. 72, 18 September 1894, p. 463.
77. Womanhood Suffrage League of New South Wales, Annual Report, 1896.
78. William Willis, *NSWPD*, vol. 83, 30 June 1896, p. 1182.
79. Womanhood Suffrage League of New South Wales, Annual Report, 1898.
80. John Fegan, *NSWPD*, vol. 94, 11 October 1898, p. 1301.
81. Womanhood Suffrage League of New South Wales, Annual Report, 1895.
82. Dowell O'Reilly to Rose Scott, 29 November 1896, Woman Suffrage Correspondence, 1887–1899, ML:NSW, MSS A2271, item 228.
83. Womanhood Suffrage League of New South Wales, Annual Report, 1898.
84. Australian Women's Franchise Society Leaflets, ML:NSW, Q324.3/1, item 24.
85. Womanhood Suffrage League of New South Wales, Annual Report, 1899.
86. ibid., 1897.
87. ibid., 1896.
88. ibid., 1898.
89. Rose Scott, Woman Suffrage Correspondence, 1900–1902, ML:NSW, MSS A2272, item 274.
90. Womanhood Suffrage League of New South Wales, Annual Report, 1900.

91. ibid.
92. ibid.
93. ibid.
94. ibid.
95. *NSWPD*, vol. 103, 12 June 1900, p. 3.
96. *Evening News*, 13 June 1900.
97. *NSWPD*, vol. 104, 17 July 1900, p. 1003.
98. WCTU of New South Wales, Annual Report, 1901.
99. Circular letter dated 29 October 1900, in Rose Scott, Woman Suffrage Correspondence, 1900–1902, ML:NSW, MSS A2272, item 480.
100. Womanhood Suffrage League of New South Wales, Annual Report, 1901.
101. *NSWPD*, vol. 107, 9 November 1901, p. 5058.
102. Womanhood Suffrage League of New South Wales, Annual Report, 1901.
103. ibid.
104. Womanhood Suffrage League: note-books of the Secretary, and newspaper clippings, ML:NSW, MSS 38/35, item 3:24.
105. Two of Gandon's leaflets are in Australian Women's Franchise Society Leaflets, ML:NSW, Q324.3/1.
106. N. J. Collier to the *Sydney Morning Herald*, 12 September 1900.
107. Elizabeth Ward, *Out of Weakness Made Strong*, p. 70.
108. P. J. Gandon to Rose Scott, 20 August 1900, Woman Suffrage Correspondence, 1900–1902, ML:NSW, MSS A2272, item 457.
109. P. J. Gandon to Rose Scott, 17 October 1900, ibid., item 473.
110. Undated, unsourced newspaper report of a public lecture given by P. J. Gandon, 'The Woman Suffrage Bill—Why it Should be Rejected by the Upper House', Womanhood Suffrage League of New South Wales: note-books of the Secretary, and newspaper clippings, ML:NSW, MSS 38/35, item 6;75.
111. P. J. Gandon to the *Evening News*, 8 October 1900.
112. *Woman's Sphere*, 6 October 1902.
113. These problems are not reflected in Rose Scott's Annual Reports, but details are gathered from Womanhood Suffrage League of New South Wales: note-books of the Secretary, and newspaper clippings, ML:NSW, MSS 38/35, items 1, 2, and 3.
114. *Dawn*, November 1901, reports the first meeting of the Women's Progressive Association.
115. Sylvia Lawson in 'Edited, Printed and Published by Women', p. 18, reports that after the *Dawn* ceased publication in 1905 Louisa was a Vice-President, but when she became so is not clear.
116. Details of the Golding sisters are gathered from the following sources: *Daily Telegraph*, 3 March 1915, article in a series on 'Our Public Women'; 'Miss Annie Golding', in *Woman's Voice*, May 1905; 'Miss Annie Golding', in *Cyclopaedia of New South Wales*, 1907, p. 672; 'Miss Belle Golding'. ibid., p. 672; Judith Allen, 'Breaking into the public sphere: the struggle for women's citizenship in New South Wales, 1890–1920' pp. 111–17; 'Miss Annie Golding', *Daily Telegraph*, 20 August 1902.
117. *Worker* (Brisbane), 7 November 1903.
118. 'Mrs Martel', *Daily Telegraph*, 7 November 1903.
119. Womanhood Suffrage League of New South Wales, Annual Report, 1901.
120. *Sydney Morning Herald*, 3 July 1901.
121. *NSWPD*, Second Series, vol. 11, 11 September 1901, p. 1220.
122. ibid., p. 1219.
123. ibid., p. 1222.
124. William Lyne to Rose Scott, 25 September 1901, Woman Suffrage Correspondence, 1900–1902, ML:NSW, MSS A2272, item 664.

125. Womanhood Suffrage League of New South Wales: note-books of the Secretary, and newspaper clippings, ML:NSW, MSS 38/35, items 1, 2 and 3.
126. *Sydney Morning Herald*, 24 June 1902.
127. ibid., 4 July 1902.
128. *NSWPD*, Second Series, vol. 6, 17 July 1902, p. 1248.
129. *Dawn*, 17 July 1902.
130. Letter to Rose Scott, 25 July 1902, Woman Suffrage Correspondence, 1900–1902, ML:NSW, MSS A2272, item 705.
131. *NSWPD*, Second Series, vol. 6, 6 August 1902, p. 1661.
132. William Lyne to Rose Scott, 25 August 1902, Woman Suffrage Correspondence, 1900–1902, ML:NSW, MSS A2272.
133. ibid.
134. *Truth*, 21 September 1902.
135. Vida Goldstein has a comprehensive report of this meeting in *Woman's Sphere*, 10 October 1902.
136. Gertrude O'Connor, 'Louisa Lawson, her life and work', part 1, ML:NSW, MSS A1897, p. 31.
137. *Dawn*, October 1902.
138. WCTU of New South Wales, Annual Report, 1902.
139. A. N. Farrell to the *Sydney Morning Herald*, 2 September 1903.
140. Dowell O'Reilly to Rose Scott, 18 August 1902, Woman Suffrage Correspondence, 1900–1902, ML:NSW, MSS A2272, item 717.
141. *Sydney Morning Herald*, 9 October 1902.
142. ibid.

6

TASMANIA, 1903

For fifty-one years, from 1803 to 1854, Tasmania (then Van Diemen's Land) was a convict colony, and when its Constitution was drawn up in 1856 half of its population was either convict or ex-convict. The Constitution shows a determination to limit the voice of this ex-convict element in the legislature, for its property qualifications gave the vote for the Assembly to only 10,000 males in a total population of 65,000, and of these only 1500 could vote for the Legislative Council.[1] Special provision was made for 'respectable' males (graduates, army officers, doctors, ministers of religion) to vote even if they did not fulfil property qualifications, and there was plural voting for each House. The qualifications were lowered in 1870, but the colony's continuing preoccupation with respectability allowed the politicians to leave an estimated 16,000 adult males without a vote for the Assembly. There was little demand for manhood suffrage because surplus population—and with it the radical element—was siphoned off from Tasmania's depressed economy into colonies which were more prosperous. It was not until the early 1880s that mining discoveries in the north-west of the island gave birth to a small and struggling Labor movement.

In 1884, when the Government announced that it intended to lower the franchise still further, the new Trades and Labor Council united with those Liberals who believed that it was time for manhood suffrage and held a large protest meeting in Hobart which extended over two nights.[2] The bill introduced by Premier William Giblin lowered property qualifications for Assembly voters to those of municipal voters and extended its wage and salary qualifications; but it still left large numbers of males without a vote. Those who spoke for full manhood suffrage in the House were easily silenced by the claim that 'any honest, industrious and energetic man'[3] could have a vote, and by the fear of many that 'the tramp or the loafer'[4] might be enfranchised. The great surprise in

Giblin's bill was that it enfranchised unmarried women with property for both Houses. Giblin quoted J. S. Mill's opinion that a woman needed a vote because she was in greater need of protection than a man, but did not explain why for that reason he did not include all women, and then he went on to expand on the theme that the unattached woman's property should be represented. Opponents claimed that Giblin was including these women because their conservative voice might counteract the widening of the franchise for men, and then the same fear that had denied the vote to disreputable men surfaced in the horrified suggestion that prostitutes with property might be eligible.[5] There was some tentative support for the woman suffrage clause, but when Giblin dropped it from the bill he was the only one who lamented its passing. Eleven years were to elapse before another move was made in Parliament, and by then the Woman's Christian Temperance Union had taken up the cause.

The pattern of development of the WCTU in Tasmania paralleled that in other colonies: founded in 1886 by Mary Leavitt and enthused by Jessie Ackermann in 1889. It was not until 1892, when Ackermann as Australasian President spent four months touring the island, that the movement developed any impetus of its own. A central Union and eleven branches were represented at the 1893 Convention. The President, Grace Soltau, recommended the adoption of votes for women, and the newly elected Suffrage Superintendent, Miss Ethel Searle, read a 'lengthy paper on female suffrage [which] aroused great interest and was ordered to be printed'.[6] The next Convention in 1894 was presided over by Elizabeth Nicholls from South Australia, visiting in her capacity as Australasian President.[7] Once again a large public meeting was held at which the women claimed their vote on the grounds of justice, and linked it to two major objectives: stricter liquor controls, and the repeal of the Contagious Diseases Act which allowed suspected prostitutes to be arrested and forcibly examined for venereal disease. This Act was to be a matter of concern to the Tasmanian women for the whole of their campaign.

From November 1894 to March 1895 a WCTU Australasian organiser, Miss Ada Murcott, spent five months spreading the temperance and suffrage gospels, rocking her way around the island by coach.[8] During her stay an Intercolonial Temperance Convention was held in Hobart, at which the women were represented, and the Temperance Council arranged a woman suffrage meeting as part of its activities. Several members of Parliament attended, and Andrew Inglis Clark, then Attorney-General in Sir Edward Braddon's Government, was chairman. He promised that he would bring in a bill in the next session giving the women their vote.[9] Inglis Clark and those in the intellectual circle of which he was the centre were the epitome of the emerging Liberalism which would eventually challenge the long hegemony of the Conservatives in Parliament. With such a promise from a member of the ministry the women must have felt they had come a long way in a very short time. Their 1895 Convention fairly hummed with woman suffrage emphasis, and they held another suffrage meeting which was supported by an impressive array of members of Parliament, aldermen and clergy.[10] Then they waited for the opening of the next parliamentary session and their expected bill.

When Parliament met in July 1895, Premier Braddon did introduce a measure to amend the Constitution, but it made no mention of votes for women.[11] It further lowered qualifications for electors of both Houses but still left many males voteless.

Braddon claimed, though, that the new provisions 'practically meant manhood suffrage'.[12] Manhood suffrage supporters, now strong in the Assembly, attacked. 'Why not go the whole way?' they asked. Braddon replied that doing so 'would introduce elements into the franchise which they all desired to be kept out of it'.[13] Then the woman suffrage supporters, from all parts of the House, entered the debate. 'Why not a vote for every man and every woman?' asked those who approved of manhood suffrage. 'Why not a vote for women on the same wages and property qualifications as men?' asked those who supported the limited male suffrage. The shifting currents of the debate which washed across the chamber demonstrate the state of Tasmanian politics at the time. Neither the Government nor the Opposition was held together by any coherent policies: they were groups of supporters ranged around a leader for factional or personal reasons. Politicians within factions could be divided on aspects of the franchise question, as was the ministry itself. When the debate reached committee stage Andrew Inglis Clark, true to his promise to the WCTU, went against the Premier and moved that a vote be given to every man and woman in Tasmania, but this was quickly rejected.[14] An amendment giving women the vote on the same conditions as men was accepted. It seemed as if the bill might go forward in this reasonably coherent form when a member pointed out that women who were married—'the mainstay of houses and the true educators of children'[15]—would be without a vote because few earned wages or owned property, while 'a lot of servant girls and members of a very undesirable class'[16] would have it. Further, sons and daughters who worked only for food, lodging and clothing would be voteless. The Assembly, unwilling to concede full adult suffrage, which would have solved the problem, then almost tied itself in knots trying to manufacture an income for married women and daughters at home in order to balance the dubious vote of some females who earned their own living. The bill which emerged, with an elaborate table of values for services provided, would have been such a nightmare in administrative terms that it was no wonder the Legislative Council rejected it out of hand. Tasmania's pathological concern with excluding the undeserving from the franchise had produced a piece of legislation which the Hobart *Mercury* said was 'in the nature of make-believe'.[17]

At their 1896 Convention the Union reviewed the 1895 parliamentary debate, and Georgiana Kermode, now Colonial Suffrage Superintendent, proposed an aggressive propaganda initiative to support any future moves politicians might make on their behalf.[18] The resulting 1896 'winter campaign' was launched at a public meeting in Hobart. One of the speakers was Jessie Rooke, a Scottish-born former New South Wales suffragist who had moved to Burnie with her doctor husband in 1894, and had appeared at the Convention as the Union's press correspondent. Rooke and Kermode then undertook a series of public and drawing-room meetings which embraced the island. One of the suffragists, possibly Jessie Rooke, described the campaign.

> The drawing-room meetings have done much to engage the interest and sympathy of the upper classes and were well attended by leading people in each district. These were chiefly addressed by ladies but the public meetings [were addressed] by Members of Parliament and prominent citizens . . . In nearly every place where the resolution was put to the meeting 'That the franchise be extended to the women of Tasmania as an act of common Justice', not more than three, and sometimes only one, hand was raised against.[19]

At district centres like Burnie, Campbell Town and Ross, the halls were crowded. At all meetings petitions were available to be signed. To support the large Launceston public meeting, the women took to the streets to gather signatures and 'were delighted to find public opinion so far advanced that instead of opposition they met with respectful support and appreciation of their just claim.[20]

The petition, of 2278 signatures, not large but creditable considering the small and scattered population, was presented to both the Assembly and the Legislative Council in August 1896 just before the Government introduced a bill which gave more males—but still not all—the vote. It did not contain woman suffrage, but in committee a successful amendment put by William McWilliams struck out the word 'male', making the bill apply to both men and women.[21] An attempt again to manufacture an income for married women was defeated, as was a proposal for full adult suffrage. The bill went to the Council, which counteracted the move to give women their suffrage by reinstating the word 'male'. Then they passed the bill. During the debate in the Assembly, Braddon referred to 'a lady of enormous debating power'[22] who had been addressing meetings around the island; this was probably Jessie Rooke, who was to be the most prominent speaker in the whole campaign.

In January 1897 there was an election and the *Mercury* wrote that it was difficult to say whether the Government was strengthened or weakened, for no-one knew on which side of the House some members would take their seats.[23] When the post-election bargaining was over, however, the anti-suffrage Braddon was again Premier but it was apparent that there was a strong Liberal element in the House which favoured manhood suffrage. In the lead-up to the 1897 Commonwealth Constitutional Convention in March it also became clear that unrest outside Parliament at the exclusion of some males from the vote was growing stronger. There was particular concern that the Commonwealth Convention might confirm the 1891 Convention proposal that each colony should use the franchise of its own Assembly as a qualification to vote for the coming Commonwealth Parliament. If it did, the voteless males in Tasmania would find themselves voteless in the federal sphere. In April a large Launceston meeting sent a petition to the Convention asking that it would adopt, not just manhood suffrage, but full adult suffrage for the Federal Parliament.[24] Braddon presented this at the same time as he presented a small petition against allowing women the federal vote; it contended that women were unfit to vote and that they did not want to anyway.[25]

In spite of concern within and without Parliament, Braddon made no move for manhood suffrage when the first session opened in 1897. He did, however, introduce a bill in August to deal with certain aspects of the electoral machinery. Although amendments to the franchise were not allowed in such a bill, William McWilliams, by now recognised as the women's chief spokesman, seized the opportunity to attack the Government. He claimed that the electoral bill should not be necessary; that the difficulties of administration would disappear if the Government would introduce adult suffrage.[26] The resulting 'lengthy and acrimonious debate'[27] centred on whether manhood suffrage or womanhood suffrage would be good for Tasmania. A correspondent castigated the Parliament in the *Mercury* for discussing votes for women in the wrong terms. Discussions, she said, 'seem to have left wholly out of view the justice of the measure'.[28] Her comment was a perceptive one; Tasmania from the beginning had formulated its franchise on a judgment of worth rather than justice.

The peripatetic Elizabeth Nicholls arrived for the 1898 Annual Convention of the WCTU, and afterwards accompanied Jessie Rooke (now Colonial President) on another island tour.[29] They had meetings at thirty centres, distributed masses of suffrage leaflets, and collected a commendable total of 12,605 signatures which some members, they reported, worked 'arduously' to obtain.

In July 1898 a bill to create an extra Upper House electorate was presented to the Assembly, and the doughty William McWilliams again seized his opportunity.[30] He first attacked the existing male franchise. The Premier, he said, claimed that every adult male in Tasmania had a vote, but because of complicated registration provisions ten per cent of wage earners were still denied it. Braddon retorted angrily that 'manhood suffrage already existed'.[31] McWilliams moved an amendment which would have given the vote for both Houses to 'every person, male or female, of twenty-one years'. Before the debate on the amendment, the WCTU petitions were presented by the members in whose electorates they had been collected by Nicholls and Rooke. There was much merriment as one after another was laid on the table, for some presenters (including the Premier) were strong opponents.[32] The Premier tried to retrieve his dignity in the debate: 'nine out of ten of those who signed it do not want it (Oh!) They will do anything to be obliging (Laughter).'[33] The amendment was carried 20–8, a statutory majority of the thirty-seven members. With a Premier who opposed both, the Assembly was overwhelmingly in favour of votes for all men and all women. When the amended bill went to the Council, Henry Rooke (not Jessie's husband) presented an anti-suffrage petition from Launceston of 1045 names. It took a side swipe at Elizabeth Nicholls, Ada Murcott and Jessie Ackermann by claiming that the agitation was 'kept up by a few individuals, some of whom are imported for the purpose'.[34] The women countered with their second barrage of petitions and the laughter was as loud as it had been in the Assembly, for Rooke himself was obliged to present one. Debate on the bill in the Council was almost non-existent; McWilliams' amendment was removed and the measure for an extra electorate passed.

The women were deeply disappointed by the Legislative Council's summary rejection of their claim in 1898; they had worked very hard in the five years since they had adopted the cause, and it was now clear that they had the Legislative Assembly on their side. In her address to the 1899 Convention Rooke trenchantly criticised Legislative Council members, but noted that they (unlike their counterparts in Victoria) were at least 'free from the stigma of insulting the women who are so deeply interested in this important question'.[35] Rooke's rhetoric had always concentrated on the injustice of women being without the vote, but in the face of continued Upper House antagonism she now began to emphasise the benefits which the WCTU claimed would flow from their suffrage, and declared: 'Time will not permit me to tell of the testimony given by men of authority of the good that has come to the States and the Colonies which have enfranchised their women ... they publicly declare that woman's vote has brought stronger moral forces to bear on social and political life.'[36] Because of the great hostility shown in the Parliament and the press to the idea of women as candidates, Rooke also began to play down any idea that women might want to be elected: 'they wanted the men to rule there—the good men.'[37]

In May 1899 Mrs Emily Dobson (wife of a Legislative Council member) who was so involved in charity work that she had a secretary to help her with her correspondence, moved to form the National Council of Women.[38] Thirty-three philanthropic organisations, many of which Emily Dobson had helped form, affiliated with it. The WCTU joined, and members of the Union were on its council. The list of office-bearers was impressive: it included Lady (Georgina) Gormanston (wife of the Governor), Lady (Alice) Braddon (wife of the Premier), and Mrs Montgomery (wife of the Bishop of Hobart). Because records have been lost, there is no way of knowing whether the National Council of Women took an active part in the remaining four years of the suffrage campaign. It seems unlikely: Braddon's and Dobson's husbands were strong opponents, and Emily Dobson replied to a request for support from the British women in 1906 (when Tasmania had already given all women and men the vote) that the National Council of Women, while it was in favour of some women having the vote, disapproved of universal suffrage for either sex.[39] She would hardly have replied in this imperious manner if the council had taken any significant part in the Tasmanian movement.

As well as women's philanthropic organisations, there were in Hobart and Launceston in the 1890s groups of upper-class women who were concerned with their own self-development. One of these was the Hobart Itinerants, so called because meetings were held in rotation in the homes of members.[40] As in other such clubs, individual members prepared and presented papers on literary and historical topics and current affairs. In October 1899 a joint meeting was arranged of the Itinerants and two other such groups. Mrs Ida McAuley (whose husband and son were both professors of mathematics) was approached to give a paper on woman suffrage. She said in her introduction that it was with surprise and regret that she had learnt that she was the only member in favour of women suffrage, and she was astounded that 'so intelligent a group of women should . . . help to block one of the paths to upward mobility of themselves and their sisters.'[41] McAuley then went on to give an able defence of woman suffrage, and claimed that she and her fellow suffragists wanted the vote 'on exactly the same terms as men, whatever that may be'.

The franchise which the 1897 Convention had adopted for the coming first Commonwealth election was that of each colony's Assembly. This meant that Tasmania, already anxious that it would have less federal bargaining power than other states because of its size and geographical position, would be further disadvantaged because it was without full male suffrage for its Lower House. Braddon therefore did an about-face and in July 1899 introduced a bill to give every man a vote. McWilliams moved that woman suffrage be included.[42] There was opposition even from the women's supporters because they thought that such an amendment would jeopardise the passage of manhood suffrage in the Upper House. The woman suffrage amendment received only a small majority from an Assembly that the previous year had been overwhelmingly in favour. As had been the case elsewhere in Australia, votes for women were expendable if it seemed that they might hold back a vote for every man. Not only the amendment, but the bill itself, was rejected by the Upper House.

There was another election in 1900 but the new Premier, Neil Lewis, was not a supporter of votes for women. Almost immediately, however, he introduced a bill giving manhood suffrage and abolishing plural voting for the Assembly.[43] This time the Lower House rejected a move to insert votes for women in the bill, and the Upper House yielded. Tasmania now had one-man-one-vote for its Assembly, but a property qualification for the Upper House. The property qualification was to continue till 1968, a memorial to Tasmania's respect for property and to its fear of radicalism.

There had always been great tension between the Upper and Lower Houses in Tasmanian politics, and in 1902 Sir Neil Lewis (he had been knighted in 1901) introduced a bill to try to bring the Upper House to heel.[44] The two Houses were to be amalgamated, and voting in the new Assembly was to be by orders. In spite of Lewis's opposition, woman suffrage was inserted into the bill and the vote to do so was greeted with cheers by an Assembly which had regained its enthusiasm now that the male suffrage question had been settled.[45] The Council rejected the move for amalgamation, and so, incidentally, the amendment giving women votes. This was the fifth time that women suffrage had been inserted in a bill by the Lower House and promptly rejected by the Upper. No bill, however, had ever been proposed which contained woman suffrage unfettered by any other cause.

By 1903 the Labor party, tardy in Australian terms because of Tasmania's late emergence from an almost exclusively rural economy, had taken shape. Five of its candidates for the Assembly were returned in the 1903 state elections, enabling William Propsting's Liberal-Democrats to form a coalition with Labor and begin a programme of Liberal reforms after forty years of Conservative stagnation. The Governor's speech opening the new Parliament announced that 'a measure will be introduced for extending the franchise to women'.[46] In mid-September Propsting laid it before the Assembly with an able apologia,[47] and it passed the House without a division. The bill did not debar women from sitting in Parliament. The WCTU, aware that there was still strong opposition to their vote in the Upper House, made an appeal to every Council member.[48] The Upper House reluctantly capitulated, but not necessarily because of the women's appeal. The press thought that Councillors were swayed by the fact that women already had the Commonwealth vote, and by the feeling that it should 'regretfully and reluctantly'[49] fall into line with other states. The Upper House asserted its supremacy by inserting a clause debarring women from a seat in Parliament, and the Hobart *Mercury* breathed a sigh of relief that Tasmania had been spared the 'strange happenings' which might otherwise have resulted.[50]

On 10 September 1903, a few days before the bill was passed through the Assembly, Jessie Rooke called a meeting to inaugurate the Tasmanian Women's Suffrage Association.[51] It may have been envisaged as a society which would fight for the state vote outside the WCTU, and so attract supporters who were not sympathetic to other aims of the Union. By the time the first public meeting was held under the presidency of Ida McAuley, however, the Upper House had assented to votes for women. The new association went ahead as a non-party organisation 'to interest women in all laws relating to women and children' and to educate members on wider political questions.[52] As a lead-up to the Commonwealth elections, the association held a series of meetings at which candidates of different persuasions put their point of view and at which mock elections were held to familiarise members with the mechanics of voting. Because the name Tasmanian Women's Suffrage Association was now inappropriate—and always had been in view of the fact that the vote was granted while it was being formed—it was changed at the first annual meeting to the Tasmanian Women's Political Association, and the association continued as a non-party educational and lobbying organisation.[53]

Other Tasmanian women were quickly subsumed into the new party structures. Lilian Locke, a Victorian Labor organiser, had visited Tasmania in the lead-up to the Commonwealth election and organised Labor women into the Workers' Political Leagues,[54] and by 1905 there were branches of the Liberal organisation, the Tasmanian National League,[55] with Lady Lewis (wife of the former Premier, Sir Neil Lewis) as President and Georgiana Kermode (who had been a Colonial Suffrage Superintendent in the WCTU) as 'a prominent worker'.[56]

Jessie Rooke, the hardest-working and most prominent Tasmanian suffragist, left the presidency of the Tasmanian WCTU in 1903, when she became Australasian President. When in February 1902 the International Women's Suffrage Committee was formed in Washington, Rooke, although she did not attend the international conference with Vida Goldstein, was appointed as an Australian committee member with her. She died in early 1906, before she could exercise the state vote for which she had worked so hard.[57]

Notes

Tasmania did not publish its parliamentary debates (Hansard) until 1979. The only records of parliamentary proceedings till that year are in the *Mercury*, a Hobart newspaper.

1. Lecture by P. O. Fysh, 'The Representation of the People', *Mercury*, 25 June 1884.
2. *Mercury*, 27 June, 1 July 1884.
3. This and similar phrases used by parliamentary members, Report of Parliamentary Proceedings, *Mercury*, 30 July 1884.
4. ibid.
5. ibid.
6. WCTU of Tasmania, Annual Report, 1893.
7. ibid., 1894.
8. ibid., 1895.
9. ibid.
10. ibid.
11. Report of Parliamentary Proceedings, *Mercury*, 25 July 1895.
12. ibid.
13. ibid.
14. ibid., 17 August 1895.
15. Editorial, *Mercury*, 17 August 1895.
16. ibid.
17. ibid., 5 September 1895.
18. WCTU of Tasmania, Annual Report, 1896.
19. A handwritten and undated account of the woman suffrage movement in Tasmania, Woman Suffrage: Miscellaneous papers on Australian and Overseas movements, 1888–1920, ML:NSW, MSS 38/38, items 514–18.

20. WCTU of Tasmania, Annual Report, 1897.
21. Report of Parliamentary Proceedings, *Mercury*, 27 August 1896.
22. ibid.
23. Editorial, *Mercury*, 31 January 1897.
24. *National Australasian Convention Debates, First Session, Adelaide, 1897*, p. 637.
25. ibid.
26. Report of Parliamentary Proceedings, *Mercury*, 28 August 1897.
27. Editorial, *Mercury*, 2 September 1897.
28. 'A Tasmanian Woman' to the *Mercury*, 5 September 1897.
29. WCTU of Tasmania, Annual Report, 1899; Womanhood Suffrage League of New South Wales, Annual Report, 1898.
30. Report of Parliamentary Proceedings, *Mercury*, 25 June 1898.
31. ibid.
32. ibid., 29 June 1898.
33. ibid., 30 June 1898.
34. ibid., 6 July 1898.
35. WCTU of Tasmania, Annual Report, 1899.
36. ibid., 1899.
37. ibid., 1900.
38. *A History of the National Council of Women of Tasmania, 1899–1968*, compiled to mark the 80th Anniversary of the National Council of Women, no author credited, no publisher given, pp. 2, 3.
39. Vicki Pearce, '"A Few Viragos on a Stump": the Womanhood Suffrage Campaign in Tasmania, 1880–1920', p. 154.
40. Cynthia Alexander, 'The Itinerants: a Ladies Literary Society', pp. 146–50.
41. Ida McAuley, a handwritten paper on woman suffrage, for a combined meeting of the Itinerants, Hamilton, and For Divers Reasons clubs, McAuley, Ida: Papers, Tasmanian Archives, NS331/9.
42. Report of Parliamentary Proceedings, *Mercury*, 6 July 1899.
43. ibid., 1 August 1900.
44. ibid., 4, 5 September 1902.
45. ibid., 4 September 1902.
46. Report of the Governor's Speech, *Mercury*, 19 August 1903.
47. Report of Parliamentary Proceedings, *Mercury*, 16 September 1903.
48. WCTU of Tasmania, Annual Report, 1904.
49. Editorial, *Mercury*, 9 October 1905.
50. ibid.
51. Women's Suffrage Association of Tasmania, Report, 1904.
52. ibid.; *Examiner*, 22 September 1903.
53. Women's Suffrage Association of Tasmania, Report, 1904.
54. *Worker* (Brisbane), 3 September 1903.
55. Vicki Pearce, '"A Few Viragos on a Stump"', p. 159.
56. *Daily Mail*, 28 October 1904.
57. Amelia Pemmell, 'Jessie Rooke', in an In Memoriam edition of *White Ribbon Signal*, 1 February 1906.

7

QUEENSLAND, 1904

In late 1859 the vast and sparsely populated northern part of New South Wales was separated and given the name of Queensland. Early that year all males over twenty-one had voted in the New South Wales Assembly elections under manhood suffrage, and they expected that they would have the same privilege in their new colony. This was not so, for the Queen had signed the Order of Separation before manhood suffrage was granted in New South Wales. The first Queensland election went ahead in 1860 with a New South Wales electoral roll from which one-third of the names had been expunged. With a property qualification for electors and little manufacturing or professional wealth, it was inevitable that the new Government would favour conservative pastoral interests. A further bulwark to these interests was provided by the new Legislative Council, for appointees (for life and unpaid) were such as would resist Liberal or radical encroachment. The Parliament refused to restore manhood suffrage until 1871, by which time the pastoral interests controlled thirty of the forty-two electorates. Bitterness and confrontation had become endemic to Queensland politics, and were to be intensified by the colony's formidable electoral problems. These problems existed up to and during the period of the struggle for votes for women.

In the first thirty years Queensland's population increased eightfold. In response to aggressive Government policy there was a constant flood of predominantly British migrants. These were augmented by 35,000 men—a high proportion of them Chinese—attracted from interstate and overseas onto Queensland's newly discovered goldfields in the 1870s, and by 13,000 Pacific Islanders (Kanakas) brought in to work the cane fields in the north. White females were in the minority and were concentrated in the towns; in the vast rural areas there was a large itinerant male population which moved from one mining town to another, or serviced beef, pearling, shearing and timber industries. Even after manhood suffrage was conceded, these men were without a vote because of residency restrictions.

The problems of adapting the electoral system to the rapidly changing demographic situation were daunting. Periodic redistributions were occasions for hostile recriminations between the developing society's three interest groups: the pastoral, the strongly emerging Liberal opposition based in the growing towns, and the labour force. As the century progressed, the itinerant work force demanded that it be given the franchise, but politicians claimed that it was impossible to solve the mechanical problems, for most did not stay long enough in one spot to qualify for registration. The labour force, and an increasing number of Liberal voices, saw the plural vote as the greatest injustice of all, and claimed that it was manipulated more in Queensland than in any other colony. As a result of this ferment of electoral discontent, labour agitation and unionism were early and vigorous in Queensland. In 1885 the various threads coalesced into the Trades and Labor Council. The Legislative Council thundered that it had 'socialist' objectives, but like other such organisations in Australia its socialism was vague and inchoate. In Queensland, however, the very word 'socialism', reinforced by the occasional theoretical socialist like William Lane, served to widen the deep divisions in Queensland society. Into this electoral complexity in the late 1880s was thrown the demand for female suffrage.

The first articulated support came from William Lane, who helped to form the Trades and Labor Council in 1885. In 1887 he began his weekly paper, the *Boomerang*, in which he stormed against the plural vote, inequitable electoral distribution, the pastoral employers, and cheap Chinese and Kanaka labour. In his invectives about wages and conditions of employment he extended his concern, as few did, from those of men to those of the 20,000 working women in Queensland. Lane's first tentative approach to votes for women must have made suffragists like Rose Scott and Louisa Lawson furious. (Both read his journal.) Under the name of Lucinda Sharpe, supposedly an American woman married to an Australian and corresponding with a friend back home, he wrote

> Woman's rights, indeed! I want a vote in theory, but I don't really care whether I get it or not. I'd like to have things fixed so that I—the wife and mother—was the recognized head of the household ... but why should I enthuse over it when I *am* so to all intent. The woman who can't manage a man must be somewhat dim-witted.[1]

Soon, however, 'Lucinda' was claiming that women needed the vote to improve their legal position, and by 1889 Lane, resuming his own identity, was supporting woman suffrage as a principle: 'It is as citizens only that the right to take part in the making of the laws which all must obey can be claimed.'[2] By 1891 he had again modified his position to that which the Queensland Labor Party was to adopt until the vote was gained in 1905: 'the most ardent advocates of woman suffrage must be content to hasten slowly ... we have first to clear the electoral ground of other obstacles to good government ... we have to abolish plural voting to make manhood suffrage complete.'[3]

In late 1889 Leontine Cooper, one of the main figures in the later suffrage campaign, began to write for the *Boomerang*. Background information about Cooper is fragmentary,[4] but it is known that she had an English mother and that her French father structured her education (it is not clear where) 'under the principles and views of Rousseau'. What emerged from this environment was not the subservient woman of Rousseau's precepts on women's education, but a cultured woman with literary and artistic tastes. Cooper is said to have had a 'slow, graceful manner' and a 'gentle, low and refined voice', but the letters and articles she wrote on woman suffrage show that she also had strong opinions and great force and vitality. The *Worker* described her as 'a leader in thought, a distinguished pen-woman, and a wise exponent of women's work',[5] and she was enough of a public figure to be asked by the Legislative Council in 1891 to be one of the six women among the Commissioners appointed to inquire into conditions of work in shops, factories and workshops. Her obituary writer speaks of her 'brave, steady work as a journalist, working for a living', so she was evidently writing professionally well before her articles and stories first appeared in the *Boomerang*, when she was fifty-one years old. Cooper was to found her own journal, the *Star*, probably in 1894, which ran for sixteen months, 'paying a little over its expenses'. No copies of it are extant, but Louisa Lawson wrote in the *Dawn*: 'We have received an interesting number of the *Star* which announces itself as "The Only Woman's Journal in Queensland". The subject of woman suffrage is treated in a leading article and a special column is given to temperance work.'[6] Articles on leading women in Australia and overseas, stories and poems, and advice about cooking were part of the paper, so the *Star* seems to have been very much like Lawson's own journal, the *Dawn*. As well as occasionally reporting on the Queensland movement for Lawson, Cooper corresponded spasmodically with Rose Scott on the subject of votes for women.

In her first article for the *Boomerang* Cooper challenged the assumption that all women should be regarded as potential wives and mothers, and pointed to the large numbers of Queensland women earning their own living.[7] She attacked the system which did not protect the woman from violence, excluded her from higher education, and did not give her a say in the laws under which she lived. She pointed out that the dominant order (in this case the male) would always frame the laws to protect its own interests, and therefore it was essential that the subordinate group (the female) should have the vote to rectify its position. In later articles Cooper supported equal wages and 'freedom to compete in the labour market for all kinds of labour'. This was in line with Lane's personal beliefs, but not necessarily in line with the Labor movement's ambivalent rhetoric. She was never to see eye to eye with Lane and the Labor movement in their timetable for gaining votes for women. She did not accept plural voting, but she did not consider that the woman's vote should wait until the plural vote had been abolished.

The first suffrage group, the Queensland Women's Suffrage League—known for a short time as the North Brisbane Women's Suffrage League[8]—was formed at a meeting in the home of a Mrs Edwards in February 1889, the year that Cooper went into battle in the *Boomerang*. It is quite likely that Cooper was a member of the short-lived society. Mrs Hannah Chewings, of the South Australian Women's Suffrage League, is said to have had some part in its formation,[9] but it is possible that Louisa Lawson was also a moving force. Sylvia Lawson, Louisa's grand-daughter, claims that about this time, fresh from the formation of the Dawn Club (the first New South Wales franchise association), Lawson went to Brisbane to form a suffrage group there.[10] Reports of the Queensland

MARY HAD A LITTLE LAMB.

The Queensland Premier Robert Philp, having killed moves for one-man-one-vote and early closing, prepares to do the same to woman suffrage.
Worker (Brisbane), 11 August 1900. Mitchell Library, State Library of New South Wales.

Women's Suffrage League have not been preserved, but some details are available from press reports. The *Women's Voice* claimed that it had as its special object the raising of the age of consent and the abolition of the Queensland Contagious Diseases Acts,[11] and the oration given at its first annual meeting on 28 July 1890 would imply that it was concerned about the plight of 'those women who had to fight the battle of life themselves'.[12] But when it canvassed for signatures to a petition in July 1889, Lane lampooned it in a cartoon in the *Boomerang* which implied that it was concerned with perpetuating the property vote rather than fighting for the rights of working women.[13] This may be doing the league an injustice; it was probably agitating for the vote for women on the same grounds as it was possessed by men.

The first annual meeting of the league,[14] and as far as we know the only one, was addressed by Alderman J. A. Clarke, whose wife was elected Vice-President at the meeting. He contended that political leaders were afraid of women; they thought that if women secured the franchise they would claim the right to sit in Parliament. 'What is there against women being elected to Parliament?' he asked. Mrs Edwards moved quickly to correct him; women were happy with male representatives, she said; they wanted only the vote. By the middle of 1891, the league was dying. Lawson reported in April: 'The Queensland Women's Suffrage League is in a moribund condition, several of the most active members of the League having resigned. It is possible that a new society having the same object may be formed, but nothing is arranged as yet.'[15] It is likely, in the light of future developments, that the resignations and consequent demise of the Queensland Women's Suffrage League were due, not to apathy, but to differences within the movement about whether the demand for the woman's vote should be linked to the demand for the abolition of the plural vote. In 1891, when the resignations took place, the political wing of the Queensland Labor Party was emerging as the unions, bitter after their defeats in the maritime strike of 1890 and the shearers' strike of 1891, sought an alternative power base. With woman suffrage in the air, labour had already considered its possible electoral implications. It was clear that if women gained the franchise under existing conditions, the conservative influence of the plural vote could be intensified. The *Worker* (which Lane founded as the successor to the *Boomerang*), on 13 June again articulated what was to be the Labor party's position. The vote for women would be passively supported on the grounds of justice, but the party would not campaign for it until it had one-man-one-vote.[16] Lane by this time was very much preoccupied with organising his ill-fated Utopian settlement in Paraguay, and his voice faded from the campaign.

While the Queensland Women's Suffrage League was running its course, there were some incidental mentions of woman suffrage in Parliament. Then in July 1890 Richard Hyne introduced a private member's bill which gave votes to women on the same conditions as men.[17] Hyne claimed that his pockets were 'full of letters ... on the subject' from women. He gave an able outline of his case: the principle of justice, no taxation without representation, and the argument that women had to obey the laws. Boyd Morehead, a pastoral representative, was Premier and he ridiculed the proposal, drawing much laughter with his sallies. He raised the spectre of women standing for Parliament: 'I say that if a good-looking girl from Maryborough stood against the honourable member [Hyne] he would not have a chance against her.'[18] In spite of the merriment, there was strong support for Hyne. The bill was shelved in favour of Government business without a vote being taken. Apart from a few incidental mentions, nothing more was to happen in the political arena until late 1894.

In 1890 the Queensland Woman's Christian Temperance Union took up the cause. The WCTU had been brought to Queensland by Mrs Leavitt, who had established one Brisbane branch and four country ones. In 1890, after Jessie Ackermann's visit, there were seventeen. At its zenith, at the turn of the century, there were to be thirty branches scattered over the colony, with an average of thirty members each. Two of the important temperance women in the franchise struggle had appeared by 1888; Elizabeth Brentnall was Colonial President and Agnes Williams was Vice-President. Elizabeth Brentnall was the wife of a clergyman who had resigned from the Methodist ministry because of throat trouble and been appointed to the Legislative Council. His appointment to the prestigious Upper House would have enhanced the influence Elizabeth was able to exert in the WCTU through her own considerable skills. She was a capable and forthright woman with outstanding organisational ability, having been mistress of a large girls' school in Lancashire before she married and migrated to Australia. Agnes Williams, her Vice-President, became the WCTU's best-known public speaker on votes for women. The *Worker*, not usually fulsome in its praise for women outside the ranks of committed Labor, spoke of Williams in 1903 as 'perhaps the best-known speaker in the State'.[19] When in 1902 she disclaimed any ambition on the part of women to sit in Parliament, the *Worker* asked: 'Why this excessive modesty or prejudice? Mrs Williams herself would make an ideal representative of women in Parliament.'[20] Williams was also the wife of a clergyman, and she carried on her WCTU work from his various bases in the colony.

Brentnall first suggested in her 1888 presidential report that the WCTU should adopt woman suffrage to achieve its temperance objectives.[21] There was resistance to the idea and, in spite of the fact that Jessie Ackermann also urged its adoption in 1890, the 1890 Convention was still divided on the issue: 'A warm discussion on the woman suffrage question ensued, a good number present taking part, and it was decided that the Colonial Union cannot take it up as a department, but the local Unions are free to do so.'[22] In 1891 a letter was read to the Convention from Ackermann, who was then Australasian President, 'a lively discussion took place', and the Convention reversed its decision[23] and formed a Colonial Suffrage Department. By 1893 the subject again figured prominently in the Annual Convention, and Annie James, Suffrage Superintendent for that year, reported: 'several Unions have taken up this work methodically and energetically, papers having been read and discussed with great interest ... Other Unions, though not seeing their way to making Woman's Suffrage a department of work, have had the matter under consideration.'[24]

There was a great deal of discussion in the Queensland press when New Zealand women voted for the first time in November 1893, and suffragists held a public meeting on 17 December at which May O'Connel, before 'a crowded and enthusiastic audience' delivered 'an able, instructive and exhaustive address'. There was 'a lively debate' and it was resolved: 'That this meeting views with pleasure the results of woman suffrage in New Zealand, and hopes that this desirable reform will soon be extended to this Colony.'[25] May O'Connel (as May Jordon) had been a committee member of the 1889 society and was active in the Labor party affairs. She helped form a large Female Workers' Union in Queensland in 1890, and was involved in the women's section of the Australian Labor Federation.

The success of the meeting evidently inspired the suffragists to form a new society. A group of twenty-five women met with Leontine Cooper in the chair to formulate resolutions to be put to another open meeting. The *Brisbane Courier* reported their deliberations:

> It was urged by some members of the Committee that the resolutions should embody the idea of 'one person, one vote' but after prolonged discussion it was decided to seek simply an affirmation of the principle that the franchise of the Colony, whatever it may be, should be extended to women. In this way the controversial matter involved in the claim for one man one vote is for the time being set aside and the question of getting the women the right of voting is allowed to stand on its own merits.[26]

The public meeting to consider the committee's deliberations was held on 28 February 1894, and as the men and women assembled Sarah Bailey, a Labor party supporter, distributed a circular which began

EQUAL RIGHTS FOR ALL

> Ladies and Gentlemen,
> As it appeared to me the resolutions to be moved at this meeting are not definite enough, and would give many sympathisers the impression that there is a desire on the part of the promoters of this meeting to give some ladies two or more votes, and some women no votes at all, if you and the Chairman will permit me I will move ... amendments in order that all doubts may be set at rest.[27]

The choice of Dr William Taylor as chairman would have heightened the tension generated by Sarah Bailey's circular. He was a member of the Legislative Council and in 1892 had made a suggestion (but did not embody it in a motion) that propertied women only should be put on the colony's electoral roll.[28] After Taylor's opening remarks, Leontine Cooper addressed the large mixed audience. She then moved the first of the committee's resolutions: 'That this meeting of British citizens is of the opinion that the time has come when the electoral laws of the Colony should be so altered as to extend to women the privilege of a political vote.'[29] Sir Charles Lilley, a Liberal and recently retired as a judge of the Supreme Court, seconded the motion. Sarah Bailey jumped to her feet and proposed an amendment which would alter the last words of the resolution to read: 'to extend to women the right to one vote, and one vote only, in parliamentary and municipal elections'.[30] There was confusion in the hall as the chairman tried unsuccessfully to suppress the speeches of a seconder and of supporters. Sir Charles Lilley and others urged Sarah Bailey to withdraw her amendment as it would cause dissension in the new society if carried. Bailey and the Labor party women hesitated but, urged on by speeches and loud cheers from their male supporters, decided to persevere. The amendment was carried, but large numbers abstained from voting. Mrs Moginie (as Miss Allen a former member of the New South Wales Womanhood Suffrage League) moved successfully that the name of the association should be, not the Woman's Franchise Association, but the Woman's Equal Franchise Association. The meeting then elected Mrs Eleanor Trundle as President and Leontine Cooper as Vice-President.

A few days later Leontine Cooper resigned from the Woman's Equal Franchise Association. She wrote to the *Worker*:

> If we desire a speedy recognition of the claim of women to political representation I think it unwise to clog the movement with the huge political revolution which one man one vote subtends. I consider the latter the Labor Party's battle and I think they are quite strong enough to fight it without clinging to our petticoats for help.[31]

Cooper followed her resignation with a leading article in the *Star* supporting her stand, and before the end of the month she and a group of twenty-nine women formed the Woman's Suffrage League.[32] There were unsuccessful efforts in the month after the split to reconcile the Woman's Suffrage League and the Woman's Equal Franchise Association, but a prolonged exchange of letters in the *Brisbane Courier* showed how much at variance they were. When the Woman's Equal Franchise Association at the end of that month prepared a petition which asked the Government for a vote 'for all white women' on the basis of 'one vote and one vote only' it was mutually understood that a merger was impossible.[33] Both suffrage societies proceeded to form branches in Brisbane and country towns, and soon there was a network spread over Queensland's major centres. Working only from newspaper reports in the absence of official records of either organisation, it is sometimes difficult to tell to which society a group was connected. It would even appear that some were spontaneous non-aligned groups.

In April 1894 the Woman's Equal Franchise Association held new elections for office bearers. Eleanor Trundle, President for less than two months, was defeated. She took her considerable abilities to the Woman's Christian Temperance Union, where she became the energetic and dedicated Colonial Suffrage Superintendent until 1905.[34] A remarkable Labor woman, Mrs Emma Miller, took her place as President of the Equal Franchise Association, and was to continue in office for the eleven years of the campaign.

Miller was forty years old when she migrated to Queensland in 1879 with her second husband, and after his death she married her third, Andrew Miller, in 1886. She had had strong labour connections in Derbyshire; her father was a Chartist agitator, and she, when widowed for the first time, had had to support her four children by working twelve hours a day for six days a week as a seamstress. Her activities within the Queensland Labor movement were wide-ranging and impressive: she had shared with May O'Connel in forming the 1890 Female Workers' Union, gave evidence to the 1891 Royal Commission into conditions in shops, factories and workshops, and was a travelling organiser for the Australian Workers' Union. Miller was physically tiny but had a colourful, forthright personality and was not afraid to be confrontational. She was 'never more delighted than when playing a vigorous part in election campaigns'.[35] She was so ardent a supporter of Labor that in 1891 she had marched in the streets with the shearers' leaders after they were released from the imprisonment which broke their 1891 strike.

The Woman's Christian Temperance Union's reaction to the political wrangling of 1894 was steadily to expand its suffrage work through its branches and to emphasise its non-political stance. The three societies all presented petitions to Parliament to support two bills containing woman suffrage which were introduced into the Assembly later in 1894. The largest petition, for one vote and one vote only, with 7781 women's and 3575 men's signatures, was tabled by Thomas Glassey (leader of the sixteen Labor members of the Assembly) when he introduced an electoral bill in August.[36] The bill aimed to give the vote to women (it did not specify in what form) and to all itinerants. There was a short ideological debate on votes for women, but the discussion centred on the ambiguity of the bill and on Glassey's quite impractical proposals to make it possible for nomads to vote. The bill was shelved, but for the rest of his life Glassey basked in the glory of what he incorrectly labelled the first attempt to give Queensland women the vote.[37]

Miffed that Glassey's bill had been put to the Assembly before his, Charles Powers (an independent opposing the Government) in September of the same year introduced an Electoral Acts Amendment Bill which abolished plural voting and gave women the vote.[38] Powers made it clear that Parliament could pass one without the other. The way was open for a debate on woman suffrage, but the only responses to Powers' ideological arguments—natural rights and no taxation without representation—were facetious and trivial:

> I find that the only women in favour . . . are . . . the ugly women and the plain women. The fair . . . and the beautiful are either indifferent to the proposed extension of the franchise or opposed to it . . . if there is a good-looking man he will get their votes irrespective of politics'.[39]

Powers' bill was also shelved. Similar bills by both Glassey and Powers in 1885 fared no better. Woman suffrage was barely mentioned in the debates before they degenerated into the familiar angry litany on inequalities of representation for men.

The three suffrage groups worked to consolidate their position in 1895 but, in the face of the then Conservative Government's opposition, there was little they could do until the elections in early 1896, when efforts could be made to influence candidates. In the pre-election period there were attempts to coordinate strategy.[40] Leontine Cooper approached Emma Miller to arrange a joint public meeting which would 'show that women of differing views wanted the vote'. Two women from the Woman's Suffrage League and two from the Woman's Equal Franchise Association would make quarter-hour speeches, and each speaker would be free to put her own point of view as to the basis on which the vote should be granted. The public meeting was not held, for Cooper says that before she went ahead she conferred with 'a gentleman of conservative influence in the political world who took part in the movement two years ago'. This could have been the Labor party's bête noir, Dr William Taylor. He advised her against the move as 'if a disturbance occurred it would discredit the movement'. The male politicians had once more thwarted the women in their desire to cooperate.

The Woman's Equal Franchise Association now made a move to embrace the Woman's Christian Temperance Union, and wrote 'asking if they could see their way clear to co-operate with us as their sisters had done in South Australia'. The WCTU *had* cooperated in South Australia, but with a non-partisan Suffrage League. The Union would have had a problem with the Labor organisation because of the basic WCTU tenet that it should stay clear of party politics. The Woman's Equal Franchise Association reported that the letter they sent 'was not even acknowledged, although we know that it was received and read'.[41]

In spite of differences, all suffragists worked very hard for this, their first election. They attended meetings, interviewed individual candidates and sent questionnaires. The Woman's Equal Franchise Association asked 'Are you in favour of extending the vote to women on a single vote basis?' and the *Worker* published the replies. Some approved the vote 'according to the aims of your Association', but others, like John Tozer, the Colonial Secretary, did not. 'If you ask me whether I am in favour of an absolutely indiscriminate suffrage to all women, I say again: certainly not.'[42]

Eleanor Trundle, of the WCTU, attacked the Premier, Hugh Nelson, for not even mentioning woman suffrage in his election speech, and at one of his election meetings Nelson was asked if he believed in it. He replied flippantly: 'I have consulted my matrimonial authority, who thinks that women would be better without it.'[43] The challenger wrote to the *Brisbane Courier* that the Premier's wife 'would seem to be an apathetic and passive member of her unjustly treated sex'.[44] Another member of the outgoing Government, the Attorney-General Thomas Byrnes, advised women to wait for the vote until men had proved that they were incapable of running the country, and then waxed lyrical about individual liberty. He too was attacked by a suffragist in the *Brisbane Courier*. 'Where is woman's individual liberty? ... [the woman] must rank with the horses, dogs and machines made for his use ... Does it ever occur to him, I wonder, that all women do not care to live exclusively for men?'[45]

Nelson, Tozer and Byrnes all retained their positions in the new 1896 Conservative Government. The Labor party increased its representation from sixteen to twenty. Several attempts were made by Liberal and Labor members to reform aspects of the electoral system in the three years of the Government's life, but with no success. The plural vote remained entrenched, and woman suffrage was mentioned only briefly in Parliament. The women continued to work in spite of the political stagnation. In early 1897 the Third Triennial Australasian Convention of the WCTU came to Brisbane and leading suffragists from all over Australia were in town for a week. Elizabeth Nicholls, as Australasian President, addressed a public franchise meeting which resolved: 'That in each Colony where woman's franchise has not been won, the Colonies be asked to circulate petitions in favour of the franchise being granted to women on the same terms as it is now or may hereafter be granted to men.'[46]

When the Queensland WCTU drafted its next petition, no mention was made of the controversial plural vote; it asked for 'the rights and privileges of citizenship so that women can protect themselves from unjust laws'. There was one petition list for women and one for men. They circulated as far north as Thursday Island, and not only Union members went canvassing. Women in Charters Towers and Townsville stood with their lists for four successive Friday nights in what were probably boisterous and rowdy streets. A total of 4000 names was presented to the Assembly on 14 July 1897, but Eleanor Trundle reported dryly that they 'met the usual fate of petitions'.[47]

In early 1898 Hugh Nelson transferred to the Legislative Council, where he continued to oppose woman suffrage, and Thomas Byrnes, who had spoken against the subject on the hustings, became Premier. Byrnes began his term with a tour of country centres, and at Rockhampton the local WCTU sent a deputation. Byrnes' reply was evasive and muddled: 'in times past he was opposed to it ... the logic of the appeal was inexorable

... the women of Queensland did not want it.'[48] The Woman's Equal Franchise Association attacked Byrnes at a special public meeting in Brisbane and asked: 'Does he in future propose only to submit legislation when he is satisfied that it is desired only by the majority so affected?'[49]

A WCTU organiser, Mrs Payne, toured Queensland in 1898 and held eleven public meetings in country centres. The meetings drew good crowds: in some cases the mayor of the town presided and the local member of Parliament attended. Encouraged, the Union decided to step up pressure on Byrnes and wrote asking him to receive a deputation. There was no need for one, replied Byrnes. He had changed his mind on the subject and 'he would take an early opportunity in Parliament of declaring his intentions'.[50] The WCTU, hopeful of a Government bill, held a public franchise meeting as part of its 1898 Convention in September. Their hopes that Byrnes would be their champion were dashed, however, when the 38-year-old Premier died of pneumonia while they were in Convention.

For the 1899 elections all three societies canvassed as they had done in 1896. The WCTU circular promised to assist any candidate 'irrespective of party' who guaranteed to vote for female suffrage if elected. On the Darling Downs, where the Labor party was particularly strong, the WCTU branch objected to the phrase 'irrespective of party' and sent out their own circular, possibly stipulating that candidates should support one-adult-one-vote.[51] All policy speeches were closely vetted by the women, and there was a flurry of letters to the press. James Dickson, the outgoing Premier, aroused their anger with this statement.

> He did not believe in those political platitudes circulated in connection with electoral reform and woman suffrage. There were a great many of these ideas circulated which had no practical application. Whether they had one man one vote or woman suffrage, it would not make two blades of grass grow where there was one before; it would not produce any wool or any more employment for artisans.[52]

'Halcro' accused Dickson of insulting Queensland women: 'The Premier of Queensland has the temerity to refer to this important and world-wide question as one of "sentimental fireworks and political platitudes" ... the question is not one of expediency but justice, and must be treated as such.'[53] The WCTU organised a large protest meeting which was attended by members of the Woman's Equal Franchise Association.[54] It is not known whether women from the Woman's Suffrage League joined in. This was, however, the first sign of cooperation in five years. A Mr Vale attacked Dickson: Wool and blades of grass were important, he said, but the Government which brought in measures to increase productivity was only valid if its powers were derived from the consent of the governed.[55]

Dickson was reinstated as Premier after the 1899 election, leading a Liberal–Conservative Government. He was opposed by eight 'oppositionists' and twenty-one Labor party men led by Anderson Dawson. In September 1899 Queensland males voted in a referendum on the Commonwealth Constitution which gave a one-man-one-vote franchise or, for South Australian electors, a one-adult-one-vote franchise. (Western Australia did not hold its referendum until July 1900.) In the lead-up to the referendum the existing Queensland suffrage was a major discussion point. The female suffragists were angry that they could not have a say in the referendum, and those opposed to the plural vote argued that Queensland's male suffrage should not be different to the Commonwealth suffrage. In the face of this changing climate Dickson promised, if federation were accepted, that he would abolish the plural vote. The Governor's speech when Parliament opened confirmed his intention, but there was no mention of introducing votes for women.[56] The WCTU convention sent a deputation in September asking that the bill be altered, but they 'avoided all mention of disputatious matters'.[57] In his reply Dickson used the vague 'political' language which did not commit himself to action: 'He was certainly taking a broader view and if the other Colonies fell into line he would, or it might be that he would take the lead.'[58] The bill which the Government drafted in October abolished the plural vote, but it did not give women votes. The Home Secretary, Justin Foxton, a staunch opponent of one-man-one-vote, bewailed his fate in having to introduce a bill containing the abolition of plural voting, and went on: 'it would scarcely have done for the Government at the present time ... to adopt the principle of female suffrage ... it is a question which can be properly decided by a poll of the people of Queensland.'[59] When the bill was debated, parliamentary supporters of votes for women did not press for it to be included in case the inclusion endangered one-man-one-vote. In a strange irony, however, the bill to abolish plural voting, so ardently desired by the Labor party, fell victim to a political upheaval which allowed Labor leader Dawson to form the first Labor Government in the world; it lasted eight days before the dismayed Liberals and Conservatives regrouped under Robert Philp.

In June 1900 the new Premier, following a Queensland tradition, made his northern pilgrimage. When challenged by the women in Cairns, he said that perhaps he would put votes for women in the next bill to abolish plural voting.[60] The Labor party at its Convention in Brisbane later that month demanded that he should do so, and on 13 July the three suffrage societies buried their differences to form a deputation led by Cooper, Miller and Trundle. The *Worker* reported that Philp 'positively promised' them a one-adult-one-vote bill. Eleanor Trundle, when she reported back to the WCTU, however, cautioned: 'We must still watch parliamentary proceedings, for the principle has strong opponents in both Houses, and we shall do well to use all our influence with our masculine friends that they in their turn influence their friends in the Legislature.'[61] This was 'backstairs influence' with a vengeance—influencing those who were to do the influencing. The *Brisbane Courier* did not approve of the Premier's soft line: 'Show us the advantages accruing from the existing women's franchises, and we shall consider whether they balance the disadvantages.'[62] The interdenominational Christian Endeavour Youth Convention meeting in Brisbane expressed surprise at the *Courier's* attitude,[63] and the editor was stung to reply that woman suffrage was only a ploy by the Labor party which was trying to abolish plural voting 'behind the petticoats of their households'.[64] Letters poured in attacking the editor (he printed them) and the Christian Endeavour told him that the vote was a right, not a gift.[65] Others protested indignantly that women with the vote might at least have a chance of changing the laws which victimised them and their children. At the height of the controversy Leontine Cooper, as President of the Woman's Suffrage League, wrote a long letter justifying the vote for

BREAKING-UP!
But imagine the consternation of some of the Bold Bad Boys at finding they have to come back so soon!

Premier Arthur Morgan forces the Queensland Legislative Council to reconvene in special session in January 1905 to pass the one-adult-one-vote bill which the Council had rejected in late 1904.
Worker (Brisbane), 17 December 1904. Mitchell Library, State Library of New South Wales.

women.[66] It was an elegant and balanced apologia which puts her in the company of women like Rose Scott, Vida Goldstein and Elizabeth Nicholls. Cooper's letter was the last word in the press controversy, for by now it had become apparent that Philp had no intention of introducing the bill to abolish plural voting in that session, let alone including woman suffrage. For nearly a year he left the one-man-one-vote bill aside, explaining suavely that it existed and he would eventually do something about it.

In August 1901 the promised bill appeared. It abolished the property vote and gave the vote to women, but it also gave an extra vote to a man with two children born in Queensland and 'in lawful wedlock'.[67] The bill was an attempt to give greater voting power to the man who was making Queensland his home, as distinct from the nomad who was perhaps only passing through. There was no hint that the 'baby vote' was to give the husband a 'plural' or superior vote in the family, although it would certainly have done so. There was much merriment in Parliament when the bill reached the debating stage. One member drew a picture of each male elector turning up at the polling station with his wife and children (or perhaps someone else's) to prove that he was entitled to the vote:[68] an interjector called it 'the law of procreation';[69] and another claimed that it was a form of 'phallic worship'.[70] The women were not impressed, either. Elizabeth Nicholls, in Brisbane at the time, called it 'extremely silly',[71] and Emma Miller said the women wanted no 'baby vote', that women had been 'treated as babies and lunatics long enough'.[72] A *Worker* cartoon showed a dummy-brandishing baby holding forth to an audience of toddlers wheeling prams, playing with toys, or just sitting sucking their thumbs.[73] Another justification for the 'baby vote' came from the London *Daily Mail*, which commented just before the bill's introduction: 'In consequences of the steady fall in the birth-rate in Queensland, an Electoral Bill will shortly be introduced, proposing to give every man with two children, born in wedlock, two votes instead of one.'[74] Queensland, like the rest of Australia, was concerned about its falling white birth-rate, but it is doubtful, to say the least, that Queensland men would have valued the extra vote so highly as deliberately to have children in order to gain it. There was so much opposition to the bill that it was shelved without a division.

In March 1902 there was another election. The Philp Liberal–Conservative ministry was returned with a clear majority. Labor's numbers crept to twenty-five, but this was still not enough to threaten Philp's supremacy. Shortly after the new Parliament assembled, William Kidston introduced a private member's bill giving women the vote, but the Government gave it only a short time for debate before it was shelved.[75] In August a combined deputation from the three societies waited on Philp, asking for a Government bill with no nonsensical clauses in it. He smoothly promised them a vote for the next election, but he did nothing.[76] In spite of all his promises, the guileful Philp had done, and would do, nothing to facilitate votes for women in his term of office. One-man-one-vote, promised to the democrats since the Commonwealth referendum in 1899, fared no better.

The fragile cooperation which had existed between the woman suffrage groups since late 1899, when it seemed that the abolition of plural voting was assured, was shattered in 1903, in the lead-up to the first federal elections in which Queensland women could vote. Two new organisations, opposed to each other, were formed to harness the women's votes. The first, the Queensland Women's Electoral League, claimed to represent women's interests and to be apolitical, but it was formed by women with Liberal party connections, guided in its early stages by two Liberal members of the Legislative Assembly, and funded by the Queensland National Defence League, a Liberal–Conservative organisation.[77] Although its stated aim was to work 'to advance political knowledge among women' and 'to promote their interests and guard those of children', another aim emphasised its anti-Labor attitudes: 'To encourage and preserve private enterprise, and to combat unnecessary interference by the State with the individual rights and liberties of its citizens.'[78]

Labor women had attended the public meeting at which the Queensland Women's Electoral League was launched, but deserted when it became apparent that its agenda put it in the Liberal–Conservative camp. Emma Miller and her associates then formed its Labor counterpart, the Women Workers' Political Organisation.[79] Its platform, too, was a mixture of women's issues and party aims: it included equal marriage and divorce laws, equal pay for equal work, and nationalisation of monopolies.[80] The WCTU reacted to the formation of the two new societies by emphasising that its own members must not be biased by 'the venom of party politics', and Agnes Williams in her lecture tour of the north before the Commonwealth election hammered this point.[81]

In October 1903 the Queensland Women's Electoral League invited Rose Scott to visit the state to organise 'in the interests of the League',[82] but those who instigated the visit had misjudged Scott if they thought that she could be coopted for the advantage of any political group. Fresh from the formation of her own non-party group in 1902, after women in New South Wales gained their state vote, Scott accepted the expenses but would not be bound by any limitations:

> I made one thing clear before leaving Sydney, and that was that I should be absolutely free in using my own discretion as to what I would say and making it a sine qua non that nothing in the shape of party politics would be imported into my meetings.[83]

Scott addressed the league's meetings in Brisbane and the major Queensland towns, travelling long distances on her tour. Country meetings usually turned into general meetings for women of all persuasions who had heard of her work for women in New South Wales. In Brisbane she went out of her way to talk to Woman's Equal Franchise Association groups and to WCTU meetings. She told an interviewer when she returned to Sydney: 'At Brisbane I was the guest of two parties, as it were ... the Conservative and the Democratic, and I fancy I must have kept the balance between them fairly well, for on the eve of my departure I received congratulatory messages and floral tributes from both sections.'[84] Perhaps deliberately naive, Scott chose not to see the plural vote as a party issue: 'she was shocked to learn that ... [it] still existed; she called on the women ... to use all their influence to induce the new Government to bring in an Electoral Reform Bill abolishing the iniquitous plural vote and giving one adult one vote.'[85] Whether Scott discomfited her host organisation by her stand we do not know; they treated her as an honoured guest. She certainly endeared herself to the Labor women both by her condemnation of plural voting and by her grasp of economic issues affecting women.

In October 1903 the Philp ministry fell and was replaced by another Liberal ministry led by Arthur Morgan. Although it was not a suffrage organisation per se, the Queensland Women's Electoral League, perhaps influenced by Scott's admonitions, sent a deputation to the new Premier. Mrs E. Harris, the Vice-President, told Morgan that they came from 'a newly-organized society to show that a large body of women who had not been included in former deputations were now wishful to have the State Franchise'.[86] Morgan promised that an electoral reform bill including woman suffrage would be introduced the following year, but before next year came there had been a dissolution and the colony went to an election.

In the August 1904 election Labor returned thirty-four members—the largest group in Parliament. It was not large enough for Labor to govern in its own right, but it was able to form a coalition with the Liberals, with Morgan as Premier. Many enemies of woman suffrage were defeated in the election, and the Woman's Equal Franchise Association felt so certain now of one-adult-one-vote that they held a celebration social. The Morgan ministry did not disappoint them; in October 1904 it introduced a bill giving adult suffrage and abolishing the plural vote.[87] The bill passed the Assembly on the voices, but was thrown out of the Council on a vote of 19–12.[88] Frederick Brentnall, Elizabeth's husband, voted against it because he did not approve of the abolition of plural voting. The Political Labor Council, outraged at the Legislative Council's defiance, held a large protest meeting on 2 November, at which Emma Miller moved one of the resolutions presented to the Premier the following night.

> We, the women of Brisbane in meeting assembled, desire to enter our protest in the strongest possible manner against the action of a majority of members of the Legislative Council, which has resulted in a rejection by that Chamber of the Franchise Bill, and we call upon Premier Morgan and his following in Parliament to brook no delay from the irresponsible nominee Upper House, as it is high time that the stain was removed from the fair name of Queensland of having for so long penalized her women by denying them their just political rights.[89]

The *Worker* launched a vitriolic attack demanding the abolition of 'this House of Prejudice, Privilege and Property',[90] and even the *Brisbane Courier*, while still reflecting its ambivalence towards the measure, was critical of the Council's 'disrespect':

> The principle of one-man-one-vote has been demanded by the people of this country, and the extension of the franchise to women is undoubtedly a policy of the Government returned to power by so large a majority that it is useless to treat such a measure with anything but the proper respect.[91]

It was out of order to submit the bill again in the same session, so the Labor–Liberal Government announced that a special 'franchise' session of both Houses would be called during the summer recess. On 5 January a reluctant Parliament assembled, in a temperature of forty degrees Celsius, to hear the Governor announce that he had called them together because 'my advisers are of the opinion that the will of the people with regard to electoral reform ... should be carried into effect without delay'.[92] Watched by a gallery of women 'wearing simple white costumes in keeping with the great heat',[93] the Assembly quickly passed the Electoral Franchise Bill giving one-adult-one-vote. It went to the Council, where it was passed with only a few grumbles of dissent. The Council was well aware that the Assembly had the power to flood the chamber with nominees who were sympathetic both to adult franchise and to the abolition of the Upper House. The jubilant suffragists were again in the gallery to watch the Upper House yield. Premier Morgan then asked them to afternoon tea and himself helped to hand around the cakes.[94] There was, sadly, one important figure missing from the tea party. Leontine Cooper died in 1903, after some years of ill-health. The *Worker* reported:

> The friends of Mrs Leontine Cooper, the pioneer woman suffragist in Queensland, will regret that she did not live to see the vote granted to women of this State. Mrs Cooper wanted the vote at any price, and she did not see eye to eye with Labor women, but she kept the suffrage flag flying by the spoken and written word for many years.[95]

The Woman's Equal Franchise Association had a celebration social and disbanded itself, and the Woman's Christian Temperance Union later in the year held a 'thanksgiving service'. In the absence of records we do not know whether the Woman's Suffrage League, of which the late Leontine Cooper had been President for so many years, held a celebration.

When Queensland women first went to the state ballot box in 1907, Elizabeth Brentnall was an invalid and voted by post. Agnes Williams and Eleanor Trundle helped to form the National Council of Women in 1905, and Williams served as President for two years and Vice-President for fifteen. Emma Miller,[96] who was sixty-six when the vote was granted, lived till 1917, conspicuous in the Labor movement till the last. During the 1912 general strike she led a contingent of women in a march on Parliament House which confronted mounted police and foot police with batons. In the melee she is said to have caused the Commissioner's horse to throw him by plunging a hat pin into its rump. She was still helping Labor candidates on the hustings in 1915 and campaigned against conscription during World War I. She was seventy-eight when she died, and the Labor movement mourned its 'Mother Miller' with due ceremony: the Labor Premier gave the funeral oration and the Trades Hall flew its flag at half mast.

Notes

1. *Boomerang*, 24 December 1887.
2. ibid., 16 May 1889.
3. ibid., 18 July 1889.
4. Most of the information about Leontine Cooper comes from an obituary article in *Woman's Sphere*, April 1903.
5. *Worker* (Brisbane), 21 July 1900.
6. *Dawn*, March 1894.
7. *Boomerang*, 8 December 1888.
8. *Dawn*, August 1890.
9. Pam Young, 'The struggle for woman suffrage (Queensland)', p. 1.
10. Sylvia Lawson, 'Edited, Printed and Published by Women', *Nation*, 25 October 1958.
11. *Woman's Voice*, July 1895.
12. *Brisbane Courier*, 28 July 1890.
13. *Boomerang*, 27 July 1889.
14. *Brisbane Courier*, 28 July 1890.
15. *Dawn*, April 1891.

16. *Worker* (Brisbane), 13 June 1891.
17. *QPD*, vol. 61, 31 July 1890, p. 438.
18. ibid., p. 441.
19. *Worker* (Brisbane), 6 June 1903.
20. ibid., 11 October 1902.
21. WCTU of Queensland, Annual Report, 1888.
22. ibid., 1890.
23. ibid., 1891.
24. ibid., 1893.
25. *Brisbane Courier*, 18 December 1893.
26. ibid., 24 February 1894.
27. *Worker* (Brisbane), 3 March 1894.
28. *QPD*, vol. 66, 19 July 1892, p. 68.
29. *Worker* (Brisbane), 3 March 1894.
30. ibid.
31. ibid., 7 March 1894.
32. *Brisbane Courier*, 23 March, 4 April 1894.
33. ibid., 28 April 1894.
34. ibid., WCTU of Queensland, Annual Report, 1895.
35. Obituary of Emma Miller, *Daily Mail*, 23 January 1917.
36. *QPD*, vol. 71, 6 September 1894, p. 464.
37. 'Extracts from a speech on woman suffrage given at the Locke Memorial Hall, Bedlington, by Thomas Glassey, June 1 1912', Glassey, Thomas: Papers, OL:Q OM 64-2.
38. *QPD*, vol. 71, 28 September 1894, p. 716.
39. George Thorn, ibid., p. 718.
40. Details of these moves are in Woman's Equal Franchise Association, Report of the Second Annual Meeting, in the *Brisbane Courier*, 1 April 1896, and the *Worker* (Brisbane), 4 April 1896; letter from Catherine Hughes to the *Brisbane Courier*, 3 March 1896; letter from Leontine Cooper to the *Brisbane Courier*, 2 April 1896.
41. *Worker* (Brisbane), 4 April 1896.
42. ibid., 14 March 1896.
43. *Brisbane Courier*, 20 March 1896.
44. ibid.
45. ibid., 24 March 1896.
46. WCTU of Australasia, Report of the Third Triennial Convention, Brisbane, 1897.
47. Details of this petition and the canvassing are in WCTU of Queensland, Annual Reports, 1897, 1898.
48. *Rockhampton Daily Record*, 31 May 1898.
49. From a resolution passed by the Woman's Equal Franchise Association and reprinted in Womanhood Suffrage League of New South Wales, Annual Report, 1898.
50. WCTU of Queensland, Annual Report, 1898.
51. ibid.; letters to the *Brisbane Courier* from Mrs Eleanor Trundle and Mrs Agnes Williams, 20 February 1898.
52. A summary of the Premier's 'Address to the Electorate', in *Brisbane Courier*, 21 February 1899.
53. 'Halcro' to the *Brisbane Courier*, 22 February 1899.
54. *Brisbane Courier*, 24 February 1899.
55. ibid.
56. *QPD*, vol. 82, 12 September 1899, p. 1.
57. WCTU of Queensland, Annual Report, 1899.

58. ibid.
59. *QPD*, vol. 82, 7 November 1899, p. 846.
60. Unidentified, undated newspaper clipping in Womanhood Suffrage League of New South Wales: note-books of the Secretary, and newspaper clippings, ML:NSW, MSS 38/35, item 4:151.
61. WCTU of Queensland, Annual Report, 1900.
62. *Brisbane Courier*, 28 July 1900.
63. ibid., 27 August 1900.
64. ibid., 1 September 1900.
65. ibid., 31 August 1900.
66. ibid., 1 September 1900.
67. *QPD*, vol. 88, 13 November 1901, p. 1815.
68. William Maxwell, ibid., p. 1818.
69. An interjector, ibid., p. 1820.
70. Joseph Turley, ibid., p. 1843.
71. *Worker* (Brisbane), 21 September 1901.
72. ibid., 30 August 1902.
73. ibid., 23 November 1901.
74. Quoted by William Browne, *QPD*, vol. 88, 14 November 1901, p. 1843.
75. *QPD*, vol. 89, 7 August 1902, p. 265.
76. *Worker* (Brisbane), 23, 30 August 1892.
77. Minutes of Meetings, July–December 1903, in Queensland Women's Electoral League: Papers, July 1903–August 1908, OL:Q, OM 7147; *Worker* (Brisbane), 18 July, 15, 22 August 1903.
78. Anne Wood, 'Women's Organizations in Queensland, 1859–1958', *Royal Historical Society of Queensland Journal: Centenary Issue*, p. 192.
79. *Worker* (Brisbane), 15 August 1903.
80. ibid., 29 September 1903.
81. WCTU of Queensland, Annual Report, 1903.
82. Minutes of meetings on 10 and 12 September 1903, Queensland Women's Electoral League: Papers, July 1903–August 1908, OL:Q, OM 7147.
83. Rose Scott, quoted in an unsourced, undated newspaper clipping, Women's Political and Educational League of New South Wales: Papers and newspaper clippings, ML:NSW, MSS 38/43, item 93.
84. 'The Women's Movement in Queensland', undated newspaper clipping from the *Daily Telegraph*, Women's Political and Educational League of New South Wales: Papers, 1902–1903, ML:NSW, MSS 38/40, item 95.
85. *Bundaberg Daily Times*, 17 October 1903.
86. *Our Federation*, 15 November 1903.
87. *QPD*, vol. 93, 18 October 1904, p. 121.
88. *QPD*, vol. 94, 20 October 1904, p. 454.
89. *Woman's Sphere*, October 1904.
90. *Worker* (Brisbane), 20 October 1904.
91. *Brisbane Courier*, 21 October 1904.
92. *QPD*, vol. 94, 4 January 1905, p. 1.
93. *Daily Mail*, 5 January 1905.
94. *Worker* (Brisbane), 4 February 1905.
95. ibid.
96. Pam Young's biography, *Proud to be a Rebel: the life and times of Emma Miller*, is to be launched while this book is in press.

8

VICTORIA, 1908

Within a year of its election on a property franchise for both Houses in 1856, the first Victorian Parliament had granted manhood suffrage for its Assembly. This early democratisation of the Lower House, however, was balanced by the retention of an extremely high property qualification for the Upper House, and by the introduction of plural voting for both Houses based on property. Even though there were to be modifications of its franchise in 1869 and 1881, the Victorian Upper House would still be, when organised woman suffrage agitation began in the 1880s, the most representative of power and privilege of all the Australian Upper Houses. The confrontation between the two Houses which was built into the Victorian parliamentary system by the polarity of their franchises was to be one, but only one, of the factors delaying votes for women until 1908.

When the bill to grant manhood suffrage was before the Assembly in 1857, the first voice was raised in support of votes for women. George Higinbotham was editor of the then radical *Argus*. He applauded manhood suffrage, but wrote that only when 'every man' and 'every woman' had a vote would the limits of electoral reform be reached.[1] He was not proposing that votes for women be included in this bill; it was an ideal to be striven for in the future. The Irish-born Higinbotham, who had arrived in the colony only a year before, was then an idealistic young barrister of thirty. He was to remain three years with the *Argus* before clashing with its more conservative owner, Edward Wilson.[2] When he relinquished its editorship Higinbotham turned his attention to politics, so was there when Victorian women ratepayers were given the state vote by mistake.

In 1863 an Act was passed which lowered the property qualification for plural voting for the Legislative Assembly to that required for the municipal franchise. It was decided that the municipal rolls would be used as a basis for compiling the state electoral rolls. The Act which validated this procedure used the phrase 'all persons' when referring to those on the municipal rolls whose names were to be transferred.[3] Overlooked by those who drafted the bill and by those who voted on it was the fact that propertied females were given the municipal vote in the 1863 Act, and their names would thus be transferred. The resulting state enfranchisement of female ratepayers came to light in the 1864 Assembly elections. Women turned up to record their votes and some candidates, realising that here was a possible source of support, wooed them by conveying them to and from the polling booths.[4]

A bill came before the Assembly in 1865 to remove some of the anomalies of the 1863 Act. It made no mention of the phenomenon of women having voted. John Dane, however, moved an amendment that 'all persons' in the 1863 Act should be altered to 'all male persons' and the women's names expunged from the state roll.[5] Higinbotham, although now known to favour votes for women, supported the withdrawal of the privilege because it 'should not have been conferred upon them inadvertently'.[6] The women lost their vote, but there was a surprising amount of support in the Assembly for leaving the position as it was. The debate was short, but for the first time in any Australian Parliament arguments which were to become well-worn were aired. Graham Berry cast the first of a long line of hostile aspersions which were to be particularly characteristic of the Victorian campaign: 'it was an unmitigated evil ... It was generally the worst type of female who had voted ... many of these women, after voting once, personated other women who were on the roll.'[7] The oversight had enfranchised only a small number of women, for male ratepayers outnumbered females by ten to one.[8] Nevertheless the Victorian suffragists in later decades were able to create a myth from what had happened to sustain them in their struggle: women had once entered the Promised Land, but had been driven out of it.

In 1873, during the passage of a bill for the redistribution of electorates, John Richardson tried in an amendment to restore the vote to female ratepayers who were, he said, usually single women or widows.[9] He claimed that he had received letters urging the reversal from 'several ladies, some of them holding a high position in the colony'. Higinbotham supported Richardson in a long speech claiming that woman's lack of a political voice was 'a badge and a result of the degraded position of the sex'.[10] Richardson's amendment passed by two votes, so Higinbotham decided to go further. He moved that a clause be added to the bill to give *every* adult female a vote.[11] There was a long debate on Higinbotham's move, but the bill was defeated 40–16. Henry Wrixon's remarks give a clue as to why Richardson's move was accepted and Higinbotham's was not. Richardson's franchise, being mainly for single or widowed property holders, was not looked upon as a franchise for women as such; it was for unrepresented property: 'The question now before the Committee was simply whether female ratepayers, who had no one to vote for them, should be enabled to exercise the rights of property.'[12] The Assembly debate was academic, for the Legislative Council, vehemently opposed to the electoral redistribution in the bill, rejected it out of hand. Higinbotham's move was to be his first and only for female suffrage in Parliament. In 1876 he resigned, in 1880 he was appointed to the Supreme Court, and in 1886 became Chief Justice. From these offices he was to be a consistent supporter of the early suffragists, but was to die in 1892, just as the struggle was gaining in intensity.

There were unsuccessful moves in 1876[13] and 1888[14] to restore the lost vote by amendments to electoral bills, and incidental mentions of the subject in Parliament, but by the time the first woman suffrage bill per se was introduced in the Assembly in 1889, the women themselves had entered the arena.

By the mid-1880s 'Marvellous Melbourne' was the largest city in Australia and the seventh largest in the British Empire. The great gold rushes of the 1850s had swelled the population of the colony from 77,000 to 540,000 in ten years, and by 1881 it had 862,000 inhabitants, two-fifths of the population of the whole continent. This fortuitous immigration from all over the world which fed back into Melbourne meant that the city in the 1880s was the least insular in Australia. It was prosperous and showy, and exuded optimism about its own future. A rich life of theatre and opera and a winter season of spectacular balls gave the affluent the opportunity for opulent display through the finery worn by their wives and daughters. The most wealthy built themselves palatial homes with sweeping lawns and conservatories, and in the 1870s and 1880s a building boom was transforming the city into one of substantial business houses, luxury hotels, coffee palaces (for the great number of temperance adherents) and handsome churches and public buildings. In this atmosphere many levels of cultural life thrived, not necessarily exclusive of each other. There was the life of books, intellect and ideas for the well-educated and widely read; social and reformist Christianity flourished as well as temperance and evangelical Christianity; and there was a strong current of secularism and free thought searching for moral and philosophical alternatives to the Christian ethic. All these levels were to provide support for woman suffrage, leading to a surprisingly harmonious diversity which existed nowhere else in Australia. The city was also the most industrialised on the continent. It and the large mining centres of Ballarat and Bendigo nourished a substantial proletariat with a growing working-class consciousness. A strong male trade union movement existed and, in certain areas of work, concomitant female trade unions. The political Labor party which grew out of the unions was, as elsewhere, to provide another recruiting ground for suffrage supporters.

In the Victorian Legislative Assembly shifting factional alignments were just beginning to settle into a loose division between Constitutionalists (vaguely Liberal) and Conservatives. The Constitutionalists were waging an unremitting war against the power of the Upper House to obstruct change which might in any conceivable way erode members' and supporters' privileges, and the Conservatives were determined that the Upper House should retain its powers. Many of the Conservatives, however, were in favour of lowering the Legislative Council franchise to a level which would give greater representation to urban wealth as compared to rural. The woman suffrage question was to be caught up and buffetted about by these shifting parliamentary currents.

The complex and heterogeneous world that was Victorian society was served by a concurrently diverse press. Two major dailies provided opposing comment on day-to-day colonial and world events. The *Argus* had been converted to a conservative mouthpiece after its short run under Higinbotham in the 1850s, while the *Age* had gained itself the reputation of being the champion of the radical Liberal cause and the scourge of the

Upper House. The *Argus* was to oppose woman suffrage and the *Age* to support it, but there were complications in this neat division in 1903, as we shall see. Smaller publications—exported to other colonies which could not support their own—served every taste, from the satirical to the acquiescent, and from the subversive to that entrenched in custom and tradition. Topics chosen by debating groups and suffrage societies reflected the controversies of the press and society. Among the multiplicity of subjects, that of 'women's rights' loomed large: whether women belonged in the home only, in public life, in the factories or the professions; whether they should be educated and if so, how far and for what; what their legal rights in marriage were, and so on. In Victoria the question of whether women should vote was set more firmly in the wider debate than it was in the still largely frontier societies of Queensland, Tasmania and Western Australia, or in the more conciliatory societies of South Australia and New South Wales. Because of this, Victorian suffragists were to attract more odium from those who were concerned about the effect which 'the new woman' might have on the established structures of society.

Henrietta Dugdale, very much a woman of the wider movement, claimed to be the first female suffragist when she began agitating in 1859.

> I was the first—for sixteen years previous to the formation of our Victorian Women's Suffrage Society—and only woman who publicly advocated the moral right of woman to her share in political power; also, to other human rights, University learning, and possession of her property after marriage. Of course male opponents showed fight; but, during the controversy, no woman offered public argument for or against, so I had to combat inane and insulting opposition unaided by the sex I was defending. To the press I was greatly indebted for support in always granting space for publication of my opinions on the franchise for women, then considered dangerous, revolutionary. I frequently received private letters of thanks, which proved to me how far extended was the ambition among women for legal justice in their lives.[15]

As 26-year-old Henrietta Davies, Dugdale had migrated to Victoria in 1852 with a husband she had married when she was fourteen years old. By 1859 her first husband had died, she had married William Dugdale, and she had a son and two daughters. Perhaps her observation of the early Chartist movement was what gave her strong feelings about the equality of all in society; she claimed in later life that one of her most vivid memories was of the Chartist riots.[16] Perhaps the law which subsumed all property of the married woman into that of the husband had adversely affected her, for it was to be the focus of her most stinging attacks. A clue that she had been affected in some way by discriminatory legislation comes in a passage from *A Few Hours in a Far Off Age*, which she published in 1883, the year before she helped to form the first Victorian suffrage society. She was then in her late fifties: 'My [sic] suffering has been borne; no alteration of the laws could now benefit me; but there are thousands enduring the pain I have experienced through man's injustice, and thousands to follow before there be just legislation.'[17]

By the time Dugdale published *A Few Hours in a Far Off Age* she was a member of both the Eclectics (devoted to the discussion of controversial subjects), and the Australian Secular Association (which attracted those who considered themselves to be freethinkers on religious and moral questions). She was also a friend and admirer of Higinbotham, to whom she dedicated her book. Dugdale used *A Few Hours in a Far Off Age* as a vehicle for her radical ideas about education, marriage, Christianity and rational dress. She herself adopted the long tunic worn over loose trousers, known as the bloomer in America, after Amelia Bloomer who first advocated the costume. The protagonist in Dugdale's book travels forward in time to a country where all the problems of women in society have been solved. This Utopian progress was put in train when a man called Higinbotham gave women the right to vote. The woman's vote leads to a world where there is complete equality between the sexes, and marriage partners relate to each other as loving companions rather than as antagonists. Children are obedient and respectful and are educated to become 'benevolent, courageous and intelligent adults'. Women despise corsets and stilt heels which restrict the body's movements. War is unthinkable, prostitution does not exist. Neither does drunkenness and its corollary, ill-treatment of women. There are no neglected children and no suffering animals. Women do not have to do heavy work and are not paid lower wages than men.

This distilled Utopia was to be the stuff of Australian suffragists' dreams, although few would have imagined Dugdale's flying machine which could fly a hundred and forty miles per hour between Melbourne and Sydney! The element of secularism in her life and work, however, was to place Dugdale at variance with many in the later suffrage movement. In her book and her life she placed much of the blame for women's subjection on the Christian church—a possibility which few Australian suffragists were willing to explore. Nevertheless the Victorian movement was, as will be seen, able to accommodate her and others of like mind. She was to live through the agitation, marrying for the third time about 1903—when she was seventy-seven[18]—and exercising her vote several times before she died in 1918, aged ninety-two.

A friend of this iconoclastic Utopian was the gentler, but just as dedicated, Annie Lowe.[19] She, then in her early fifties too, was to help Dugdale form the Victorian Women's Suffrage Society in 1884, and to grow old with her in the subsequent twenty-four years of agitation. Annie Lowe was a second-generation Australian whose grandfather had been one of the earliest settlers on the Hawkesbury River in New South Wales. She gave her father the credit for her social and political landscape: 'He discussed politics before his boys and girls. We imbibed his broad and liberal views. Boys and girls, we were trained equally. We girls were taught that what was good for the boys was good for us to know.' Among the snippets of information about Lowe's early life (the only sources are a few interviews given when she was an elderly woman) are that she had witnessed the first election under responsible government in Australia (she would have been twenty-one and living in New South Wales) and that she was a friend of the poet Henry Kendall. He had, she said, written to her, and poems about her. One cannot but surmise an early romance. She bore at least two children to the husband who took her outback to live, 'seven hundred miles further than others had been ... [we] crossed rivers on a raft of logs or a tree dug-out ... The blacks came in swarms to look at me.' The year is not known, but she said that when she came to Melbourne 'where whispers of it were in the air', the woman suffrage cause appealed to her naturally: 'I applied my father's arguments for manhood suffrage to the women's cause.'

Lowe was to work actively for woman suffrage, as an office holder in societies and as one of the movement's most valuable speakers, until 1908, two years before her death at seventy-six. She has been overshadowed by Vida Goldstein's spectacular participation in the last eight years of the campaign, but she should be put in her rightful place as one of the most important and committed women of the Australian movement. Comments draw a picture of a thoroughly likeable person with a sharp mind, persuasive manner and optimistic disposition. She mixed easily with suffragists from Dugdale to the Woman's Christian Temperance Union women. In 1909 the *Weekly Times* described her as 'an intellectual, a woman with a broad mind and a most delightful wit. Her manner is natural, warm and breezy ... [she has] courage and independence of spirit ... Australian—that is the word for it.' To her is credited the reply to the charge that the suffragists were like 'shrieking old cockatoos'. It was the male cockatoo which did the shrieking, she said 'very sweetly, very politely'.

Precipitating the formation of the Victorian Women's Suffrage Society in 1884 could have been the wave of crimes of violence against women in that year, and anger at the legal stratagems used by the accused to avoid trial or, if arraigned and convicted, at the leniency of the sentences handed down on them. In June an *Age* editorial accused the legal system of abrogating its responsibility to protect women,[20] and a few weeks earlier Dugdale had attacked the courts in a letter to the *Melbourne Herald*.[21] Contrary to popular belief, she wrote passionately, 'nice' women *were* discussing these cases (many involved rape), and their anger was compounded by the fact that those who inflicted the violence on women had a share in the making of the laws while their victims did not.

Annie Lowe said that the genesis of the society lay in a meeting between her and Dugdale at which they spoke of votes for women and decided to contact others to discuss it.[22] The resultant meeting of 'that gallant pioneer band of twenty women'[23] (although there were men present) was held at the home of a Mrs Rennick on 25 May 1884. Dugdale was in the chair and the meeting formed itself into a committee with a sub-committee to draw up a Constitution. Vida Goldstein later reported that their early champion Higinbotham was not there, but sent 'a handsome donation'.[24]

The committee formed on 25 May called a general meeting on 22 June, which was attended by fifty women and twenty men.[25] The Reverend Dr Bromby, the Canon of St Paul's Anglican Cathedral, snowy-haired but sparse and fit from his strict health regimen, chaired the meeting. He was a well-known supporter of higher education for women and he favoured female suffrage, but he showed in his introduction that he was very much a man of his times. Condemning the moves of the 1860s to confer the vote on female ratepayers only, and reasoning from the dubious premise that women would hold the same opinions as their husbands, he argued that it was right for the family, as the bedrock of society, to have double representation:

> It was said that married women would have a double vote with their husbands and that would tell against single men and place them at a disadvantage, but as a married man possessed a greater stake in the country by reason of his marriage he was deserving of another vote.[26]

Lowe and Dugdale both spoke, and both emphasised that women needed the vote to gain greater protection from violence: 'The laws for offenses against property were very severe, but for brutal offenses against women they were not.'[27]

The platform proposed by the committee and presented to the meeting by Dugdale was for votes for women on the same conditions as men, but 'with the restriction of an educational test by writing legibly the name of the candidate on the ballot paper'—a provision which was quite lost sight of in future agitation.[28] The platform gave women plural voting rights as well as the primary vote, but no attempt was made, as in Queensland, to entangle woman suffrage with the plural voting issue. A motion to limit the vote to female ratepayers had little support, although the mover, a Mrs Webster, claimed that it would have more chance of success. Seconding the latter, a hapless Mr Black wanted to know whether the meeting proposed to place the vote 'in the hands of the courtezan': 'What the speaker had intended to say could not be heard amid the indignant interjections.'[29] Neither Lowe nor Dugdale were elected to office at the meeting, although both became committee members. Dugdale became President the following year.

The women of the new society were both enthusiastic and optimistic. Dugdale wrote a few days after the meeting: 'the men of Victoria are certainly going to lead the way, by setting Conservative Old England the example by granting *justice to woman* [sic], so idiotically denied to her by the wooden heads of the past!'[30] The new organisation operated on the usual levels: public meetings which formulated resolutions,[31] letters to the press, and distribution of literature. Deputations also waited on politicians and prominent citizens for support. At its public meetings Dugdale, Lowe and Brettena Smyth, who became a member of the committee a year after it was formed, were the chief speakers. The numbering system of leaflets scattered through collections indicate that its propaganda was extensive; one is labelled no. 27. By June 1885 there were 195 members and an attendance of a hundred at the first annual meeting.[32] For all the exuberance and high hopes of these early women, there was to be no parliamentary response until after the formation of a second organisation, a breakaway from the first, by Brettena Smyth in 1888.[33]

Smyth had developed as a vigorous and valued speaker under the auspices of the Victorian Women's Suffrage Society, but it is possible that by 1888 the direction her public life was taking was causing tension between her and some of the other members. Like her English torchbearer Annie Besant, she had become convinced that the most pressing inequality faced by the great mass of women was not public, but private: overwork, economic deprivation, and ill-health—all caused by frequent and involuntary child-bearing. When she launched the Australian Women's Suffrage Society, which was to be linked in the public mind with her advocacy of the right of every woman to advice about, and access to, contraceptives, Smyth had been a widow for seven years. She had earned a living for herself and her family by converting the greengrocery and confectionery business she had managed with her husband into one combining drapery and druggist lines.[34] In 1887, when she was forty-five years old, she had enrolled as one of the first female students in the Medical School of the Melbourne University. Forced to drop out after passing her first exams because her savings were lost in one of the late 1880s financial crashes, she was to save some more, lose her money again, and drop out again. In 1893, when she was fifty-one, a Melbourne journal reported, 'Mrs Smyth has again risen above her misfortunes, and hopes to save the University fees at no distant date.'[35]

The formation of the Australian Women's Suffrage Society was not the only initiative Smyth took in 1888. A judgment in Sydney that year made it possible to advertise and sell contraceptives. She immediately took advantage of the ruling, indiscriminately mixing drapery, babies' needs and 'preventatives' in her advertisements.

Best Female French Preventatives or Contraceptives, 10/6. English, 5/6 ... French Preventatives (male), 10/6 and 15/6 per dozen ... Ingram's Improved Seamless Enema and Syringes, highly polished, 12/6 ... Ladies Silk Stockings: all sizes, from 8/6 upwards ... Baby Charms and Comforters.[36]

By the early 1890s she was writing moderately priced booklets on women's health and birth control: ' "Love, Courtship and Marriage", with 50 illustrations, 1/- ... "Limitation of Offspring", illus, 1/6 ... "The Causes of Sterility and Barrenness", 1/-.'[37]

Her books were eagerly bought by those desperate for such information; 'Limitation of Offspring' went to eight editions. Smyth also launched into public lectures, for which she charged a fee. Some of them were for women only. One newspaper said that her very name meant 'BUMPER HOUSE'.[38] Surrounded by her 'life-sized skeletons and large diagrams',[39] she must have been a striking figure on the platform, for she was described as being 'well-nigh six feet in her evening shoes'[40] and 'muscular and well-developed ... with a perfect disdain for a broomstick waist'.[41] Lectures usually ended with a 'delineation of character' using phrenology, one of the pseudo-scientific obsessions of the age. Although women in large numbers read her books and attended her lectures, the gospel preached by Smyth was not a popular one with officialdom when politicians were pontificating about the need to build up a defence force and fill Australia's empty spaces. Many suffragists either rejected her stand or found it impolitic. In 1897 at least two of the large societies disowned her.[42] They particularly objected to the fact that she was distributing her advertisements for contraceptives with literature from the Australian Women's Suffrage Society.

Among those who became members of Smyth's organisation were two writers visiting Melbourne, the Swedish Axel Gustafson and his American-born wife. In the year they were there Axel Gustafson wrote at least three rather prolix pamphlets for the Australian Women's Suffrage Society,[43] but in spite of early propaganda with these the society does not seem to have been a strong one. It limped along through the 1890s, overtaken by other organisations. In 1897 Smyth, encouraged by the success of her books and lectures (she did not go back to university) closed down her business and prepared for an Australian and overseas tour. She became ill just before she was due to leave and died in Melbourne in 1898, and her society seems to have died with her. Of the three outstanding pioneers, Smyth's 'commanding presence'[44] was to be missed when Lowe and Dugdale were lauded at the 1908 victory celebrations. One of those who helped Smyth form the Australian Women's Suffrage Society was a colourful 34-year-old socialist medical practitioner, Dr William Maloney,[45] who was elected to the Victorian Legislative Assembly in 1889 on behalf of the Workingmen's Political League. Elected with him was William Trenwith, President of the Melbourne Trades and Labor Council. These two were the first directly to represent the Labor movement in the Victorian legislature. On 24 September 1889 Maloney rose in the House and asked leave to introduce a bill 'for removing all sex disabilities in regard to voting'.[46] If he appeared in his usual bohemian style that day, he would have waxed his moustache—but not his goatee beard—and would have been wearing a cream silk suit with a red or yellow tie. His panama hat would have been in the cloakroom.[47] The sober-suited Assembly greeted Maloney's bill with 'jeers, sneers and cat-calls'.[48] If there were any supporters on the Liberal benches, they were silent. When it seemed that there would be no seconder, a latecomer to the chamber, the elderly Colonel Tom Smith, rescued him,[49] but the bill died, as the Conservative Government gave it no time for discussion in the session. To Maloney, however, belonged the honour of introducing the first specific woman suffrage bill in Victoria. The suffragists showed their gratitude for this and for his later support when 20,000 of them signed a testimonial to him in 1908.[50]

In November 1890 the Government fell to a no-confidence motion, and the financier George Munro became Premier. The Woman's Christian Temperance Union, now well established, rejoiced; Munro was a strong temperance man and might be persuaded to take kindly to votes for women.

Mary Leavitt established the WCTU in Victoria in 1885. By 1887 there were twelve branches and the first Colonial Convention was held. The progress from then on was rapid: twenty-three branches in 1888, thirty-two in 1889, and by 1891 fifty-seven branches.[51] The credit for this rapid growth lies with another American WCTU woman, Mary Love, who arrived in 1886, not as a missionary but, having been recently widowed, to stay with her sister-in-law's family.[52] By 1888 she had become President of the Colonial Union and had travelled 200,000 miles throughout the colony, forming new branches and forestalling Jessie Ackermann by putting them on a sound organisational basis. Love's statements on suffrage show a progression of thought; in 1888 and 1889 she was saying that women should influence male voters to choose men who would put controls on liquor traffic, but by 1890 she was claiming 'the more effective voice at the ballot-box for women'[53] and the 1890 Convention passed a resolution:

> That as men and women are alike in having to obey the laws, this meeting declares its conviction that they should also be equal in electing those who make the laws; and, further, that the ballot in the hands of women would be a safeguard to the home, in which the interests of women are paramount, and as what is good for the home is also good for the State, the enfranchisement of women would be conducive to the highest national welfare.[54]

It was the classic WCTU resolution: benefits to the State wedded to abstract justice. Mrs McLean, to be a major WCTU voice in the Victorian movement, read a paper which the Union published as a pamphlet to launch its campaign.

When Parliament resumed in 1891 the WCTU combined with the Victorian Alliance (a male temperance organisation) in a deputation to Munro, the temperance Premier. He promised only that he would bring the matter before his Cabinet. Munro had good reason to be cautious; he led a fragile coalition of those Liberals who were disenchanted with the Conservatives' handling of the economy, a few Independents, and the two Labor men. He asked whether the women wanted the vote for female ratepayers only and they replied: 'We are asking for and expecting to get the same privileges as our brothers.'[55] In that case, replied Munro, perhaps hoping to be relieved of any responsibility, there would need to be united and representative agitation.

The WCTU approached the two suffrage societies, and to show that women were indeed in earnest a combined effort was launched to gather signatures for what was to become known in Victorian suffrage lore as 'the monster petition'. Vida Goldstein, twenty-two years old and then only in the rank and file of the movement, gave a rare vignette of the kind of canvassing work carried out by suffragists in other colonies also.[56] The women went from house to house in Melbourne and in many of the country towns. It was not practical, she said, to cover the whole of Victoria, 'for the canvassers had to be well-equipped to deal with the arguments for and against'. Although the women were sometimes rebuffed by 'those whose interests ended at the garden gate', those women who took part in charitable or philanthropic work welcomed them. Wives of working men were enthusiastic and their husbands, if present, sympathetic. 'Wherever the workers went', she said, 'they found the great majority of women in favour of the vote, and of being on a footing of equality with men in every respect.'

The united canvassing for the great petition gripped the city's imagination. Never before had large numbers of women, armed with pencil and paper, taken to the streets to knock on the doors of rich and poor alike. Goldstein wrote later that it was the largest petition which had ever been presented to the Victorian Parliament, and that 'tremendous interest was aroused when the bulky document was carried by several attendants into the Legislative Chamber'.[57] From 1891 votes for women could not be dismissed as the idea of a few radicals—although the politicians were to keep trying. The WCTU reported that it was henceforth discussed 'in the daily press, on the streets, in social gatherings.'[58] In the coming seventeen years of the campaign the monster petition would be referred to as incontrovertible proof that Victorian women were not apathetic on the question and, like the lost vote of 1865, would develop a certain mythic ambience for the suffragists. The petition became a symbolic banner which could be flourished to enthuse flagging spirits.

Munro yielded, and the 30,000 signatures were presented on 29 September to support the second reading of a bill which gave woman suffrage and abolished plural voting.[59] The Premier was so strongly attacked by his supporters for risking the abolition of plural voting by linking it to woman suffrage, however, that although the two provisions were actually passed 39–13 in the Assembly, he dropped votes for women before the bill went to the Council. In spite of the sacrifice, the Upper House rejected one-man-one-vote. The women were bitterly disappointed that this should happen after all their hard work. The WCTU reported: 'your self-sacrificing efforts did not receive the success they deserved ... We feel that a great error was made when it [woman suffrage] was tacked onto the Bill seeking to abolish plural voting.'[60] Munro may have been making a token gesture to placate the WCTU women, with some of whom he must have come in contact socially. For all the Premier's moral pretensions, there were questions asked the following year about his probity in financial matters when his business interests collapsed like a pack of cards, leaving him bankrupt and discredited.[61]

By 1894 there was an array of organisations supporting woman suffrage, with different ideological and political flavours. The obvious ones were the Woman's Christian Temperance Union which linked its demands to prohibition or limitation of the drink traffic; the 1884 Victorian Women's Suffrage Society which had been associated over the years with Dugdale's aggressive free thought and secular pronouncements; and the 1888 Australian Women's Suffrage Society which was in accord with Smyth's birth-control work. The last two groups had a preponderance of members with Labor sympathies. Then there were the Women's Progressive Leagues. Scattered through the suburbs and country towns, they were not suffrage organisations as such. The members seem to have been a mixture of Liberal reformist and Labor women interested in municipal reform and state laws which affected women and children. By the turn of the century their support was to become so vocal that they could almost be termed de facto suffrage societies. A Labor organisation, the Women's Social and Political Reform League, agitating for federation and free trade, also appeared in 1894 and it favoured 'equality of political rights for both sexes on the basis of one-adult-one-vote'.[62]

On 1 March 1894, a public meeting was held at WCTU headquarters to launch yet another suffrage organisation, the Victorian Woman's Suffrage League. The President of the meeting explained that 'although the League was initiated by the WCTU it would be apart from that organization, no other qualification being required than that of securing the franchise for women'.[63] The new league passed a resolution which explained why members thought that a new organisation was needed: 'it is desirable to form a League to be based on the lines of Christ and morality, but quite apart from party politics.'[64] The Victorian Woman's Suffrage League would be able to bring together those who did not think that votes for women should be associated with Dugdale's or Smyth's creeds, with the left-wing inclinations of the Women's Progressive Leagues, or with the prohibition campaign of the WCTU. It was, however, to have its own partisanship; it was to be 'Christian' and 'moral'. 'Christian' would have excluded freethinkers like Dugdale, but would 'moral' have excluded advocates of birth control? There are no records of the league with which to pursue the question. The WCTU gave the league good coverage in its annual reports and from them we know that there was cross membership of the two organisations. The league and its branches were still active when the vote was won in 1908.

With so many organisations agitating for woman suffrage, it is hard to be sure which one is being referred to in press reports. Even the suffragists themselves used different titles at different times, sometimes referring to the 1894 organisation as the Woman's Franchise Society. The multiplicity of organisations does not seem to have weakened the Victorian movement; it seems rather to have diffused tensions such as those which built up in Rose Scott's tightly controlled Womanhood Suffrage League in New South Wales and which led to two antithetical groups in Queensland. A Victorian suffragist, whatever her special interest might be—the Labor Party, temperance, municipal reform, birth control, or none of these—could join a society linked to the struggle for votes for women.

At this stage Annette Bear-Crawford, the next major figure in the Victorian movement,[65] proposed that a central organisation be set up to coordinate strategy. Annette Bear, as she was until 1894 when she married and she and her husband adopted the joint name, was one of six daughters (there were also three sons) of John Pinney Bear, a member of the Victorian Legislative Council from 1863 to 1878. In that year he resigned from the Council and took his family to England, where he stayed for ten years.

Annette's education in Australia by governesses was continued at a ladies' college in Gloucestershire. She also spent time on the Continent before studying as a social worker and using her skills in the slums under the auspices of the Bishop of London. She mixed with others engaged in philanthropy (Beatrice and Sidney Webb were her friends), became involved in the woman's movement, and took part in the British woman suffrage campaign under the moderate leader Millicent Garrett Fawcett.

By the time Annette's parents returned to Victoria in 1888, she and some other members of the family had established independent lives for themselves in England. (Two of her sisters were to win international acclaim as fencers.) Annette might have spent the rest of her life in England if her father had not died at his Victorian vineyard soon after his return. In 1890, an independent and hard-working woman of thirty-seven, she arrived back to join her widowed mother in Melbourne. She immediately involved herself voluntarily in the work she had been trained to do. Her crowded interests took in agitating for the raising of the age of consent, and the appointment of women as factory inspectors and police matrons. She helped to launch the Society for the Prevention of Cruelty to Women and Children and, arising from her deep concern for the plight of unmarried mothers, with Vida Goldstein and Vida's mother in 1897 launched the 'willing shilling' drive to build the Queen Victoria Hospital for women and children.

The United Council for Woman Suffrage which Bear-Crawford nursed into being was made up of three representatives from each group advocating reform. It organised public meetings and deputations, lobbied parliamentary candidates and organised petitions. Bear-Crawford's logical mind and conciliatory nature were responsible for the success of the early years of a venture which involved so many women from disparate backgrounds. She was the first President, Secretary for her five years of involvement, and one of the council's most eloquent speakers. Vida Goldstein often went with Bear-Crawford on speaking engagements and observed in her friend the skills of oratory and repartee which she would use herself in the last eight years of the movement.

Soon after the formation of the United Council in 1894, William Maloney broke the three years of silence with a bill which, perhaps to placate the antagonistic Upper House, gave women the Assembly franchise only.[66] The bill had a short debate but did not complete its stages in the Assembly before the colony went to an election. George Turner was returned as Premier and, with a short interregnum under Allan McLean, was to remain so until 1901. Turner began his Liberal reign in harmony with his left-wing progressives and with the support of the seventeen Labor members who were elected with him. In 1895[67] and 1896[68] he introduced bills to give women the vote, but both were yoked to the abolition of plural voting. As usual with such bills, he pleased neither the suffragists nor those who wanted one-man-one-vote. Both bills were rejected by the Legislative Council. The women attended the debates and were deeply offended by the hostile remarks made by their opponents in both Houses, for attacks were made on them personally rather than on their arguments. The WCTU reported that at the ruling against the 1896 bill, 'silently we arose and left the House in a body; in a few moments not a woman's form graced its cushioned seats.'[69]

During the years of Turner's unpassable bills, the Victorian movement was expanding and changing shape. The two earlier societies still existed but were beginning to slide into the past, while the Victorian Woman's Suffrage League burgeoned. The Women's Progressive Leagues grew stronger and more vocal. Deputations to members of Parliament could be organised by individual groups, but larger ones were orchestrated by the United Council. Public meetings were held in individual suburbs by the particular group operating there, and the United Council arranged others in central locations in which all the groups could take part. Many competent speakers were needed to fuel these meetings. Two more highly articulate women emerged to join those who had already distinguished themselves: the Labor woman, Lilian Locke, and Janet Michie, the elder daughter of the now aged Sir Alexander Michie (former Attorney-General and long-time correspondent of J. S. Mill).

Frustrated in Parliament, the women succeeded elsewhere. The United Council campaigned in 1896 to have women elected to School Boards of Advice, and returned ten.[70] In Prahran, where four women were successful, it was reported that 'the battle ran high [and] the greatest excitement prevailed.' Then, realising that municipal council membership was a stepping stone to the legislature, the United Council turned its attention to the municipal elections for, it said, 'if we do not put in men favourable to our cause, we shall have a majority against us [in the Legislature].'[71] All municipal candidates were quizzed on their attitudes to woman suffrage, and the women who owned property were marshalled on election day: 'it was said that more women voted than men. Cab loads of our sex were going to and from the Town Hall all day. Women were trotting about canvassing and bringing in their dilatory sisters, and making things lively generally.'

Even if women's votes did not determine the outcome of the municipal elections, some evidently felt that their seats had been placed in jeopardy, for at a gathering of successful candidates in November woman suffrage was venomously attacked. As in Parliament, the women were abused rather than their arguments refuted. The WCTU was pleased to note that some men walked out of the meeting in protest.

In early 1898 the Commonwealth Constitutional Convention, which had at the end of 1897 met in Adelaide, came to Melbourne. The suffragists seized the opportunity to hold a large public meeting, with the Attorney-General, John Isaacs, in the chair. Dr John Cockburn and Frederick Holder gave glowing reports of how woman suffrage had worked in South Australia. There had been, said Holder, 'a marked change in the attitude of the South Australian Parliament towards all questions dealing with the interests of women and children'.[72] Towards the end of the meeting the audience demonstrated the rumbustious vitality and camaraderie which had developed in the wide-ranging Victorian movement. The chairman began: 'That in the opinion of this meeting ...', when the platform was invaded by a Mr Flynn crying 'Rot! Rubbish!' When he tried to go on, 'the audience, including many of the ladies, started stamping their feet, and made his remarks quite inaudible.' Flynn was obliged to retire, unheard.[73]

In August 1898 Premier Turner, pressured by the women and by those who wanted the abolition of plural voting, introduced two bills. The Plural Voting Abolition Bill was defeated in the Legislative Council. The bill giving women the vote had a long debate in which a move to put a referendum to the colony was defeated. Malcolm McKenzie, in answer to a supporter quoting J. S. Mill, claimed, referring to the Married Women's

Property Act of 1884, that 'the last shred of injustice' had been removed from women, and that if Mill had been alive in 1898 he would not think that women needed the vote.[74] The bill was passed 52–29 in the Assembly. For the first time in all the years of discussion about votes for women in Victoria—and fourteen years after the first society was formed—a bill was to go unencumbered to the Legislative Council.

To support the bill's passage, the United Council organised a deputation for the night of 6 September, and more than 300 women[75] crowded into Queen's Hall in the parliamentary building. Although the deputation had been prearranged, the women 'were kept standing for three quarters of an hour while Councillors swilled champagne'.[76] When the leaders were finally given a hearing in another room, the speeches were interrupted by 'low jests and idiotic exclamations such as "Who'll mind the babies?", "New Woman" and others not fit to print'.[77] Annie Lowe seems to have been the chief speaker, and she and the others retained their dignity and put forward their arguments in a controlled and rational manner. One newspaper said that Sir William Zeal, President of the Legislative Council, was conciliatory. It is more correct to say that he was suffocatingly patronising. He was sure, he said, that the women 'would excuse the Council if they did not at once give a reply . . . [it] would be dealt with in the Council . . . in a kind and considerate way . . . in the best interests of women . . . The question was "Is it desirable?"'[78] Meanwhile some of the women in Queen's Hall were being subjected to what would now be called sexual harassment. One member of Council

> accosted two of the younger members of the deputation with the following indecent remark which should have been followed by his being consigned to the lock-up. 'You girls—you don't want votes. You want—something else.' His leering pause deserved six months without the option. One woman remonstrated with him and he slunk off like a whipped mongrel.[79]

News of the affronts caused anger among suffragists in Victoria and elsewhere. The *Age* commented: 'had the deputation represented voters, its reception would have been punctual, courteous and possibly obsequious.'[80] The New South Wales Womanhood Suffrage League passed a resolution of indignation which it asked the United Council to forward to Zeal with its own protests.[81]

Zeal was on the defensive when he introduced the Woman Suffrage Bill in the Upper House, and petulantly protested that press reports were 'unfair'. Then he caused further anger in the galleries packed with women by criticising their formally correct deputation: 'there is an Act of Parliament which sets itself against any large number of persons appearing in Parliament House with the object of influencing honorary members.'[82] The chief speaker against the bill was Henry Wrixon, who claimed that a logical corollary would be that the women must be given the right to sit in Parliament. He then centred his long speech on the discord that a woman's independent point of view might cause in the family.[83] These points were hammered mercilessly by him in Legislative Council debates until 1908. (It is worth noting that Wrixon owed his prominent position in Victorian society to the fact that he had married a widow who had inherited considerable wealth from both her father and her husband.)[84] When James Campbell rose and claimed that the vote was 'only asked for by extremists and by women of improper character', there were cries of 'shame' from the women in the gallery.[85] The bill was defeated in the Council 19–15.

The United Council for Woman Suffrage printed a propaganda leaflet in the form of a reply to Wrixon's long speech, claiming that 'No husband owns a wife body and soul' and that 'It is insulting to call her a dependent considering the work she does.'[86] The *Age* attacked the Legislative Council for its rejection of the bill, claiming it had 'superciliously snapped its fingers in the faces of the people at large'. It showed, the *Age* said, the danger of a Constitution which gave 'impregnable' power to its Upper House.[87]

Brettena Smyth's death in early 1898 had left no real gap in the movement, for by then her energies had been channelled into her lecture work, and the society she had founded was moribund. The next death of a leader, however, was a bitter blow. In November 1898, after a farewell meeting at Prahran Town Hall, Annette Bear-Crawford left for England to attend the Women's International Congress. Her husband joined her three weeks before she died of pneumonia in London in June 1899, only forty-six years old. The women mourned her in a service at St Paul's Cathedral, Melbourne, on 4 July. Her international standing can be gauged from the facts that her English friends contributed to have a memorial plaque placed in her home church at South Yarra, and that a statue was unveiled to her memory in London in 1902.[88]

Someone with the organisational abilities and enthusiasm of a Bear-Crawford was needed to fill her place in the United Council. The woman with the personality and training was there—the 29-year-old Vida Goldstein, the greatest of the Victorian, and perhaps of the Australian, suffragists. Goldstein's contribution was to be both scintillating and dramatic, but it should be noted that she was in a leadership role only for the last nine years of a hard-fought campaign which lasted for twenty-four years—if one measures the length of the campaign from the formation of the first society. Goldstein was the only major figure in the Australian movement who was a second-generation suffragist. She was born in 1869, the year Dugdale began to speak up for votes for women, and she was sixteen and had graduated from her governess's instruction to Melbourne Presbyterian Ladies' College when the first society was formed by Dugdale and Lowe. Between then and 1891, when she helped her suffragist mother collect signatures for the great petition, she had matriculated with honours in French and English and enjoyed a busy round of balls and parties in the prosperous middle-class stratum of society to which her parents belonged. In these years she developed an elegant style in dress and (aided by her natural beauty of face and figure) a capacity for presenting herself well—qualities which were to be frequently commented on in her public life.

Goldstein's education had ranged much further afield than the academic subjects and deportment which were taught at the Presbyterian Ladies' College. Her father (an Irish-born Protestant) and her Australian-born mother set their four daughters and one son an example of involvement in social reform work through Dr Charles Strong's First Scots Church. When Vida was fourteen, Strong, a Labor-oriented suffragist himself, left the Presbyterian fold after a doctrinal dispute and formed his independent Australian Church, and the Goldsteins went with him. The Australian Church was heavily involved in the relief of distress and backed the doctor's chief philanthropic passion, agitation for the clearance of the slums and their replacement with clean, sanitary housing.[89] Vida, the eldest daughter, often accompanied her mother when she dispensed aid in the poorest parts of Melbourne, and her sympathies with the problems of working-class men and women had their roots in these early years.

Through the 1890s Goldstein was in the ranks of the suffragists, but she involved herself in other issues too: the National Anti-Sweating League, the Criminology Society, the Jubilee Appeal for the building of Queen Victoria Hospital. She may have come to prominence in the movement before 1899 if it had not been for the eroding of the family's income in an 1893 bank crash. She and her sisters, forced to earn their own livings, set up a coeducational preparatory school which absorbed most of her energy. Goldstein had, however, attended suffrage meetings with her close friend, Bear-Crawford, and observed her lucidity and her capacity to handle hecklers. She was to develop her own logical clarity of speech and to combine it with a talent for witty repartee with which she could handle the most abusive of interjectors. Her niece gives no date but says that her first speech was made to friends at a drawing-room meeting. She was extremely nervous, and stipulated that there were to be no questions, but afterwards found herself vivaciously discussing points with her audience.[90] In 1899, then, Goldstein was a well-educated and experienced social worker of twenty-nine, with a clear understanding of the problems of women. When Bear-Crawford died, she was there, ready to bring her shining enthusiasm to the leadership of a movement whose early high priestesses were either dead (Smyth and Bear-Crawford) or elderly (Dugdale and Lowe).

Two months after Bear-Crawford's death, Goldstein became Organising Secretary for the United Council for Woman Suffrage. By January 1900 she had given up her school, and her position as Secretary had become a paid one. By the end of 1900 affiliated associations had grown from twelve to thirty-two, including such diverse organisations as the Victorian Lady Teachers' Association, the Central Methodist Mission and the Trades Hall Council.[91] The United Council's executive was now made up of one representative from each member group, and it had an Organising Committee, a Literature Committee and a Parliamentary Committee. While member organisations were still free to agitate under their own names, activities of the United Council were more tightly controlled. Goldstein wrote to Rose Scott that there were some 'ill-advised' people in the Victorian movement who were 'dangerous in interviewing members and speaking at public meetings', and for that reason the Organizing Committee arranged all the central meetings.[92]

Heavily represented still in the reorganised Council were the Women's Progressive Leagues which, Goldstein said in 1900, had woman suffrage as the main plank in their platforms, although they took up any issues which involved the welfare of women and children. Their tactics were similar to the organisations which described themselves specifically as suffrage societies: public meetings, drawing-room meetings, and canvassing door to door for signatures to suffrage petitions.[93]

Although Women's Progressive Leagues were not affiliated to a political party, the word 'progressive' was widely used in Australia at the time to indicate a position to the left of Liberal and to the right of Labor. So Labor men like Maloney, Strong and Henry Champion (Vida's brother-in-law) were members of the Women's Progressive Leagues, but Goldstein herself, who refused to define herself politically, was also a member.

The suffragists had little reason to complain of Government responses while the expansion of the United Council was taking place under Goldstein in 1899 and 1900. In 1899 the long-running Turner Government introduced a Plural Voting Abolition Bill[94] and a Woman Suffrage Bill[95] and ran them in tandem through the Assembly. This time the Legislative Council, influenced by the fact that one-man-one-vote would be the franchise for the Commonwealth Parliament, accepted it reluctantly for Victoria. Now the Labor party was free to support woman suffrage unreservedly. Victorian Labor, however, had not become as strong a political force as in Queensland and New South Wales, so its support was to be of little help. In fact, from 1903 to 1908, as we shall see, its advocacy was to be a distinct hindrance in the context of Victorian party politics.

Suffragist support for the 1899 Woman Suffrage Bill included 'a monster demonstration' of approximately one thousand people at the Melbourne Town Hall, and large regional meetings. The imperturbable and tenacious Annie Lowe parried interjectors at the Town Hall and Goldstein had her first blood-letting before an audience at Prahran. At Ballarat an ebullient crowd almost drowned out with 'derisive cheers' a Councillor Elliot who tried to move an amendment to the meeting's resolution in favour of votes for women. When in characteristic Victorian fashion he fell back on what he and the suffragists evidently thought was slighting personal comment—'women who do their washing on Saturdays'—'the hostile demonstration became almost deafening'.[96] In spite of the women's campaign, the Legislative Council rejected the bill,[97] as it rejected two similar bills the following year.[98]

Mid-1900 saw the emergence of an Anti-Suffrage League which probably had its roots among the Conservatives in the Legislative Assembly; the league's founders, Freda Derham and Carrie Reed, were both daughters of Assembly members.[99] The league gathered 22,978 signatures and submitted them when the Legislative Coucil was due to consider the second of that year's bills.[100] Petitions from various groups poured in to counter those of the Anti-Suffrage League but Goldstein, scornful of the efficacy of petitions since the mammoth 1891 effort, did not organise a united canvass.

This orchestrated opposition was nourished by the *Argus*, and July to December of 1900 saw a battle royal in *Argus* and *Age* editorials, with each editor publishing letters to support his own point of view. The *Age* started up a women's suffrage fund, but it is not clear where donations were channelled. Goldstein challenged Derham and Reed to debate, but they made excuses: 'We simply have no organization and can attempt nothing beyond what we are doing at present.'[101] The *Argus* said they were 'shunning the platform as not belonging rightly to Woman's Sphere'.[102] The *Age* rejoined gleefully that in gathering signatures Derham and Reed had already moved into the public sphere and were inciting other women 'to do the very thing which they tell them they are incapable of doing'.[103]

The anti-suffrage canvassers were accused of unscrupulous tactics in asking questions like 'Do you want women to neglect their homes and become members of Parliament?'[104] and 'Are you in favour of all the bad women of Melbourne getting into Parliament?'[105] More serious allegations were made in the Legislative Assembly and in letters to the *Woman's Sphere*. It was claimed that pressure was being put on 'girls' to sign the anti-suffrage petition by the owners of the factories in which they worked.

> The proprietor's daughter and another lady called at our factory on Thursday, July 19th, and spoke to some of the girls, asking them to sign. When they said that they would not sign what they did not understand, Miss——[sic] and friend seemed quite cross ... The clerk now has the petition ... a good many have signed in fear ... I expect [the rest] will have to sign or get things made unpleasant for them now, or in the future.[106]

In September 1900, at the height of the anti-suffrage campaign, Goldstein launched her monthly paper, the *Woman's Sphere*. Below the title on the cover she printed a quotation from a fifteenth-century manuscript attributed to Terence: 'I am human, and nothing human is beyond my sphere.' The greater part of the magazine was devoted to woman suffrage: reports of the various societies and of the United Council, and analysis of parliamentary debates. There were significant differences between the *Woman's Sphere* and Louisa Lawson's *Dawn*, the only other radical women's paper in Australia at the time. Both publicised the legal disabilities of women, but the *Dawn* ventured further into an analysis of covert discrimination and the conditioning which made women feel inferior. It was thus more critical of the social mores of the period. This may have been the reason why Rose Scott, who rarely ventured from legal disabilities into this more dangerous territory, felt free to give the *Woman's Sphere* the recognition she had always withheld from the *Dawn*.[107] Goldstein's paper, like Louisa Lawson's, travelled all over Australia and, through contacts which the Australian suffragists had, overseas. The *Woman's Sphere* claimed not to be aligned to any political party, but as it gave very good coverage to Labor's support of the cause, and because it was so ardent in reporting and extending the activities of the Women's Progressive Leagues, which were seen to have a Labor bias, the paper itself was seen as having Labor leanings. This impression was to be intensified when, in late 1900, Goldstein began to attack the parliamentary Liberal party for its lack of ardour in advancing woman suffrage.

By 1901 votes for women had been an issue in two elections. Four bills unencumbered with any other provision had passed the Assembly and been promptly rejected by the Legislative Council. All the suffragists and reformers of the period castigated the Upper House and accused it of obstructing the will of the people. Goldstein was as loud in her condemnation as any, but she had developed into a more perceptive political observer than most. It seemed to her that the Legislative Assembly debates, although occasionally shot through with their old fire, had now become a ritual. There was a placid expectation that after a short debate in 'the other place' a bill would be returned. In September 1900 she claimed that the Cabinet was clearly not serious about woman suffrage, even though it had allowed so many bills to pass. If it wanted votes for women it would fight the Legislative Council on the question.[108] The *Age* thought as she did, for it commented: 'If the Legislative Assembly does nothing, and tamely submits, the Council will keep on rejecting it.'[109]

By January 1901 the reluctance of the Liberal party to confront the Upper House had been discussed by the United Council for Woman Suffrage and they issued a manifesto, printed in the *Age*. The title was 'Who Rules Victoria?'[110] and it castigated the Assembly for 'the grovelling spirit' with which the Assembly meekly accepted the rejection of this and other measures, and it demanded reform of the Council. A paragraph which the *Age* omitted was evidently too strongly worded for the paper's liking. Goldstein published it in the *Woman's Sphere*: 'If . . . the present leaders of Victorian Liberalism do not take this course, it will be evident that they will be accessories before the fact to the strangling of Victorian Liberty. Whatever they may call themselves, they will, in truth, be accomplices of Conservatism.'[111]

In the latter half of 1901, after a two-year stint, Goldstein resigned as Secretary of the United Council and another important figure, Lilian Locke, took her place. Locke, the daughter of an Anglican clergyman, earned her own living as 'A Town Shopper and General Agent'—a joint business of 'the Misses Locke'. She selected goods for country clients on a commission basis and supplied 'Companions, Governesses, Housekeepers, Nurses, Lady-Helps . . .' She was active in the Women's Progressive Leagues,[112] and shortly before she became Secretary of the United Council had persuaded the previously autonomous Leagues to form a Union, of which she was also Secretary.[113] A great deal of her time had also been given to the Women's Political and Social Crusade, a women's group which had worked with the Labor party campaigning against aspects of the Commonwealth Constitution proposed in 1897-8.[114] Since then it had struggled along as a loose organisation committed to a mélange of Labor ideals. It was anti-imperialist and opposed to 'the insane craving for titles and dignities'; it called for justice for the working class instead of 'a disgusting patronage of the poor which goes by the name of charity and slum work'; and it urged its members 'to make the women's vote, when it comes, a solid democratic vote, that is to say, a Labor vote'.[115] Locke was a vivid and forthright speaker—her platform addresses, the Brisbane *Worker* said, were as fiery as her hair.[116] Although herself a clergyman's daughter, she had little time for the jargon in which many, but not all, WCTU women felt compelled to wrap up their agitation, castigating it as 'obtrusive and wholly unnecessary piety'.[117]

In February 1902 the International Woman Suffrage Conference met in Washington, and Vida Goldstein went as Australian delegate. She carried a commission from the Victorian Government to inquire into methods of dealing with neglected children, one from the Criminology Society to study the penal system, and one from the Trades Hall Council to inquire into trade unions.[118] She travelled via Sydney, where the New South Wales Council of Women appointed her delegate to the International Council of Women Convention to be held after the Woman Suffrage Conference. In Sydney she stayed with Rose Scott, who gave a reception for her the night before she embarked, and some of the women gathered at the wharf to farewell her when she sailed.[119]

Goldstein had a stimulating and exciting time in America.[120] She was given a reception in Salt Lake City on her way to the conference and her portrait appeared in the *New York Herald*. With other conference delegates she addressed both Houses of the United States Congress and she had an interview with President Roosevelt, who questioned her about the position women held in Australian politics. He was particularly interested in the granting of Commonwealth voting rights, which had occurred after Vida left Australia.

In the address of welcome to the delegates at the Conference, Goldstein heard herself described as 'a full [sic], up-to-date representative woman, widely [sic] awake to all the refinements of life, and fully cognizant of all the rights of her sex'. The speaker was seizing the opportunity to counter world-wide disparagement of suffragists as unfeminine.

The *Boston Woman's Journal* showed the same preoccupations when it published this piece about the Australian delegate.

> We see her slender, girlish grace,
> Her vivid, keen, and sparkling face;
> From her clear eyes, intelligence
> Looks forth, with wit and common-sense;
> No manly air can we perceive,
> She looks as womanly as Eve;
> We think the 'Antis' must be doting,
> For girls are *not* unsexed by voting.

At the conference Goldstein gave an address on 'The Australian Woman in Politics'. She was appointed Secretary, and a member of the committee to organise a convention in Berlin in 1904 at which a permanent international organisation would be formed. With Carrie Chapman Catt (America) and Florence Fenwick Miller (England) she drafted the proposed Constitution and Declaration of Principles for the international body.

The declaration, which Goldstein proudly published in the *Woman's Sphere*, was not at all conciliatory. It proclaimed the liberty of the individual woman, and took no account at all of the interests of the State. With its catechism of independent political, social, legal and economic rights, it would have confirmed the worst fears of the Conservatives in the Victorian legislature that the patriarchal stability of the Australian home and State would indeed be undermined by these contentious women.

> self-government in the home and the State should be the inalienable right of every normal adult, and in consequence no individual woman can 'owe obedience' to any individual man, as prescribed by old marriage forms, nor can women as a whole owe obedience to men as a whole, as prescribed by modern governments.[121]

Although Goldstein was important to the Victorian movement by 1902, its impetus did not depend on her alone. In her absence a large meeting was held at the Melbourne Town Hall to celebrate the granting of the Commonwealth vote to all Australian women.[122] Alfred Deakin, who had moved from the Victorian Parliament to become Acting Prime Minister of the new Commonwealth, was chief speaker. Annie Lowe, Catherine Helen Spence (who was in town from South Australia) and Mrs Press from the WCTU followed him. The meeting turned into a demand for the Victorian Legislative Council to capitulate when next a woman suffrage bill came before it. The veteran Annie Lowe was greeted with loud cheers when she moved 'That this meeting expresses its gratification that the Commonwealth Parliament has affirmed the principle of woman suffrage in the passage of the Uniform Franchise Bill, and naturally concludes that the Legislative Council will now no longer withhold the State franchise from the women of Victoria.'[123]

Since the 1894 elections, the composition of the Victorian Legislative Assembly had gradually changed. Labor had not kept up its early promise in 1894 when it increased its membership from eleven to seventeen. Although Labor members gave their support to woman suffrage, the Labor party as a whole had little political clout. At the same time as Labor declined, Liberalism moved to the right and became more cautious about reforms.

This did not mean that the new Liberalism found itself in harmony with that bastion of privilege, the Legislative Council. When the dour William Irvine became Premier in mid-1902 he made an attempt to limit the power of the Upper House by lowering its franchise and providing for a double dissolution in case of deadlocks. As a sop to the women, who were pestering him with delegations, he tacked on woman suffrage.[124] After four bills in which woman suffrage had been treated as a separate issue, Irvine was once again entangling it with political power play. The bill did not reach the Legislative Council before Irvine called an election which gave him a large majority over twelve Labor members and fifteen reformist Liberals.[125] The new Cabinet included Thomas Bent and several other committed anti-suffragists. With his position now unassailable, Irvine tackled the power of the Council in earnest. The Constitution Reform Bill to which he again tacked woman suffrage in late 1902 was an immensely complex one: it reduced the number of members for both Houses, lowered the qualifications for electors and elected for the Upper House, and provided for a joint sitting or double dissolution to resolve deadlocks. At the last moment a clause was added which gave public servants and railway employees their own representatives in each House, thus depriving them of a vote (and reducing the power of Labor) in the electorates in which they lived.[126] The bill, because of the last clause, was angrily opposed by Labor in the Assembly, which meant that support for woman suffrage was also withheld. It had a stormy passage through both Houses, with a bewildering array of amendments and counter amendments. When it finally returned from the Council to the Assembly in 1903, it had no woman suffrage clause. In other respects the bill had been altered to such an extent that the Assembly accused the Council of giving back 'a torn and tangled measure' and refused to accept it.[127] A conference was arranged of representatives from both Houses and in the bargaining the Assembly representatives agreed to drop votes for women in return for the Council's capitulation on some other aspects of the bill.

The women had followed the progress of the bill closely. In February 1903, when the Legislative Council amended the woman suffrage clause out of it, they held 'a grand suffrage demonstration' at the Melbourne Town Hall. In her speech Lilian Locke, as Secretary of the United Council, accused the Upper House of denying women any political privileges while fighting to protect their own wealth and exclusiveness—'a system of lopping off everybody's head but their own'. Annie Lowe, the United Council President, moved amid cheers that the Assembly should 'make the suffrage clauses vital principles of the Constitution Reform Bill ... and resist to the utmost any further attempt by the Legislative Council to refuse this measure of simple justice to the women of Victoria'.[128]

When the Assembly did not resist to the utmost, but dropped the woman suffrage clause in the bargaining between the two Houses, the women were furious. Another Melbourne protest meeting was held which preceded meetings in the suburbs and large country towns. A *Melbourne Punch* cartoon showed Irvine over a stool being beaten by one woman, while others waited their turn.[129] Goldstein stingingly attacked the Legislative Assembly in the *Woman's Sphere*. That the women were aiming their attacks in the right direction is shown by the comment of a Legislative Council member: 'the very easy manner in which the matter of female suffrage had been allowed to drop caused him to suspect whether the gentlemen who had seven times passed woman suffrage were really so much in earnest in the matter as it was thought they were.'[130]

The confirmed supporters of the women in the Assembly were also angry. Two of them, Dr Maloney[131] and Donald Mckinnon,[132] tried to repair the damage by introducing private members' bills later in the session, but Irvine blocked both, claiming that a certain stability had been achieved in the Victorian electoral system, and he did not mean it to be upset by votes for women.

In this period of frustration, all Australian political parties began marshalling their forces for the Commonwealth election late in 1903—the first in which women were allowed to vote. The Labor party, at meetings in the Trades Hall in April and May, urged all women with Labor sympathies to join either the Women's Progressive Leagues or the (until now male) Political Labor Councils.[133] As the battle for the woman's vote intensified, Labor went further and constituted a women's committee of the central Political Labor Council and Lilian Locke was conscripted to travel Victoria recruiting women into the councils to act as canvassers and 'housekeepers' for specific Labor candidates.[134]

Goldstein, not now holding any office in the United Council for Woman Suffrage, threw her formidable energy into forming the apolitical Women's Federal Political Association, to educate women in electoral procedures and issues. By August it had a membership of three thousand, and auxiliary branches in the suburbs and country areas. It issued pamphlets and held drawing-room meetings and large public meetings of which mock elections were a part.[135] The mock elections aimed to make women familiar with all aspects of an election. Those women who had agreed to go on the list of candidates made election speeches and then the procedures for marking a ballot paper, and what constituted an informal vote, were explained. Votes were cast at a mock polling booth set up in the hall, and were placed in the ballot box provided; the presence of a returning officer and scrutineers at the booth made the familiarisation procedure more realistic.[136]

The Women's Federal Political Association was not a suffrage organisation, but inevitably suffragists were its most enthusiastic members and office-bearers. Goldstein was President, and Lowe Vice-President. Lilian Locke, in spite of her arduous workload elsewhere, was an active member, and so was Henrietta Dugdale-Johnson. The membership, however, was of two different persuasions. There were those like Goldstein, who believed passionately that women should not be conscripted into party structures, but should remain free to vote for candidates who best represented their interests. These non-party women had their stance reinforced when Rose Scott visited Melbourne in 1903 and extolled the virtues of being non-aligned.[137] There were women like Lilian Locke, however, who saw no contradiction in belonging both to a party and to a group with a purely educational purpose.

In September 1903, comparatively late in the Commonwealth campaign, the two sections of the Women's Federal Political Association came into conflict. The majority non-aligned membership carried a motion asking Goldstein to stand for the Senate as its candidate, and she accepted. Locke, believing that Goldstein would attract votes which would otherwise go to Labor, withdrew the Labor women. Other women with party affiliations may have withdrawn too, for the association now threw itself enthusiastically into Goldstein's election campaign. The Victorian WCTU was critical of Goldstein's decision to stand. It thought that she would hinder the gaining of the state vote:

> One of the first things an opponent often says in arguing the subject of granting the franchise to women is 'Women will be wanting to sit in Parliament next'. However logical and even desirable this may be, it is not wise to force the matter before the time is ripe.[138]

The opinion of the Victorian WCTU was not necessarily shared by the Unions in other states. Elizabeth Nicholls, in *Our Federation*, the monthly Australasian organ of the WCTU, criticised the Victorian women and wrote, 'this is contrary to the traditions of the Union, which has ever stood for no sex in citizenship.'[139] Scott wrote from Sydney approving Goldstein's candidature. Lowe, now seventy-one, was also asked to stand 'by several of the women's organizations',[140] but it is not clear which organisations these were. Lowe declined, citing Catherine Helen Spence's failure to be elected as a delegate to the 1897 Commonwealth Convention. Mrs Evelyn Gough, a member of the United Council for Woman Suffrage, was among the list of announced candidates, but she withdrew and gave her support to Goldstein.[141]

There was a flurry of anxious activity among politicians at the prospect of a woman candidate.

> The announcement that the Women's Federal Political Association has invited Miss Vida Goldstein to become a candidate for the Senate has caused much questioning of Sir William Lyne by Federal members as to the legality of female Federal candidature. The Home Secretary says that he has no doubt that women are eligible, because the Federal Acts Interpretation Act provides that 'he' means also 'she' in all legislation, unless the contrary is expressly mentioned.[142]

With the *Woman's Sphere* for publicity—she handed it over to an editor for the duration of the campaign—and an election committee from the Women's Federal Political Association behind her, Goldstein threw herself into the two and a half months on the hustings with customary gusto. Her apologia, 'Should Women Enter Parliament', was published in the *Review of Reviews*,[143] and her committee issued leaflets setting out her platform. Although she charged one shilling admission to cover expenses, she had crowded meetings in Melbourne and country towns, with enthusiastic responses from her audiences. The papers, especially the country ones, seemed to be astonished that this particular political woman had none of the characteristics lampooned so mercilessly in the Legislative Council. They exclaimed at her 'charming voice, modest manner, and absence of anything masculine',[144] at her 'easy delivery of speech',[145] her 'smooth tongue and ready wit',[146] and her plain common sense. The *Bulletin* reported: 'Miss Goldstein laid down the political law to a Town Hall crowd the other night in a smart turn-out and a bright piece of coquettish millinery.'[147]

Goldstein certainly passed the tests of oratory, of an approved platform, and the 'womanliness' prescribed for a female in political life. But there were powerful forces at work which made her defeat inevitable. With the opening up of the Commonwealth theatre for political players, party lines had hardened. Other Independents were standing for the four Senate seats, but Vida's candidacy posed the greatest threat to the three political groups: four Liberals (backed by the *Age*), four Conservatives (backed by the *Argus*), and four endorsed Labor candidates. The *Age* and the *Argus* gave her good coverage, but became increasingly critical of her as they became more anxious about her erosion of votes. Because her policies were so akin to those of the Labor party, campaigning against her was most intense from that quarter. With a catch-cry of 'Labour, not Sex', voters were warned that votes for her were votes thrown away: 'we would like to signalize the occasion by giving a vote to such a capable woman reformer as Miss Goldstein if there were any to spare. But there are not!'[148]

Goldstein may not have been very optimistic when she began her campaign, but must have become increasingly so as she progressed. At one meeting 'the cheering and applause which punctuated her address, and the attentive hearing she was accorded, would have been welcomed as a happy augury of success by many an old campaigner steeped deep in political life. The hall was crammed in every part, and numbers had to stand.'[149]

On the morning of the election Goldstein arrived at the polling booth at 7.20, and 'before the Carillons had ceased their jangling the first vote ever cast by a woman in Victoria under the Commonwealth Franchise Act had been cast by the first female candidate for the Federal Parliament.'[150] When results were posted, Goldstein was fifteenth, but with 51,497 votes. There were consolations. She had letters congratulating her on her 'moral courage' in standing and on her 'splendid polling'. The *Age* called her final figure 'astonishing'.[151] Carrie Chapman Catt, a leading figure in the American movement, had written in November: 'We are so proud of you, and so happy that you have this honour, even if you are not elected.'[152]

The fragmentation of the women in the 1903 Commonwealth elections changed the shape of the Victorian suffrage movement. In February 1904 Lilian Locke resigned her position as Secretary of the United Council for Woman Suffrage to take up a paid career within Labor structures, and Annie Lowe took her place. Most of Locke's time in her Labor party position was spent consolidating the women's committees of the Victorian Trades and Labor Councils, but she spent periods in other states enthusing their Labor women and receiving accolades in their Labor presses. She was effectively lost to the wider suffrage campaign, confining herself to advocating state votes for women—albeit vigorously—in the course of her other work. She achieved distinction as the first woman member of the Victorian Trades Hall Council,[153] and the first to be appointed to an Intercolonial Trades and Labor Conference.[154] There is a photograph of this conference showing her in her high-necked blouse and wide-brimmed flower-bedecked hat, among forty-four dark-suited men.[155] Her brief career in the party organisation came to a halt in 1906, when she married George Burns, a Labor member of the Tasmanian Legislative Assembly. Goldstein, still a friend in spite of Locke's defection in 1903, joined prominent Labor men in giving one of the eulogies at her wedding.[156] In spite of the Brisbane *Worker's* hope that her work 'would not be strangled by a wedding ring',[157] she resigned and left for Tasmania to follow her husband's political fortunes. In 1907 she went with him to Queensland where she was when the Victorian vote was granted. She was to continue to work within the Labor Women's Organising Committees there and when she and her husband shifted to New South Wales, but not again in a paid capacity.

The Labor success in drawing women into its fold was not lost on the Liberals. A meeting was held in the Melbourne Town Hall in March 1904 by 'six public-spirited women who held Liberal opinions'. The new organisation, the Austalian Women's National League, had as its aims:

1. To support loyalty to the throne and Empire.
2. To combat socialism by strongly advocating equality of opportunity for all classes, and opposing the nationalization of industries.
3. To educate women in politics.
4. To safeguard the interests of the home, women and children.[158]

The order in which the four platform planks are placed is significant. Liberal, anti-Labor principles are enunciated first, and then women's interests. Nothing is said about the state vote for women.

The men behind the formation of the Australian Women's National League envisaged the women's organisations as adjuncts of the male Australian National Leagues, which were concerned with electing right-wing Liberal men to Parliament, but the movement quickly took on a life of its own. Its rapid growth reflects the strength of Liberalism in Victoria in the period. By September 1905 (only eighteen months after its formation) it had eighty-three branches, providing social activities for its 10,000 members as well as working for the party. The Women's National League was to become a strong influence in Victorian Liberal affairs. The women secured equal representation with men in the joint affairs of the leagues, and thus were able to have a say in forming Liberal policy. The Women's National League claimed later that it helped to secure the state franchise for women, but in fact it was to remain conspicuously silent on the issue in the following critical years. When an abortive private member's woman suffrage bill was before the Victorian Parliament in 1904, Goldstein challenged the league to state its attitude to the bill.[159] The league remained silent. Goldstein was still challenging it in 1908, with the same result. The Liberal organisation, according to Goldstein, was devoted only to 'herding the women to the [Commonwealth] polls like so many sheep'.[160] Speakers at its meetings, she went on, were men, 'all of whom bitterly opposed the granting of the franchise to women, and are opposed to it still'.[161]

Goldstein's Women's Federal Political Association, still spurning party allegiances, dropped the word 'Federal' in 1904 and became the Women's Political Association. It extended its self-imposed task of educating women in electoral matters to making them familiar with political procedures. Elections were held within the framework of the association's branches and a Women's Parliament was convened, with a female Premier, and women as members and Cabinet Ministers. The Parliament introduced, discussed, and rejected or passed bills—and those aimed at improving the lot of women and children figured prominently.[162] For the anti-suffragists within Parliament, who had been darkly muttering for years that the woman's vote would lead to females on the parliamentary benches, the Women's Parliament must have raised further fearful apparitions. Not only women members, but women with portfolios! And a woman as Premier!

One of those with such a phobia about women politicians was Thomas Bent and in 1904, when Irvine went to the Commonwealth Parliament, Bent became Premier. The

Government called itself Liberal, but was actually a Liberal–Conservative coalition. Those Liberals who were so reformist in their beliefs that they could not support Bent moved into opposition with Labor. The Bent Cabinet contained several confirmed anti-suffragists besides Bent, and Goldstein labelled it as Conservative, not Liberal, with a reactionary Premier who was 'a past master in parliamentary tactics and the art of bluff'.[163]

Bent and his Cabinet were to block votes for women in Victoria until 1908. Bent refused to introduce a Government bill and did everything he could to hinder private bills. Bent's stand was not inconsistent with his earlier expressed opinions, but one must look further for an explanation of his entrenched obstinacy in the years when Victorian women were the only white Australians without a state vote. The answer is not hard to find. Bent and his Liberal and Conservative colleagues were afraid that the woman's vote would strengthen Victorian Labor. In the 1903 Commonwealth elections Labor did so well overall in Australia that in 1904 John Watson was able to form the first Commonwealth Labor Government—although it lasted only for four months. Several times in the years 1904–8 Bent made it clear that he blamed the women for Labor's federal successes: 'It is through the women voting that we have three parties in the Federal Parliament, and everyone deplores the condition into which *that* [sic] Parliament has got.'[164]

When the United Council for Woman Suffrage made its first approach to the new Government in November 1904, Bent set the tone for his future relationships with the women: 'I am directed by the Premier to acknowledge receipt of your letter . . . for a deputation on the desired introduction of a woman suffrage bill. I am to say that Mr Bent has no time for such a deputation.'[165] Goldstein, looking on from outside the United Council for Woman Suffrage, soon became impatient with its lack of success in dealing with the Premier. She accused it of not being forceful enough with the Government, and of expecting the state suffrage to simply fall into its hands now that the Commonwealth vote had been won. The Women's Political Association would therefore, she said, become a suffrage society as well as an educational body, and with a more vigorous campaign would 'assume control of suffrage forces throughout Victoria'.[166] In order to direct this campaign through the Women's Political Association, she wound down the *Woman's Sphere* to an eight-page pamphlet and within two months it had gone out of existence. With it went the historian's most valuable source of information about the late Victorian suffrage movement.

Goldstein was being less than just to the United Council. She soon found out for herself that Bent was an arrogant and obdurate opponent, and resistant to all agitation. He sent curt and evasive answers to approaches by letter, and refused to see delegations until 1906. Although five private bills were passed through the Assembly with large majorities in the years 1904–8, he foredoomed to failure the two which he allowed to go to the Upper House by speaking against them in the Assembly. One example of his boorishness and contempt for the women themselves will suffice. Having accepted an invitation to be present at a suffrage meeting in Brighton Town Hall, he sat in the front row and ostentatiously went to sleep while Lowe (President of the United Council) and Goldstein (President of the Women's Political Association) addressed the meeting:

... an occasional remark about the men not having made a howling success of politics, or a chance reference to women possessing the powers of moral suasion, rousing him only to momentary attention.

Mr Bent was invited to speak, but as he did not respond, although roused from his apparent slumber, Miss Goldstein inquired if he did not want to say anything. 'No' came the blunt rejoinder.[167]

The Women's Political Association did not 'take over' the Victorian movement, although it did function as a staunch suffrage body from 1905 to 1908. It was one more organisation working alongside, and in concert with, the Woman's Christian Temperance Union, and with the United Council and its affiliated organisations. The stagnation between Bent and the suffragists continued throughout 1906, when women again went to the Commonwealth polls. Goldstein considered standing again for a Senate seat but decided against it. The party women went to the hustings on the lines drawn up after the 1903 Commonwealth elections: Miss Powell, successor to Locke as Labor party 'lecturess', addressed mass rallies of Labor women, and her counterpart, Mrs Andrews, addressed rallies of the Australian Women's National League. Goldstein's Women's Political Association continued to berate all Victorian women who put party issues before women's issues when choosing candidates.

In October 1906 the apolitical Victorian branch of the National Council of Women, which now represented thirty-four women's organisations in the state (some of them suffrage groups), had its Fourth Annual Convention and decided to enter the suffrage fray.[168] Bent was not enthusiastic about receiving their delegation, and there was correspondence about whether he could fit them in at night as they wished; working women could not attend during the day. Bent finally yielded to their request for a night meeting. When the 'large and representative deputation' asked him to introduce a Government bill, he claimed the fault was not his that it had not been done before; the opposition came from within his Cabinet.[169] He would approach the Cabinet on their behalf. Nothing happened. As Goldstein had said, Bent was a master in the art of bluff.

In 1906 the *Age* gave good coverage to the British women's suffrage struggle (which was just entering its militant phase) and one of the items featured was that individual women were being asked to sign 'declarations' to say that they believed women should have the vote.[170] In 1907 the Victorian women took up the idea. Thirty-six women from eighteen societies 'specially interested in securing woman suffrage' met at the Woman's Christian Temperance Union offices, with Goldstein presiding.[171] The meeting decided to form a Woman Suffrage Declaration Committee which would issue forms on which men and women would declare their support.[172] The forms were to be held by the committee and presented to Parliament at an appropriate time. The scheme was, in effect, an ongoing petition. The Declaration Committee also decided that it would take other steps to secure woman suffrage. This last organisation spawned by the Victorian movement is further evidence that Goldstein's Women's Political Association did not control the suffrage campaign in its last years. Under the Presidency of Eleanor Hobbs, also Superintendent of the State Suffrage Department of the WCTU, and with Eugenie Davidson as its Secretary, the Declaration Committee earned its name on a collective level by its continued reiteration of the women's claims, especially in the lead-up to the Victorian elections in 1907.

> It might be necessary to drive the point home on the Premier.
>
> SUFFRAGETTE.—"Yes, sir, we have damaged your motor-car, but this is no wanton act. We are determined to draw attention to our wrongs."

How *Melbourne Punch* saw the Victorian women's threat to take militant action in early 1908. The male figure is Sir Thomas Bent.
Melbourne Punch, 27 February 1908. State Library of New South Wales.

The Liberal and Conservative forces fought the 1907 state election under their new name, the United Liberal Party. The United Liberal Party had drawn some of its reformist Liberals back into the fold and was now a large, unwieldy conglomerate ranged against the declared Labor policy of the nationalisation of the means of production, distribution and exchange. Two results of the 1907 election were significant for the rest of the suffrage campaign: Labor was crushingly defeated,[173] and the number of Liberals in the Assembly who were committed to woman suffrage increased.[174]

In May 1908 Bent attended a gathering of Premiers of all Australian states. A motion came before them that the electoral laws of the states should be made uniform with those of the Commonwealth. Bent maintained that there was no possibility of making the electoral laws uniform while other states retained woman suffrage. Victoria, he said, was not going to do anything so 'foolish' as to give its women votes.[175] The Woman Suffrage Declaration Committee, in order to keep its finger on the political pulse, had been meeting weekly as the opening of the new Victorian Parliament approached. It reacted immediately by calling on Bent to resign because of his arrogant assumption 'that because he is opposed to woman suffrage, therefore the whole State is opposed to it'.[176]

> The Committee begs to remind the Premier that the State has declared in favour of woman suffrage by overwhelming majorities at six general elections, that the Legislative Assembly has passed the woman suffrage Bill thirteen times in thirteen years, that now only two voices are required to pass it in the Legislative Council, and that five of the members of his own Cabinet are in favour.[177]

The Declaration Committee also attacked Bent in the *Age*, declaring that 'the only block to reform is Mr Bent', and that by continuing in his opposition 'he does, unconstitutionally, constitute himself the State ... he is too good a parliamentary tactician to deny that a private member's measure dealing with an alteration to the Constitution is foredoomed to failure'.[178] Bent, as he always did when the blame for women not having the vote was placed at his door, reacted with an air of bewilderment. He could not understand what all the resentment was about, he said. He had never assumed that 'l' état, c'est moi'. He was surely entitled to his opinion, 'if those who wanted woman suffrage had the votes—well, there was nothing to stop them in making the principle the law'.[179]

Goldstein was busily engaged in debates and public speaking at this period, and she seems to have been acting as spokesperson for the Woman Suffrage Declaration Committee as well as the Women's Political Association. At one of these debates a ballot was taken on who should be Premier of Victoria: Bent, Prendergast, Alexander Peacock or George Swinburne. Bent was placed last with 20 votes out of 222![180] The attacks on Bent gained in intensity as the new Parliament neared its opening date in mid-1908. A campaign of meetings was held all over Melbourne in June. Bent was attacked for calling Victoria 'God's own Country' when women were excluded from citizenship,[181] and for a speech in which he said, 'We have made representative Government an actual fact.'[182] The last claim was made at a public meeting at which the Premier protected himself from his vociferous male and female challengers behind a chairman's ruling that no questions could be put. The Woman Suffrage Declaration Committee challenged him to attend a suffrage meeting and refute their arguments.[183] Not all the women's organisations were joining in the campaign against Bent; even at this stage the Women's National League was maintaining 'the strictest silence'.[184] On 8 July 1908 Goldstein wrote to Mrs

Shepparton of the league asking how the organisation dared to call itself national—and claim that it was working in the interests of women and children—when it declined to speak up for the state vote.[185] An article in the *Advertiser* commented that it was 'strange that members of the Australian Women's National League can take such an enthusiastic interest in the Federal franchise and yet content themselves with having no vote in the State Parliament'.[186]

In June a new and threatening note began to sound in the suffrage agitation. Since 1906 the *Age* had been giving good coverage to the militant British 'suffragettes'. (The paper always put the word in quotation marks to distinguish them from their more peaceful British colleagues.) Victorians had read about Lady Steel, who had her furniture confiscated because she refused to pay taxes, and about the great Hyde Park rally where 35,000 demonstrators gathered before 350,000 spectators to hear motions carried simultaneously from twenty platforms condemning the British Parliament for its refusal to introduce a Government bill. The arrests and imprisonments had been reported, and in June the *Age* commented on the women in prison garb (to protest against the imprisonment of their colleagues) who had been ejected from one of Lloyd George's meetings when as many as twenty scrimmages broke out simultaneously in the hall. The editor went on to suggest that Victorian women themselves might have reached the stage when more 'strenuous' action would have to be taken against 'the hybrid of Liberals and Conservatives from which has naturally evolved the party of stagnation'. The *Age* editor stopped short of advocating violence, but hinted that there *was* one way Victorian women could protest, 'and surely that way need not be pointed out to them'. Bent's coffers, he said, relied on the taxes of more than 144,000 women who were breadwinners . . .[187] Such considerations had not been absent from the deliberations of the suffragists. In a motion attacking Bent for refusing to include woman suffrage in the Government programme for the coming session, and for refusing to debate the issue with them, the Declaration Committee congratulated the British women for 'adhering to their militant policy until the Government gives a distinct pledge that it will include women suffrage in the Government programme'.[188]

On 30 June a group of male suffragists called on Goldstein, and offered their help in forcing Bent to introduce a Government measure. Goldstein wrote that they urged the women to 'demonstrate along the lines of the militant suffragists in England'.[189] The deliberations resulted in a decision to form a Men's League for Woman Suffrage, which was constituted within one week.[190]

When Parliament opened the Labor leader, George Prendergast, in the absence of any Government move, tabled a bill,[191] but he and the women agreed that it should be a reserve bill while the women continued to put pressure on Bent.[192]

In August Eleanor Hobbs, President of the Woman Suffrage Declaration Committee, saw the State Secretary, William Edgar, in the course of the committee's lobbying of the Ministry and of Legislative Council members. Edgar suggested that he and she should beard the lion in his den, so they went together to visit the Premier in his office, where Hobbs made a 'magnificent' plea urging Bent to change his mind and make votes for women a Government measure.[193] Bent, who was having trouble with the left-wing elements of his disparate and monolithic anti-Labor party, was less devious than usual in his reply. He told the two that he would be ridiculed as 'weak' if he changed his mind after so many years of opposition, and he 'could not go against his old friend Campbell who was so dead against it'. Hobbs parried all his arguments and finally Bent said that he 'would think on it'.[194]

As Bent still procrastinated, the National Council of Women sent another delegation.[195] Then the Men's League for Woman Suffrage decided that it would have to act, even though the women had wished to carry the point on their own. The men planned their deputation for 18 August, and Goldstein sent letters to prominent male supporters, Liberal and Labor, urging them to join the delegation. The account of the men's approach to Bent makes interesting reading.[196] Even though some members of the delegation were his political enemies, there was a relaxed atmosphere and a camaraderie that never existed when politicians were dealing with women. Federal Senator Trenwith and Dr Maloney told the Premier bluntly that he had no right to stand in the way of the will of the people, Maloney speaking 'in a vein of moderation and sweet reasonableness, on which the Premier commented later with astonishment'. The Liberals in the group were not quite as blunt. There was a good deal of flattery (or irony) in comments like that of Sir William Zeal, who had been so discourteous to the delegation of 300 women in Queen's Hall in 1898. He was 'certain that no one had greater sympathy with women and their aspirations than the Premier'. The Reverend Bevan 'contrasted the patience and longsuffering of the women of Victoria with the demonstrative behaviour of the suffragettes in England'. Bent said his Cabinet was the problem, even if he were willing to yield. He would think the matter over and approach them. Bent's Cabinet was yielding even then. Goldstein wrote in her diary that same day that one of the Cabinet members told her 'under pledge of secrecy' that the Government would shortly sponsor a bill.[197]

Six weeks passed. On 2 October Goldstein was in the waiting room of a photographic studio when Bent came out after a sitting. Goldstein seized her opportunity. She called out and demanded 'What about that woman suffrage Bill?' The startled Premier turned around. 'Hmph! It's you, is it?' he said when he saw Goldstein. He walked on, but then came back and told her that when the bill was introduced she ought to have her photograph taken holding a copy of it. Goldstein replied that she would 'be delighted to do so' if he supplied the bill. Bent laughed and told her that he was still trying to persuade 'Old Pitt', one of the Legislative Council members, and he would let her know what was happening later in the week.[198]

Five days later Bent announced to the House that the Government intended to bring in a bill providing for adult suffrage.[199] Goldstein was attending a meeting of the National Council of Women that night and made the announcement. It was greeted with cheers.[200] Then, showing that her sense of humour was still intact even after such bitter opposition, she wrote to Bent and 'asked him if he did not think we were "good fighters!"' She requested a signed copy of the bill,[201] but I can find no evidence that she had her photograph taken with it—or even received it.

On 15 October Prendergast handed over his measure, and five days later Bent himself moved the second reading of the Government's version of the bill.[202] It gave women the vote for both Houses on the same conditions as men. Only women ratepayers would automatically be put on the state roll; like the man who was not a ratepayer, his female counterpart would have to make special application and would be issued with a voter's right. This electoral provision dated back to 1865, and it had come under strong attack in the years preceding 1908, opponents claiming that a completely new state roll should be compiled in the same way as the Commonwealth roll had been—by a census of households within each electorate. Prendergast, for the Labor party, now attacked the old provision in the context of the Woman Suffrage Bill, claiming that it disadvantaged women who had no property (and, by inference, Labor voters) for these women would have to go to a great deal of trouble to put themselves on the roll.[203] As it happened, the women were not disadvantaged. Although there was an Assembly election in 1908, shortly after woman suffrage was granted (at which Bent lost office), women were not eligible to vote in it because the bill had not received royal assent. Great numbers of them did take out electoral rights, but by the time the next election was held in 1911 a new state roll had been compiled, by canvass of households, under the Electoral Act of 1910.

Bent had a great deal of difficulty in explaining his change of mind to the more cynical section of the Parliament, and had to endure considerable banter. He introduced the bill with such a glowing outline of the support it had had over twenty years that one would have thought that he had been among the most ardent of advocates. When challenged, however, he attributed his change of mind to 'the great work that women are doing in connection with charitable institutions', the part women were playing in business, and their achievements at the university. He claimed that he had been favourably influenced by the opinions of the other Premiers at the Premiers' Conference (although it was there that he had described woman suffrage as 'foolishness'). He was ready, he said, 'to confess, on my bended knees if you like, that I have changed my original views'.[204] In committee an opponent of the bill, Norman Bayles, moved an amendment to allow women to sit in Parliament.[205] The Government opposed him, and the amendment was defeated with a minimum of discussion. Even ardent supporters of women's right to candidature were not willing to endanger the suffrage now that it was almost within their grasp.

In the month when the bill was waiting to go to the Upper House, Goldstein wrote sixty-one letters to members of Parliament on its behalf,[206] and the women submitted 21,000 'declarations' which the Declaration Committee had been gathering since early 1907. Councillor Thomas Harwood announced that he would present a petition *against* the woman's vote which he was sure would have 40,000 to 50,000 names.[207] Three weeks later he produced 1207. Goldstein scoffingly called his document a 'Declaration of Dependence'.[208]

John Davies, the Attorney-General, introduced the bill in the Legislative Council on 18 November, and the *Argus* described the scene: 'Ladies flocked to the galleries yesterday to hear the debate on the Adult Suffrage Bill. Miss Vida Goldstein, who occupied one of the front seats, was an intent listener.'[209] Not all women were content to be mere listeners. When Harwood quoted Ruskin as saying that 'a woman's best influence was a guiding, not a dominating, one', a woman in the gallery jumped to her feet and joined the debate: she 'was dragged back to her seat by her companions, but it was evident that she was annoyed that her speech had been terminated—after conversing with her companions in an excited undertone for a few moments, she suddenly left her seat and

The Celebration Meeting of the Womanhood Suffrage League of New South Wales after the state and Commonwealth vote were granted in 1902. Note that there were almost twice as many men on the platform as there were women.
Mitchell Library, State Library of New South Wales.

Jessie Rooke, the 'lady of enormous debating power' in the Tasmanian campaign.
Archive Office of Tasmania.

Elizabeth Brentnall, the capable President of the Queensland Woman's Christian Temperance Union for the whole of the suffrage campaign.
Mitchell Library, State Library of New South Wales.

Mary Love, the American visitor who galvanised the Victorian Woman's Christian Temperance Union into action in the late 1880s.
Mitchell Library, State Library of New South Wales.

Annie Lowe, who with Henrietta Dugdale formed the Victorian Women's Suffrage Society in 1884, the first organisation of its kind in Australia.
Mitchell Library, State Library of New South Wales.

Brettena Smyth, the Victorian birth control writer and lecturer, who formed the Australian Women's Suffrage Society in 1888.
Mitchell Library, State Library of New South Wales.

Henrietta Dugdale, who claimed that she was the first Victorian woman, in 1859, publicly to advocate woman suffrage. She lived to exercise her vote several times after the right was granted in Victoria in 1908.
Mitchell Library, State Library of New South Wales.

Right: Marie Kirk, Secretary of the Victorian Woman's Christian Temperance Union for the period of suffrage agitation.
Mitchell Library, State Library of New South Wales.

Below: Annette Bear-Crawford, who united the various Victorian organisations under the banner of the United Council for Woman Suffrage in the early 1890s.
Mitchell Library, State Library of New South Wales.

Above: Vida Goldstein, the shining light of the Victorian suffrage movement from 1899 to 1908.
Mitchell Library, State Library of New South Wales.

Left: Dr William Maloney, the flamboyant supporter who introduced the first specific woman suffrage measure into the Victorian Parliament in 1889.
Mitchell Library, State Library of New South Wales.

Lilian Locke, the most notable Labor woman in the Victorian movement. She withdrew her support for Vida Goldstein in 1903 because she though Goldstein's non-party candidature for the Commonwealth Senate would divert votes from the Labor party team.
Mortlock Library, State Library of South Australia.

Sir Thomas Bent, the intractable opponent of the woman's vote until 1908, when he thought that it would serve his own interests.
Mitchell Library, State Library of New South Wales.

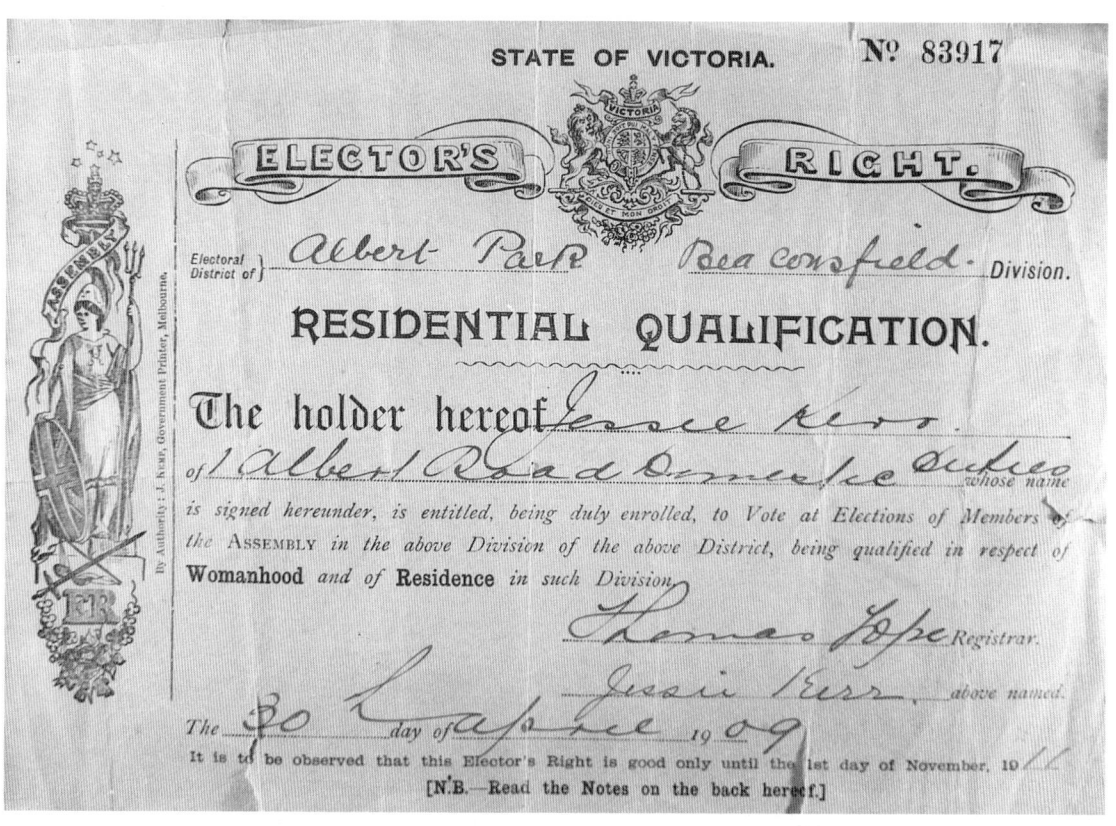

A voter's right taken out after the Victorian women's vote was granted in 1908.
By courtesy of the Victorian Woman's Christian Temperance Union.

Alice Henry and Miles Franklin, both of whom took part in the American woman suffrage campaign.
Mitchell Library, State Library of New South Wales.

11,950. GREAT SUFFRAGETTE DEMONSTRATION in LONDON. Mrs. Fisher. Mrs McGowen and Miss Vida Goldstein from Australia.

Margaret Fisher (wife of the Australian Prime Minister), Emily McGowan (wife of the New South Wales Premier) and Vida Goldstein dressed for the coronation suffrage march in London in 1911.
La Trobe Collection, State Library of Victoria.

walked out of the gallery.'[210] No division was called for when the bill was passed, but Goldstein noted that there were twenty-three supporters and five opponents.

On 5 December the leading suffragists had their photograph taken in the Botanic Gardens, and two days later they held their victory celebration, which they called a Commemoration Conversazione. It was attended by 'a large and enthusiastic audience'.[211] Eleanor Hobbs (the hard-working Superintendent of Suffrage in the WCTU since 1898 and President of the Declaration Committee since its formation) was in the chair, and the meeting gave pride of place to the two early pioneers, Lowe and Dugdale-Johnson, who reviewed the early days of the struggle. Dr Maloney, honoured because he introduced the first bill, was loudly cheered when he told the meeting he hoped they would not rest until women had the right to sit in Parliament. Mrs McLean, President of the WCTU, thanked the Men's League for its support, and Janet Michie said the women's first aim should now be to gain equal pay for equal work. The last speaker was Goldstein, who read a long honour roll of workers over the years; one hopes Brettena Smyth had a prominent place on the list. No-one, as far as we know, thanked Sir Thomas Bent.

At the victory celebration it was suggested that there should be a memorial to honour the Victorian women who had fought for the vote. Suggestions poured in which Vida recorded in her diary: an obelisk, a bed in the Women's Hospital, a Women's Centre, an annual garden party, a free kindergarten ... The most interesting was that there should be erected a white marble statue of an upright Goldstein, with her foot on the neck of a prostrate black marble statue of Thomas Bent.[212] I have been unable to uncover any evidence of a memorial.

Annie Lowe did not live to exercise her franchise. Although she had continued her public speaking to the very end of the campaign, her health was already causing concern when the bill was passed in 1908. She died, aged seventy-six, in 1910. Dugdale-Johnson voted several times in state elections before she died in 1918, at the grand old age of ninety-two. Goldstein's achievements and failures as a post-suffrage woman activist are too complex to list here, but a few details do have direct links with this history. She owned and edited another paper, the *Woman Voter*, between 1910 and 1919, which always maintained its independence from party politics. The *Voter* was the vehicle for her campaigning when she stood as an 'Independent Woman Candidate' four more times (unsuccessfully) for the Commonwealth Parliament between 1910 and 1917. The right to stand for the Victorian Parliament was given in 1923, but Goldstein never did so between then and her death in 1949. Her connections with the British movement in the immediate post-suffrage period are detailed later in this book.

The late arrival of woman suffrage in Victoria has been blamed on two things: the opposition of a strongly entrenched Upper House, and the more forceful tactics of the suffragists in that state. The answer is not so simple. It was the Liberal–Conservative Government in the Lower House rather than opposition in the Upper House which delayed the bill; the Upper House yielded soon enough when Bent introduced a Government bill. The tactics of the Victorian women (public meetings, petitions, deputations, lobbying) were not to blame either; they were as conventional as those in other states. The composition of the movement, however, was more radical than it was in other states. Organisation began earlier in Victoria than in other colonies, and from the beginning was associated with a more critical analysis of the woman's place in society, and involved a preponderance of members sympathetic to an emerging Labor party. Although apolitical and more conciliatory agitation appeared when the Woman's Christian Temperance Union spoke up in 1892 and when it instigated the Victorian Woman's Suffrage League in 1894, this was negated by the United Council's toleration of many shades of feminist expression and by the rise of the left-leaning and vocal Women's Progressive Leagues. When Goldstein came to prominence, she added her radical critique of society which was akin to Labor's; and Lilian Locke's short prominence further linked woman suffrage to Labor's ambitions for change.

Although Victorian Labor supported woman suffrage from the time plural voting was abolished in 1899, its support had little to do with the granting of the vote in 1908. Labor was vocal and pugnacious, but did not develop enough political strength in the 1890s to have any sway in the House. As the century turned, the Liberals moved to an alliance with the Conservatives against Labor. The majority of Liberals clearly believed in votes for women, as evidenced by the eleven unencumbered bills passed through the Assembly between 1898 and 1908, but any determination to push the measure through the 'House of Obstruction'[213] was sapped by the desire to placate their Conservative colleagues and by their own fear that the women's vote would give Labor an advantage. The execration of Thomas Bent by the suffragists was well-deserved. For the last five years his personal opposition both personified and guaranteed the inertia of the Legislative Assembly.

Why did Bent and his Cabinet finally yield in 1908? The most persuasive factor was probably the meteoric rise of the Australian Women's National League which convinced the parliamentary Conservatives that the woman's vote would not be radical. A speaker at a National League meeting of 800 women in July 1908 urged it to support state suffrage for women because members could use their votes to combat socialism.[214] Legislative Councillor William Edgar told a Woman's Christian Temperance Union meeting the same month that some of 'the most rabid Conservatives in the House ... believed the woman's vote had a leaning towards Conservatism'.[215] There were other reasons: pressure from the apolitical Council of Women, and from within Bent's largely factional coalition to acknowledge 'the accomplished fact' of woman suffrage in the rest of Australia. Not least may have been the fear that the Victorian 'good fighters' might metamorphose overnight into dreaded suffragettes, and so bring condemnation on Victoria from the rest of Australia.

Notes

1. *Argus*, 18 May 1857.
2. *Australian Dictionary of Biography*, vol. 4, p. 391.
3. The two measures which resulted in propertied women being given the vote were the Local Government Act of 1863 and the Municipal Constitutions Act of 1863.
4. Graham Berry, *VPD*, vol. 11, 1 March 1865, p. 418.
5. John Dane, ibid., p. 416.
6. George Higinbotham, ibid., p. 416.
7. Graham Berry, ibid., p. 418.

8. Alfred O'Connor claimed this in *VPD*, vol. 24, 24 September 1876, p. 747.
9. *VPD*, vol. 16, 8 July 1873, p. 656.
10. ibid.
11. ibid., 5 August 1873, p. 952.
12. Henry Wrixon, ibid., 8 July 1873, p. 660.
13. Alfred O'Connor, *VPD*, vol. 24, 14 September 1876, p. 747.
14. William Stanbridge, *VPD*, vol. 59, 18 December 1888, p. 2537.
15. Henrietta Dugdale-Johnson, *Woman's Sphere*, August 1903.
16. *Table Talk*, 20 October 1899.
17. Henrietta Dugdale, *A Few Hours in a Far Off Age*, p. 57.
18. *Australian Dictionary of Biography* places this marriage about 1905, but a letter enclosing membership fees for Goldstein's Women's Federal Political Association, published in *Woman's Sphere*, August 1903, is signed H. A. Johnson.
19. The following material on Annie Lowe is from an interview in the *Weekly Times*, 26 May 1909, and obituary in the *Weekly Times*, 23 April 1910.
20. *Age*, 24 June 1884.
21. *Melbourne Herald*, 30 May 1884.
22. *Weekly Times*, 23 April 1910.
23. ibid., 26 May 1909.
24. *Woman's Sphere*, January 1902.
25. *Age*, 24 June 1884; *Argus*, 24 June 1884.
26. *Argus*, 24 June 1884.
27. Annie Lowe, ibid.
28. It is possible that this provision was repealed later, but no papers of the society are available to confirm this.
29. *Woman's Voice*, 20 April 1895.
30. *Melbourne Bulletin*, 27 June 1884.
31. *Woman's Voice*, June 1895, reports that four were held in the second half of 1884, at South Yarra, South Melbourne, Collingwood, and in the Melbourne Coffee Palace.
32. *Argus*, 1 July 1885.
33. Brettena was a corruption of Bridegetena, the name given Smyth by her Irish mother.
34. In 1888 Smyth argued for the vote because 'Through the death of my husband I have had to pay all taxes just the same as when he lived', *The Liberator*, 16 September 1888.
35. *Table Talk*, 3 November 1893.
36. Brettena Smyth, *Limitation of Offspring*, p. 9 of introduction.
37. ibid.
38. *North Melbourne Advertiser*, 7 October 1892.
39. *South Melbourne Record*, December 1891.
40. *North Melbourne Advertiser*, 7 October 1892.
41. *Essendon Chronicle*, 21 October 1892.
42. 'Not Now A Suffragist' to the *Argus*, 14 April 1897; *The Champion*, 24 April 1897.
43. Australian Women's Franchise Society Leaflets, ML:NSW Q324.3/1.
44. *Essendon Chronicle*, 2 October 1892.
45. Maloney sometimes chaired Smyth's lectures; as a medical doctor he would have added to their credibility.
46. *VPD*, vol. 61, 4 September 1889, p. 1261.
47. The clothes Dr Maloney usually wore are described in *Australian Dictionary of Biography*, vol. 10, p. 389.
48. Alice Henry, 'Marching towards Citizenship', p. 102.

49. ibid.
50. *Australian Dictionary of Biography*, vol. 10, p. 389.
51. An outline of the early years of the Victorian Union is in WCTU of Australasia, Report of First Intercolonial Convention, 1891.
52. Mary Love's brother-in-law was Cornelius Ham, a member of the Victorian Legislative Council.
53. Mary Love's presidential addresses are in the WCTU of Victoria, Annual Reports, 1888, 1889 and 1890.
54. WCTU of Victoria, Annual Report, 1890.
55. ibid., 1891.
56. Vida Goldstein, 'The Struggle for Woman Suffrage' in Isabel McCorkindale, *Pioneer Pathways*, pp. 116–17.
57. Vida Goldstein, *Woman Suffrage in Australia*, p. 2.
58. Australian Women's Franchise Society Leaflets, propaganda leaflet of the WCTU of Australasia, ML:NSW Q324.3/1.
59. Munro presented this petition himself, *VPD*, vol. 67, 29 September 1891, p. 1613.
60. WCTU of Victoria, Annual Report, 1891.
61. *Australian Dictionary of Biography*, vol. 5, p. 314.
62. *Age*, 9 June 1894.
63. *Age*, 26 February 1894.
64. ibid.
65. The sketch of Bear-Crawford is drawn from *Australian Dictionary of Biography*, vol. 7, pp. 230–1; *The Webbs' Australian Diary*, 1898, ed. Albert Austin, p. 118.
66. *VPD*, vol. 74, 19 July 1894, p. 911.
67. George Turner, *VPD*, vol. 79, 26 November 1895, p. 3475.
68. Robert Best, *VPD*, vol. 82, 6 September 1896, p. 1860.
69. WCTU of Victoria, Annual Report, 1897.
70. ibid., 1896.
71. All details of these municipal involvements are in ibid.
72. Womanhood Suffrage League of New South Wales, Annual Report, 1898.
73. Unsourced newspaper clipping, 3 March 1898, Womanhood Suffrage League of New South Wales: note-books of the Secretary, and newspaper clippings, ML:NSW, MSS 38/35, items 4:282 and 4:283.
74. *VPD*, vol. 88, 10 August 1898, p. 805.
75. Jean Curlewis, Two Hundred Women in the House, LTL:V typescript, box 179/9, no. 11379. This source says there were 200 women, but other sources agree that it was 300.
76. *Tocsin*, 22 September 1898. *Tocsin* was a Labor publication with an addiction to purple prose.
77. ibid.
78. *Age*, 7 September 1898.
79. *Tocsin*, 22 September 1898.
80. *Age*, 8 September 1898.
81. Womanhood Suffrage League of New South Wales, Annual Report, 1899.
82. *VPD*, vol. 89, 13 September 1898, p. 1435.
83. ibid., p. 1442.
84. *Australian Dictionary of Biography*, vol. 6, pp. 445–6.
85. *Argus*, 14 September 1898.
86. Woman Suffrage, Leaflets and Press Cuttings on Australian and Overseas Movements, ML:NSW MSS 38/39, item 103.
87. *Age*, 16 September 1898.
88. *Australian Dictionary of Biography*, vol. 7, p. 231.

89. ibid., vol. 6, p. 208.
90. Leslie Henderson, *The Goldstein Story*, p. 70.
91. *Woman's Sphere*, December 1900.
92. Vida Goldstein to Rose Scott, 16 December 1900, Woman Suffrage Correspondence 1900–1902, ML:NSW MSS A2272, item 563.
93. *Woman's Sphere*, December 1900.
94. *VPD*, vol. 91, 2 August 1899, p. 427.
95. ibid., 8 August 1899, p. 499.
96. *Argus*, 29 August 1899.
97. *VPD*, vol. 91, 6 September 1899, p. 115.
98. *VPD*, vol. 95, 26 September 1900, p. 1653; vol. 96, 20 December 1900, p. 433.
99. *Argus*, 22 September 1900.
100. *Woman's Sphere*, October 1900.
101. *Age*, 4 August 1900.
102. *Argus*, 25 September 1900.
103. *Age*, 6 August 1900.
104. 'A Working Woman' to the *Age*, 17 August 1900.
105. Unnamed correspondent to the *Woman's Sphere*, October 1900.
106. ibid.
107. Womanhood Suffrage League of New South Wales, Annual Report, 1901.
108. *Woman's Sphere*, September 1900.
109. *Age*, 14 August 1900.
110. *Age*, 8 January 1901.
111. *Woman's Sphere*, July 1901.
112. ibid., December 1900.
113. ibid., November 1901.
114. *Tocsin*, 9 June 1898.
115. Lilian Locke (attributed), 'Address to the Victorian Women's Political and Social Crusade', presumed to be late 1903 or early 1904, LTL:V, handwritten paper, Women's Political and Social Crusade folder, Merriefield Collection.
116. *Worker* (Brisbane), 7 October 1905.
117. Lilian Locke (attributed), 'Address to the Victorian Women's Political and Social Crusade'.
118. Leslie Henderson, *The Goldstein Story*, p. 76.
119. *Woman's Sphere*, February 1902.
120. The following details of Goldstein's time in America come from *Woman's Sphere*, April 1902.
121. *Woman's Sphere*, December 1902.
122. *Age*, June 1902.
123. ibid.
124. *VPD*, vol. 100, 29 July 1902, p. 216.
125. D. W. Rawson, 'Victoria', p. 92.
126. *VPD*, vol. 101, 15 October 1902, p. 570.
127. *VPD*, vol. 103, 1 April 1903, p. 3247.
128. *Woman's Sphere*, March 1903.
129. *Melbourne Punch*, 6 April 1903.
130. Joseph Abbot, *VPD*, vol. 103, 1 April 1903, p. 3272.
131. *VPD*, vol. 105, 9 September 1903, p. 101.
132. ibid., 28 October 1903, p. 991.
133. Janice Brownfoot, 'Women's Organizations and the Woman Movement in Victoria, 1890–1908', BA (Hons) thesis, p. 58.

134. The *Tocsin* throughout December 1903 reported on Locke's movements.
135. From the time of its formation Goldstein publicised the aims and activities of the Women's Federal and Political Association in the *Woman's Sphere*.
136. *Woman's Sphere*, November 1903.
137. ibid., June, July 1903.
138. *White Ribbon Signal*, September 1903.
139. Elizabeth Nicholls, quoted in ibid.
140. *Melbourne Herald*, 8 July 1903.
141. *Federal Co-operative News*, 24 September 1903.
142. *Age*, 5 August 1903.
143. *Review of Reviews*, 20 September 1903.
144. *Avoca Mail*, 27 November 1903.
145. ibid.
146. *Bendigo Evening Mail*, December 1903.
147. *Bulletin*, 20 August 1903.
148. 'Labor Ticket, December 9 1903', an unidentified newspaper clipping, Goldstein Vida: Papers, 1902–1919, LTL:V, MSS 7865.
149. *Ballarat Echo*, 8 December 1903.
150. *Argus*, 17 December 1903.
151. Quoted in *Woman's Sphere*, 15 January 1904.
152. ibid.
153. *Weekly Times*, 15 July 1905.
154. ibid., April 1905.
155. ibid.
156. *Tocsin*, 11 June 1906.
157. *Worker* (Brisbane), 16 December 1905.
158. Dame Elizabeth Couchman,'The Australian Women's National League', no date given, LTL:V, typescript, MSS 871.
159. *Woman's Sphere*, October 1904.
160. ibid., September 1904.
161. ibid.
162. ibid., October 1904.
163. ibid.
164. *VPD*, vol. 110, 13 July 1905, p. 592.
165. Quoted by George Prendergast, *VPD*, vol. 109, 22 November 1904, p. 3114.
166. *Woman's Sphere*, January 1905.
167. *Age*, 12 September 1905.
168. ibid., October 1906.
169. WCTU of Victoria, Annual Report, 1906.
170. *Age*, 12 December 1906.
171. *Age*, 20 March 1907.
172. WCTU of Victoria, Annual Report, 1907.
173. D. W. Rawson, 'Victoria', p. 103.
174. WCTU of Victoria, Annual Report, 1907.
175. *Age*, 21 May 1908.
176. *Argus*, 16 May 1908.
177. ibid.
178. *Age*, 21 May 1908.
179. *Argus*, 18 May 1908.

180. *Argus*, 25 May 1908.
181. Miss C. Kilkelly to the *Melbourne Herald*, undated newspaper clipping, Goldstein, Vida: Papers, 1902–1919, LTL:V, MSS 7865.
182. *Argus*, 25 May 1908.
183. *Argus*, 17 June 1908.
184. Diary of Vida Goldstein, 4 August 1908, LTL:V, MSS 7865.
185. ibid.
186. *Advertiser*, 20 June 1908.
187. *Age*, 24 June 1908.
188. *Argus*, 6 June 1908.
189. Diary of Vida Goldstein, 30 June 1908, LTL:V, MSS 7865.
190. ibid.
191. *VPD*, vol. 119, 9 July 1908, p. 114.
192. Diary of Vida Goldstein, 4 July 1908, LTL:V, MSS 7865.
193. WCTU of Victoria, Annual Report, 1908.
194. Diary of Vida Goldstein, August 1908, LTL:V, MSS 7865.
195. WCTU of Victoria, Annual Report 1908.
196. *Age*, 19 August 1908.
197. Diary of Vida Goldstein, 18 August 1908, LTL:V, MSS 7865.
198. ibid., 2 October 1908. 'Old Pitt' was William Pitt, a member of the Legislative Council.
199. *VPD*, vol. 119, 7 October 1908, p. 1078.
200. Diary of Vida Goldstein, 7 October 1908, LTL:V, MSS 7865.
201. ibid., 13 October 1908.
202. *VPD*, vol. 119, 20 October 1908, p. 1269.
203. ibid., p. 1273.
204. ibid., p. 1272.
205. ibid., p. 1285.
206. Diary of Vida Goldstein, 29 October 1908, LTL:V, MSS 7865.
207. ibid., 27 October 1908.
208. Unsourced, undated American newspaper clipping in which Goldstein gives her account of the final debate, Woman Suffrage: Leaflets and press cuttings on Australian and overseas movements, ML:NSW, MSS 38/39, item 131.
209. *Argus*, 19 November 1908.
210. ibid.
211. *Age*, 8 December 1908.
212. Diary of Vida Goldstein, 7 December 1908, LTL:V, MSS 7865.
213. Unsourced, undated American newspaper clipping, Leaflets and press cuttings on Australian and overseas movements, ML:NSW MSS 38/39, item 131.
214. Mr S. Jacoby, reported in the *Age*, 16 July 1908.
215. *Age*, 3 July 1908.

PART II

SYNTHESIS AND BEYOND

9

THE POLITICIANS AND THE WOMEN

The Constitutions of the Australian colonies were based on the British electoral system and its underlying political philosophy. Except in South Australia they were postulated, not on the premise that every man should have a voice in electing members to the Lower House of the legislature, but that the male with property should have a voice. All colonies except Tasmania, using the powers written into their Constitutions, conceded manhood suffrage very soon after they were given responsible government, but property retained its representation through restrictions on electors and those elected to the Upper Houses and by plural voting (again with the exception of South Australia) for both Assemblies and Legislative Councils.

The rationale that the man with property should have more voting power than the man with none took several forms in Australia. One which had common credibility was that possessions equalled wisdom, and a second was that possessions indicated an interest in the ongoing development of the country. But more often the defenders of the property vote spoke only of the admitted principle that property should be represented.

Even before the Married Women's Property Acts of the 1880s and early 1890s, a small but significant number of women in Australia possessed property in their own right. They were widows who lived in houses or managed businesses or farms left to them by their husbands; or they were independent single women who had had property left to them by relatives or, more rarely, had leased or purchased it with their own earnings. The early attempts to grant female suffrage were not based on the ideology that the woman, like the man, should have a vote by virtue of her humanity; they were based on the premise that the property of these women 'irrespective of sex' should have representation. So conservatives, not radicals, were responsible for the first attempts to give votes to women. They moved bills and amendments to bills in attempts to give propertied women a vote, while at the same time roundly condemning woman suffrage as a principle.

The first of these attempts was in Victoria, where women with property in their own right were given the municipal vote in 1863 and it was decided to use the municipal roll as the basis of the electoral roll for the Victorian Parliament. Those males not on the municipal roll who were entitled to a vote under manhood suffrage granted in 1857 would have to make special application for a voter's right. Because the bill confirming this decision did not specify that women's names were not to be transferred from the municipal roll, women with property found themselves with a vote for the Victorian Parliament—or votes if they owned property in more than one electorate. Those who were in favour of leaving these women with the franchise maintained that they were not advocating votes for women; they were simply rectifying the anomaly that there was in the colony property which was unrepresented.[1] A similar rationale was used when William Giblin included votes for propertied Tasmanian women in an 1884 bill. Female property attracted taxation, he said, so why should it not be able to look after its interests in Parliament?[2] In Western Australia Cookworthy and Sholl made like attempts in 1893 and Dr Edward Stirling's bill in South Australia in 1886 was followed there by Caldwell's limited bills.

These early moves to give propertied women the vote were attempts to counteract the growing radicalisation of Australian Assemblies in the late nineteenth-century. Sometimes movers openly admitted their intention, as did Cookworthy and Sholl when they argued in the Western Australian Assembly that the conservative voice of propertied women would counteract the undesirable electoral influence of the goldfields. More often moves were veiled in language about the legitimate representation of property.

Most of these bills and amendments to bills, all of which were unsuccessful, excluded the married woman. In some cases the justification was that few married women owned anything in their own right; before the Married Women's Property Acts of the 1880s and 1890s a marriage settlement was necessary to prevent the possessions of the woman passing to the husband on marriage. The other reason given was that the husband's vote represented not only his own, but his wife's property. Thus William Stanbridge, in a Victorian debate, explained that he 'only proposed to give the vote to those [propertied] females who had not a parliamentary voice through their husbands'.[3]

Those who were attempting, by giving votes to a few women, to increase the representation of property in the Assemblies (or, in the case of South Australia, to introduce such representation where it had never been) were going against the ideological tide in Australia. Progressive Liberalism in the nineteenth-century came to view the property vote in any form in the Assembly as a denial of democracy, although most were willing to concede the rights of property in the Legislative Councils, either through election or nomination. Labor, when it found its collective voice in the 1880s and 1890s, vehemently opposed the representation of property through whatever mechanism. Where manhood suffrage no longer needed its championship, Labor made common ground with progressive Liberalism to eradicate the plural vote. The battle for one-man-one-vote became one of parliamentary Conservatism trying to protect its interests against democratic Liberalism and Labor, and was part of the process which led to the Australian party system.

When Australia is lauded for its early recognition of the woman's right to vote for its Assemblies, the restrictions in the Upper Houses are rarely acknowledged. In New South Wales and Queensland the Upper Houses were nominated, so the question of women voting for them did not arise. Queensland abolished its Legislative Council in 1921, before any women had been nominated for it, and New South Wales did not have a female Councillor until 1931, when Ellen Webster was appointed by a Labor Government. In the other four states, although women were given voting rights on the same property qualifications as men, they were greatly disadvantaged. Fewer women than men owned property in their own right and, unless a house were in the joint names of husband and wife, the family residence was presumed to be owned by the husband. The property qualifications remained in Victoria until 1950, Western Australia until 1964, Tasmania until 1968, and South Australia until 1973. Tasmania in 1954, however, gave a vote to the householder's spouse. The suffragists did not seem to consider the franchise for the Legislative Council important, and it must be presumed that, unless they had an identification with the Labor party, they too accepted the principle that property rather than the individual should be represented there. The lack of any considerable say in the election of Councillors, however, was a limitation on women's overall political power until the second half of the twentieth-century.

When the women formed their own suffrage societies in the 1880s and 1890s, the first question they had to settle was the basis on which they would ask for a vote. All rejected the proposition that votes should be given to propertied women and that other women should have none. The 1888 the South Australian Women's Suffrage League, however, although its platform stipulated that the qualifications for women 'should be the same as those which apply to men', was beguiled into supporting a property bill proposed in 1890 by Robert Caldwell on the basis that it would be 'the thin end of the wedge' leading to votes for all women. By 1891 they were less credulous and withdrew their endorsement of any such future bills. It was apparent by then that Caldwell was trying, with the introduction of a propertied vote into a House which had never had one, to counteract increasing Labor representation.

Having decreed that a vote should be given to every woman, suffrage societies then had to decide whether they would allow their claim to be entangled with the bitter controversy over the plural vote. Members of societies were divided on the issue of the plural vote and, in a climate where opinions for and against were helping to delineate political groupings, a suffrage society could not take a stand without aligning itself with one party and against another. The WCTU did not need to wrestle with the problem; their Constitution forbade them to affiliate with any political party and so they demanded the vote 'on the grounds that it is, or shall be, granted to men'. The open societies, with a wider-ranging membership, had no ready-made solution, but to avoid internal tensions they all, with the exception of Queensland, decided to do as the WCTU was doing. Such a decision, they thought, would keep them clear of political turmoil and persuade politicians, whether they backed the plural vote or not, to be sympathetic to their claims. They soon found out they were mistaken in the case of Labor. Trades and

Labor Councils, and Labor parties as they were formed, although they expressed sympathy with the women's aspirations, refused to give them any official support until the plural vote had been abolished. Labor politicians who did vote for bills which gave woman suffrage when Labor was still trying to achieve one-man-one-vote, like Arthur Rae in New South Wales and William Maloney in Victoria, were going against the policy of their party.

Every colony could point to abuses of the plural vote, but in none was its manipulation more blatant than in Queensland. It was claimed there that men with money and influence were not only multiplying votes for themselves and male members of their families by the judicious purchase of land, but were taking advantage of the plural vote in other ways. In 1899 Francis Kates told the Legislative Assembly that he had lost an election because of his opponent's deviousness: 'My opponent had a paddock on the Downs, a very large paddock. He cut it up into very small portions and issued leases to his friends in Brisbane to put them on the roll. When the polling day came round they got a special train and came up and outvoted me.'[4] 'A paddock on the Downs' was a colloquialism of the time for a large property on the Darling Downs.

Queensland's strong Labor movement, nurtured on acrimonious confrontation over the electoral system, saw in the granting of woman suffrage an increase in opportunities for abuse of the plural vote. Not only would a landholder by subdivision be able to bestow multiple votes on his sons, but perhaps on his wife and daughters. Using women active in their party's affairs, Labor in 1894 subverted efforts by the suffragists to form a united society, and forced into being a Labor organisation, the Woman's Equal Franchise Association, which not only agitated for one-adult-one-vote, but made it clear that it would oppose woman suffrage on any other conditions.

In Western Australia the very vocal opposition of Frederick Illingworth should not be allowed to overshadow the support for the *principle* of woman suffrage expressed by other radical politicians in that colony. But though it supported the concept, incipient Labor there opposed woman suffrage bills not only because of the plural voting issue, but because the woman's vote would work against it in other ways. The mass influx of males onto the western goldfields created new 'male' electorates. Woman suffrage would mean that the Government could legitimately give greater representation to the coastal areas, which would balance the radical voice of the goldfields. Representatives from the goldfields therefore did all they could to hinder woman suffrage bills.

There is perhaps some justification for Labor's opposition to votes for women because of the abuses of the plural voting system, although there had been no question in any colony of rejecting manhood suffrage because plural voting existed. No vindication can be conceded, however, for its opposition in Western Australia on the grounds that a perfectly legitimate division of urban electorates could take place because the names of women would swell the electoral rolls there. Labor could be as opportunistic about votes for women as Conservative parties had been in their early attempts to give only propertied women the vote.

The Labor party in Australia had emerged from the trades unions via their Trades and Labor Councils, and the attitude of the councils paralleled that of political Labor: in all colonies they refused to back woman suffrage until plural voting had been abolished. In Western Australia the first Trades and Labor Congress which met at Coolgardie in 1899 did not even support votes for women conditional on the abolition of the plural vote, although the national body of Trades and Labor Councils had done so in 1896. For all that it formally endorsed female suffrage after the abolition of the plural vote, however, the male trade union movement was markedly unenthusiastic when it came to active support. Leontine Cooper in Queensland put her finger on the reason for their inertia:

> Labour has never yet shown sympathy with woman, but with the cry 'Woman's competition means lower wages' has kept us out of their unions and other trades, indifferent to the fact that they thus thrust us into the sweater's den, or a still lower hell. When woman has political power, no matter on what basis or what terms, it will be seen that she will fight for the cause of her fellow-women, irrespective of race or creed.[5]

Conservatives in Australian Parliaments, once they were defeated in their efforts to give only propertied women a vote (or votes if they were entitled to them on a plural voting basis), aggressively opposed bills granting womanhood suffrage. In the Assemblies they fought to prevent them reaching the Upper Houses, and in the Legislative Councils, where their representation was much greater, refused to ratify them until they were forced to do so. South Australia and Western Australia must be excepted from this generalisation: in South Australia the Legislative Council itself was radicalised by the 1894 elections and initiated the bill which gave women votes; and in Western Australia the Upper House considered only one bill, which it passed without demur because it thought the woman's vote would counteract the electoral threat of the goldminers.

Conservative politicians had ideological reasons for opposing a measure which would, they rightly thought, alter the woman's view of herself in society, but they had political reasons, too. The first of these had to do with the rural–urban distribution of political power. Colonial Constitutions, drawn up at a time when the prosperity of Australia was envisaged as residing in the soil—and when power lay with the large landowners—gave varying degrees of weighting to rural electorates at the expense of urban. In the late nineteenth-century the rural property owners, who provided the Conservative backbones of both Upper and Lower Houses, were fighting to retain their favoured position against urban Liberal forces. With women concentrated in the towns, they saw woman suffrage as a weapon placed in the hands of their enemies who were fighting for electoral redistribution, for the woman's vote could be used to centralise political power in the cities. The other reason, and a related one, was their fear of the creeping radicalism in Australian society. This was manifesting itself in radical Liberalism which was willing to make common ground with Labor's demand for the abolition of the plural vote and for electoral redistribution; in the centralisation of trade union power in the Trades and Labor Councils; and in the rise of political Labor. It is true that the woman's vote was an unknown electoral quantity (some on the left were afraid that it would be conservative) but it was concentrated in the towns where radicalism fermented. Samuel Staughton cautioned his Conservative party colleagues in an 1890 Victorian debate: 'Do Honorary members for a moment think that the Labor Party would advocate woman suffrage if they thought that the woman's vote would be a conservative one?'[6] A South Australian conservative observer was less temperate and more colourful in his warning about what would happen if the Labor suffragist Mary Lee and her colleagues had their way:

> If Mrs Lee obtains the power she desires and is permitted unrestrained to stir the seething cauldron of class discord I may live to see her knitting, counting the while the bleeding heads of the thrifty and learned as they fall beneath the strokes of the guillotine. Then by brute force, the best intellects removed, she may have scope for political experiments.[7]

The Liberal, or middle, ground in Australian politics, at a time when parties as such were only beginning to solidify, is harder to categorise in its attitude to votes for women. There were those, like Thomas Bent and John Forrest, who defined themselves as Liberals (and have been defined as such in Australian political history because of the parliamentary measures they successfully espoused), who vigorously opposed votes for women. But the further to the left the politician can be placed on the Liberal spectrum, the more likely he was to support the women's demands. Because it was electorally impossible in any colony for Labor on its own to give women votes, the bias of a particular colony's Liberalism was vital to its prospects for woman suffrage. In Victoria and Western Australia, where Liberalism had common cause with parliamentary Conservatism, and no unanimity with Labor, the woman's vote was granted only when it appeared that it would favour the interests of the Conservative party. In the other four colonies, where Liberalism was more progressive in its predilections, the measure was passed by a conjunction of Liberal and Labor forces.

Even though the suffragists refused to accept a vote for propertied women only and, except in Queensland, rejected involvement with the plural vote, party divisions put great strains on the unity of their societies. The WCTU, because members wanted the vote for a specific purpose, was the most successful in containing tensions between women with different political convictions. The South Australian WCTU expressed the attitude of the Temperance Unions everywhere: 'Though we may differ on many subjects, we agree on those most important. Let us, therefore, put them before party politics.'[8]

The WCTU did have some problems in staying clear of party politics, however. In Victoria in 1897 several candidates wrote to Union branches asking for support in the coming election. The central Union gave this rather naive advice. The 'cause' referred to in the quotation is votes for women:

> In the country it is easier to choose your candidate, to support and stick to him, than in the town, where so many men are in favour of our cause that it is hard to decide on the best man to work for. I would advise women to be very true to the sitting member if he has been true to them, and try to get the other good men who oppose him to retire and stand for places where the sitting member is known to be unfavourable to our cause.[9]

The Women's Suffrage League of South Australia was the only open society which appears to have avoided tensions in its varied membership. Theirs was a relatively short-lived society, however; if the vote in South Australia had been delayed until the late 1890s or the early twentieth-century, when politics in that colony became more confrontational, the story might have been different. In the eastern colonies tensions resulted in a proliferation of groups: in Queensland the Labor women broke away to form a separate society in 1894; in New South Wales, even though plural voting was abolished in 1893, the Womanhood Suffrage League maintained unity with difficulty until 1901, when a group broke away to form the Women's Progressive Association, with left-wing leaning; and in Victoria, as in Britain and the United States, groups multiplied to suit the needs of the political and ideological stances of the women.

Most suffrage organisations, whatever the political composition of their membership, insisted that they were non-party. Even the Woman's Equal Franchise Association in Queensland claimed that it had no party affiliations,[10] and this was true in so far as the official Labor party had no voice in its affairs after the association was formed. But it was not true in that the Woman's Equal Franchise Association followed the Labor party line and those with any other affiliation would have been out of place among its membership. Agnes Williams lasted less than two months as its first President before she was replaced in a special election with the strong Labor woman, Emma Miller. Williams then went to work with the apolitical WCTU.

Large numbers of suffragists not only owed no allegiance to any party; they declared themselves to be non-aligned on principle. Some condemned the party system but others, while recognising its historical imperative, thought that women should refuse alignments in order to become a powerful lobbying force on women's issues after their vote was won. Divisions between the women on party lines, and between party women and non-aligned women, became glaringly apparent at the first Commonwealth elections in 1903, both in states with woman suffrage for their own Assemblies and in states without.

The right to stand as candidates for both Houses of the Commonwealth Parliament was conceded in 1902 when all white Australian women were given the Commonwealth vote. Only in South Australia, however, was the right of state candidacy given at the same time as the vote. The prospect of women occupying their hallowed parliamentary benches seemed to frighten most nineteenth-century Australian parliamentarians out of their wits. The spectre was raised early in the campaign in every colony, and haunted most debates thereafter. Opponents argued that if women were given the franchise, the natural corollary was that they would have to be allowed to become members. As Henry Rooke in an 1896 Tasmanian parliamentary debate put it: 'if they once allowed them the vote, the women would next elect themselves.'[11]

The fear of women in the legislature was not confined to the parliamentarians. Dr Edward Stirling, in his masterly apologia for woman suffrage in 1885, told the South Australian Parliament that 'of all the objections, this was the one he'd heard used more than any other',[12] and when the opposition press in all colonies fulminated against votes for women they would predict the possibility as one of the measure's most dire consequences.

Comments about women in Parliament ranged from witty pleasantries through to acrimonious denunciations. Stirling in 1885 was only being whimsical when, contending that parliamentary representation could come some time in the future, he conjured up a mixed Assembly where all calculations would be upset by 'a member of the Government marrying the leader of the Opposition and so giving rise to a coalition Ministry'.[13] The editor of the Adelaide *Observer* commented at the time:

> The idea of a Parliament composed of men and women rather staggers the imagination, especially if the women who sit in the legislative halls must be either maids or widows ... the natural influence of sex would give rise to some frightful perplexities at times ... extraordinary elections in consequence of the enforced resignation of lady members ... No Government would be safe against the persistent attacks of a feminine opposition.[14]

Not all comments were jocular. Adye Douglas in the Tasmanian Upper House asked his fellow Councillors scornfully: 'Do you want to bring them in here with their babies and their bottles?'[15] A Victorian paper declared:

> Can we, as sane people, subscribe to such a preposterous possibility as that of being governed by a Legislature and a Cabinet of females—most of them women who have failed in the pursuit of woman's great object in life—man—and whose intellectual attainments and individual attractiveness would not, as a matter of course, be of a high order?'[16]

Supporters of woman suffrage, both inside and outside Parliament, reacted in different ways when the bogy of female representation was raised. Some, while not actually defending women in Parliament, could reply that the idea might not be such a bad one, at that. Elizabeth Nicholls told a South Australian public meeting in 1893 that 'even if some women did get into Parliament she did not think that women would be any the worse for it'.[17] Sometimes, but not often, supporters vigorously defended the proposition. In 1902 the Queensland WCTU protested strongly against a suffrage bill which specifically excluded women from Parliament, and called the exception an 'insidious clause' which carried a 'sex stigma'.[18] They then sent a deputation to the Premier asking that Queensland women be put 'in the same position politically as the Federal Parliament has placed the women of Australia'.[19] In 1903 the Brisbane *Worker* attacked a Legislative Councillor who had spoken against women in Parliament:

> Mr F. I. Power said that women should not take a seat in Parliament because Nature had provided certain functions for her which would make the situation awkward at times. To hear this inspired 'fossil' anyone would think that all women were the mothers of young families. The women who will someday seek representation in Parliament will be mothers of grown-up families, or single unattached women.[20]

The most common reaction of the women to the philippics against them was to deny that they wanted the right of candidature, at least for the time being. They not only did this before 1894, when the South Australian bill was passed, but continued their denials in the years following. These disavowals could mean that they thought the demand for candidature would hinder the granting of their suffrage, or that the time was not yet ripe for such a step. But they could also mean that the women themselves did not believe that they should aspire to the Houses. At a New South Wales WCTU meeting soon after the 1894 South Australian bill had given women the right to be elected in that state, the President, Sara Nolan, vigorously repudiated any intention of Union members in New South Wales wanting to enter Parliament. There were 'quite enough good and true men' in that state to fill the parliamentary benches, she said.[21] Elizabeth Ward spoke in the same vein, and when later in the meeting a proposed message of congratulation to the South Australian women was discussed, many were critical of the South Australian Parliament for going so far. This was evidently reflected in the message which was sent, for Elizabeth Nicholls who, like most South Australian women, was proud that they had been given more than they asked for, wrote back:

> I am sorry that any of our New South Wales sisters object to women having the right to sit in Parliament; we did not venture to ask for it yet but are very glad to have it, for while we are not anxious to avail ourselves of the right, we believe we shall be far more successful in securing laws for the good of our people if legislators know that in case they fail us we can enter Parliament and make the laws ourselves. One New South Wales sister said that if women had such a right in New South Wales the worst women would be nominated and elected. I would fain think she is mistaken, and in South Australia, I am sure, such a thing would not occur ... The New Zealand women are already asking the right to sit as members. It must eventually come to that, for justice demands completely equal political rights and opportunities for men and women, and the world will never be properly governed until the right to rule is not decided by sex or class, but by character and ability.[22]

It is apparent when one overviews the movement that the WCTU, with its mutual support structure crisscrossing the continent, figured very prominently. In Tasmania it *was* the movement; in Western Australia it carried the agitation until three months before the vote was conceded; and in other colonies it worked beside the open franchise societies in varying degrees of balance and harmony. When the National Conventions to plan a Constitution for the new Commonwealth gave the suffragists the opportunity to lobby for woman suffrage in the federal sphere, the WCTU, unlike the open state societies, was able to speak with a national voice.

The burgeoning of the Australian WCTU in the 1890s is best explained by the fact that the American women who brought it to Australia tapped into an existing Australian male temperance movement. Since the 1850s temperance campaigners had been declaiming against colonial drinking habits, and by the 1890s there was an array of male organisations (in the larger colonies affiliated to Temperance Alliances) which held periodic 'missions' to persuade drinkers to 'sign the pledge'. Most of these, as well as imposing total abstinence on their members and converts, advocated prohibition, but they probably saw this as only a distant possibility. Their immediate concerns were restrictions on the number of liquor outlets, shortened trading hours, and local option laws. The men welcomed the formation of the Union, and drew the women into their lobbying work via petitions and deputations. Membership of the Union would have come from families in which the males were either active in, or sympathetic to, the temperance cause. This meant that the women came mainly, but not exclusively, from the nonconformist churches, and many of them took an active part in their churches' affairs through Sunday school teaching, women's groups and charity work. The Union provided them with an opportunity, acceptable even to convential husbands and fathers, to move out 'into the world'—an opportunity which they seem to have seized with alacrity.

The WCTU, by aggressively declaring that women would use their votes to impose prohibition or at least local option, aroused the opposition of the liquor interests to woman suffrage. They frequently claimed that the victuallers were bringing pressure to bear against bills in the legislatures, and in New South Wales it was contended that liquor interests lay behind the formation of the Anti-Suffrage League in 1900. The claims could be true, but they are hard to substantiate. In 1895 the New South Wales Licensed Victuallers' Association discussed and supported a motion: 'To grant the suffrage to women would lead to the ruin of the trade',[23] and they may have then moved to lobby the New South Wales Government, although their concern is not reflected in the New South Wales debates. In Victoria in 1901, however, Vida Goldstein made a more specific accusation:

> There is always a close connection between anti-suffrage and the liquor traffic. In Victoria it is an open secret that at the bottom of the hostility to woman suffrage of many members of the legislature who are largely interested in breweries and hotels, is the deadly fear that when women get the vote prohibition will rule the land.[24]

Goldstein may have been right. There may well have been members in either the Council or the Assembly who were afraid that their investments would be threatened by the proselytising zeal of female teetotallers, of whom Goldstein, though not a member of the WCTU, was one. But the opposition of Conservatives to votes for women involved many other complex factors. The possibility that women would impose prohibition seems to have been given little credence in parliamentary debates in any colony and it is unlikely that the involvement of the WCTU delayed either state or Commonwealth votes, or inhibited support in the wider community. Agitation coming from women who were seen as moral and conservative in other ways may even have calmed the fears of some who were afraid that 'women's rights' would threaten the structure of Australian society. All Australian states had given their women votes before the great prohibition debate intensified in Australia, but in the United States the last ten years of the woman suffrage campaign coincided with the ten years before prohibition was imposed in 1920, and these years were marked by a highly organised and overt campaign by the brewing interests to block woman suffrage moves in Congress and in those states where it had not already been granted. In Australia efforts to impose prohibition in the 1910s and 1920s were all defeated.

Most, if not all, WCTU women were members of churches, as were many suffragists in the open societies, but they could not always rely on their churches to encourage them in their franchise work. Churches heavily involved in social work and reform, like the Victorian Labour Church, and Dr Strong's Australian Church (to which Vida Goldstein and her parents belonged) backed the movement. Unitarianism and Christian Science, regarded by the mainstream as aberrant, allowed women to preach and would have had no quarrel with women in public life. (Catherine Helen Spence was a preacher for the Unitarian and Vida Goldstein, when she became its convert, for the Christian Science.) The nonconformist churches were generally supportive, but could be unpredictable. Individuals and congregations were free to hold their own opinions, but central gatherings (male) often issued rulings, especially if approached by the suffragists. The South Australian Women's Suffrage League, with many clergymen involved in its formation, was able to marshall most nonconformist churches behind it; in Victoria in 1896 a circular was sent 'to all leaders of religious thought' and 'favourable replies' were received;[25] and Rose Scott had many affirmations of support when she lobbied New South Wales leaders. In Queensland, however, although the Christian Endeavour Convention (an interdenominational youth organisation) had a verbal sparring match with the editor of the *Brisbane Courier* when he opposed votes for women, the Brisbane Ministers' Union refused to endorse the Christian Endeavour stand.[26] The fact that woman suffrage was so entangled with party politics worried the Salvation Army in New South Wales (the only state for which I have a reference). It replied to Scott's approach: 'as the Constitution of the Salvation Army does not favour us as a body taking part in political questions, we do not see our way clear to accede to your request.'[27] The writer of this letter, however, went on to assure Scott that the women had the support of the majority of Salvation Army members, and wished her every success. The Church of England seems to have thought that silence was the wisest policy, but in 1903, after the vote was granted, the President of the Anglican New South Wales Mothers' Union made an interesting comment: 'Besides their other duties, women now have the burden of the vote, as if wives and mothers have not quite enough to do without that.'[28]

There appear to have been few Catholic women active in the organisations; there were certainly none in prominent positions in the WCTU, and only Annie and Belle Golding can be confirmed among leaders of the other societies. Vida Goldstein claimed that the Catholic Church was against woman suffrage,[29] but this was not universally so. Cardinal Moran sent a letter of support with a deputation to the New South Wales Premier in 1898,[30] and in 1902 he wrote: 'For many years I have been in favour of extending to women the same powers enjoyed by men in the matter of suffrage. I consider that they are entitled to the right.'[31] Other Catholic men disagreed. At the second Australasian Catholic Congress held in Melbourne in 1894 a paper written by Annie Golding (which because of her sex she was not allowed to read) pleaded 'that the enfranchisement of women recognized the true rights and capacities of women'.[32] Its reception was cool, and Mr P. W. Crowe claimed in a later paper that 'It is a matter of grave doubt whether the extension of the franchise adds to the exaltation of women, or whether such power is within the compass of her life and duties.'[33] Father T. A. Fitzgerald wrote that Catholic women felt 'an innate repugnance to exercising their privilege of voting. It seems antagonistic to the established traditions as to women's place in the world, utterly inconsistent with [their] retiring disposition'.[34]

Generalisations from the announcements of church conventions and prominent male churchmen do not, however, tell us what the ordinary men, and especially women, of the congregations thought. The truth is that among church members, as among non-church members, opinions were divided. Two incidental reports are illuminating. Vida Goldstein claimed that a secret ballot was taken at a Catholic fête in 1900 and the result was 328–281 in favour.[35] James McCulloch said in an 1896 Victorian parliamentary debate:

> At Wodonga a large Presbyterian bazaar was held, and a barrister who was in favour of woman suffrage challenged another barrister who was strongly opposed to it to engage in a debate on the subject. After the debate a count of the women was taken, and they were 2–1 in favour.[36]

What were the women like who encouraged their supporters, pitted themselves against their adversaries, and lobbied both in the maelstrom of Australian political life in the period? They show a considerable diversity if examined according to the Australian class structure. Rose Scott and her select group in Sydney, the women with wealthy husbands or parents (like Rosetta Birks in South Australia, Annette Bear-Crawford in Melbourne, and the women of the Karrakatta Club in Perth) were all from the upper echelons of their societies. Some of these upper-class women, like Lady Mary Windeyer in New South Wales and Mrs Oakley-Fysh in Tasmania, worked through the Woman's Christian Temperance Union, but the women in the WCTU tended to belong on the middle rungs of the social ladder. Some of them may have been in quite straitened circumstances, for what held these women together was not social and economic position, but respectability and membership of a church. The women with Labor sympathies, or active in the Labor movement, were not those who stitched till late at night for the 'sweater', or who worked for long hours in factories. They were in modest financial circumstances, but their life experiences had confirmed them as Labor supporters. Women like Mary Lee and Augusta Zadow in South Australia, Emma Miller in Queensland, Lilian Locke in Victoria, and the Golding sisters in New South Wales, however, must be seen as representing the great number of 'invisible' suffragists at the bottom end of the scale who were so overworked in the labour market or in striving to make their husband's meagre wages stretch to the needs of their usually large families that they could only sign the petitions brought to them by their sisters, or perhaps occasionally swell the numbers at a public meeting. 'A Busy Mother' writing to the *Brisbane Courier* in 1900 put it this way: 'It is rather hard that because many of us mothers have not time to fight for a vote, it should be taken for granted that we do not want it.'[37]

The claim that the woman suffrage movement was an urban one is correct in that it began in each capital city and had the greatest number of adherents there, but the suffrage organisations did spread their tentacles out into the country towns. Many of the country branches of the WCTU formed suffrage departments, and even those which were too small to do so contributed signatures to the Union's petitions. In the Queensland mining towns, where the number of Labor adherents was high, there was much support for what the Woman's Equal Franchise Association was doing. The New South Wales Womanhood Suffrage League had healthy branches in Newcastle and on the south coast, and smaller branches scattered through the areas further out; in Deniliquin, where Mary Glyde was Secretary, the league reported a public meeting which attracted two hundred and a petition which measured sixteen feet;[38] and Frances Paul wrote from Orange to Rose Scott in 1900: 'Oh what a commotion we've made in this sleepy little place! . . . there are no more any apathetic ones (or I don't meet them!) but either enthusiastic "Franchise women" or strenuous opposition to the Franchise.'[39] Arthur Rae gave some indication, too, of the non-organised support in the country when he wrote to Scott from Wyalong, a New South Wales mining centre, that in his electioneering speech every reference to woman suffrage was received with cheers.[40] In Victoria large public meetings were held in provincial centres like Ballarat and Bendigo, not only in support of the state vote, but in support of Goldstein's Senate candidature in 1903.

The age range of active suffragists is significant. The married women tended to be those whose health had survived the rigours of their child-bearing years and who, in late middle life, were left with enough energy to move into public life. The younger women—Vida Goldstein, Annette Bear-Crawford, Annie Golding, Lilian Locke—were usually single or childless. Quite remarkable are the sturdy elderly women who chose the speaking platform instead of the chimney corner: Mary Lee, who helped to form the South Australian League when she was sixty-five and lived till she was ninety-six; Emma Miller, whose public life continued for twelve years after the crowning of her suffrage efforts when she was sixty-six; Annie Lowe, prominent in the Victorian movement from the time she was fifty until the vote was granted when she was seventy-four; and Catherine Helen Spence, who was seventy-two when she stood for election to the 1897 Federal Convention three years after the South Australian vote was conceded. When assessing the women who wanted the vote, as distinct from those who joined societies, one must add not only those single women whose battle to earn a living left them with no energy to take part, but those married women who in their post-child-bearing years did not enjoy the health and vitality of an Emma Miller or an Annie Lowe.

Although there was some cross-membership, especially in Victoria, the suffragists fall for the most part into two groups: Union women and those in the societies. The women who took the initiative in forming the open societies were generally, because they had no pre-existing movement to launch them, more individualistic. They were also more widely read and more sophisticated than those in the Union. They were city women from backgrounds as diverse as those of Henrietta Dugdale and Rose Scott, but they had personally reached two interconnecting beliefs: that the woman was a citizen of the State and so entitled to a share in its government, and that with the vote woman's legal and social status could be upgraded. Some, like Dora Montefiore and Rose Scott, could point to conversion experiences around which these beliefs pivoted, but others had reached their position through thought and reading. Several gave credit to J. S. Mill's *The Subjection of Women*, but their speeches and propaganda also show a wide knowledge of the suffrage movements in England and the United States, and of the writings of the women in these movements.

The numerous organisations and the complex mix of women which made up the Australian movement knew that there was only one way they could gain their suffrage: a majority must vote in favour of it in both Houses of their particular legislature. They therefore saw their mission as the education and conversion of the politicians, the male electorate, and other women. To this end a mass of pamphlets and tracts was distributed to supplement their rhetoric in deputations to Parliaments and on the speaking and debating platforms. An examination of the arguments they presented—and the counter-arguments these generated—will throw some light on why Australian women had the vote when every other nation except New Zealand denied it to their women.

Notes

1. *VPD*, vol. 11, 1 March 1865.
2. *Mercury*, 23 September 1884.
3. *VPD*, vol. 59, 18 December 1888, p. 2537.
4. *QPD*, vol. 83, 8 November 1889, p. 869.
5. *Brisbane Courier*, 30 April 1894.

6. *VPD*, vol. 96, 11 December 1900, p. 115.
7. E. Young, *Advertiser*, 10 October 1893.
8. WCTU of South Australia, Annual Report, 1897.
9. WCTU of Victoria, Annual Report, 1897.
10. *Worker* (Brisbane), 4 April 1896.
11. *Mercury*, 24 September 1896.
12. *SAPD*, 22 July 1885, c. 330.
13. ibid.
14. *Observer*, 23 July 1885.
15. *Mercury*, 9 October 1903.
16. *Bairnsdale Advertiser*, 17 November 1903.
17. *Advertiser*, 15 March 1893.
18. WCTU of Queensland, Annual Report, 1902.
19. ibid.
20. *Worker* (Brisbane), 1 April 1903.
21. Report of a meeting of the WCTU of New South Wales, 28 December 1894, in E. Ward, *Out of Weakness Made Strong*, p. 61.
22. Elizabeth Nicholls to Elizabeth Ward, 3 January 1895, quoted in *Out of Weakness Made Strong*, pp. 62–3.
23. Licensed Victuallers Association, Report of the Annual Meeting, unsourced newspaper clipping dated December 1895, Womanhood Suffrage League of New South Wales: note-books of the Secretary, and newspaper clippings, ML:NSW, MSS 38/35, Item 167.
24. *Woman's Sphere*, August 1901.
25. WCTU of Victoria, Annual Report, 1896.
26. *Worker* (Brisbane), 8 May 1901.
27. Letter to Rose Scott, 21 November 1900, Woman Suffrage Correspondence, 1900–1902, ML:NSW, MSS A2272, item 526.
28. Quoted in S. Willis, 'Homes are divine workshops', p. 179.
29. *Woman's Sphere*, November 1900.
30. *Dawn*, July 1898.
31. *Catholic Press*, 24 May 1902.
32. Quoted in P. O'Farrell, *The Catholic Church in Australia*, p. 254.
33. ibid., p. 255.
34. Quoted in S. Willis, 'Homes are divine workshops', p. 179.
35. *Woman's Sphere*, November 1900.
36. *VPD*, vol. 96, 20 December 1900, p. 434.
37. *Brisbane Courier*, 4 September 1900.
38. Womanhood Suffrage League of New South Wales, Annual Report, 1898.
39. Letter to Rose Scott, 25 November 1900, Woman Suffrage Correspondence 1900–1902, ML:NSW, MSS A2272, item 543.
40. Womanhood Suffrage League of New South Wales, Annual Report, 1894.

10

THE ARGUMENTS AND THE ISSUES

Each side of the woman suffrage debate had its arsenal of ideological weapons which were brought out every time there was a confrontation about votes for women in Australia. The same shots were fired by deputations in the lobbies of Parliaments and in clashes in the actual legislatures. The arguments were the same in propaganda leaflets, press editorials and the letters columns of newspapers as they were in large public meetings and debates in small suburban and country Schools of Arts and temperance halls. And, with some variations of emphases, they were the same just before the vote was granted in Victoria in 1908 as they had been in scattered pockets of discussion back in the 1860s.

The basis of the pleading of the suffragists was that justice and the theory of natural rights demanded that every individual should have a say in the government of the State. Successive waves of nineteenth-century immigrants brought with them to Australia the ideals of equality and the inherent rights of the individual, which had their roots in the Enlightenment and The Declaration of the Rights of Man and of the Citizen. These ideals were being espoused in waves of revolution in Europe, in the People's Charter and unrest in England, and in the vigorous democratic enthusiasms sweeping North America. Radical Liberals brought the ideas of the British political philosophers, particularly those of John Stuart Mill expressed in his *Representative Government* of 1859. The year before he published *Representative Government*, Mill had written to Henry Chapman, with whom he had been associated in London (and who was then the Victorian Attorney-General) approving the manhood suffrage established in Victoria:

> The only thing which seems wanting to make the suffrage really universal, is to get rid of the Toryism of sex, by admitting women to vote; and it will be a great test how far the bulk of your population deserve to have the suffrage, their being willing or not to extend it to women.[1]

When Mill in *Representative Government* contended that 'the prime idea of democracy is the Government of the whole people by the whole people',[2] he included women in his definition of people. Of the difference of sex he wrote: 'I consider it to be as entirely irrelevant to political rights as difference in height or in colour of the hair.'[3] When, ten years later, Mill published *The Subjection of Women*, no-one in Australia who was keeping abreast of English political theory could fail to be challenged by the claims of women to the vote. Some supporters corresponded with Mill: Sir Henry Parkes, Archibald Michie, Catherine Helen Spence. Some had more personal links with him: Arthur Hardy, who had settled in Adelaide and was a friend of Dr Edward Stirling, was his brother-in-law, and Spence visited the philosopher when she went to England in the 1860s. Some prominent suffragists were so familiar with his work that in their rhetoric they might at times be accused of plagiarism. Two of the first pamphlets issued in Australia (by the Victorian Women's Suffrage Society in 1884) quoted extensively from *Representative Government* and *The Subjection of Women*. As the movement gathered momentum many other suffragists, perhaps entirely ignorant of the democratic theorists, nevertheless echoed their ideas as they reiterated the belief which supported all their claims: that the woman, as a citizen of the State, should share in its political processes. Supporters in every colony reaffirmed it. So Eleanor Trundle of the Queensland WCTU said in 1898: 'Our sole point is that it is our right as citizens to a voice in the Government of the country',[4] and a circular asking support from new members of the Victorian Parliament in 1892 said that 'as an act of common justice ... all women desiring to vote should be allowed to do so; those who do not to be allowed the liberty of refraining.'[5] Rose Scott echoed Mill's contention:

> We claim that as a human being, she should have from the parent state the same rights and privileges as that other section of humanity called *men*, and we affirm that the sex of a human being is, like *race* and *colour*, a secondary matter. [Scott's emphasis][6]

As Mill had done, Australian suffragists moved from abstractions to more specific arguments. Louisa Lawson contended that the laws should not be made by men only when both sexes had to obey them, and went on: 'No strong faction, however honourable they might be, ever looked at the rights and interests of a weaker party with quite the same considerations that they bestowed on their own concerns.'[7] Mary Lee wrote to the South Australian *Register* in 1890: 'it is an arbitrary, an unjust Government which compels its support from those whose will in relation to it is never consulted; that as women assist in maintaining the Government they have a right to say how and by whom they shall be governed.'[8]

That they were forced to pay taxes when they had no representation angered those women who were prosperous enough to be levied. When it was argued that the plea of 'no taxation without representation' was not valid because so few owned property, the suffragists retorted that a woman paid indirect tax every time she spent money on the multitude of items which attracted customs duty. Her opponents then claimed that *she* was not paying the tax; her husband was paying it through her.[9] The WCTU Superintendent of Suffrage in Western Australia, Christine Clark, wrote in response that a wife keeping house for her husband should be reckoned as earning part of his salary.[10]

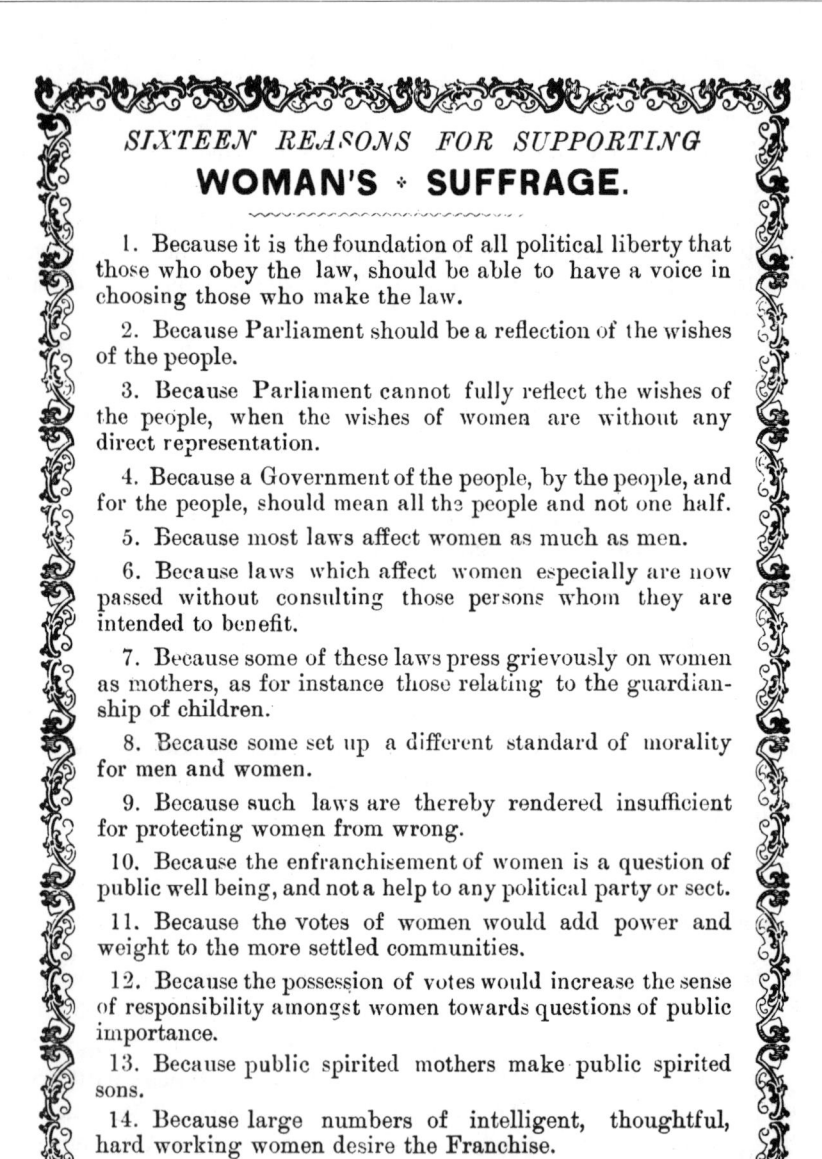

SIXTEEN REASONS FOR SUPPORTING WOMAN'S ✣ SUFFRAGE.

1. Because it is the foundation of all political liberty that those who obey the law, should be able to have a voice in choosing those who make the law.

2. Because Parliament should be a reflection of the wishes of the people.

3. Because Parliament cannot fully reflect the wishes of the people, when the wishes of women are without any direct representation.

4. Because a Government of the people, by the people, and for the people, should mean all the people and not one half.

5. Because most laws affect women as much as men.

6. Because laws which affect women especially are now passed without consulting those persons whom they are intended to benefit.

7. Because some of these laws press grievously on women as mothers, as for instance those relating to the guardianship of children.

8. Because some set up a different standard of morality for men and women.

9. Because such laws are thereby rendered insufficient for protecting women from wrong.

10. Because the enfranchisement of women is a question of public well being, and not a help to any political party or sect.

11. Because the votes of women would add power and weight to the more settled communities.

12. Because the possession of votes would increase the sense of responsibility amongst women towards questions of public importance.

13. Because public spirited mothers make public spirited sons.

14. Because large numbers of intelligent, thoughtful, hard working women desire the Franchise.

15. Because the objections raised against their having the franchise are based on sentiment, not on reason.

16. Because, to sum up all reasons in one—it is just.

Originally published by the W.C.T.U. National Franchise Department, New Zealand.
Re-Printed for W.C.T.U. of South Australia.

Holden & Strutton, Printers, Grenfell Street.

A Woman's Christian Temperance Union leaflet which is typical of the propaganda of all societies. The arguments based on justice and natural rights are placed first, and the persuasive 'expediency' arguments follow.
Mitchell Library, State Library of New South Wales.

Occasionally an adversary reacted to arguments based on political theory by claiming that the theory itself was wrong. So a correspondent wrote to Rose Scott in 1897 that the vote was not a right to be given simply because a man or a woman existed, and that to give it to some would '(a) do them harm (b) cause them to do harm to others'. 'If we have grounds for thinking we can rule better than others, then it is clearly our duty to rule', said the writer.[11] Another reaction was to claim that a woman might fulfil some of the obligations of citizenship, but she could not fulfil them all. For instance, she could not bear arms. Dr Edward Stirling responded to this contention in South Australia in 1885 when he said that 'he thought that the exercise of the material function might be looked upon as a fair equivalent'.[12] A suffrage pamphlet put it more dramatically. It quoted the American suffragist Lucy Stone: 'Some woman perils her life for her country every time a soldier is born. Day and night she does picket duty by his cradle. For years she is his quartermaster and gathers his rations.'[13]

The most common rebuttal of the natural rights theory was more wide-ranging than the woman's failure to pay taxes or to fight for her country. Opponents, particularly parliamentary ones, usually conceded that the individual had an inherent right to representation through the ballot-box, but the women was a special case: historical precedent and the woman's intellect and 'nature' made her an exception to the rules which governed a democracy. By doing this, they deflected the arguments away from the rights of the individual to specific accusations about the nature of woman and the position she should hold in society. The late-nineteenth-century suffrage movement has had much criticism for defending the woman's vote from an expediency standpoint— that the woman's participation would be of advantage to the State—instead of basing its claims more firmly on the inherent rights of the individual. To the Australian suffragists, however, the right of the woman as a person to representation was the rock upon which the whole edifice of their thoughts and claims was built, and very rarely did their rhetoric or their propaganda omit this basic contention. To make headway against the anti-suffragists, however, they then had to move on to countering the more insidious arguments being put forward, arguments designed to prove that the principles of democratic theory did not apply to them.

Some complex mental gymnastics were required to admit the theory and yet contend that it did not apply to half the population. One group of arguments saw women as an intellectually inferior species. With colonial universities opening one by one to women, and the first females into courses carrying off an astonishing proportion of honours, it was a difficult position to sustain, but adherents persevered. Dr Edward Stirling, a lecturer in medicine at Adelaide University, was aware of this contention when he introduced the subject in the South Australian Parliament in 1885. Women that year had carried off the three university prizes. 'Speaking now as a teacher of both sexes,' he said, 'he had no hesitation in saying that he could recognize no essential difference in the mental capacity of men and women.'[14] There was an occasional attempt 'scientifically' to prove inferiority. Jessie Rooke wrote to Rose Scott describing the winter campaign of meetings all over Tasmania in 1896: 'at Evandale a sudden champion of the other side in the form of the local Doctor ... maintained a woman's brain was lighter than a man's.'[15] The answer Rooke gave was that it was quality, not quantity, that counted.

Some who agreed with the Evandale doctor maintained that history proved the woman's intellectual inferiority:

> the suggestion that women are equal to men is absurd. They are as inferior mentally as physically. That they are physically goes without saying; that they are so mentally the ages have proved. Once and again there is the brilliant exception, but that only proves the rule.[16]

This rationalisation greatly riled the women. Although they were unaware that so many women *had* actually achieved and not had their achievements publicised, they knew only too well the social and educational restrictions which had kept most women from fulfilling their potential. Some, like Louisa Lawson and Rose Scott, had also gone a long way in analysing the conditioning which had robbed women of the initiative and incentive to achieve. Women everywhere were rebuked when they tried to point this out: 'Where genius has existed, neither the want of education, nor a cramping education, has been sufficient to prevent its discovery ... if they'd had the genius they'd have been encouraged ... great men have achieved in spite of difficulties.'[17]

The women were equally angered by those who claimed that they did not have the objective judgement with which to assess political issues. As late as 1904 in the Victorian Parliament Thomas Bent fulminated:

> do you mean to tell me that woman is as competent to deal with questions of public policy as man is? I deny it ... Will anyone tell me that the ordinary woman has the same business capacity as men to deal with matters affecting the State? I deny that she has.[18]

The most powerful weapon that the proponents of mental inferiority had was ridicule. They could build upon a rich Australian culture of jokes and cartoons picturing women as stupid, shallow, loquacious, hysterical, vicious, and incapable of logical reasoning. The most perceptive analyst of this culture was Louisa Lawson. In her seventeen years of editorials in the *Dawn*, she probed for the assumptions about women which permeated Australian culture. Whatever a woman does or is, Lawson wrote, she is criticised. The most innocuous qualities could be twisted to show her in a bad light. For example: if she is vivacious and enjoys social life she is a 'flirt' or a 'gadabout'; if she is quiet and of a more serious turn of mind she is 'withdrawn' and 'stupid'. Through such sneers in conversation, writings, jokes and cartoons, contempt for women was handed down from one generation to the next. Women in Australian society, Lawson claimed, were valued only in so far as they served or attracted men: there is 'no contemptuous epithet in more common use among men than "old woman". It is clear that whenever the loss of youth destroyed women's attractiveness to men, no attempt was made to hide the prevailing belief in the littleness, triviality and inferiority of women.'[19] It was time, Lawson said, for some systematic analysis of 'this constant crusade of the newspapers here in Sydney and all over the civilized world ... habitual belittlement leads women to mistrust themselves and silently tolerate jests against womankind.'[20] Lawson was doing no less than feeling her way towards the kind of feminist analysis of social attitudes which erupted in Australia in the 1960s and the 1970s.

Even before the suffrage movement gained a foothold in Australia, the 'new woman' of the nineteenth-century had been the butt of cartoonists. Lawson knew the caricature well and described her to the Dawn Club in 1889: 'The popular idea of an advocate of women's rights is this ... an angular, hard-featured, withered creature with a shrill, harsh voice, no pretence to comeliness, spectacles on nose, and "blue-stocking" visible all over her.'[21]

The 'new woman' in the Australian press was an untidy amalgam of all the feminist demands for change being made in Europe, Britain and North America: demands for a voice in the political process, for better education, for the right to enter the professions or work for a living wage, for the right to autonomy within the family and for equal divorce laws. Some feminists had demanded freedom from the constraints of fashion, so she was pictured as dowdy and unfeminine and uninterested in attracting men; attacks had been made on male power, so she became a man-hater; some women had declared the marriage institution to be repressive, so she aimed to abolish it. Because some had agitated for freely available information about birth-control, she could be labelled as selfish and valuing her own pleasure above the filling of the cradle; because women's groups protested at the conditions which forced women into prostitution and at the drunkenness which deprived them and their children of sustenance, she was determined to curb men's freedom and independent social life. The New Woman was a phantom to be feared (but hard to find in the flesh), an accretion of ideas which, if not opposed, might do great damage to the existing structure of society. When the demand for the vote erupted in the 1880s, the cartoonists, writers and parliamentarians were able to transfer their caricature of this elusive creature to the more specific 'political woman'. Canon F. Boyce of Sydney wrote in 1903: 'The barb of sharply pointed ridicule has never been more used against a principle than it was against ... woman suffrage.'[22] Derision had no roots in logic, and it could not be countered with rational argument. Mocking laughter implied that a proposition was too ludicrous even to be discussed. Parliamentarians and journalists tried to outdo each other with their witticisms. It was common to refer to a government which might be elected with woman suffrage as a 'petticoat government', and suffragists became 'freaks of nature',[23] 'platform-haunting sisters',[24] 'old frumps' and 'gawks',[25] and 'shocking emancipated gristly females'.[26] Charles Moran claimed in the Western Australian Assembly: 'There is not a member in this chamber tonight who would like to see his own wife ... go out every night during a time of political turmoil, sitting in a crowded hall, hooting and howling, and perhaps waving her hat about.'[27] A bizarre example of the use of the woolly image of the new woman can be found in a series of advertisements for Bile Beans in the Brisbane *Worker* in 1898 and 1899:

> The 'New Woman' with her mannish mode and airs, can never be a success, for the simple reason that nature is against her. Her internal organism can stand less strain and needs a great deal more attention than does the male ... Bile beans for biliousness are the only real specific that absolutely keep the system clear of waste amd impure matter.[28]

This unrelenting misrepresentation of the New Woman and the suffragist can only be understood when one knows that opponents were not attacking only her right to democratic representation; they were attacking her new independence of thought and the haze of assumptions summed up in the term 'women's rights'. This is one of the reasons why opposition was so organised in Victoria, where some suffragists openly supported the causes espoused by more radical British and American feminists. The Australian women protested about the ridicule and mockery but, as late-twentieth-century feminists were to rediscover, heated protests could simply provide more scope for their detractors to lampoon them. There was another way: they could distance themselves from the caricature by narrowing their demands, and they could emphasise their conformity to other aspects of Australian culture. It was a dangerous reaction: it led to the postponement of demands for state candidature (which was to limit the value of the woman's vote) and it stifled those voices which, like Lawson's were searching for the social assumptions which underpinned legal and economic discrimination against women.

In order to maintain the belief that the woman was so far removed from the man as not to be considered for representation, she had to be seen as possessing entirely different characteristics. The sharp dichotomy between masculine and feminine which was accepted wisdom in the nineteenth-century must be defended and reinforced. The suffragist was constantly berated for deviating from the ideal of the feminine, and taking on qualities seen as masculine. She was 'that creature of abhorrence to all true men and women—the masculine woman'.[29] Henry Hall in an 1898 Western Australian parliamentary debate claimed that the vote was sought only by 'a few women of masculine proclivities',[30] and Captain C. Salmon in Victoria declared in 1894: 'I have never found any desire for the franchise on the part of women—I mean real women. I have met he-women—who ought to have been born men, but nature made a mistake—who were in favour of the so-called woman's suffrage.'[31] It was feared by some that the Australian woman might undergo a wholesale personality change if she were allowed to vote:

> They must certainly face all the possibilities of the change, and he feared that as woman approached nearer to the male type she would lose some of the affectionate weaknesses which are her strength ... if mathematical precision of thought took the place of that charming wilfulness of temper man would lose a great source of pleasure and woman a great source of power.[32]

In her most extreme form the masculine woman wore male clothing. The staunch nonconformist Henrietta Dugdale seems to have been the only Australian suffragist publicised for wearing the 'bloomer' suit for ordinary wear, but Australian women cyclists in the 1880s and 1890s wore a form of trouser costume. Many leading Australian suffragists, however, paralleled their claim to political freedom by condemning the physical restraints of corsets and long skirts. Freedom from restrictive clothing became for them a metaphor for freedom from social and political limitations. During a lively discussion of dress reform in her short-lived paper in 1895, Maybanke Wolstenholme wrote that some aspects of women's clothing were 'akin to Chinese foot-binding',[33] and Henry Champion in his journal wrote: 'The Woman Movement aims at the emancipation of half the human race from all disabilities, physical, intellectual, social and political—either in the form of corsets that cramp the body or prejudices that distort the mind.'[34]

Detractors constantly brushed aside suffrage petitions and dismissed agitation, claiming that 'the true woman' did not sign or take part. There were many proposals for referenda of all females which, it was claimed, would prove that those agitating did not represent the mass of women. Suffragists were divided on whether referenda should be held. Some, like Rose Scott, were quite happy with the idea, convinced that the women

THE WILD WOMAN IN POLITICS.

How *Melbourne Punch* saw women on the hustings.
Melbourne Punch, 22 November 1906. State Library of New South Wales.

would ask for the vote. Most workers, however, opposed referenda on principle. Goldstein wrote to Scott that 'the question of whether the majority of women want suffrage or not has nothing whatever to do with it.'[35] Serena Lake, writing to the South Australian *Advertiser* in 1891, agreed that some women did not want their suffrage, but contended that the vision of these women had been obstructed by 'centuries of oppression and limitation'[36] and that the opinions of these women were irrelevant, for the vote should not be withheld from those who wanted it because some did not; no referendum had been held before manhood suffrage was conceded in each colony. There were letters to the press from supporters who did not have time to join organised protest. Miss Tilley pointed out the fallacy of interpreting silence as opposition; it reminded her of the little girl who would not share her cake, for 'them as asks is impudent and shan't get any, and them as don't ask don't want'.[37]

The 'natural' qualities of the 'true woman' who opponents said did not desire and should not have the vote were interminably discussed. The woman was, it was claimed, naturally weak and dependent and could not cope with the demands of the outside world. She needed a man to cling to and lean upon. The man of integrity shielded, protected and honoured her, and was unfailingly chivalrous to her. She only had to ask for what was reasonable and men would give it to her. The 'Busy Mother' who wrote claiming a vote on behalf of all those who did not have time to agitate was advised by the *Brisbane Courier*: 'Would she not serve the Colony better by training her sons so that they would always remember her at the ballot box and so most effectively cast her vote as well as their own?'[38] This vision of the ingratiating female persuading the gallant male to make decisions in her favour led to long parliamentary speeches of sentimental twaddle, usually including in their obfuscations the assertion that no man loved and honoured women more than he, the speaker, did—and ending with the repetition that the woman did not need the vote. Suffragists came out strongly against what Rose Scott called 'the clinging ivy and oak business'.[39] Mary Lee and others claimed that history did not bear out the chivalry contention; that opponents were wilfully blind to the realities of the nineteenth-century world in which many women were subjected to domestic violence and countless others were obliged to work long hours for low pay to support themselves—and often dependants as well.[40] Annie Lowe declared in a suffrage speech in the Melbourne Town Hall: 'I say that not the most chivalrous deference or the most constant attention from man to woman should usurp the place of truth and justice.'[41]

Women expected to wheedle their own way from their indulgent menfolk were also supposed to be too innocent and modest to take part in 'the slough of public life', too pure even to attend political meetings and mix with men at the polling booth. Although Australian suffragists rejected the contention that their 'innocence' and 'purity' excluded them from the political process, they did not reject the nineteenth-century concept that women were morally superior to men. This dictum was a weapon which could be wrested from the hands of their opponents and used in support of their suffrage. Tracts in Victoria claimed that the woman's vote had had 'a purifying and elevating effect' in Wyoming (which had had woman suffrage since 1869) and 'a superior effect' in New Zealand, and that the same results had been observed in South Australia. The judgments were subjective; leaflets of the short-lived Anti-Suffrage League in New South Wales claimed that the woman's vote in these places had been *injurious* to the particular states. The credo that the woman's superior morality would bestow great benefits on society can, however, be discerned in the speeches and writings of the majority of Australian supporters, male and female. It was at the core of the WCTU propaganda, and Liberal politicians like Sir William Lyne and Walter James believed it: Lyne asked the first Commonwealth Parliament: 'Is it not a gross wrong to cut off from the right to the franchise half of the people in this country, possessing three-fourths of its moral fibre?'[42]

Scott never doubted that women by their goodness could transform the world. To her the era of the voting woman was 'the advent of the mother-woman's world—the wide, loving heart and sheltering arms'.[43] Louisa Lawson, too, was unable to resist this hyperbole when she wrote that the woman 'will be a power for good in every place and she will conquer error by truth and love'.[44] Even Catherine Helen Spence, more moderate in her views and language, thought most women would be guided by moral issues when making their choice of representatives.[45] As it became apparent that the Australian colonies would enter the new century as 'the youngest nation in the world', the suffragists were able to link several factors into one comprehensive claim: the voting woman's moral influence would help to make the new nation a Utopia in the southern seas. The irony of the contention that they could change the world by electing righteous males to do it for them seemed to be lost on the women. They had rejected the indirect influence of one woman on one man, only to embrace the collective female influence on the composition of a male parliament.

There were dissenters from the moral superiority belief. Annie Golding had no time at all for it. 'The only pedestal' for a woman, she told a Granville meeting in 1898, 'was what her self-respect placed her on.'[46] A Queensland woman columnist was caustic: 'Why, there is hardly a quality a man will readily credit women with save one, and that is—virtue. No doubt, he would also reserve that for himself, did he not consider it rather a beastly nuisance and altogether an unmanly commodity.'[47] Some males, supporters *and* opponents, were also sceptical. The editor of the Brisbane *Worker* expressed doubts that women would 'wash, boil and blue the moral atmosphere'[48] and his counterpart on the Hobart *Mercury* wrote: 'no one, we suppose, actually believes all that is said upon ... the old nonsense about the absolute purity, honesty and morality of women.'[49]

The South Australian champion, Dr John Cockburn, was not only sceptical, but critical, as Arthur Rae was in New South Wales, of the women's extravagant claims. 'There is no need to claim the franchise for women on the ground that the use of it would bring the millennium suddenly upon us ... Woman is no more a political Solon than man.'[50] One male believed in women's moral superiority, but thought they should keep it to themselves: 'The prospect of being reformed by the accumulated vote of irate and declamatory womanhood has no charms for the average man.'[51]

The woman's supposed moral superiority had some sub-characteristics which could also be enlisted on both sides of the debate. Her powers were said to be not analytical, but intuitive, and to her opponents her lack of rationality prevented her from making informed judgments at the ballot-box. Most women did not reject the 'feminine logic' attributed to them; it was, after all, some compensation for what they were told they lacked in so many other areas. When acknowledging this attribute, however, they were often obliged to yield some of the analytical powers which in other contexts they claimed to have to the same degree as the male. The woman's instinct, these suffragists claimed, would make up for any lack of logic and enable her intuitively to assess an issue or a candidate: 'two heads are better than one and we will find that men will have a better and clearer perception of the right when they allow their calm reason to be assisted by women's instincts.'[52] An occasional suffragist disdained to engage in such sophistry: 'The sooner we alter our idea of what is womanly the better. We, as women, should leave off trusting to instinct, which is often only a combination of women's mental laziness and other people's extinct thought resuscitated.'[53]

Some of the lustre of the woman's halo was supplied by another property of moral superiority, that of self-sacrifice. The nineteenth-century dichotomy of characteristics vindicated male ruthlessness and self-interest because they were considered essential in a world seen to be governed by social Darwinism, and it allocated to the woman tenderness and the sacrifice of the self in the interests of others. The average woman did, indeed, need to submerge her own interests or she would never have coped in a world in which she not only reared the children but (in the absence of government welfare, and with no hospitals except for the very poor) cared for the sick and elderly and carried out most charitable work on behalf of the family. At first glance the allocation of the virtue of self-sacrifice would seem to have little to do with whether a woman should register a vote, but in every colony opponents provided the link. In a Victorian parliamentary debate women were told that public life in any form was not for them: 'The high and noble work of woman was to watch the cradle of the infant, to care for the aged and infirm, and to attend to the sick.'[54] The myth of the woman's 'natural' wish to submerge her own interests in the service of others was to be alive and kicking long after the suffragists were buried, but some nineteenth-century Australian women were clear-sighted enough to object to the unctuous bombast which was a camouflage for denying the woman any right to self-development or to participation in the challenging outside world. Louisa Lawson considered the doctrine pernicious, and another suffragist retorted: 'Women need today not so much the teaching of self-sacrifice as the inculcation of self-respect.'[55]

Not only was the woman to be excluded from the vote because of the given characteristics which made up her feminity, but because of the sphere which nature decreed she should occupy in the life of the State. This sphere was private, firmly centred in the home as a wife and mother, although many anti-suffragists did allow by the 1890s that she could make a brief sortie into feminine employment before she settled down to her real vocation. Opponents were not usually arguing that she could not spare the time away from her home to record her vote, for women, especially in the prosperous echelons of Australian society, spent considerable time socialising outside their homes and working for philanthropic organisations. The woman was being castigated for wanting to take her first step into the arena of public life which men reserved for themselves. A Victorian politician, with a flair for mixing metaphors, put it this way: 'We are expected to make a leak in the Ship of State which will eventually wreck the whole social fabric.'[56]

Victorian marriage was supposed ideally to function on a neat division of labour and responsibility; the man provided the money, and the woman took responsibility for

How *Melbourne Punch* saw the threat of women in Parliament in 1901.
Melbourne Punch, 26 September 1901. State Library of New South Wales.

children and the home. In the prosperous stratum of society from which most male opponents (inside and outside Parliament) came, the system worked very well for the man, providing him with support and sexual gratification but giving him flexibility in that the home functioned in his absence and was there to welcome him when he returned. The woman, and only the one whose husband was prosperous, had no more than the daily flexibility which servants and child-carers might provide, and contacts which might lead to infidelity were limited. No wonder Victorian males did not want their wives to take that first crucial step over the threshold. Rhetoric denying the woman the vote because of her sphere in society was long-winded, lyrical and, as the suffragists indicated, had little relevance to making a mark on a ballot paper: 'the duties useful and ornamental at present performed by the matron must be otherwise allotted. There is still the home to be exalted ... Who is to exalt it?'[57] asked one and 'Who will cook the dinner?' was the plaint of another.[58]

Opponents could be ungracious and even abusive on the subject of the woman's separate sphere. Ebenezer Ward, of South Australia, objected to women being allowed into the gallery of the House to waste their time listening to suffrage debates.[59] It must have been galling for the women to listen to hostile parliamentary speeches when they had no right of reply; one parliamentarian said:

> I have no doubt that the homes of some of these women who are the advocates of woman suffrage are in a very miserable state. The type of women who frequent this Chamber when the woman suffrage Bill is being discussed is enough to terrify anyone. We have only to look at them—and my word! What a good thing it is that we are not related to any of them![60]

One particularly churlish member of the Victorian Parliament told the Assembly: 'They come to us and say, "Oh, Mr Gaunson, do on this occasion let us have the franchise!" But I say to them, "Get out; cook a chop, and learn to dress your baby if you have one".'[61]

To those who argued against the vote on the grounds of separate spheres, the woman who did not marry was such an abnormality that she did not deserve consideration. As a correspondent to the *West Australian* put it: 'if they are not married they ought to be'.[62] During the debate on whether women should have a Commonwealth vote in 1902, a rambling Senator warned that this was the first step in opening up all male occupations to women, and that these opportunities would then discourage them from marrying:

> I admit that the denial of certain occupations is very hard on many women with intelligence, character and energy, who have not been fortunate enough either in obtaining husbands or in finding means of livelihood that are deemed appropriate to the sex, or who have had husbands; but we must remember that it is our duty to legislate for the whole class, and not for the exceptions to it.[63]

All suffragists, male and female, were scornful of this claim that the separate sphere of homemaker excluded the woman from the franchise. Just as they had turned the 'moral superiority' argument on its head, they now contended that the married woman's concern for the well-being of her home dictated that she should have some influence on political decisions. Sir William Lyne, introducing the bill giving the Commonwealth vote in 1902, argued that the women of the new nation should share in parliamentary decisions which affected their husbands and children as well as themselves.[64] Some suffrage propaganda used the housework analogy: 'It is your duty to help in the national housekeeping. Qualities which will make you a good wife, good sister, good daughter, good housekeeper, will serve to keep the National Household in order.'[65]

Although the suffragists argued so strongly for a say in legislation which affected homes and families, the leading women, at least, did not see the world as neatly divided into the private sphere for women and the public sphere for men. Because these women were aware of the intolerable burden carried at that period by the woman who had to rear the children and earn the money as well, it was rare in Australia for one to advocate the right of the married woman to work in paid employment. To them, as to their opponents, the husband's obligation was to support his family. They spoke up strongly, however, against the contention that the unmarried woman was an anomaly and that her rights and interests should not be taken into account. The women advocated the opening up of opportunities (and equitable pay) so that the woman would not have to fall back on marriage because she could not support herself. Rose Scott, Catherine Helen Spence and Vida Goldstein had all rejected marriage, and Louisa Lawson's experience of it had not been encouraging. Scott, able to make the choice because her father had left her financially independent, defined marriage as 'friendship under difficult circumstances'.[66] Lawson saw it as 'a clear, defined, but limited career'.[67] She advised mothers to ensure a good education for their daughters so that they had freedom of choice, and warned girls to think carefully before they chose.[68] Yet the women were of their time and had divided hearts. Lawson idealised the good marriage in other issues of her paper, and Jessie Ackermann, that successful career woman and inveterate globe-trotter, still maintained that 'Home is, and ever will be, the chosen kingdom of woman. She could not, if she would, eradicate the instincts which make her the homemaker of the race.'[69]

When women argued that their position as homemakers was not incompatible with the ballot, they sometimes drew the rejoinder that the woman's interest in political matters would lead to dissension between husband and wife. It was an echo of the English common law which had decreed that in marriage the woman was absorbed into the existence of her husband and had no rights, or even existence, of her own:

> Over the breakfast and dinner table wife is to quarrel with husband and sister with brother. Political faction is to divide the home, and drive man's helpmeet from his side . . . We are perfectly sure that in the end it will be for evil, and by and by history will repeat itself in the banding together of the best of our womanhood to cast it out.[70]

Goldstein scornfully called such arguments 'a plea for despotism',[71] and thought that the vote would hardly initiate dissension where none had existed before. She and many others thought that politics would provide husband and wife with an interesting subject for discussion and would make marriage more of an equal partnership.[72]

The debate about whether the vote would disturb the social order by confusing the obligations of, and the relationship between, male and female highlights the late-nineteenth-century tension which, with the rise of nationalism, existed between the rights of the individual and the interests of the State. Opponents condemned the vote because it would harm the State by undermining the existing order of function and responsibility or, at the very least, it would not confer any benefit on it. The *Mercury* of Tasmania summed it up in this way: 'The only question worth discussing is whether the work of the country would be better done if women vote, for the object of voting is to get the work done in the best manner. Voting is not an end, but a means to an end.'[73]

With Australia moving towards nationhood, the argument that the needs of the State were more important than the rights of the individual carried considerable weight in Australian society. The suffragists exploited it by arguing that the woman should have the vote in order to bring her moral influence to bear on parliamentary affairs, but their opponents argued that she had a different function to perform in the new nation. As its child-bearer she was to fill its empty spaces and provide healthy units for the army which would protect it against Asian encroachment. If women, encouraged by any political participation at all, became disenchanted with their private sphere, the birth-rate would drop. Opponents of suffrage sentimentalised 'the crowning glory of motherhood', and told women that they should seek their satisfaction in its repetition. It is quite clear that many women were unimpressed by this propaganda. The large numbers who flocked to Brettena Smyth's lectures and bought her books on birth-control indicate that they were seeking some reliable method of controlling their fertility other than sexual abstinence. Births fell steadily in the 1890s and into the new century; a subsequent New South Wales 1903-4 Royal Commission on the Birth-Rate blamed the fall on the women's movement, which they said encouraged women to think of their own interests rather than their duty to the nation.[74] Scott attacked the Royal Commission because no women were included on its bench, and accused it of calling only the evidence it wanted to hear.[75] Restrictions were placed on the importation and advertising of contraceptives in the early century, and this made it impossible for a woman to plan her pregnancies, thus circumscribing her public role.

Because it was accused of undermining the family by asking for the vote, much of the movement's propaganda was concerned with justification and reassurance. It assured antagonists that enfranchised married women would be just as committed to their roles as homemakers and mothers. That commitment, in fact, was one of the primary reasons for requesting it: 'It is not to take women from their homes but to protect them we ask for the ballot. While here and there is one who by peculiar gifts and circumstances is fitted to do public work, the great work is done by individuals, quietly.'[76] The enfranchised homemaker and mother would, the women contended, be more contented with her lot because she would be held in higher esteem. Scott, while she fought for better conditions for employed women, at the same time claimed the vote 'that we may change the conditions of life so that at any rate every mother may be able to stay in the home, and make it most truly her sphere of work and rest'.[77] The women were not only going to 'protect the home'—a vague but reassuring phrase—but they were going to raise the standards of Parliament and society: 'give us the power and sacredness of the ballot, and we will lift ourselves and our brothers to a higher civilization.'[78] In 1896, when women were voting for the first time in South Australia, a suffragist put her Utopian pen to paper.

> Ye women of Australia
> Arise in all your might;
> Your country calls you to her side
> To stand up for the right.

> A house without a woman's care
> Is desolate and drear;
> The State is but a larger house
> With ever-widening sphere.
>
> Then raise the flag of Womanhood
> And let its motto be—
> 'For honor, truth and righteousness
> And heavenly purity'.[79]

Some suffragists dreamed not only of changing Australia with their vote, but of changing the world. Annie Preston wrote: 'Fighting and rioting are cruel and clumsy ways of settling a difference and I hope that women's vote will persistently make for international and domestic peace.'[80] Many Temperance Unions formed Departments of Peace and Arbitration which developed similar abstract rhetoric, but they failed to arouse great enthusiasm among members. The South Australian President Elizabeth Nicholls reported to the 1894 Union Convention that the Superintendent 'has year after year urged the claims of her department, but I fear without awakening in you the active sentiment against the war spirit which should possess every Christian.'[81] While most suffragists were content with a vague vision of a war-free world, the commitment of some to woman suffrage was followed by a lifelong allegiance to pacifism. Vida Goldstein and Rose Scott both became leaders of women's pacifist movements, and Goldstein's political following was to be greatly eroded when she carried her anti-war stand into the years of World War I.

Suffrage propaganda about the woman's vote raising the status of the home and improving society was full of soothing abstractions, but when the rhetoric dealt with the lot of working women it was both specific and denunciatory. In 1891 in Victoria 114,229 women were earning their own living and their wages, like those of women all over Australia, were sometimes as low as 40 per cent of those earned by males doing comparable work. Women who were forced to provide shelter, food and clothing for themselves and at the same time care for and support aged or incapacitated dependants or young children were particularly disadvantaged. Because they could not leave those for whom they were responsible, they were forced to do piece-work for factories at prices so low that the term 'sweated labour' was used to describe their plight. The suffragists, whatever social stratum they belonged to, took it upon themselves to publicise the position of all women exploited in industry and commerce. Scott in 1903, in a paper titled *Why Women Need the Vote*, denounced unscrupulous employers who grew rich on the profits of cheap female labour: 'girls who are paid wages so low that they can hardly live upon them ... and yet their employers are men, well-fed, well-clothed, and not ashamed to ask the ill-paid, half-starved girl, to come back at night and do overtime without pay'.[82] The vote was to be the weapon to put pressure on male Parliaments to end this discrimination: 'all experience proves that the rights of the labouring man are best preserved in Governments where he has possession of the ballot, we therefore demand on behalf of the labouring woman the same powerful instrument, that she may herself protect her own interests.'[83]

The women were not only concerned about the plight of their sisters who were capable of, or who had only the qualifications for, unskilled work. They wanted equality of

A SENATORIAL SISTER.

Melbourne Punch was kinder to Vida Goldstein in 1903, but managed to bring in the stock caricature by providing her with a chaperone from the Woman's Christian Temperance Union if she were elected to the Commonwealth Senate.
Melbourne Punch, 13 August 1903. State Library of New South Wales.

education so that women could take their place in more skilled occupations: 'Let our girls be given equal opportunities with boys to fit themselves for an independent life, and grow up with the knowledge that so long as they have health they can always support themselves by their own labour.'[84] Australian universities were opening their doors to women in the 1880s, before the suffrage movement developed its momentum, but taking advantage of the opportunity depended not only on the family's prosperity (as it did for young males) but on the father's attitude to education for girls. By the turn of the century there was a significant group of Australian women with degrees in arts and medicine, and law and science followed. But for those who held that important piece of paper, new barriers awaited. Medical graduates, for instance, were not accepted as residents at Sydney Hospital until 1909. Women could go overseas or interstate, as many did, to gain their obligatory residential qualifications and then return to practice. But the first woman to graduate in law in New South Wales in 1902 could not apply for admission to the bar until 1918. When she was admitted as barrister in 1921 she declined to accept briefs because she had been so long away from her discipline. If a woman with a degree could use her qualifications in a profession where she was self-employed—as a medical practitioner or as principal of her own private school—she could expect to make a good living, but a woman graduate employed in either the public or private sector could be the victim of the same wage discrepancy which worked against her sisters in factories and shops.

For the woman who had been able to develop skills to enable her to do the same work as men, as in teaching, tailoring and the public service, the suffragists demanded 'equal pay for equal work'. The tailoresses' unions made some gains for themselves in the period, but little improvement was made in the parity of teachers. An isolated but short-lived victory was achieved in 1902 for women in the new federal public service by Vida Goldstein and her co-workers. The Federal Public Service Bill was due to go before the Australian House of Representatives meeting in Melbourne in 1903. Goldstein wrote in her election manifesto of that year that in order to get the principle of equal pay written into the bill she and her friends wrote letters to the papers, organised petitions and spent days lobbying members at the Houses of Parliament. 'Had there been women in the House there would have been no need for such tactics', she claimed.[85] The story did not have a happy ending; the equal pay provision was later quietly withdrawn from the bill.

Most women in the work force were not doing the same work as men. They worked as hard, but in areas of labour which had been designated as women's work, and therefore paid at a much lower rate. For these women the suffrage movement demanded a wage which would at least enable a woman to support herself: 'no man or woman should be allowed to sell his or her labour for less than can secure them a comfortable shelter, sufficient clothing, and good wholesome food to sustain the whole body'.[86] Some, like Annie Golding and Brettena Smyth, demanded 'equal pay for work of equal merit',[87] a system within which women's work would not be devalued 'because of that old idea that what a woman does is of less value than what a man does'.[88] A century later, this concept is only reluctantly gaining acceptance.

During the suffrage period male trade unions, notably those in South Australia and Queensland, helped women to form unions of their own to fight for some improvement in wages and conditions in their spheres of work, but were firmly against wage parity. Where women did the same work as men and belonged to the same union, as in teaching, they were able to block demands for 'equal pay for equal work' at their source because of male numerical strength within the unions and their monopoly of office-bearing positions. There were occasional anomalies of attitude within the mixed unions, however; the Brisbane *Worker* in 1890 described women telegraphers on lower wages than men as 'a standing menace'[89] because, costing less, they were being employed in preference to males. Unions firmly resisted any attempts by women to break into occupations deemed to be exclusively male, and thus paid at a higher rate, by refusing them membership of the particular union. The boycotting of Louisa Lawson's *Dawn* in 1889 illustrates the tactics employed. Lawson proudly boasted that her magazine was produced solely by women, among them typographers. The Typographers' Union refused to allow the women to join, and then boycotted the *Dawn's* premises because it was employing non-union labour. Lawson was able to survive the boycott and the months of harassment because her paper sold mainly by subscription and because her female employees refused to be intimidated.

The optimistic and inexperienced women who contended that with their votes they could change this whole structure of wage relativity were being simplistic. They were to learn that the battle for wage parity had to be fought not only in Parliament but against employers and against the attitudes of the whole male work force. The work they did in publicising the plight of working women should not be downgraded, however; they began the long struggle which other women were to continue.

Women like Dora Montefiore and Rose Scott were emboldened to launch the suffrage movement when some specific experience made them realise how the laws of the nineteenth-century could be used to disadvantage them or other women. They then took it upon themselves to educate others who, because legal sanctions had never impinged on their lives, were unaware of discrimination. The women were convinced that even well-intentioned men could not see the world from their point of view (and many men were far from well-intentioned) and therefore would not legislate in women's interests without electoral pressure: 'It is feared that human nature is not to be trusted to deal impartially with interests running contrary to its desires, especially when the opponent is entirely unrepresented and powerless to make her voice heard.'[90] Belle Golding put it more succinctly: 'Man never had, nor will, nor can represent her.'[91]

By the time of the most intense suffrage activity, legislation had been passed in every colony which gave the married woman the right to hold property, to retain her earnings, and to make a will. The women were concerned about the wide range of issues which remained, and few speeches or writings were free of references to legal discrimination. By 1902, when Rose Scott sent a questionnaire to leading women in other states,[92] a little had been achieved in areas other than property, but much remained to be done. As a result of the lobbying of the Vigilance Association founded in Victoria by Annette Bear-Crawford and Dr Constance Stone, the age of consent had been raised there from fourteen to sixteen, although there was strong parliamentary opposition to the move. In 1902 it was seventeen years in South Australia and Western Australia, but fifteen in Tasmania and, in spite of the efforts of Scott and her associates, fourteen in New South Wales. The

WOMAN'S SUFFRAGE!

No. 1.—"Are you going to vote for Mr. Blank to-day, Miss Butterfly?"
No. 2.—"Indeed, I am not; he is not my ideal of a member of Parlia[?]
ent to hear him speak the other night, and, do you know, he's quite bald!"

Women, especially attractive women, were usually pictured in the cartoons as unable to understand political issues.
Bulletin, 4 July 1891. State Library of New South Wales.

age of consent was an issue that particularly roused the anger of the suffragists for, as Jessie Ackermann pointed out in 1913, the pregnant girl (let alone the pregnant child) in Australia faced great difficulty in proving paternity, and maintenance was pitiful in the rare cases when it could be obtained.[93]

Although the women protested for the whole period about the injustice which gave the sole guardianship of the married woman's children to the father, the situation which had so angered Dora Montefiore in the late 1880s was still the same (except in South Australia) until 1912, when Victoria gave the mother automatic guardianship of the children on the death of her husband. It was not until 1934 that the last state (Tasmania) passed a similar law. Anger about the situation in New South Wales in 1903 shows in Scott's *Why Women Need the Vote*:

> children belong—not to you—oh dear no! but to the father ... If he dies, he can, by his Will, have more power over the children though dead and in his grave, than their living mother has! ... he can, by his Will, have more power over the children though dead and in his grave, than their living mother has! ... he can leave the mother without a penny! The law cannot interfere. The law regards the mother merely as a wife who is the property of her husband.[94]

In Western Australia in 1902, when Scott made her survey, the Government had made what it considered a magnanimous concession: the wife, if the husband appointed another guardian in his will, could, if of 'good character', keep them with her until they were six years old.[95]

No issue illustrates the complexity and fragmentation of Australia's legal system more than that of divorce. It was not until 1975 that divorce law became uniform in every state when the Family Law Court was established by the Commonwealth Parliament. In 1902 grounds for divorce were the same for male and female only in Western Australia and Tasmania. In the others, although the woman could be divorced for one act of adultery, the man had to be guilty of aggravated adultery—repeated acts, or adultery with violence, desertion, rape (of another woman), sodomy, or incest. The cavalier attitude of many politicians in this area is well illustrated by a statement made when the bill to give women their Commonwealth vote was being debated in the Senate in 1902. Women did not need the vote to gain easier divorce, he said, 'What has been said with respect to the divorce laws is only a cry. Woman is the first to forgive all the past misdeeds of man if he is at all a decent sort of fellow.'[96]

The suffragists were very concerned about the treatment of women in the prison system, and as a result of their efforts a few police matrons had been appointed in some states by 1902 to oversee the court appearances and imprisonment of women and children. It was true, as Scott's survey indicated, that sentences for women were usually less than those for men when they were arraigned for the same offence (and they were never whipped, as men were), but it was reported of an address given by Rose Scott in 1904: 'that which has aroused the greatest interest, the deepest feeling in Rose Scott's paper ... was when she compared the punishments inflicted upon men who commit crimes against property with those inflicted upon men who perpetrate the most hideous crimes against women and children.'[97]

Prostitution was first entangled with woman suffrage in 1865 when the Victorian Legislative Assembly was debating whether or not the vote given inadvertently to women two years before should be withdrawn. A member contended that in the intervening election 'the worst type of the other sex'[98] had flocked to the ballot-box. From then until the early century there was no lack of parliamentary and extra-parliamentary spokesmen who opposed votes for all women on the ground that prostitutes would thus be enfranchised: 'there are in Melbourne and the suburbs six thousand of a certain class of females, and this Bill makes the monstrous proposal that we are to enfranchise these women.'[99] The suffragists pointed out the double standard involved in such reasoning: 'It has been contended that, at all events, our unfortunate sisters should not have a vote, but, if that is so, why should our brothers, who are equally guilty, have a vote given to them.'[100] The WCTU women, and many others who advocated a high standard of sexual morality for both men and women, blisteringly attacked the double standard as such. In order to keep intact their ingrained belief in the superior morality of the female, they were obliged to always see the prostitute as the victim—in the first place of man the seducer, and in the second instance of the economic system which did not allow the woman to earn 'an honest living': 'To her certain knowledge men were the corruptors of women ... [anti-suffragists] seek to deny the right [of the vote] to the victim, while the victor retained the political power.'[101] The WCTU also attacked the women who complacently accepted the double standard: 'They will extend the hand of friendship to a man of wealth and position without regard to his character, and turn with disgust from his victim.'[102]

The Contagious Diseases Acts of Queensland (1868) and Tasmania (1879)—and clauses in the Health Acts in other colonies which could be used for the same purpose—led to further confrontations between the suffragists and their legislatures. The Australian Contagious Diseases Acts had their roots in nineteenth-century European legislation to regulate prostitution in response to the widespread incidence of venereal disease. In 1864 the British Government established Lock hospitals in garrison towns throughout the British Empire. Women suspected of being infected prostitutes could be forcibly detained, examined and treated there, albeit with the limited treatment then available. Josephine Butler, as the World Superintendent of the Moral Purity department of the WCTU, led the campaign against the British measure which, she said, served to 'deprive women of their natural and civil rights, drive them outside the law, and make a slave class of them that men may sin more comfortably'.[103] The Queensland Act followed closely upon the British and was applicable to the whole population, and the Tasmanian Lock Hospital was established in 1879 in response to pressure from the British Navy, which used Hobart as a summer base. The navy threatened to discontinue its visits unless a clean prostitute population could be guaranteed—a move which would have meant a considerable economic and, in the upper ranks of society, social loss to the town.

The first abortive suffrage society in Queensland in 1889 had as one of its main aims the abolition of that colony's Act, and the open societies in other colonies protested sporadically. But it was the WCTU, both in its colonial branches and as a national body, which declared that its women would use their votes to abolish these 'obnoxious' and 'iniquitous' measures.[104] Technically any woman could be apprehended and forced to undergo a gynaecological examination, so the measure was seen as an unjustified intrusion on the common-law rights of all women, without any comparable intrusion on the rights of men. The protests of the suffragists seem to have had little effect. Contagious Diseases Acts in their various guises remained to bedevil the Australian women's movement throughout the twentieth-century. The 1915 Western Australian measure, for instance, split the thriving movement which had grown out of the suffrage campaign in that state. Edith Cowan and her supporters spoke for the Act because it was applicable to both men and women, but Bessie Rischbieth (of the Women's Services Guild) and her supporters vigorously opposed the measure as such.

The arguments the Australian suffragists used to support their suffrage were basically the same as those being used in Britain and North America in the period. It is true that much emphasis was placed on the benefits which would accrue to the Commonwealth and the home by virtue of female suffrage, but the women were true daughters of the Enlightenment in that they contended that as citizens of the State they had the right to share in its political processes. They were our first feminists, for in arguing for their suffrage they analysed the way society discriminated against all women socially, politically, economically and legally. They vowed that through the ballot-box they would eliminate all these forms of discrimination. They thought the battle would be easy, but they were to find that some of the arguments they used were ambiguous; that they had handicapped themselves by not holding out for direct state representation (for most laws which discriminated against them were enshrined in state legislation); and that their vote did not give them automatic access to the male power structures which underpinned political, economic and legal decision-making in Australia.

Notes

1. John Stuart Mill, quoted in Marian Sawer and Marian Simms, *A Woman's Place*, p. 2.
2. John Stuart Mill, 'Representative Government', p. 247.
3. ibid., p. 290.
4. WCTU of Queensland, Annual Report, 1898.
5. WCTU of Victoria, Annual Report, 1892.
6. Report of a debate between Rose Scott and Miss Badham, in *Australian Economist*, vol. 4, no. 16, 21 June 1895, p. 496.
7. *Dawn*, July 1899.
8. Mary Lee, 'Letter to Women', *South Australian Register*, 21 March 1890.
9. Frederick Illingworth, *WAPD*, vol. 12, 10 August 1898, p. 917.
10. Christine Clark to the *West Australian*, 6 August 1898.
11. Letter to Rose Scott, 9 September 1897, Woman Suffrage Correspondence, 1887–1899, ML:NSW, MSS A2271, item 269a.
12. *SAPD*, 22 July 1885, c. 327.
13. 'A suffrage question box', pamphlet in Woman Suffrage: Leaflets and press cuttings on Australian and overseas movements, ML:NSW, MSS 38/39, item 51.
14. *SAPD*, 22 July 1885, c. 323.
15. Jessie Rooke (deduced) to Rose Scott, undated letter, but presumed to be 1896, Woman Suffrage: miscellaneous papers on Australian and overseas movements, 1888–1920, ML:NSW, MSS 38/38, items 514–518.

16. *The Country*, quoted in *Worker* (New South Wales), 16 May 1896.
17. H. Hart, *Woman Suffrage, a National Danger*, p. 42.
18. *VPD*, vol. 110, 13 July 1904, p. 329.
19. *Dawn*, November 1891.
20. *Dawn*, February 1891.
21. *Dawn*, July 1889.
22. Introduction to Elizabeth Ward, *Out of Weakness Made Strong*, p. 4.
23. Frank Madden, quoted in the *Age*, 13 October 1896.
24. *Argus*, Editorial, 11 September 1900.
25. David Gaunson, *VPD*, vol. 113, 15 August 1906, p.930.
26. George Meredith, quoted in the *Age*, 13 October 1896.
27. Charles Moran, *WAPD*, vol. 12, 17 August 1898, p. 1043.
28. *Worker* (Brisbane). This and other advertisements using the theme of the 'New Woman' ran for several months in the second half of 1900.
29. W. Montague Whitney, 'Womanhood Suffrage', p. 35.
30. Henry Hall, *WAPD*, vol. 12, 24 August 1898, p. 1202.
31. *VPD*, vol. 74, 19 July 1894, p. 930.
32. *SAPD*, 30 October 1889, c. 1382.
33. *Woman's Voice* (New South Wales), 12 January 1895.
34. 'Nausica' to the *Champion*, 2 May 1896, vol. 2, no. 46, p. 171.
35. Vida Goldstein to Rose Scott, 5 August 1899, Woman Suffrage Correspondence, 1887–1899, ML:NSW, MSS A2271, item 397.
36. *Advertiser*, 3 September 1891.
37. *Dawn*, 2 May 1892.
38. *Brisbane Courier*, Editorial, 5 September 1900.
39. *Woman's Sphere*, October 1902.
40. 'Letter to Women', *South Australian Register*, 14 April 1890.
41. Report of a Melbourne Town Hall meeting, *Age*, 13 October 1896.
42. William Lyne, *CAPD*, vol. 9, 23 April 1902, p. 11931.
43. *Woman's Sphere*, October 1900.
44. *Dawn*, January 1890.
45. Catherine Helen Spence, Address to the Old Scholars Associations of Ladies' Schools, 13 April 1896, Australian Women's Franchise Society Leaflets, ML:NSW, Q324.3/1.
46. Unidentified newspaper report of a public meeting at Granville in June 1898, Womanhood Suffrage League of New South Wales: note-books and newspaper clippings, ML:NSW, MSS 38/35, item 4.
47. 'Through a Woman's Eyes', *Worker* (Brisbane), 12 August 1899.
48. *Worker* (Brisbane), Editorial, 6 September 1902.
49. *Mercury*, Editorial, 24 September 1896.
50. Unidentified newspaper clipping, 4 March 1898, Womanhood Suffrage League of New South Wales: note-books of the Secretary, and newspaper clippings, ML:NSW, MSS 38/35, item 4:281a.
51. A. Weaver, 'Objections to the Extension of the Franchise to Women', in Woman Suffrage: South Australian Papers, ML:NSW, MSS 3007, item 7.
52. *The Elector*, 30 November 1895.
53. Janet Michie, a printed leaflet, 31 August 1894, in Woman Suffrage: Press cuttings, ML:NSW, 396.3/S, item 1.
54. William McLellan, *VPD*, vol. 16, 5 August 1873, p. 962.
55. Mrs C. Wallace, WCTU of Victoria, Annual Report, 1891.
56. *VPD*, vol. 67, 29 September 1891, p. 1636.
57. *Argus*, Editorial, 12 August 1899.

58. *Advertiser*, Editorial, 4 June 1894.
59. 'Deborah' to the *Advertiser*, 30 May 1889.
60. *VPD*, vol. 96, 11 December 1900, p. 117.
61. David Gaunson, *VPD*, vol. 113, 15 August 1906, p. 930.
62. 'E.E.B.' to the *West Australian*, 4 July 1898.
63. *CAPD*, vol. 9, 9 April 1902, p. 11488.
64. William Lyne, ibid., 23 April 1902, pp. 11929–11935.
65. A. Lista, 'Why women should use the vote', leaflet in Woman Suffrage: leaflets and press cuttings on Australian and overseas movements, ML:NSW, MSS 38/39, item 143.
66. Miles Franklin, 'Rose Scott, some aspects of her personality and work', p. 100.
67. *Dawn*, June 1889.
68. *Dawn*, March 1893.
69. WCTU of Australasia, Report of Second Triennial Conference, 1894.
70. *Brisbane Courier*, Editorial, 1 September 1900.
71. *Woman's Sphere*, September 1900.
72. ibid.
73. *Mercury*, Editorial, 29 June 1898.
74. 'Royal Commission on the Birth Rate and the Mortality of Infants in New South Wales, 1904', in *Royal Commissions, Select Committees of Parliament, and Boards of Inquiry, part 4, New South Wales, 1854–1960*, pp. 225–6.
75. Rose Scott, Presidential Address, August 1904, Women's Political and Educational League of New South Wales: Papers, 1904–1910, ML:NSW, MSS 38/41, p. 323.
76. Catherine Wallace, Paper to be read to the Second Triennial Conference WCTU of Australasia, 1894, Australian Women's Franchise Society Leaflets, ML:NSW, Q324.3/1.
77. Rose Scott, 'Why Women Need a Vote' (1903), in Women's Political and Educational League of New South Wales: Papers, 1904–1910, ML:NSW, MSS 38/41, p. 195.
78. *Herald* (Victoria), 10 June 1891.
79. *Worker* (New South Wales), 11 January 1896. This poem is signed C.E.C., and is presumed to be the work of Caroline Emily Clark, of South Australia.
80. Annie Preston to the *Brisbane Courier*, 23 May 1895.
81. WCTU of South Australia, Annual Report, 1894.
82. Rose Scott, 'Why Women Need a Vote' (1903), Women's Political and Educational League of New South Wales: Papers, 1903–1910, ML:NSW, MSS 38/41, p. 193.
83. ibid., p. 193.
84. 'Hope On' to the *Woman's Voice*, December 1894, p. 119.
85. Vida Goldstein, 'Should Women Enter Parliament?', p. 135.
86. WCTU of Victoria, Annual Report, 1895.
87. Unidentified newspaper report of a public meeting at Granville in June 1898, Womanhood Suffrage League of New South Wales: notebooks and newspaper clippings, ML:NSW, MSS 38/35, item 4.
88. Brettena Smyth, Address to the Fourth Annual Meeting of the Victorian Women's Suffrage Society, *Liberator*, 16 September 1888, p. 259.
89. William Lane writing as 'Lucinda Sharpe', *Worker* (Brisbane), March 1890.
90. Mary Lee, 'Letter to Women', *South Australian Register*, 14 April 1890.
91. *Dawn*, April 1899.
92. Womanhood Suffrage League of New South Wales: Papers 1892–1902, ML:NSW, MSS 38/36, item 247.
93. Jessie Ackermann, *Australia from a Woman's Point of View*, p. 171.
94. Rose Scott, 'Why Women Need a Vote', (1903), Women's Political and Educational League of New South Wales: Papers, 1904–1910, ML:NSW, MSS 38/41, p.–201.

95. Womanhood Suffrage League of New South Wales: Papers, 1892–1902, ML:NSW, MSS 38/36, item 247.
96. *CAPD*, vol. 9, 10 April 1902, p. 11559.
97. *Woman's Sphere*, November 1904.
98. Graham Berry, *VPD*, vol. 11, 1 March 1865, p. 418.
99. *VPD*, vol. 67, 30 September 1891, p. 1700.
100. Dr William Maloney, *VPD*, vol. 97, 3 November 1901, p. 2667.
101. Henrietta Dugdale, Report to the First Annual Meeting of the Victorian Women's Suffrage Society, *Woman's Voice*, May 1895, p. 223.
102. WCTU of Tasmania, Annual Report, 1896.
103. Josephine Butler, quoted in WCTU of Australasia, Third Triennial Conference Report, 1897.
104. Elizabeth Nicholls used these words in ibid.

11

'THE KNIFE WITHOUT THE BLADE': THE GIFT THEORY AND THE LEGACY

The details of the suffrage campaigns were slotted away in *Parliamentary Debates*, in Louisa Lawson's *Dawn* and Vida Goldstein's *Woman's Sphere*, in correspondence between suffragists, in newspaper columns, in the minute books and annual reports of the Woman's Christian Temperance Union in all states and in those of the Womanhood Suffrage League in New South Wales. (Those of suffrage societies in other states have not survived.) All were soon submerged in Australian history. Some attempts were made to record state movements, but no chronicler of the period had access to the information which might give an overall picture. In the absence of collated historical evidence to the contrary, the myth grew that Australian women did not struggle for their vote, that it was handed to them gratuitously, sometimes because of the strength of politicians' democratic beliefs, and sometimes because of political expediency. The myth was first expounded by William Pember Reeves in 1902 when commenting on the New Zealand, South Australian, Western Australian and federal movements,[1] and it was seized upon and expanded by later commentators. Jessie Ackermann, puzzled by the lack of women in political life in 1913, concluded that the Government placed the vote 'freely in the hands of the women',[2] a strange claim when one considers how much pressure came from the WCTU suffrage departments which she had helped to set up in all colonies. On a visit to Australia the following year Adela Pankhurst, comparing the British militancy to what seemed to her to be an uneventful Australian campaign, told a reporter from *Lone Hand*: 'Australian women obtained their vote so easily, that's why they do not value it.'[3] The myth was still being reiterated as late as 1973, when Ross Paulson wrote in *Women's Suffrage and Prohibition*: 'The fact that the vote came to Australian women more or less fortuitously rather than by their own efforts and organizational skill and political pressure may help to explain their subsequent timidity about enhancing their status.'[4]

Politicians, even erstwhile obstructionists like Sir John Forrest in Western Australia, were only too happy to bask in the praise heaped upon them, and rarely reciprocated by acknowledging the hard work and lobbying done by the women. As the years passed, the gift-without-pain theory seemed to offer an explanation for the puzzling phenomenon of a nation which had been second in the world to give its women the vote, but in 1921 had not had one woman in any of its seven Parliaments. The theory was credible also in that it could be linked to Australia's reputation as a 'social laboratory', as Reeves did in his *Social Experiments in Australia and New Zealand*. It was plausible in that it was a half-truth, for in no country in the world could the vote be anything *but* a gift from men; only male parliamentarians had the power to grant it. In this sense manhood suffrage in Britain was a gift from the men with power to the men without, although it was preceded by a long and bitter campaign; and woman suffrage in Britain was also a gift from men to women, although it was preceded by more than half a century of agitation, with angry and violent confrontation in the eight years before World War I. Now that the history of women's agitation in Australia has been put on record we must acknowledge that, although Australian women did not resort to militancy, they worked hard for their vote, and the propaganda they distributed and the pressure they put on Governments was of prime importance in gaining it so early. It is necessary, however, to recapitulate aspects of the campaigns to come to some conclusions about why politicians in Australia were more susceptible to pressure than those in the two great democracies from which our suffragists drew their inspiration. British women were given only partial suffrage in 1918, and all women were not enfranchised until 1928. In the United States women did not achieve their national vote until 1920.

Politically there can be no doubt that the strength of democratic Liberalism in Australia, the rise of the Labor party in the critical period of the women's agitation, and the comparative amity between the two, were crucial. Woman suffrage was part of the democratic vision of both radical Liberalism and Labor. So in four states—South Australia, New South Wales, Tasmania and Queensland—the vote was given when the two formed coalitions which were able to push it through essentially conservative Upper Houses, South Australia being aided by a temporary radical element in its Legislative Council. But the equation between the gaining of power by those who held woman suffrage as a principle, and their granting of it, is not as neat as it appears on the surface. In all states with plural voting Labor was content to bury its principles until one-man-one-vote had been achieved; in Western Australia and Victoria right-wing Liberalism allied with Conservatism, which had opposed the vote on principle, were also quite prepared to bury *their* principles when it appeared that woman suffrage might favour them.

The gaining of the South Australian vote in 1894 was critical to the national suffrage gained in 1902, for South Australian delegates to the 1897 Commonwealth Convention, lobbied by their women, threatened to forgo federation rather than have their women disenfranchised in the national arena. The national suffrage is the one which gained international prestige for Australia. The federation movement, backed by progressive Liberalism and gaining its momentum in the 1890s, gave all Australian suffragists and their supporters a unique opportunity which they were quick to perceive. In their petitions to the 1897 Convention they were able to argue that the new nation which would be born on 1 January 1901 had the opportunity to lead the world in political innovation. The women, and their political spokesmen at the 1897 Commonwealth Convention, knew that the ruling of that Convention was vital. If suffrage could not be written into the Constitution, provision must be made for it to be granted by a simple Act of the new Parliament, for a Constitutional amendment would require a national referendum in which not only must a majority of voters give their approval but so must a majority of states. Agitation in the United States had stagnated in the late nineteenth century precisely because women were fighting this complex battle to amend *their* federal Constitution. It should not be assumed, however, that the victory gained at the 1897 Convention was an easy one, or that it would have been won without the political pressure which suffragists in all states put on their candidates for election to the Convention. And although Kingston and Holder from South Australia were able to gain a ruling that the new Commonwealth could fix its own franchise—and that it could not disenfranchise women who already had the state vote—both WCTU women and those from the open societies then challenged candidates for the first Commonwealth Parliament to include in their platform the federal vote for all Australian women.

Australian suffragists, then, worked in a political framework which was ideologically and constitutionally easier to manipulate than the entrenched privilege and custom which stood between British women and their vote, and the complex requirements for amending the United States Constitution which were frustrating their counterparts there. But this certainly does not mean that the vote was handed to them as a gift, as Reeves and others would imply. The debates within and without Parliament and the course of the state campaigns show that, without the vigorous lobbying through public meetings, propaganda and petitions, the women would have had very few active supporters.

The political elements can be more precisely measured than the social factors which caused Australian politicians to be more receptive to the demands of their women. Although without a comprehensive Australian study from which to draw conclusions, analysts of the wider woman suffrage movement have commented on what might or might not have been the reason for early female suffrage in New Zealand and Australia. They have taken the assertion of Reeves—that the vote was a gift—as axiomatic, and compared the two nations with two American states: Wyoming, which gave women the vote in 1869, and Utah, which did so in 1870. The possible unique characteristics of the two territories have been assessed: that in Wyoming the male lawmakers thought that the presence of women at polling booths might replace anarchy with civilised conduct, and that in Utah the Mormon men, in response to an attack on polygamy in Congress, may have been trying to illustrate that they were not oppressive to women, and at the same time strengthen their influence in the territory in relation to non-Mormons. Two interlocking factors which are said to be common to both states, and to New Zealand and Australia, emerge from the discussion: that on the frontier women, because of their visible contribution, have had a higher status than in sophisticated and urban social groupings; and that the vote was given in order to bring women's influence to bear to create stability in highly volatile populations.[5]

Peter Biskup, writing of the Western Australian movement in 1959, applied the higher-status ingredient of what has become known as the frontier theory to the granting of woman suffrage in 1899 in that state, and by inference extended it to apply to the whole of Australia. Women, he said, were valued more highly here than in England because of their contribution to colonial life and because Australian immigrants (being predominantly lower middle class or working class) 'did not insist on absolute subordination' of their women.[6] It is true that the argument that women had benefited the colonies figured in debates in Queensland and Western Australia, but opponents could, and did, argue that the woman's valued contribution to society could continue only if she stayed out of public life. Some, like Forrest in Western Australia, would not even acknowledge the contribution of women. His parents had arrived as indentured servants, and his mother had borne ten children in the years when they were establishing themselves as independent farmers, but Forrest claimed that the woman should not have the vote because 'She can't do the heavy work that building up the Colony requires.'[7] The claim that Australia's immigrants thought more highly of their women because of their class structure would be very hard to quantify, too. Biskup's higher-status theory is dubious in view of the systematic exclusion of women from decision-making processes in Australia after the vote was won.

The other aspect of the frontier theory does, however, have validity for Australia: that women were given the suffrage so that their vote could be used by the male decision-makers to create and maintain stability. The suffrage period coincided with that in which each Australian colony was attempting, through social legislation, to impose some order on societies which were the end results of the convict system, gold-rushes and massive waves of immigration. The patterns of order to which they aspired were predominantly those of the Anglo-Saxon culture from which most settlers had come, but although parliamentarians had a reverence (to a greater or less degree) for the traditions and example of 'the mother country', they did not feel completely bound by them. They felt free to experiment—to break free of the old model and ask what was best for the colony or, in the case of the Commonwealth, for the new nation. Dr Edward Stirling, when introducing his 1885 motion, told the South Australian Parliament:

> It would be another creditable page in the record of South Australia if from the legislature of this distant colony there should proceed yet another measure based upon equality and justice which should serve as a precedent for the law-makers of other countries, whom we were usually accustomed to imitate rather than to instruct.[8]

Giving women votes would, in other words, enhance Australia's status in the eyes of the world.

When Liberal legislators (predisposed by progressive Liberal theory to grant the women's request) asked whether their suffrage would help to stabilise and regulate Australian society, they were reassured by the answers which came back from the movement. The women too wanted a stable society in which to bear and rear their children. They would elect 'righteous' men to Parliament (whatever that meant) and so raise the tone of parliamentary proceedings and the standard of social legislation. Through the men they elected, they would in some unspecified way bring their superior morality to bear to raise the moral standards of Australian society; the woman's vote might even help to control the drunkenness which was destroying or immobilising so many human units of production. These arguments, vague as they were, were particularly acceptable in view of the rise of nationalism all over the Western world in the last half of the nineteenth century. The eighteenth and early nineteenth century had seen the State as existing to meet the needs of the individual, but the citizen now was increasingly seen as having a responsibility to serve the needs of the nation. The editor of the *Brisbane Courier* reflected this when he wrote in 1900 of the Queensland suffrage movement: 'Show us the advantages accruing from the suffrage and we shall consider whether they balance the disadvantages.'[9] The vote could certainly be seen as an advantage to the nation in one way; it would be a tool with which legislatures could achieve a stable and well-ordered society.

But would these advantages—the vote as a symbol of Australia's progressiveness and the vote as a tool for control—be cancelled out by disadvantages? Would women, given encouragement, demand a greater share in political and public life and so create instability in that sacred foundation of the new nation, the home? The arguments used in the campaigns were reassuring. Although women insisted that the laws which discriminated against them must be changed, few were interested in challenging the male domain of political decision-making (not yet); and married women were not trying to abrogate their responsibility for bearing and rearing children. Particular conclusions could be drawn, too, to allay the male terrors which surfaced in cartoons showing large (and therefore powerful) females departing for or taking part in political meetings while small (and so less powerful) males tried vainly to cope with the disorders of domesticity. The women's message was that the sexual division of labour within the family would be undisturbed: houses would still be cleaned, socks mended, and clean shirts find their way back to drawers; children would be dressed, fed, and have their noses wiped, and the baby would be presented only when smiling and sweet-smelling.

This strand of private-sphere feminism in suffrage propaganda was vital in soothing the fears of politicians and the community, but the arguments it encapsulated were not used by the suffragists only for reasons of expediency. Private-sphere or domestic feminism, although it based the married woman firmly in the home, sought a reappraisal of the relationships between male and female within the family; it demanded that the woman be recognised as an independent entity entitled to consideration in political, social and legal terms, but not necessarily in economic terms. The separate vote was to be both the symbol of this recognition and the tool by which changes were to be brought about to make it a reality. Rose Scott summed up the attitudinal change which had to take place:

> Men have come to look upon a woman as a sort of appendage to themselves, a sort of tail that has only to wag when man—the dog—is pleased. And many men's attitude on the woman question is that of serious and painful surprise such as might reasonably overcome a respectable dog if he was informed that in the future his tail would assert its own individuality.[10]

There was, however, another major strand in the women's suffrage propaganda which, if it had proved threatening in Australia, might have given the politicians pause. Mill had in 1868 expressed the hope that Australia would lead the way in votes for women,[11] but he wrote some time later to Catherine Helen Spence that he thought the smaller numbers of unmarried women seeking employment opportunities meant that Australia would *follow* Britain: 'it is likely, I think, to be successful in the colonies later than in England, because the want of equality in social advantage is less felt in colonies owing, perhaps, to women's having less need of other occupations than those of married life.'[12] Mill was wrong in thinking that Australia's high marriage rate would delay the suffrage. The fact that most women married *helped* them to gain their vote. Open-sphere or occupational feminism, demanding wider work opportunities, higher pay and better conditions in the workplace was strong here, and ran parallel with domestic feminism, but Governments, and the male unions, did not need to fear an electorate of unmarried females who, facing a lifetime in paid employment, would bring strong pressure to bear to change the sexual division of labour, and the wages differential, outside marriage. At any one time there were large numbers of women in paid employment outside the home, but it was a changing group as girls moved into it from school, and women moved out of it to marry. Female trade unions found it difficult to survive, let alone develop militancy, with such transient membership. It was not until World War II, when Australian women flooded into industry to replace men who had gone into the armed forces, that the fight for equal pay, kept alive since the suffrage period by numerous women's associations, was able to gather strength. Then the slow climb, not yet complete, began towards wage parity for women doing the same work as men, and for those doing work of equal value.

Australian suffragists, then, were able to prevail in their agitation for the vote for several reasons: the strength of radical Liberalism in Australia which recognised the right of the individual to a share in the government of the State; the happy coincidence of Australia's federation movement in the period of most intense suffrage activity; the desire of Australians to show the world, and especially Britain, that Australia was a progressive society; and the perception that the woman's vote would be a tool which the politicians could use to impose order and morality on the emerging nation. The strong strand of occupational feminism in the suffrage movement, demanding a reappraisal of the sexual division of paid labour, with wage parity and the opening up of work opportunities, was able to be ignored. In the absence of male union support, a transient female work force posed neither a political, social or economic threat to the established ordering of Australian society.

The complex pressures on feminism all over the Western world in the first half of the twentieth century are now receiving serious attention from historians of the women's movement, who are questioning the glib assumption that feminism died when the vote was gained. Such an in-depth analysis, taking into account two world wars and the great depression, lies outside the scope of this study, but two main themes of the Australian suffrage movement need to be followed through: the reinforcement of domestic feminism at the expense of that which was fighting for justice and parity for women in the labour market, and the harnessing of the votes and energies of women to serve the male political machines.

Domestic feminism in the suffrage period and the early century, fighting for economic security and legal and social rights within marriage must, I contend, be seen as a valid manifestation of the women's movement. It was to achieve important improvements for women who were circumscribed within their child-bearing role—such as child endowment, family allowances, widows' pensions. But writers in the early century, here and overseas, began to give private-sphere feminism an extra dimension through philosophical assertions of biological determinism and the theories of the eugenists. Using the dangerous assertions of the suffragists that men and women were equal but different and complementary, the woman was told that biology was her destiny; she was free and equal but within the confines of domesticity. Sigmund Freud and his fellow travellers were to provide a pseudo-scientific base for these philosophical assertions and create a stereotype of the 'normal' woman as one who did not want to share in the masculine world.

The writings of the new philosophers like Havelock Ellis, Ellen Key and Karl Pearson were seductive insofar as they encouraged the woman to feel proud of her biology and championed her right to be recognised as a sexual being, but they found fertile ground in Australia for other reasons. The new nation was anxious to increase its white population as a bulwark against the 'hordes of Asia'—this anxiety, in fact, was one of the reasons for its unification. It was also increasingly anxious that the health and vitality of each white human unit should be improved and safeguarded. By means of the theories of eugenics and the philosophies of biological determinism, responsibility for maintaining the dominance of the Anglo-Saxon race by restoring its vigor and increasing its numbers was placed firmly on the shoulders of the woman. Motherhood was defined as a career, and it was urged that all girls should be educated with this in mind. One of the foremost exponents of education for motherhood in Australia was Maybanke Wolstenholme, a founding member of the New South Wales Womanhood Suffrage League, who became Maybanke Anderson when she married Professor Anderson of Sydney University in 1899. With her blessing and that of others of like mind, the new philosophies were translated in Australia into compulsory domestic science instruction for girls, and even in some attempts to establish chairs of domestic science in universities. Although the movement was particularly strong in Australia because of the country's preoccupation with quantity and quality of population, Australia was paralleling what was happening in the rest of the Western world. Rebecca West commented tartly in 1912: 'Just at present we are in the midst of a renaissance of domestic service. At King's College the home science course has been started with an endowment of £100,000 to teach middle-class women how to scrub floors and feel perfect ladies while doing it.'[13]

This conditioning of girls to accept marriage as a lifelong vocation was reinforced in Australia as the century progressed by the proliferation of articles in women's magazines on motherhood, housework and cooking. The efficient full-time housewife was elevated to a position of honour approaching veneration and the Australian version of the 'feminine mystique' emerged. By the 1920s the woman was back on her nineteenth-century pedestal with new accoutrements—a book on domestic science in one hand and one on mothercraft in the other. Without any compensatory emphasis on the possibility of a career outside marriage (let alone a career *and* marriage), most Australian girls until World War II, internalised a vision of their time in the paid work force as only a bridge between school and domesticity.

The extension of domestic feminism into vocational marriage and motherhood dampened, but did not entirely drown, opposition in Australia to the institutionalising of economic discrimination against women in the paid work force. A wages system based on the family was inaugurated in the Harvester Judgment in 1907. This fixed the minimum wage for a married man with three children, and then assessed a single woman as needing only 54 per cent of that. This differential was perpetuated through later basic-wage decisions. The system was based on the premise that all women married and that the male was always benevolent enough to provide adequately for his wife and children, and it discouraged women from seeking paid work outside marriage (and so 'taking jobs from men') or from leaving an unhappy marriage to fend for themselves and their children. It was particularly hard on widows who had to bring up children on their own and on women who had the disabled or aged dependent on them, and it validated economic discrimination against those who chose not to marry, or who were never asked. Bessie Rischbieth, the Western Australian feminist whose work spanned more than forty years, wrote in 1963: 'the basic wage finding was one of the hindrances to equal pay and ... the necessity for reassessment of the basic wage is still a burning question and endeavours to solve it cannot be relaxed.'[14] A comprehensive account of this occupational feminism in Australia from the turn of the century until the 1960s is still to be written.

Australian twentieth-century feminists did not quarrel with tax concessions for families with children, or child endowment and maternity allowances (provided that the last two were paid directly to the mother), but they contended, as did so many of the suffragists before them, that the basic wage should be based on the individual. They found themselves, however, excluded from the structures—the male trade unions and the political parties—where decisions were made about their economic situation. Trade unions, when they did not allow women membership, showed no inclination to fight for improvements in the female wage structure. The Harvester Judgment and consequent basic-wage decisions relieved them and the politicians from any obligation to the woman in the work force. When the basic wage went up, did not the woman's wage rise proportionately?

Firmly relegated to the private sphere by the new conditioning, and discouraged from remaining in the labour market by a discriminatory and now institutionalised economic system, the Australian woman was also circumscribed in politics. In the lead-up to the 1903 Commonwealth elections, the first in which all white Australian women could vote, the parties waged aggressive campaigns to attract as large a share of the new electorate as possible. They were competing, not just for women's votes, but for their energies. Where auxiliary party organisations of women did not exist, they were formed; where they did, moves were made to strengthen them. In each case women loyal to the party's platform were used to enlist other women. No party considered a woman for candidature although in the Commonwealth arena they had the right to stand, and although both Liberal and Labor parties had female adherents who had demonstrated their abilities during the suffrage campaigns. Labor, Liberal or Conservative, the women were to bolster the campaigns of male candidates. The Queensland Woman's Equal Franchise Association had been doing this for Labor's state candidates in the 1890s. Emma Miller told a meeting of members in 1897:

> During the general elections, in several of the Constituencies, members of the Association were very active workers, both before the polling day in canvassing from house to house, and on the polling day. From each candidate helped very hearty thanks was received, and, with one exception, all candidates for whom women worked were returned.[15]

The use of the women as servants to the male political structures continued and expanded in subsequent federal and state elections. Muriel Heagney wrote of the first Victorian Conference of Labor Women in 1909, at which women passed resolutions they would urge the party to adopt: 'In the 1910 Federal Election Campaign selected women speakers were sent by the Central Executive all over the State. The women also raised over £1,000 at a bazaar at the Trades Hall which went a long way towards success in Political Labour Council electioneering.'[16] Heagney's statement neatly encapsulates the kind of work done by the women of all parties in the post-suffrage period. They not only raised money for campaigns and catered for conferences; they acted as speakers and organisers and were, in scattered numbers, elected as representatives to predominantly male conventions. In some states there were strong women's organisations, like the Australian Women's National League in Victoria and the Women's Electoral League in Queensland, which lobbied their own parties on required legislation. But no matter what her abilities or what service she may have given to her party, the woman was not seriously considered until well into the second half of this century as a possible representative of that party in Parliament. As late as 1949 Elizabeth Nicholls wrote: 'Women have the vote, but it is made exceedingly difficult for them to achieve positions of public importance. The majority have been organised to serve parties and win elections for men.'[17]

In the fragmentation of 1903 many women refused on principle to follow political parties. One reason given was opposition to the party system itself. To these women the system which had taken shape while they were campaigning for their vote did not present itself as an historical imperative consequent on Labor finding itself a political voice; to them the confrontation which was its corollary was a deterioration in the standards of government. Rose Scott, one of the chief apostles of the non-party creed, denounced the party system's 'government by contradiction',[18] and in an address to her Women's Political and Educational League she said: 'Our place as women was not that of camp followers to a corrupt system of party politics, but as women to be man's inspiration to higher and nobler methods of governing a country.'[19] Scott and her fellow believers clung obsessively to this Utopian vision of women vicariously transforming the world, although it was so much empty rhetoric in the light of the party system—and perhaps in any light. Rather than give up their entrancing vision and face reality, they condemned the party system itself.

The second reason the women gave for standing aloof from party politics had more validity and it did not presuppose the elimination of the party system itself. Women, it was said, should withhold their allegiance in order to put pressure for reform on all parties. From this point of view women's non-party-political organisations can be seen as the forerunners of the present Women's Electoral Lobby. Women in many organisations based on this premise were to fight laboriously for improvements throughout the century, supplementing the lobbying of women working within the party framework.

Research into the painstaking work done by party women *and* non-party women will eventually give a clearer picture of this agitation from the turn of the century until the blossoming of the 1960s. The material now available is enough to refute the claim that Australian feminism died with the suffrage movement.

The question of how women voted has preoccupied Australian political commentators since the first woman exercised her vote in the 1896 South Australian election. Because the Kingston Government was returned then with an increased majority, women were assumed in the main to be democrats.[20] After the 1903 Commonwealth election Thomas Bent blamed the women for the fact that Labor polled so well, and this was one of the reasons he gave for the delay in giving the state vote to Victorian women.[21] In 1908 when he allowed women their vote, however, he had become convinced by the strength of the Australian Women's National League that women would be a conservative force. Later commentators, too, have had varied opinions. In 1921 the British political analyst James Bryce thought that Australian women favoured the Labor party,[22] but a 1977 Labor party inquiry held women responsible for keeping Labor out of office for most of this century.[23] It is hard to escape the impression that it has been convenient to blame women for, or credit them with, any changes in Australian patterns of voting. For instance, since the 1916 and 1917 conscription referenda women had been held vaguely responsible for the 'no' vote, but this conclusion does not take account of several factors: the overwhelming rejection of conscription by the soldiers in the trenches (the only group whose vote could be accurately assessed); the support for conscription by the numerically strong Australian Women's National League; and the opposition of the rural sector in which farmers feared that they would be left without labour. Murray Goot's 1984 analysis of the problem concludes that there is no way of measuring how women voted.[24]

Without proof there is only conjecture. It is likely that in the first half of the twentieth-century most women voted as the males of their households did, not because of pressure to do so, but because their economic interests were bound up with those of their husbands and fathers. Changing patterns attributed to women can just as validly be seen as changing opinions over the whole of the society. The *Brisbane Courier* as early as 1893 thought that the women's vote would be predictable. The editor was commenting on the granting of woman suffrage in New Zealand: 'it is hard to see how she can be expected to differ much from the views held by her male relatives . . . as a rule the same party or class opinions dominate all the members of every domestic circle.'[25] Vida Goldstein, having twice tried unsuccessfully to wrest enough women's votes from party allegiances to give her a seat in the Senate, wrote in 1911: 'To add a million women to the register is the same as to add a million men. Each party gets its share.'[26]

Since World War II, however, the picture cannot be so simplified. The mass movement of women into the work force consequent on reliable birth-control and advances in domestic technology has sounded the decline of domestic feminism and the invigoration of a feminism which had been kept simmering by dedicated groups of Australian women—that which demanded that the woman be considered as a separate economic unit apart from the family. In the 1990s we have reached a situation which would have delighted our suffragists—one in which women's issues could well decide the outcome of an election.

That most women in the post-suffrage period voted for party candidates rather than for women who stood as Independents is borne out by the fate of the large numbers of women who, either for ideological reasons or because they could not gain party preselection, stood without party backing. Feminists all over the world who had applauded the early grant of the vote to Australian women were astounded by the nation's intransigence when it came to electing them to the legislatures. Only nine women were elected to state Parliaments before the beginning of World War II. South Australia, which in 1894 gave women both the right to vote and to stand as candidates for its legislature, did not elect a women until 1959—a gap of sixty-five years. Although Australia in 1902 was the first in the world to give its women the right to sit in its national Parliament, no woman was elected to either the Senate or the House of Representatives until 1943—a gap of forty-one years. Ada Holman, an Australian suffragist and successful journalist, was mortified when she visited England in 1925 with her husband, the former Labor Premier of New South Wales, to find eight female members in the House of Commons, one of whom was a minister in Britain's first Labour Government. 'It was exciting, though painful in contrast to our own womanless legislatures',[27] she wrote.

Some random comparisons will show how quickly Australia lost its lead in giving women political participation and how backward it was by the 1920s. In Finland in 1906, the first year in which their women were allowed to vote and stand, nineteen women of a total of two hundred were elected. This increased to twenty-five in 1908. Denmark elected nine women in the first election after it gained the vote in 1918, Germany and Austria elected thirty-six and eight respectively after they gained the vote in 1919, Czechoslovakia seventeen at its first woman suffrage election in 1920, and Sweden five in its first in 1922. In 1922 Australia had had only one woman parliamentarian, Edith Cowan of Western Australia.

A more comprehensive overview of Australia's female representation as compared to other countries is needed, however, before longer-term generalisations can be made, and I do not have access to all the statistics required. To go further and draw conclusions about the *reasons* for variations of representation from country to country, one would have to take into account some important interrelated variables: the relative strengths of twentieth-century ideological factors governing women's place in a particular society: how many Parliaments there are in its political system: the concentration or dispersion of population; and the strength and organisation of party structures within the national unit. By no means the least important factor to be considered would be the method of election in the countries to be compared. For instance, Australia since the 1940s has had a much higher percentage of women members in the Commonwealth Senate (which is elected on a proportional basis) than in the House of Representatives or in any of the state Parliaments which are elected by preferential voting. The following examination of some of the reasons for Australia's poor record of female representation might contribute to such a comparative overview.

It is important to note that until after World War I Australian women could be nominated only in South Australia and for the Commonwealth Parliament. Candidature became possible in New South Wales and Queensland in 1918, Western Australia in

1920, Tasmania in 1921, and Victoria in 1923—Victoria thus maintaining its record of giving political rights only when forced to do so by the situation in the rest of the nation. Parliamentary debates during the suffrage period show that even supporters of the vote could be opposed to giving women the right to sit in Parliament. In nearly every case amendments to allow them to do so were moved by those trying to wreck the suffrage bills. Goldstein's right to stand for the Senate in 1903 was challenged (unsuccessfully), and although the South Australian Parliament gave the right to stand in 1894, that state was the last to elect a women. It is quite likely that the clause allowing candidacy was left in the South Australian suffrage bill in 1894 because some members in that state held the same view as R. K. Pilkington did in Western Australia in 1920 when the right to stand was being debated: 'It is because honorary members recognize that the public know the unwisdom of such a course that they are prepared to put this Bill upon the statute book.'[28] The suffragists themselves must bear some of the responsibility for the delay in granting candidature. Some, it is true, believed that women should not enter Parliament, but more often denial of interest was made in order not to endanger the granting of the vote. Politicians who did look with favour on women in Parliament had little incentive to fight for it in view of these disclaimers.

The most obvious blame for Australia's intransigence, even after candidature became possible, lies with the political parties. They refused to nominate women or, if they stood as Independents, actively campaigned against them. Female Independents were particularly threatening to the entrenched and confrontational Australian party system, for they had the potential, campaigning on women's issues, to attract the votes of half the electorate. So Goldstein in 1903 found ranged against her the Liberal, Conservative and Labor press, each of which was backing a Senate team. The opposition to her was particularly bitter from the Labor Party, to whose platform she was closest. The 51,497 votes she polled confirmed the fears of all parties that women candidates were a threat to party unity. She stood four more times as an Independent for the Commonwealth Parliament—for the Senate in 1910, for the House of Representatives in 1913 and 1914, and for the Senate in 1917. All attempts were unsuccessful. She polled well in the first three of these four elections but, probably due to her pacifist stand during the war, very badly in 1917.

The unwillingness of Australian parties to nominate women from within the ranks of their female supporters or, on the rare occasions they did so before the 1970s, to nominate them for any but unwinnable seats, owes much to their fear that women, once in Parliament, would put women's issues before party solidarity. An examination of the campaign, election and parliamentary record of Edith Cowan, the first woman to gain a seat in any Australian Parliament, encapsulates these party attitudes. Cowan was a member of the socially prestigious Perth Karrakatta Club, helped to form the Western Australian Woman's Franchise League just before the vote was won in 1899, and had since then lobbied on women's issues from within women's organisations. In 1921, a year after women's candidature was made possible in Western Australia, she asked for nomination by the Nationals, a group to the right of the Liberal spectrum which, in spite of its denials to the contrary, was in effect a party. Nationals were fielding two candidates in most electorates to maximise their share of the votes cast, confident that the second preferences of one would flow to the other. The party granted Cowan nomination to a blue-ribbon National seat, as second candidate to the sitting Attorney-General. It was thought that she had no chance of election, but women's organisations in which she had worked backed her campaign, her electorate was a prosperous one in which many members of these organisations lived, and no Labor candidate complicated the situation. There was considerable consternation within the National party and the consequent National Government, but jubilation within the ranks of the women, when the sitting Attorney-General lost his seat to her. The National Council of Women held a public meeting in her honour,[29] and Cowan presented brooches cast in the form of a cracked gumnut to her committee members[30]—the press had remarked when she nominated that her constituency would be a hard nut to crack. The galleries were crowded at the opening of Parliament to view the first swearing in of a female member in Australia.

Cowan made it clear in her first speech in Parliament that she would feel free to dissent from the National party's policies, especially when it came to measures affecting women.[31] From the beginning she was an embarrassment to the Government. In her maiden speech she castigated the Minister for Railways for his imposition of a one-shilling charge for prams on suburban trains, and said he should be sentenced to an afternoon tramping the city with a heavy baby on his hip and a bag of purchases in his free hand.[32] For the most part she was able to handle dissent from Government measures by abstention from voting, but the whole Parliament was taken aback during discussion of the Arbitration Act Amendment Bill to limit working hours for employees, including domestic servants. She moved that wives should be considered to be employed by their husbands,[33] thus dramatising the fact that wives could, in fact, be worse off than their own servants. They were entitled to no money, but only to the board, food and lodging husbands thought fit to provide—and there was no limitation on their working hours. This situation had concerned the suffrage movement: Rose Scott in 1903 had expressed the hope that ultimately wives would be entitled to a set portion of their husband's income.[34] The New South Wales *Bulletin* reacted to Cowan's suggestion with a page of cartoons showing what might actually happen if the wife decided to limit her unpaid working day to ten hours. Cowan achieved some significant gains for Western Australian women, the most important being the Act which made it unlawful for a single woman to be prevented by reason of her sex from holding civil or judicial office, or from practising any profession.[35] She was unsuccessful in extending this to include women who married. She stood as a National for a second term, but this time aggressive campaigns were waged against her by the favoured National candidate and by Labor, which had decided to contest the seat.

There were other reasons for low representation of women in Australian Parliaments. Although the municipal vote was given very early to women—South Australia was the first to give it in 1861 and Tasmania the last in 1884—women could not sit on municipal councils until during and after World War I, and so could not utilise the pathway to Parliament which had served men so well in Australia and elsewhere. Another was that female representatives could come from only three areas: the small group of women who did not marry and could afford to cease work and finance themselves for an election campaign; those older married women whose child-bearing and child-rearing years were behind them and whose husbands would finance their campaigns and were happy for them to be away from their homes for long periods; and those who belonged to a class so wealthy that a supervisory housekeeper, servants and nursery staff could be employed. This very wealthy class was small in Australia, and even in its ranks the Australian version of the 'feminine mystique' dictated that the 'true' woman should take responsibility for her own home and children. There were other practical factors, too. Those women who lived outside capital cities had the problem of distance to consider. Rose Scott, commenting with approval on Goldstein's candidature in 1903, wrote that only women in Melbourne— where the Commonwealth Parliament was then sitting—could be elected to either House and still attend to their homes.[36] When the Parliament was moved to Canberra, an isolated city built specifically for it, the 'tyranny of distance' became even more acute for women. The experience of Dame Enid Lyons, the first woman to be elected to the Commonwealth House of Representatives, will serve to illustrate the multiple problems which beset a woman aspiring to the Commonwealth Parliament.

Enid at eighteen married Joe Lyons, then Minister for Education in the Tasmanian Labor Government and her senior by eighteen years. In spite of the fact that she bore twelve children in twenty-five years (one died in infancy) she appeared on most platforms with her husband, attended conferences with him, and even stood once as an Independent for a Tasmanian seat. Her biography tells of her perpetual exhaustion, even though she was able to secure that scarce Australian commodity, good domestic help. Joe Lyons became Premier of Tasmania for two periods, and then moved to Commonwealth politics. In 1931 he turned his back on Labor and was largely instrumental in welding together the anti-Labor forces into the United Australia Party. Then a year later he became Prime Minister and brought their brood to the Lodge in Canberra, where he died in office in 1939. In 1943 Enid Lyons, back in Tasmania and with five children still at school (the youngest ten years old) sought the United Australia Party nomination for the electorate in which she had grown up. She said she did so because 'Joe had always cherished the wish that I should be the first woman elected to Federal Parliament' and because 'I believed with all my heart in the right of women to a place in Government.'[37] Her request presented the pre-selection committee with a dilemma, for they had tentatively chosen two men, and they did not think it possible that a woman could win the conservative rural seat. 'It was felt that in view of my extensive political services in the past, I could hardly be passed over, [so] . . . after a long debate it was decided that there should be three candidates.'[38]

With the help of her husband's reputation as well as her own, Lyons won the seat in an electorate where men outnumbered women by 1500 and, using the annuity given her by Parliament on her husband's death, settled her five children into boarding school. In Canberra she gave a great deal of thought to her 'uniform'—black dresses with removable white collars—and a code of conduct in Parliament which would be acceptable to the male members: 'Australians are a highly conservative people, and even today the tradition of male supremacy holds in a manner not matched in any country of comparable development.'[39]

Lyons tried to return to visit her children once a month and to arrange her duties so that she could be home for school holidays. At first she travelled overnight to Melbourne by train and on an overnight ferry across the Tasman. When it became apparent that the travel was affecting her health, the Prime Minister arranged that she should have precedence for plane bookings, scarce in war time. Lyons gives a graphic picture of how hard it was to be a politician *and* a woman with family obligations—even when she could afford boarding-school fees.

> By the time I had cooked the Christmas fare, had conducted the seasonal festivities, and organised the family outings; had altered all the clothes, cutting down suits and 'turning' school tunics, cleaning, pressing, and mending; and had packed the children off to school; Canberra beckoned as a place of rest. No meals to cook, no beds to make, and typists to help with correspondence! Only my stockings to wash and my clothes to press! But I would look sometimes at the men about me, and envy them for having wives. Were there any, I would ask myself, who even washed their own socks?[40]

Lyons was re-endorsed and returned in 1946, when she trebled her first majority, and in 1949 when she quadrupled it. But eighteen months into her third term, a serious operation having added to the other exhausting complications of her life, she was suffering from burn-out, and resigned from Cabinet. When Parliament was dissolved in 1951, before the end of its term, she seized with relief the opportunity to resign from her seat. 'But what of the position of women, I was asked. Would I abandon my post under such circumstances?'[41] Lyons explained that she was afraid that pushing herself as hard as the double life demanded would rob her children of their one remaining parent. Although she lived for thirty more years, she did not stand again.

Lyons was hailed by women's organisations as an example of what a woman could achieve, but she can more validly be seen as an example of the almost insurmountable difficulties which lay in the path of any woman who aspired to office in the Commonwealth Parliament, especially if she shared, as Lyons did, the Australian obsession with the low birth-rate. The press avoided taking her seriously as a politician by emphasising her motherly attributions rather than her political contributions. She was 'Australia's mother';[42] she was praised for bringing 'the homely touch'[43] to Parliament; and in 1950–1, after she had left Parliament because of ill-health and the difficulty of combining two roles, she was voted 'the outstanding mother of the year'.[44] The image of her projected by the media and her own eulogies of domesticity and the joys of having a large family[45] helped, ironically, to strengthen the very image which was helping to keep women out of Australian Parliaments.

Even though they confounded the party experts by winning what were thought to be unwinnable seats, the pre-selection experiences of Cowan and Lyons show that Australian women were caught in a circle of illogic. Because the parties would not nominate them for any but what they thought were unwinnable seats, and campaigned against the many who stood as Independents, women had little chance of being elected. The fact that they were rarely elected could then give the political parties a justification for not nominating them for seats which were winnable. The experiences of Cowan and Lyons throw doubt on the contention that women could not win seats simply because they were women. Jessie Street was another who won reluctant nomination for an 'impossible' New South Wales Labor seat in the 1943 election in which Lyons was returned, and on the primary vote she came in ahead of her Liberal rival. When the poll was declared which gave the victory to the Liberal candidate on preferences, he was so soured by the thought that a woman had nearly defeated him that he refused to shake Street's hand extended to congratulate him.[46] The myth that the Australian electorate was antipathetic to women even when they were pre-selected by political parties was to remain until well into the second half of the century, in spite of evidence to the contrary. The myth had been launched after Vida Goldstein's unsuccessful bid for the Senate in 1903. The writer of this poem ignored the large number of votes gained by her and the fact that she had been doomed because, as an Independent, all parties campaigned vigorously against her.

> She was pretty
>   She was fair:
> Tailor-made and
>   Debonair.
>
> She was clever
>   She was bright;
> And her politics
>   Were right.
>
> She was gifted
>   In her speech;
> She had mighty
>   Truths to teach.
>
> But one thing she had a-missing,
>   Which the legislator wants,
> And I almost blush to name it,
>   But she really hadn't – pants,
>   No she hadn't
>   Really hadn't
>   Poor Vida hadn't pants.
>
> For the great Australian nation,
>   Though it loves to woo and flirt,
> Will never bend its noodle
>   To unmitigated skirt.[47]

If the winning of the vote was not followed by the admission of women to a direct voice either in the Government or in the underlying power structure of political parties, it is reasonable to ask what it *did* achieve. Many women and politicians in the euphoric post-suffrage period credited it with a great deal. In a letter of introduction to Rose Scott which Edith Cowan carried to Sydney in 1900—the year after Western Australian women were enfranchised—Mrs Christine Clark wrote to Rose Scott: 'You have no idea what a difference it has made to us having the vote! They give us as much consideration now in their political calculations as men, or almost as much!'[48] Commonwealth politicians, in a resolution sent to the British Parliament in 1910, expressed the opinion that the woman's vote had 'given a greater prominence to legislation affecting women and children',[49] and Goldstein wrote in 1911 that since the vote, 'Members of the Parliament find they can make time to attend to the claims of women voters.'[50] She credited the women's vote with several measures which had been passed since 1902, including equal pay in the public service—a measure which was withdrawn. Nellie Martel (by then working for the British movement), said in an interview in England in 1905: 'Until we got the vote we agitated in vain for many reforms. Immediately the vote was granted, and fully a year before we were able to exercise it, we found member after member introducing measures which previously we had pleaded for all to no purpose.'[51] There were some improvements in state social legislation in the period immediately after suffrage was granted, but both Goldstein and Martel were exaggerating, probably to impress their British and American audiences, but perhaps also to try to convince themselves that the struggle had been worthwhile. The truth was that Australian women, emasculated by their fragmentation and by their exclusion from decision-making processes (but aided by the Liberal reforming spirit and interventionist policies of the early twentieth century) had to lobby inch by inch for improvements in their social, economic and political position, both inside and outside marriage. By 1916 Rose Scott had no illusions about the struggle which still lay ahead. In an address to the National Council of Women she listed all the laws which still discriminated against women and children, and went on

> We are enfranchised women. For fourteen years we have had the vote. Why have not women won all these rights for our fellow women and children? It is because of the Eternal Sex Question and shows that the majority of women have chosen to serve men at election time, rather than ameliorate the wrongs endured by their own sex, and have failed to insist that every Government programme has something in it for women . . . these reforms I have indicated were most of them advocated as reasons for the women's vote, and even now if women would only combine and work for these reforms and stand apart from parties and factions there is nothing that they could not accomplish for their fellow women and children.[52]

The story of twentieth-century feminism in Australia, and all over the world, was to be the story of this continuing fight for political, legal and economic equality. The hard-won reforms of sixty years were then to provide the environment in which the new feminism of the 1960s could flourish and in which other women could take up the cudgels laid down by suffragists like Louise Lawson and Henrietta Dugdale, who could discern more subtle forms of discrimination than were apparent to most Australian suffragists. Bessie Rischbieth, one of the leaders in the long haul, paid tribute to the women who began the journey when she wrote 'We are deeply indebted to those women who pioneered women's suffrage. It was they who laid the necessary foundations for our own work to obtain full citizenship.'[53]

Notes

1. William Pember Reeves, *State Experiments in Australia and New Zealand*, pp. 103-4.
2. Jessie Ackermann, *Australia from a Women's Point of View*, p. 210.
3. Adela Pankhurst, *Lone Hand*, 1 July 1914, vol. 2, no. 8, p. 96.
4. Ross Paulson, *Women's Suffrage and Prohibition*, p. 6.
5. The following sources are relevant to an assessment of 'the frontier theory': Alan Grimes, *The Puritan Ethic and Woman Suffrage*; Ross Paulson, *Women's Suffrage and Prohibition*; Aileen Kraditor, *The Ideas of the Woman Suffrage Movement 1890-1920*; William O'Neill, *Everyone was Brave*; Carol Bacchi, 'First-Wave Feminism: history's judgment'.

6. Peter P. Biskup, 'The Westralian Feminist Movement', p. 71.
7. *WAPD*, vol. 12, 17 August 1898, p. 1031.
8. *SAPD*, 22 July 1885, c. 332.
9. *Brisbane Courier*, 28 July 1900.
10. Rose Scott, 'Why women need a vote', (1903), Women's Political and Educational League of New South Wales: Papers, 1902–1903, ML:NSW, MSS 38/41, item 223.
11. John Stuart Mill to Archibald Michie, 1868, quoted in Marian Sawer and Marian Simms, *A Woman's Place*, p. 2.
12. John Stuart Mill to Catherine Helen Spence, 1868, quoted in ibid., p. 2.
13. *Daily Herald*, 22 June 1912, quoted in James Marcus (ed.), *The Young Rebecca: writings of Rebecca West*, p. 361.
14. Bessie Rischbieth, *March of Australian Women*, p. 20.
15. *Worker* (Brisbane), 30 March 1897.
16. Muriel Heagney, 'Notes on Women in the Australian Labor Movement', LTL:V, Women in Political History folder, Riley Collection.
17. Elizabeth Nicholls, *Torch-Bearers: the Woman's Christian Temperance Union of South Australia*, p. 48.
18. This phrase was used by a correspondent to Rose Scott, 1 May 1901, who mentioned that it was coined by the *Bulletin*, Woman Suffrage Correspondence, 1899–1902, ML:NSW, MSS A2272, item 616.
19. Rose Scott, 'Why women need a vote', Women's Political and Educational League of New South Wales: Papers, 1904–1910, ML:NSW, MSS 38/41, pp. 319.
20. *Bulletin*, 9 May 1896.
21. *VPD*, vol. 110, 13 July 1905, p. 592.
22. James Bryce, First Viscount, *Modern Democracies*, p. 199.
23. Penny Giles, 1982, 'Affirmative Action in the Australian Labor Party', unpublished paper quoted in Marian Sawer and Marian Simms, *A Woman's Place*. p. 116.
24. Murray Goot, 'Electoral Systems', p. 184.
25. *Brisbane Courier*, 30 November 1893.
26. Vida Goldstein, *Woman Suffrage in Australia*, p. 8.
27. Ada Holman, *Memoirs of a Premier's Wife*, p. 77.
28. R. K. Pilkington, *WAPD*, vol. 62, 17 September 1920, p. 510.
29. Peter Cowan, *A Unique Position: a biography of Edith Dirksey Cowan*, p. 167.
30. ibid., p. 166.
31. *WAPD*, vol. 64, 28 July 1921, p. 16.
32. ibid., p. 18.
33. *WAPD*, vol. 65, 16 November 1921, p. 1730.
34. Rose Scott, 'Why women need a vote' (1903). Women's Political and Educational League of New South Wales: Papers, 1904–1910, ML:NSW, MSS 38/41, p. 197.
35. *WAPD*, vol. 68, 5 September 1923, pp. 1375-6.
36. *Herald* (Victoria), 8 August 1903.
37. Enid Lyons, *Among the Carrion Crows*, p. 9.
38. ibid., p. 10.
39. ibid., p. 5.
40. ibid., p. 40.
41. ibid., p. 164.
42. 'Australia's mother', *People 5*, 6 October 1954.
43. ibid.
44. ibid.
45. ibid.

46. Jessie Street, *Truth or Repose*, p. 259.
47. Undated clipping (presumed to be early 1903) in Vida Goldstein: Papers, 1902–1919, MTL:V, MSS 7865.
48. Christine Clark to Rose Scott, 15 December 1900, Rose Scott, Woman Suffrage Correspondence, 1899–1902, ML:NSW, MSS A2272, item 526.
49. *CAPD*, vol. 59, 7 November 1910, p. 6300.
50. Vida Goldstein, *Woman Suffrage in Australia*, p. 9.
51. *Dawn*, 1 June 1905.
52. Rose Scott, 'Laws which concern women and children', 6 September 1916, National Council of Women of New South Wales: Papers 1899–1921, ML:NSW, MSS 38/39, item 377.
53. Bessie Rischbieth, *March of Australian Women*, p. 12.

12

AUSTRALIAN SUFFRAGISTS AND SUFFRAGETTES IN BRITAIN AND AMERICA

Historians have not given Australia serious consideration when assessing the nineteenth-century feminist movement and the world-wide struggle for votes for women, dismissing the early victories in Australasia as frontier phenomena. It is clear, however, that although allowance must be made for the fact that their frontier situtation (especially the coincidence of suffrage agitation and federation) was easier to manipulate than the established structures and traditions of older societies, the Australian organisations, arguments, and the issues which the arguments encapsulated, were part of the universal suffrage movement.

The influence which the early vote in Australia had on the campaigns in Britain and the United States, and the use to which it was put by overseas suffragists in their propaganda, are areas which beg exploration, but only a limited amount of material is available in Australia. We know from Goldstein's account in the *Woman's Sphere*, however, that when she went to America the suffragists there used the fact that Australian women had the vote to publicise their own demands, and they gave Goldstein the opportunity to broadcast her enfranchisement through newspaper interviews, public speeches, an interview with the President and an address to a Congressional Committee.

For several years Australian and New Zealand women were able to bask in the glory of having won their vote so early, but when Finland gave woman suffrage in 1906 and Denmark a limited female suffrage in 1908, the Australian experience ceased to be remarkable in America. Because Australia was part of the British Empire, however, the Australian vote continued to have some relevance in Britain. Until 1918 the women there were able to reproach their Parliament for being less progressive than its own colonies. Two Australian women (Goldstein and Martel) and one New Zealand woman (Lady Anna Stout) wrote booklets after 1910 which the British movement could utilise. Just how relevant were their extravagant eulogies of the moral and legislative claims for the vote in Australia and New Zealand by then would be an interesting question to pursue in British records.

In this chapter I wish to place the Australian movement more firmly in the chronological development of the movement in Britain and the United States, and to follow the fortunes of some Australian suffragists who played an active part overseas. In the process I will offer the information available in Australia about the interaction of the Australian experience with these two great movements. A more comprehensive overview of this interaction will have to wait on research in overseas libraries.

Australian suffragists were part of a world movement and they were both aware of it and proud of it. The WCTU, with its network of suffrage departments, had the strongest international ties. WCTU branches were fortified and encouraged by their American parent and by its offspring in other parts of the world, and Australian successes in turn strengthened the resolve of Union 'sisters in other lands'. Casual WCTU visitors or those who stayed longer, like the American Mary Love (who put the Victorian WCTU movement on its feet), and Jessie Ackerman and her fellow missionaries were always assured of a warm welcome anywhere in Australia. The open societies, even though they belonged to no comparable international organism, also had two-way communication with women of like minds. Rose Scott, that compulsive letter writer, kept in touch with a network of overseas correspondents. Maybanke Anderson wrote that she had 'almost a passion for acquiring and recording knowledge of the work of women in other lands, and her annual reports for both associations [the New South Wales Womanhood Suffrage League and the National Council of Women] may yet be very valuable as authentic history.'[1] Suffrage information flowed in and out of Australia via letters, newspapers and magazines. Louisa Lawson's *Dawn* and Vida Goldstein's *Woman's Sphere* both circulated overseas. In 1896 a correspondent wrote to Lawson: 'Since some months I do not receive your paper. It is of the greatest importance for the Women's Movement in Germany to hear from you and your progress.'[2] The debate about whether the woman's vote was working or not working in Wyoming (where women had had their franchise since 1869) or New Zealand (since 1893) generated long speeches in Australian Parliaments, and judgments of overseas commentators were quoted in many pro-suffrage and anti-suffrage leaflets. Not only the arguments of J. S. Mill were used by supporters, but those of prominent suffragists like Millicent Garrett Fawcett in England and Lucy Stone in America. Opponents quoted overseas anti-suffragists, especially British statesmen. Arguments for and against were adapted to suit the bias of the Australian debate.

The women from overseas who came to invigorate the WCTU campaign were predominantly American, but the open societies had many from Britain in their front ranks, either those coming to settle, or expatriates returning after a prolonged stay in 'the old country'. So Englishwomen Dora Montefiore and Nellie Martel (New South Wales), Mary Lee (South Australia), Emma Miller, Elizabeth Brentnall and Agnes Williams (Queensland), and Madeline Onslow (Western Australia), played their leading parts, and the returning Victorians Annette Bear-Crawford and Dr Constance Stone boosted the campaign in that state.

By the turn of the century the international woman suffrage movement had been launched, and Australian women were more than welcome at international gatherings. In 1900 the National Union of Women's Suffrage Societies in England wrote requesting a delegate to their convention from each Australian colony: the New South Wales Womanhood Suffrage League wrote to Miss Tilley, already in London, asking her to represent them.[3] in 1902 Vida Goldstein made her event-packed visit to Washington as the representative of Australia and New Zealand at the first gathering of the International Woman Suffrage Conference, which was to have a long history in the international women's movement. WCTU women often attended these open conferences as well as their own world conventions. Australian women were to make an honourable contribution to the international movement but their continuing participation belongs with a study of Australian post-suffrage feminism and is beyond the scope of this book.

By 1902 two prominent New South Wales suffragists were living in England. The widowed Dora Montefiore took her Australian-born children back in the mid-1890s and in 1901 Madeleine Onslow accompanied her husband when he returned there because of ill-health. They had both identified themselves with the British movement by the time the first elected Australian Prime Minister, Edmund Barton, arrived in 1902 to receive his knighthood and attend the coronation of Edward VII. Barton was no enthusiast for woman suffrage; he had been forced by South Australian delegates to yield the Commonwealth vote to their women at the Federal Convention in 1897, and he knew that this would inevitably lead to the Commonwealth vote for all Australian women. The 1902 Federal Franchise Bill was timetabled for the week after Barton sailed, perhaps because he wanted to avoid both the debate and the celebrations which he knew would follow. The bill was ratified by both the House of Representatives and the Senate soon after he arrived in England. The British women, with their movement stalled under a Tory Government since 1885, had been closely monitoring Australian developments, and they approached Barton and asked him to use his influence on their behalf. An address with the signatures of eighteen prominent suffragists, of whom Madeleine Onslow was one, was presented to him. The preamble claimed that the British case was strengthened by the adoption of woman suffrage in Australia.

> We take the opportunity of your presence among us to thank you for the lead given to the Old Country by your example, to ask you for any information you might possess as to the prospects of Women's Suffrage in such of the Australian States as have not yet adopted it (i.e. Victoria, New South Wales, Tasmania and Queensland) and to request you to extend your sympathy and support to us in our efforts to secure a similar reform in the United Kingdom.[4]

There is no evidence that Barton tried to put any pressure on the British Government or that he took any part in promoting votes for women in the four remaining Australian states. Only one, New South Wales, gave its women state rights before he left politics for the High Court bench.

In 1904 another New South Wales suffragist, Nellie Martel, returned to England with her sick husband. She was made much of by the British movement, not only as a woman with a vote, but because she was one of three New South Wales women who had stood (all three unsuccessfully) for election to the Commonwealth Senate in 1903. The *Dawn* throughout 1905 reported Martel's triumphs as a suffrage speaker. The forceful style which had been frowned upon by Rose Scott and her ladylike League was not unwelcome in the British Climate.

By 1906, when a Liberal Government ended the twenty-one years of British Tory rule, there were in Britain organisations of suffragists of all classes and political persuasions. Noticeable were the Labour groups, established either by working women or by left-wing intellectuals. One of these was the Women's Social and Political Union, which had been formed in Lancashire in 1903 by Mrs Emmeline Pankhurst and her daughter Christabel. It was envisaged as a Labour society representing the Lancashire mill girls, but it soon became a national organisation and attracted a wider membership. It adopted as its motto 'Deeds, not Words' and on the hustings for the 1906 election campaign its members aggressively challenged candidates and disrupted meetings, attracting the derogatory label 'suffragettes' from the press. On the day the new Parliament opened a large group of women staged what they termed a 'raid' on Parliament House to demand an audience with the Prime Minister, Henry Campbell-Bannerman.[5] Twenty, including Nellie Martel[6] and Dora Montefiore, were admitted to the Stranger's Lobby, but the Prime Minister sent word that he would not meet them. A protest meeting was held there and then—the speakers standing on chairs to address their audience. The officials attempted to eject them from the lobby and in the ensuing struggle ten, including the two Australians, were arrested. They appeared before a magistrate charged with 'using violent and abusive language', a term which Montefiore claimed was chosen at random.[7] The Melbourne *Age* reported that during the court hearing Nellie Martel 'shouted and gesticulated' and claimed that as an enfranchised woman and one-time candidate in Australia she had the right to enter the inner lobby of the House.[8] Like the other woman she was bound over to keep the peace for six months, but on failure to produce surety was sentenced with them to two months in prison. The ten women, all of whom 'refused to leave the dock till force was used', were in the vanguard of more than a thousand women who were to be imprisoned between 1906 and 1914. In 1908 Martel is reported to have been badly beaten up—together with Emmeline Pankhurst—in a by-election demonstration.[9] Other details about her participation are sketchy, but she was probably still active in 1913, for a propaganda pamphlet by her, *The Women's Vote in Australia*, was published by the British Women's Press in that year.

As a member of the committee of the Women's Social and Political Union, Dora Montefiore had helped to organise this protest. Earlier that year she had gained extensive publicity for the movement when she dramatised her yearly refusal to pay income tax by barricading her house when the bailiffs, as they had done the two previous years, came to seize some of her possessions for sale. The bailiffs (and newsmen seeking interviews) beseiged the house for two months until, with twenty-two police in case of resistance, they were licensed by Parliament to use force to enter. Force was not needed; Montefiore had never intended to offer resistance. During the siege frequent suffrage demonstrations were held in the street outside, Montefiore herself addressing the audience from an upstairs window. From 1906 Montefiore began her mental journey from radical Liberalism to Socialism and eventually to Communism. She moved away from the Pankhursts and the National Union of Women's Suffrage Societies, preferring to work for the woman's vote through organisations demanding adult suffrage. In *From a Victorian to a Modern* (1927) she tells how she spoke on woman suffrage in France, Germany, Holland, Denmark, Sweden, Finland, Austria, Hungary, Italy, Cape Colony, the Transvaal and the United States. She made two visits back to Australia, spending a year in 1911 working for the left wing of the Australian Labor movement, and in 1922–3 visiting the widow and two young children of the son who had settled in Australia and then died from gas poisoning suffered when serving with the Australian contingent in France.

The British women had been optimistic about their chances for the vote when the Liberals were elected to power with a huge majority in 1906; but the new Government showed no enthusiasm for female suffrage, although it was committed to manhood suffrage and the abolition of the plural vote. Henry Asquith who, as Chancellor of the Exchequer, took over the running of the Government in 1907 when Campbell-Bannerman was ill, and who became Prime Minister in 1908, thought that woman suffrage would be 'a national disaster'[10] and he became increasingly antagonistic as the woman's vote was raised to complicate every move for electoral reform. The debates in Parliament were complicated by all the complexities which had beset the Australian debates and by others peculiar to Britain. Should only widows and spinsters have the vote? Should the vote be given on the same property and residential qualifications as applied to male electors? If manhood suffrage were granted, should it be extended to all women or would doing so strengthen the Labour party whose influence, although as yet weak in Parliament, was increasing outside it? How would giving woman suffrage complicate attempts to settle the Irish question which involved dispute over Irish representation in the House of Commons? The fact that there was a large majority of women in the British population was raised, too, for adult suffrage would mean, it was contended, government by women. To put pressure on the Government whenever the subject was being debated in the Houses, the movement organised huge rallies at major cities all over Britain, and the Pankhursts' Women's Social and Political Union began its spiral of militancy by disrupting by-elections and by repeated attempts to storm Parliament and interview Asquith. At by-elections women were forcibly removed from the halls, and in Parliament Square and Downing Street they were manhandled by police, many of whom subjected them to sexual indignities by tearing their clothes and pinching and twisting their breasts. Some women chained themselves to railings in order to gain time to address the crowds. As the militancy gained in intensity, and arrests and prison terms increased, a section of the Pankhursts' Social and Political Union broke away in disapproval, leaving a comparatively small group to carry on with what the great majority of suffragists considered to be self-defeating tactics.

In November 1910 the Australian Commonwealth Parliament, perhaps influenced by reports of the brutal police treatment of 300 women who had tried to march on the House of Commons earlier that month, decided to put its finger in the British pie. In spite of protests from some members that 'a child should not tell its parent what to do', motions were passed by both Federal Houses and cabled to Asquith, whose Government's refusal to allow a suffrage bill to be reintroduced in the House of Commons had triggered this particular peak of suffrage activity. The motions of support were introduced in the Commonwealth Parliament by two who had championed woman suffrage in their own states: by Arthur Rae (New South Wales) in the Senate and Dr William Maloney (Victoria) in the House of Representatives.

> That this House is of opinion that the extension of the suffrage to the women of Australia for State and Commonwealth Parliaments, on the same terms as to men, has had the most beneficial results. It has led to the more orderly conduct of elections, and at the last Federal elections the women's vote in a majority of the States showed a greater proportionate increase than that cast by men. It has given a greater prominence to legislation particularly affecting women and children, although the women have not taken up such questions to the exclusion of others of wider significance. In matters of Defence and Imperial concern they are proving themselves as far-seeing and discriminating as men. Though disaster was freely prophesied, the reform has brought nothing but good, our women taking their places in our system of representative government and effectively promoting its development.[11]

The motions did not come up for discussion in the House of Commons. In a reply to a question by British women in May 1911, Asquith did say that one cable had been received, but that he was not aware of the other.[12] The petition caused some waves, however. In early 1911 Lord Curzon (a committed opponent in the House of Lords), in response to it and to all those who contended that the vote for women in Australia and New Zealand set a precedent for Britain, published *Fifteen Reasons Against Woman Suffrage*.[13] He followed up his contentions at a meeting on 9 May. Curzon restated the usual objections which had been used in Australia, but he also expanded on the question of imperialism which had been raised in the 1910 address from the Australian Parliament. He contended that Britain's strength as an imperial power would be threatened if her Government were elected by a population with a majority of women.

> No precedent exists for giving women, as a class, an active share in the government of a great Country or Empire, and it is not for Great Britain, whose stake is the greatest, and in whose case the result of failure would be most tremendous, to make the experiment... The presence of a large female factor in the constituencies returning a British Government to power, would tend to weaken Great Britain in the estimation of foreign powers.[14]

In London at the time to attend an Imperial Conference and the coronation of King George V and Queen Mary, were prominent politicians from all over the Empire. The British Women's Freedom League approached those from Australia and New Zealand with questions based on Curzon's arguments, and published their replies in a pamphlet titled *Colonial Statesmen and Votes for Women*.[15] To the general question as to whether the women's vote had been beneficial, Andrew Fisher, then Australia's first Labor Prime Minister, said he was 'delighted with the results', and Andrew Kirkpatrick (South Australia) proffered this surely self-evident observation: 'I doubt very much whether one single candidate could secure his return to either House of Parliament in Commonwealth or State if he proposed to repeal it.' The British women's pamphlet gave considerable space to the refutation of Curzon's contention that imperialism was in danger. Not one Australian or New Zealand delegate shared Curzon's contention, it said, and went on 'We at home have not forgotten how Australia and New Zealand sprang to our support in the South African War, not one whit behind the Colonies with exclusively male electorates.'

The pamphlet quoted W. Pember Reeves, former Agent-General for New Zealand in London, who had in 1902 written *Social Experiments in Australia and New Zealand* contending that Australian and New Zealand women had not had to work for their vote. The period in which women had voted, he said, 'coincides precisely with the growth of a feminine Imperial spirit in that country'. This growth was 'a serious recognition of participation in a great and glorious responsibility'. Reeves was by then Director of the London School of Economics, and the pamphlet was quoting the claim made at a dinner party given in May of that same year by the British Men's League for Women's Suffrage in honour of the visiting Vida Goldstein, whom the pamphlet described as 'leader of the suffrage movement in Australia'. One wonders what the guest of honour was thinking during Reeves' panegyric on the imperial spirit: Goldstein was by then a committed pacifist, so her attitude to imperialism would have been equivocal, to say the least.

Perhaps the petition of the Australian Commonwealth Parliament to Asquith in 1910 had triggered the invitation of the Women's Social and Political Union—the militant wing of the British movement—to Goldstein to visit London in 1911. She was met at Euston Station by a large welcoming committee, and on 23 March was the guest speaker before more than 10,000 at the Royal Albert Hall. Australian expatriates or those visiting for the coronation 'came from all parts of London to hear her'.[16] Goldstein in her speech used the grill separating the Women's Gallery from the Parliament in the House of Commons as a symbol of the separation of women from all important decision-making, and she identified herself with the Pankhursts' Women's Social and Political Union by claiming that 'its [the grill's] existence alone justified the militant movement'.[17]

Goldstein stayed eight months in London and her speeches and contributions were published in the suffrage organ *Votes for Women*. She probably joined other women selling the paper in London streets, for she posed thus for a studio photograph when she returned to Australia. For the first two months of her stay the militancy continued, and she was there when the women vacated their houses for all-night gatherings rather than allow themselves, unenfranchised, to be counted in the census. But when Asquith allowed a bill to move to the debating stage in the House, a truce was declared between the Government and the suffragettes, and on 17 July, the Saturday preceding the coronation, a rejoicing march was held. Forty thousand suffrage supporters, representing all groups in the movement, marched from the Embankment to Albert Hall, taking just on three hours to pass a given point.[18] In the lead were 700 women dressed in white, each representing an imprisonment for the cause, and next came contingents from Ireland, Scotland and the Dominions. The united Australian and New Zealand contingent was organised by Goldstein, Lady Cockburn (by then living in London with her husband, who was President of the newly-formed Men's International Alliance for Woman Suffrage) and Lady Stout (there with her husband, New Zealand Chief Justice, for the coronation). The contingent was preceded by women holding a large banner urging 'Mother' to trust its women as the two Dominions had done. In the contingent were Australians living in England and those there for the coronation, including Mrs Fisher, wife of the Australian Prime Minister. Those who were able to crowd into the Albert Hall heard a succession of speakers, one of whom was Goldstein.

Marching behind the Australian banner may well have been the 22-year-old Jessie

Street. She visited England with her parents in 1911 and found 'a kindred spirit' in her cousin, the actress and suffragette Winifred Mayo: 'I was a newcomer, and quite inexperienced, but I soon learned to be useful',[19] Street wrote. She canvassed from house to house for support, sold *Votes for Women* in the streets and joined processions. Street was from New South Wales and would have been in her early teens when the vote was won there. She was to become one of Australia's leading twentieth-century feminists.

In 1911 the Women's Press published Goldstein's *Woman Suffrage in Australia*, and before leaving she, Lady Stout and others launched the Australian and New Zealand Women Voters' Association through which Australian women could monitor any British legislation which might affect them or their sisters back home. It was also to be a base from which expatriates could support the British campaign. Research in the Fawcett Women's Library in London might well turn up material to give an overview of the way members of the association campaigned in Britain until the partial vote was given in 1918. One other Australian woman had some suffrage participation in 1912; Edith Cowan, the former Western Australian suffragist, who was to be Australia's first successful female parliamentary candidate, visited Madeline Onslow, who had decided to live in London after her husband's death in 1908, and she attended suffrage meetings with her.[20]

The militancy intensified from 1912 to 1914. In 1913 Emily Davidson gave the cause its martyr by throwing herself under the horses at the running of the Derby. Imprisoned suffragettes went on hunger strikes and were force fed, and when it seemed that some might die the Government passed what came to be called the Cat and Mouse Act, whereby women could be released to regain their strength and then imprisoned again for the same offence. Back in Australia many women's voices were raised in condemnation of the British militancy: Rose Scott described the suffragettes' actions as 'absolutely barbaric' and as doing 'infinite harm ... to the dignity and beauty of true womanhood';[21] in 1914 the Australian Women's National League, claiming to represent 52,000 voters, expressed 'the utmost indignation at the suffragette outrages and their insult to the King';[22] and when Dr Roberta Jull, of the Western Australian Karrakatta Club, proposed the same year that a vote of sympathy by sent to imprisoned militants, there was a spate of protests to the Western Australian papers opposing the move.[23] It would be wrong to conclude from the silence of most, however, that there was no support at all among Australian women for their more forceful British sisters; there had been hints of militancy in the Australian campaigns, especially among Labor women. One could well envisage a militant Annie Kenny (in the person of Emma Miller, Lilian Locke, Annie Golding or Mary Lee) rising from Labor ranks to be a standard bearer; and if Bent had not yielded in Victoria in 1908 it is possible that Goldstein would have heeded her male advisors and called the Victorian women to more aggressive action. When the militancy began in England, however, only one Australian state did not have the vote, and the Victorian women were convinced that their Government would soon have to yield to bring itself into line with the rest of Australia.

The outbreak of war put out the fires of militancy in Britain, although the suffrage organisations continued to exist. Involvement in war work did not prevent the National Union of Women's Suffrage Societies from organising deputations and petitions, especially when the coalition Government formed to conduct the war discussed the advisability of giving votes to servicemen to make conscription more acceptable in England. When the more sympathetic David Lloyd George replaced Asquith at the head of the wartime coalition Government, the British Act was passed in 1918 which gave votes to all adult males—with some dual voting—but enfranchised only those women over thirty who were municipal ratepayers, married to municipal ratepayers, or university graduates. Thus the British Government until 1928 was able to avoid both 'petticoat government' and the enfranchising of large numbers of women who might well have voted for the British Labour party. The suggestion that the women should be given the vote as a reward for their war service was only made in passing in the parliamentary debate; it was seized upon and exaggerated by the press.[24] It is more likely that the Government yielded because it did not want a resurgence either of peaceful agitation or of militancy by the women, who could use their wartime work as an additional argument for having the vote. It was able to pre-empt these possibilities with partial suffrage. The right to be candidates was given in a bill the same year, and in the election which took place three weeks after it received the royal assent Lady Astor was returned by the Plymouth electorate to replace her son who had become ineligible to stand for the House of Commons when he became the Viscount on the death of his father.

Although property qualifications and plural voting did not exist to hamper the struggle in the United States, Constitutional requirements for granting the vote to women were more complex than those in Britain and Australia. Any American state, provided it had the consent of the majority of males in a referendum, could change its own franchise to give women the state vote, but in spite of hundreds of state campaigns only four were enfranchised by 1906. The United States Constitution decreed that when thirty-six of the forty-eight states had woman suffrage the United States Congress could be petitioned to pass a Constitutional amendment which would impose the vote for women—state and federal—on the remaining states. There was another path to the federal vote; a Constitutional amendment could be initiated in the Congress, where it would require a majority of two-thirds in both Houses. If it passed both, it would then have to be ratified by thirty-six of forty-eight of the state legislatures and would become law for all states. By 1906, the year Susan Anthony died and four years after Elizabeth Stanton's death, an amendment in Congress had not been considered to be the best option.

One of the bewildering array of American organisations agitating for the vote was the National Women's Trade Union League which had its headquarters at the social work settlement community at Hull House, Chicago. The settlement movement began in London in 1884 and Hull House was established by Jane Addams in 1889. Like other 'settlements', Hull House was a live-in base in a deprived area from which philanthropists and social workers laboured to improve living and working conditions for the residents. They provided consultative services, formed and made facilities available for self-help community groups, and lobbied local authorities and governments on specific issues. Because the Women's Trade Union League was so concerned about conditions and wages for working women, Hull House was a centre for vigorous suffrage agitation.

Two Australian women were living and working at Hull House by 1906. The 45-year-old Alice Henry,[25] teacher, Victorian Labor party worker and journalist, had left Australia for England in 1905. In October of that year she attended the great suffrage rally in Manchester organised by the Women's Social and Political Union in the lead-up to the 1906 election which replaced the Tory Government with a Liberal. The following year she sailed for America, where she travelled and lectured on the Australian woman suffrage campaigns, and later that year found herself in Chicago speaking on behalf of the municipal vote for women in that city. She stayed on to work in the suffrage department of the National Women's Trade Union League and to edit its paper *Life and Labor*. She was to have only one trip home before she returned to Australia to live in 1930.

In 1906 another Australian woman arrived at Hull House to join Henry. The 26-year-old Stella (Miles) Franklin sailed from Australia for San Francisco earlier that year. Franklin had come to Sydney from the bush in 1901, after she published her largely autobiographical first novel, *My Brilliant Career*. The book dealt with the problem for a woman of reconciling marriage with personal and intellectual fulfilment and was an immediate success. It caught the attention of feminists and in Sydney Franklin was befriended by Rose Scott, and on a short visit to Melbourne by Vida Goldstein and her sisters Aileen and Elsie. Franklin took little part in the suffrage movement, for the New South Wales campaign was almost over when she arrived in Sydney. Between 1901 and 1905, however, she wrote *Some Everyday Folk and Dawn*.[26]

Although ostensibly a romance, *Some Everyday Folk and Dawn* is a thoroughly feminist novel in that it deals with seduction and abandonment, the double standard, legal discrimination and the vulnerability of the woman in marriage. It is also a suffrage novel, for in picturing the first election in a country town after women were given the vote it brings out the major themes of the woman suffrage movement, the most significant being the vote as a symbol: the 75-year-old Grandma Clay is elated at being 'a freed citizen and no longer rated with criminals and lunatics'[27] and she points out to her granddaughter that 'It ain't what things actually are but what they stand for.'[28] The conduct of an election is painted vividly; the biases of the press, the support for one candidate by temperance societies, the adjustment of the candidates' presentations and platforms (more apparent than real) to allow for female voters, and the limited choice for electors—there are only two candidates and each is attached to a party, so the protagonist votes informally. Readers can project themselves into the large good-natured crowds at election meetings in the halls and the open air, where the men and the women exchange banter with each other and interject during the candidates' speeches. They can experience the excitement of the women at the polling booths for the first time, and can share the suspense of the declaration of the poll to the waiting crowds from the highest vantage point in the town, the hotel balcony.

Franklin's ship berthed at San Francisco in April 1906, just after the great earthquake and fire had ravaged the city.[29] She was met by Carrie Whelan, a friend of Carrie Chapman Catt, to whom she carried a letter of introduction. Catt was then emerging as a leader of the suffrage movement to fill the gap left by the death of Stanton and then of Anthony. Because Catt was overseas, Whelan gave her an introduction to Jane Addams, at Hull House in Chicago. After helping with relief work among the 300,000 homeless

Franklin travelled, with a short stint working as a waitress to gain material for her writing, and at the end of 1906 she arrived at Hull House, where she was to work for nine years. In 1908 she became part-time Secretary of the Women Workers' Trade Union League and in 1910 full-time Secretary. In 1912 she joined Alice Henry as assistant editor of the League's journal *Life and Labor* on which she worked until 1915 when she went back to England to live for twelve years. With the League so much involved in suffrage work, Franklin had several high-points of experience. In 1909 she was in the state capital, Springfield, Illinois, to hear speakers from the suffrage train who had descended on the city for the Republican Convention after traversing the state speaking to audiences along the way. In 1912 she was in Chicago for the convention of the newly formed Progressive party when a 'grand suffrage parade' was held with the women marching behind 500 yellow suffrage banners, and she was there in 1914 when a 'suffrage festival' was held in conjunction with the biennial convention of women's clubs meeting there. Franklin went to England for a visit in 1911, but she left America on 30 June, a fortnight after the great march on the Saturday before the coronation. While in England she renewed her friendship with Vida Goldstein, who was addressing suffrage meetings in London.

Franklin later questioned the wisdom of her involvement in the work in America. In a letter to Alice Henry she wrote: 'For a literary artist to be drawn away by causes is a form of infidelity, and has its punishments.'[30] Although she toiled at her writing while she was in Chicago, she wrote nothing of worth in those years. Her first burst of creativity was before she left Australia, and she did not find its source again until she returned to her own country and its themes.

One Australian woman gives a brief glimpse of the marches, or parades, which had become a major form of agitation in America by 1914. In that year Ada Holman, a journalist, post-suffrage feminist and wife of the then New South Wales Labor Premier, was in America. She met Carrie Chapman Catt, who took her on a short campaigning tour, and invited her to take part in one of the great New York parades. Catt handed her 'a furry object' and asked her to carry it in the parade. Holman asked what it was. Catt replied that it was a kangaroo and was meant to signify that she came from Australia. Holman wrote: 'Close scrutiny revealed a certain resemblance to our leaping marsupial but it was a very wobbly and strangely heavy specimen.'[31]

In 1915 Carrie Chapman Catt took over as President of the stagnant National American Woman Suffrage Association. She had been reluctant to do so, for at fifty-five she did not feel that she had the energy required to work in this most prominent position. She proved to be a brilliant tactician, bringing most of the state societies under her banner. With neither Democrats or Republicans committed to woman suffrage and, after fifty years of strenuous campaigning, only twelve states won, Catt decided that the state campaigns must be coordinated and the war must be fought more strenuously on the federal front. She set up her headquarters in New York from which to wage a campaign to have a suffrage amendment introduced into Congress, and enlisted women to work full-time with her there. She made it quite clear that state leaders would be expected to make their contribution to the federal campaign and in return the central organisation would send a task force to each state when their periodic state

Constitutional Conventions were being held. State campaigns, even if not successful in gaining regional votes, would keep the subject alive in the event of a ratification campaign. The plan required a veritable army of dedicated and mobile workers, and a large budget. The wealthy women in the American movement made the last possible.

Catt's workers in New York were now campaigning in tandem with another large branch of the movement, the Congressional Union. The Union was under the leadership of the Quaker Alice Paul, who had worked with the British Women's Social and Political Union and had suffered imprisonment and force feeding. The Congressional Union had already been lobbying for some years for an amendment to be introduced into Congress. In 1916 it changed its name to the Woman's Suffrage Party, and the following year its members, to the disapproval of Catt and her associates, decided to adopt more harassing tactics. Since he had been elected for his second term in 1916, President Wilson had been making soothing noises about woman suffrage but had done nothing. Members of the Women's Suffrage Party began to picket the White House, holding placards with slogans such as 'What Will You Do For Woman Suffrage?' When the United States entered the war in 1917 and adopted Wilson's slogan 'Make the World Safe for Democracy', the emphasis on the slogans changed. Now they said 'Democracy Should Begin at Home', 'A Democracy in Name Only', and 'Kaiser Wilson'. The women—professionals, wealthy society women, Quakers, college graduates and working women—stood silently at their posts on either side of the White House gates throughout a bitter winter; they moved only for a march around the perimeter of the White House on Inauguration Day. Mobs of opponents, including servicemen, harassed them, tearing banners from their hands and destroying them. No attackers were arrested, although the women were very roughly handled, but many suffragists faced court and were imprisoned for 'obstructing the sidewalk'. Two hundred and eighteen women from twenty-six states went on hunger strikes and many were force fed. Public indignation at the treatment forced Wilson to release them just before the Nineteenth Constitutional Amendment (called the Anthony Amendment in honour of the Quaker leader Susan Anthony) was introduced into Congress. Wilson, the day before it came up for debate in the House of Representatives, advised all Democrats to vote for it, but it was passed 274–136, by the bare two-thirds majority. It then went to the Senate, which passed it with a larger majority in 1919. The weary suffragists were then obliged to turn their attention to the ratification campaigns. In state after state they marshalled their forces as the Amendment came before its legislature. In the southern states they were opposed by those determined to have no extension of the Negro vote, in the mid-west by the liquor lobby which poured large amounts of money into the campaigns in the face of looming prohibition, and in the industrialised east by business interests wishing to avert demands for better wages and conditions from their army of cheap female workers. But in 1920, with thirty-six ratifications, the amendment became law, and, seventy-two years after the Seneca Falls Declaration, all American women had their state and federal vote.

Notes

1. Maybanke Anderson, *Sydney Morning Herald*, 2 May 1925.
2. *Dawn*, June 1896.
3. New South Wales Womanhood Suffrage League, Annual Report, 1900.
4. 'Address presented to Sir Edmund Barton requesting his support for woman suffrage in Great Britain.' ML:NSW, Miscellaneous Addresses no. 4, MSS D386.
5. Dora Montefiore, *From a Victorian to a Modern*, pp. 92-5.
6. Dora Montefiore does not mention Nellie Martel as being among the women but she is reported as taking part in the *Age*, 17 October 1906.
7. Dora Montefiore, *From a Victorian to a Modern*, p. 94.
8. *Age*, 17 October 1906.
9. There are several secondary references to this, but I have been unable to find a primary reference.
10. David Morgan, *Suffragists and Liberals: the politics of woman suffrage in England*, p. 113.
11. Arthur Rae (New South Wales) introduced this motion in the Senate, *CAPD*, vol. 59, 17 November 1910, p. 6300. Dr William Maloney introduced it in the House of Representatives, *CAPD*, vol. 59, 25 November 1910, p. 6886.
12. Agnes Edith Metcalfe, *Woman's Effort*, p. 168.
13. Quoted in 'Colonial Statesmen and Votes for Women', ML:NSW, 324.3/2A1.
14. ibid.
15. ibid.
16. *The Life and Work of Miss Vida Goldstein*, ML:NSW Doc. 915A, p. 11.
17. Agnes Edith Metcalfe, *Woman's Effort*, p. 169.
18. ibid., p. 178.
19. Jessie Street, *Truth or Repose*, p. 39.
20. Peter Cowan, *A Unique Position: a biography of Edith Dirksey Cowan*, p. 131.
21. Letter to the editor from Rose Scott, an unidentified newspaper clipping, 7 December 191[?], quoted in Kay Daniels and Mary Murnane, *Uphill all the Way*, pp. 273-4.
22. *Daily Standard*, 30 May 1914, quoted in Marian Simms, 'Conservative feminism in Australia: a case study of feminist ideology', p. 11.
23. Gail Reekie, 'With ready hands and new brooms: the women who campaigned for female suffrage in Western Australia 1895-1899', p. 31.
24. Martin Pugh, *Electoral Reforms in War and Peace*, pp. 136, 145.
25. This sketch is drawn from the author's short autobiography, *Memoirs of Alice Henry*, and from a recently published biography by Diane Kirkby, *Alice Henry: the power of pen and voice*.
26. Although Miles Franklin wrote this book before she left for America in 1906, it was not published until 1909.
27. Miles (Stella) Franklin, *Some Everyday Folk and Dawn*, p. 256.
28. ibid., p. 288.
29. Material about Franklin's American years comes from Verna Coleman, *Miles Franklin in America: her unknown (brilliant) career*.
30. Miles Franklin to Alice Henry, quoted in ibid., p. 199.
31. Ada Holman, *Memoirs of a Premier's Wife*, pp. 178-9.

Bibliography

Primary Sources

Parliamentary Papers

Commonwealth Acts of Australia, vol. 1, 1902.
Commonwealth of Australia: Parliamentary Debates.
The Constitution of the Commonwealth of Australia, 4th edn, 1986.
The Constitutions of the the Australian States, 4th edn, 1989.
National Australasian Convention Debates, Sydney. 1891.
National Australasian Convention Debates, Adelaide, Melbourne and Sydney, 1897–98.
New South Wales: Parliamentary Debates.
Queensland: Parliamentary Debates.
Royal Commissions. Select Committees of Parliament, and Boards of Inquiry, Part 4, New South Wales, 1854–1960.
South Australia: Parliamentary Debates.
Victoria: Parliamentary Debates.
Western Australia: Parliamentary Debates.

Reports of Suffrage Societies and Woman's Christian Temperance Unions

Womanhood Suffrage League of New South Wales, Annual Reports, 1892–1903.
Women's Suffrage Association of Tasmania, Report, 1904.
Woman's Christian Temperance Union of Australasia, Triennial Convention Reports, 1891–1909.
Woman's Christian Temperance Union of New South Wales, Annual Reports, 1883–1903.
Woman's Christian Temperance Union of Queensland, Annual Reports, 1885–1906.
Woman's Christian Temperance Union of South Australia, Annual Reports, 1887–1905.
Woman's Christian Temperance Union of Tasmania, Annual Reports, 1887–1904.
Woman's Christian Temperance Union of Victoria, Annual Reports, 1886–1909.

Woman's Christian Temperance Union of Western Australia, Annual Reports, 1893–1900.
Women's Franchise League of Western Australia, Annual Report, 1900.
Women's Suffrage League of South Australia, Reports, 1891, 1894.

Manuscripts and Contemporary Pamphlets

Address presented to Sir Edmund Barton requesting his support for woman suffrage in Great Britain, ML:NSW, Miscellaneous Addresses no. 4, MSS D386.
Anderson, Maybanke (1908). 'A Refutation and an Appeal, by a citizen who has no vote', ML:NSW, 324.3/A.
Ashworth, E. 'The History of the Queensland Women's Electoral League', OL:Q, typescript, OM71/47.
Australian Women's Franchise Society Leaflets. ML:NSW, Q324.3/1.
Australian Women: Newspaper Cuttings 1895–1920, ML:NSW, A920.7/A.
Batchelor, E. L. 'The Labor Party and its Progress', lecture delivered at the Democratic Club, Adelaide, 5 March 1895, ML:SA, pamphlet, 339.9942/B328.
Couchman, Elizabeth. 'The Australian Women's National League', no date given, LTL:V, typescript, MSS 871.
'Colonial Statesmen and Votes for Women', pamphlet published by the British Women's Freedom League, 1911, ML:NSW, 324.3/2A1.
Curlewis, Jean. 'Two Hundred Women in the House'. LTL:V, typescript, box 179/9, no. 11379.
Feminist Club: Papers, ML:NSW,MSS AS75/2.
Franklin, Miles: Papers 1902–1925, ML:NSW, 364/8.
Glassey, Thomas: Papers. OL:Q, OM64/2.
Goldstein, Vida. Diary of Vida Goldstein, 1908, a handwritten journal held by the Fawcett Library, London, and reproduced on microfilm, LTL:V, MSS 7865.
Goldstein Vida: Papers 1902–19, Fawcett Library Collection, London, reproduced on microfilm, LTL:V, MSS 7865.
Goldstein, Vida: Press cuttings, LTL:V, box 2943/5, MSS 11956.
Goldstein, Vida. 'Report to the National Council of Women of New South Wales, 1902', ML:NSW, 396.3/G.
Heagney, Muriel. 'Notes on the Australian Labor Movement', LTL:V, Women in Political History folder, Riley Collection.
Intercolonial Trades and Labor Unions Council of Australasia: Official report of the seventh congress at Ballarat, 1891, ML:NSW, FM3/211.
Jull, Roberta, 'History of the Karrakatta Club, 1894–1944'. BL:WA, MSS 863 3049A/12.
Karrakatta Club: Constitution, BL:WA, MSS 863 3042A/1.
Karrakatta Club: Meetings of the Legal and Educational Department, 1894–97, BL:WA, MSS 863 3049A/3.
'The Life and Work of Miss Vida Goldstein', a pamphlet produced to support the candidature of Vida Goldstein, 1912, ML:NSW, Doc. 915A.
Lawson, Louisa: Papers and news cuttings, ML:NSW, MSS 4937.
Locke, Lilian (attributed). 'Address to the Victorian Women's Political and Social Crusade', presumed to be late 1903 or early 1904, LTL:V, handwritten paper, Women's Political and Social Crusade folder, Merrifield Collection.
Luffman, Laura (1909). 'The Principle of Women's Associations for Women Alone', ML:NSW, 396.3/L.
McAuley, Ida: Papers, Tasmanian Archives, NS/347/7.
National Council of Women of New South Wales: Papers, 1899–1921, ML:NSW, MSS 38/49.
O'Connor, Gertrude, 'Louisa Lawson, her life and work', ML:NSW MSS, A1897. This manuscript has five parts:

1. The life and work of Louisa Lawson (1920).
2. Woman Suffrage.
3. How the *Dawn* was started in 1888.

Addendum 1: Typewritten copy of a speech read to the Dawn Club, 23 May 1889.

Addendum 2: Speech made by Louisa Lawson at the first meeting of the New South Wales Womanhood Suffrage League, 1891.

Parkes, Henry: Correspondence. ML:NSW, A928.

Premiers Files, Western Australia, 1888–1889, BL:WA, MSS 863.

Queensland Women's Electoral League: Papers, July 1903–August 1908. OL:Q, OM71/47, item no. 4.

Scott, Rose. Woman Suffrage Correspondence, 1887–1899, ML:NSW A2271.

Scott, Rose. Woman Suffrage Correspondence, 1900–1902, ML:NSW MSS A2272.

Selwyn, Rose: Papers, 1890–1897, ML:NSW, MSS 201/3.

Women's Suffrage League of South Australia: 'Petition to the South Australian Weslyan Conference asking them to support woman suffrage, February 4 1889'. ML:SA, 396.3/M.

Trades Union and Labor Council of Western Australia: Minutes and proceedings of the first congress at Coolgardie, 11–15 April 1899, BL:WA, 331.8806/53.

Windeyer, Margaret: Papers, 1885–1939, ML:NSW, MSS 186/17.

Windeyer, Mary: Papers, 1854–1911, ML:NSW, MSS 186/14.

Wolstenholme, Maybanke. 'List of objects of the journal, *The Woman's Voice*', 1894 leaflet, ML:NSW, MSS AW44.

Woman Suffrage: Leaflets and press cuttings on Australian and overseas movements, ML:NSW, MSS 38/39.

Woman Suffrage: Miscellaneous papers on Australian and overseas movements 1888–1920, ML:NSW, MSS 38/38.

Woman Suffrage: Papers, collected by J. F. Fischer, ML:NSW, 324.3/F.

Woman Suffrage: Press cuttings, ML:NSW, 396.3/S.

Woman Suffrage: Press cuttings, collected by Rose Scott, ML:NSW, MSS 396.3/S.

Womanhood Suffrage League of New South Wales: Minute books, 1891–902. ML:NSW, MSS 38/33.

Womanhood Suffrage League of New South Wales: Note-books of the Secretary, and newspaper clippings. ML:NSW, MSS 38/35.

Womanhood Suffrage League of New South Wales: Papers, 1892–1902, ML:NSW, MSS 38/36.

Womanhood Suffrage League of New South Wales: Roll book, correspondence and financial note-book, 1891–1902, ML:NSW, MSS 38/34.

Woman's Christian Temperance Union of New South Wales: Papers, 1882–1978, ML:NSW, MSS 3641.

Woman's Equal Franchise Association of Queensland: Papers, OL:Q OM 87/19.

Women's Political and Educational League of New South Wales: Papers, 1902–1903, ML:NSW, MSS 38/40.

Women's Political and Educational League of New South Wales: Papers, 1904–1910, ML:NSW, MSS 38/41.

Secondary Sources

Books and Articles

Ackermann, Jessie. *Australia from a Woman's Point of View*, London, Cassell, 1913; republished by Collins in 1981.

Aitkin, Don, ed. *Survey of Australian Political Science*, Sydney, George Allen and Unwin, 1984.

Alexander, Cynthia. 'The Itinerants: a ladies' literary society'. *Tasmanian Historical Research Association: Papers and Proceedings*, vol. 32, no. 4 (1985), pp. 146-50.

Allen, Judith. 'Breaking into the public sphere: the struggle for women's citizenship in New South Wales, 1890–1920'. In *In Pursuit of Justice*, ed. J. Mckinolty and H. Radi, Sydney, Hale and Iremonger, 1979, pp. 107-17.
———. 'The "feminisms" of the early women's movements in Britain, America and Australia, 1850–1920'. *Refractory Girl*, no. 17 (1979), pp. 10-16.
———. '"Mundane" men: historians, masculinity and masculinism'. *Historical Studies*, vol. 22, no. 89 (1987), pp. 617-28.
Anderson, Francis. 'The Women's Movement'. In *Australia: Economic and Political Studies*, ed. Meredith Atkinson, Melbourne, Macmillan, 1920, pp. 266-303.
Atkinson, Meredith, ed. *Australia: economic and political studies*, Melbourne, Macmillan, 1920.
Austin, Albert, ed. *The Webbs' Australian Diary, 1898*, Melbourne, Pitman, 1965.
Aveling, Marian, ed. *Westralian Voices: Documents in Western Australian Social History*, University of Western Australia Press, 1979.
Bacchi, Carol. 'Evolution, eugenics and women: the impact of scientific theories on attitudes towards women, 1870–1920'. In *Women, Class and History*, ed. Elizabeth Windschuttle, Melbourne, Fontana Books, 1980, pp. 132-56.
———. 'First-wave feminism: history's judgement'. In *Australian Women: feminist perspectives*, ed. Norma Grieve and Patricia Grimshaw, Melbourne, Oxford University Press, 1981, pp. 156-66.
Banks, Olive. *Faces of Feminism*, Oxford, Martin Robertson, 1981.
Bernays, C. *Queensland Politics during Sixty Years, 1859–1919*, Brisbane, Government Printer, 1919.
Bevege, Margaret, James, Margaret, and Shute, Carmel, eds. *Worth her Salt*, Sydney, Hale and Iremonger, 1982.
Birke, Lynda. *Women, Feminism and Biology*, Great Britain, Harvester Press, 1986.
Biskup, Peter. 'The Westralian feminist movement'. *University Studies in Western Australian History*, vol. 3, no. 3 (1959), pp. 71-84.
Black, George. *A History of the New South Wales Political Labor Party*, Sydney, printed by George A. Jones, 1910.
Blackstone, William. *Commentaries on the Laws of England*, 16th edn, London, J. Butterworth, 1825.
Blount, Maurice J. 'Woman's sphere'. *The Australian Woman's Magazine*, vol. 1, no. 7 (October 1882), pp. 212-13.
Bollen, John. 'The temperance movement and the Liberal Party in New South Wales politics, 1900–04'. *Journal of Religious History*, vol. 1, no. 3 (1961), 160-82.
———. *Protestantism and Social Reform in New South Wales 1890–1910*, Melbourne University Press, 1972.
Brome, Vincent. *Havelock Ellis, philosopher of sex*, London, Routledge and Kegan Paul, 1979.
Brown, Louise, ed. *A Book of South Australia: women in the first hundred years*, Adelaide, Rigby, 1936.
Bryce, James. *Modern Democracies*, vol. 2, London, Macmillan, 1921.
Burke, Patti. 'Did an old and sleepy gentleman secure the vote for Australian women?'. *Women and Labour Conference Papers*, vol. 2 (1982), pp. 1-10.
Caine, Barbara. 'Woman's "natural state": marriage and the nineteenth-century feminists'. *Hecate*, vol. 3, no. 1 (1977), pp. 84-102.
Cameron, Barbara. 'The flappers and the feminists'. In *Worth Her Salt*, ed. M. Bevege, M. James, and C. Shute, Sydney, Hale and Iremonger, 1982, pp. 257-69.
Catt, Carrie Chapman, and Shuler, Nettie Rogers. *Woman Suffrage and Politics*, New York, Charles Scribner's Sons, 1923.
Champion, Henry. 'The Claim of Woman'. *Cosmos*, vol. 1, no. 9 (1895), pp. 448-52.
Chisholm, Alec. 'The lady of the treasure house'. *Life Digest*, vol. 11, no. 4 (1948), pp. 7-10.
Clark, Carrel. *The Parliament of Tasmania: an historical sketch*, Hobart, Government Printer, 1947.

Clarke, Jocelyn. 'Losing the numbers game'. In *Australian Women and the Political System*, ed. Marian Simms, Melbourne, Longman Cheshire, 1984, pp. 44-58.
———, and White, Kate. *Women in Australian Politics*, Sydney, Fontana Books, 1983. Cleverdon, Catherine. *The Woman Suffrage Movement in Canada*, Toronto University Press, 1950.
Cole, Kathryn. *Power, Conflict and Control in Australian Trade Unions*, Ringwood, Victoria, Pelican Books, 1982.
Coleman, Verna. *Miles Franklin in America: her unknown (brilliant) career*, Sydney, Angus and Robertson, 1981.
Collier, James. *Sir George Grey*, Wellington, Whitcombe and Tombs, 1909.
Combe, Gordon. *Responsible Government in South Australia*, South Australian Government Printer, 1957.
Cott, Nancy. 'Feminist theory and feminist movements: the past before us'. In *What is Feminism*, ed. Juliet Mitchell and Ann Oakley, New York, Pantheon Books, 1986, pp. 49-62.
———. *The Grounding of Modern Feminism*, Yale University Press, 1987.
———. 'What's in a name? the limits of "social feminism": or, Expanding the vocabulary of women's history'. *Journal of American History*, vol. 76, no. 3 (1989), pp. 809-33.
Cowan, Peter. *A Unique Position: a biography of Edith Dirksey Cowan*, University of Western Australia Press, 1978.
Cowie, Bessie. *One of Australia's Daughters: an autobiography of Mrs Harrison Lee (-Cowie)*, London, H. J. Osborn, 1906.
Crawford, Virginia. 'Feminism in France'. *Fortnightly Review*, vol. 67 (1897), pp. 254-534.
Crowley, Francis. *Sir John Forrest*, University of Queensland Press, 1968.
———. *Modern Australia in Documents: 1901-1939*, Melbourne, Wren Publishing Company, 1973.
———, and de Garis, Brian. *A Short History of Western Australia*, Melbourne, Macmillan, 1969.
Daniels, Kay, ed. *So Much Hard Work*, Sydney, Fontana Books, 1984.
———, and Murnane, Mary, eds. *Uphill all the Way: a documentary history of women in Australia*, Queensland University Press, 1980.
Davis, Solomon. *The Government of the Australian States*, London, Longmans, 1960.
de Garis, Brian. 'Western Australia'. In *The Emergence of the Australian Party System*, ed. P. Loveday, A. Martin and P. Weller, Sydney, Hale and Iremonger, 1977, pp. 298-354.
Dingle, A. E. 'The truly magnificent thirst'. *Historical Studies*, vol. 19, no. 75 (1980), pp. 227-49.
Dixson, Miriam. *The Real Matilda*, Ringwood, Victoria, Penguin Books, 1976.
Dugdale, Henrietta. *A Few Hours in a Far Off Age*, Melbourne, McCarron, Bird & Co., 1883.
Dillon, Gar. *A Delusion of the Australian Culture: a brief history of the clash with alcohol in New South Wales 1788-1983*, Sydney, New South Wales Temperance Alliance, 1985.
Eisenstein, Hester. *Contemporary Feminist Thought*, Sydney, George Allen and Unwin, 1980.
Eldershaw, Flora, ed. *The Peaceful Army: a memorial to the pioneer women of Australia 1788-1938*, Sydney, Women's Executive Committee, 1938.
Ellis, Havelock. *Studies in the Psychology of Sex*, Philadelphia, Davis, 1904–28.
Ellis, Malcolm. 'George Reid: why the *Bulletin* called him "Yes-No Reid"'. *Bulletin*, 21 July 1962, pp. 20-3.
Encel, S., Mackenzie, N., and Tebbut, M. *Women and Society: an Australian study*, Melbourne, Cheshire, 1974.
Evans, Richard J. *The Feminists*, New York, Barnes and Noble, 1979.
Faust, Beatrice. 'Feminism then and now'. *Australian Quarterly*, vol. 46, no. 1 (1974), pp. 15-28.
Feeney, Jennifer. 'Votes for women: the Ballarat Woman's Franchise League.' *La Trobe Library Journal*, vol. 8, no. 31 (1983), pp. 64-5.
Fernon, Christine. 'Women's suffrage in Victoria. *Refractory Girl*, no. 22 (1981), pp. 18-25.
Field, Edward Percy. 'A proposal for the extension of the franchise'. *Victorian Review*, vol. 1, no. 1 (1880), p. 745-54.

Fitzpatrick, Brian. *A Short History of the Australian Labor Movement*, Melbourne, Rawson's Bookshop, 1940.
Fitzgerald, Father T. A. 'Woman's suffrage from a Catholic viewpoint'. *Australasian Catholic Record*, vol. 9 (1903), pp. 381-90.
Flexner, Eleanor. *Century of Struggle*, Harvard University Press, 1959.
Fowler, John. 'The 1890s—turning point in Queensland history'. In *Prelude to Power*, ed. D. Murphy, R. Joyce and C. Hughes, Brisbane, Jacaranda Press, 1970, pp. 45-55.
Franklin, Stella (Miles). *My Brilliant Career*, Edinburgh, Blackwood and Sons, 1901.
———. *Some Everyday Folk and Dawn*, Edinburgh, Blackwood and Sons, 1909.
———. 'Rose Scott: some aspects of her personality and work'. In *The Peaceful Army*, ed. Flora Eldershaw, Sydney, Women's Executive Committee, 1938, pp. 90-107.
Fraser, Francis, and Palmer, Nettie, eds. *Centenary Gift Book*, published for the Victorian Women's Centenary Council, Melbourne, Robertson and Mullins, 1934.
Fry, Eric, ed. *Rebels and Radicals*, Sydney, George Allen and Unwin, 1983.
Fulford, Roger. *Votes for Women*, London, Faber, 1957.
Garden, Donald. *Victoria: a history*, Melbourne, Nelson, 1984.
Gillan, Helen. *A Brief History of the National Council of Women in Victoria, 1902-45*, Melbourne, Spectator Publishing Co., 1945.
Gilman, Charlotte Perkins (1899). *Women and Economics*, 1899; reprinted 1912, London, G. P. Pitman and Sons.
Goldstein, Vida. 'Should women enter Parliament?'. *Review of Reviews*, vol. 23, no. 2 (1903), pp. 135-36.
———. 'The Australian Woman in Politics'. *Review of Reviews*, vol. 24, no. 1 (1904), pp. 47-50.
———. *Woman Suffrage in Australia*, London, Woman's Press, 1911.
Gollan, Robin. *Radical and Working Class Politics: a study of Eastern Australia, 1850-1910*, Melbourne University Press, 1976.
Goot, Murray. 'Electoral systems'. In *Surveys of Australian Political Science*, ed. Don Aitkin, Sydney, Angus and Robertson, 1984, pp. 179-259.
Green, F. C. *Tasmania: a century of responsible government*, Hobart, Government Printer, 1956.
Grieve, Norma, and Grimshaw, Patricia, eds. *Australian Women: feminist perspectives*, Melbourne, Oxford University Press, 1981.
Grimes, Alan, P. *The Puritan Ethic and Woman Suffrage*, New York, Oxford University Press, 1967.
Grimshaw, Patricia. *Women's Suffrage in New Zealand*, Auckland, Oxford University Press, 1972.
———. 'Women and the family in Australian history: a reply to *The Real Matilda*', *Historical Studies*, vol. 18, no. 72 (1979), pp. 412-21.
———. 'Women in the 1888 volume'. *Australia 1888*, bulletin 6 (November 1980), pp. 36-9.
Hagan, J. 'An incident at the *Dawn*'. *Labour History*, no. 8 (1965), pp. 19-21.
Hancock, Dennis. *The Making of Western Australia*, Sydney, Bay Books, 1979.
Hannan, G. 'William Lane: mateship and utopia'. In *Prelude to Power*, ed. D. Murphy, R. Joyce and C. Hughes, Brisbane, Jacaranda Press, 1970, pp. 181-6.
Harris, J. *The Bitter Fight*, University of Queensland Press, 1970.
Hart, H. *Women's Suffrage and National Danger: a plea for the ascending of man*. London, Alexander Shepheard, n.d.
Hause, Steven C. *Hubertine Auclert: the French suffragette*, Yale University Press, 1978.
Henderson, Leslie. *The Goldstein Story*, Melbourne, Stockland Press, 1973.
Henry, Alice. 'The Australian woman and the ballot'. *North American Review*, vol. 183 (1906), pp. 1272-9.
———. 'Marching towards citizenship'. In *Centenary Gift Book*, ed. Frances Fraser and Nettie Palmer, Melbourne, Robertson and Mullins, 1934, pp. 101-6.
———. *Memoirs of Alice Henry*, ed. Nettie Palmer, bound multigraph, 1944; 100 copies only distributed.

Higgins, Susan. '"That singular anomaly, the lady novelist" in 1888'. *Australia 1888*, bulletin 7 (April 1981), pp. 68-73).
A History of the National Council of Women of Tasmania 1899–1968, no date and no publisher given.
Holman, Ada. *Memoirs of a Premier's Wife*, Sydney, Angus & Robertson, 1947.
Holmes, Jean. *The Government of Victoria*, St Lucia, University of Queensland Press, 1976.
Holthouse, Hector. *An Illustrated History of Queensland*, Adelaide, Rigby, 1978.
Hubbe, Rica. 'South Australian women in medicine, law, arts and science'. In *A Book of South Australia: women in the first hundred years*, ed. Louise Brown, Adelaide, Rigby, 1936, pp. 147-9.
Hyslop, Anthea. 'Temperance, Christianity and feminism: the Woman's Christian Temperance Union of Victoria 1887–1897'. *Historical Studies*, vol. 17, no. 66 (1976), pp. 27-49.
Jacombe, C. E. *God's Own Country*, London, Max Goshen, 1914.
Jaensch, Dean. *The Government of South Australia*, University of Queensland Press, 1977.
———. 'South Australia'. In *The Emergence of the Australian Party System*, ed. P. Loveday, A. Martin and P. Weller, Sydney, Hale and Iremonger, 1977, pp. 249-97.
James, K. 'The home: a private or a public place? Class, status and the actions of women'. *Australian and New Zealand Journal of Sociology*, vol. 15, no. 1 (1979), pp. 36-42.
Jones, D. *Chartism and the Chartists*, London, Alan Lane, 1975.
Jones, Helen. *Nothing Seemed Impossible: women's education and social change in South Australia, 1875–1915*, University of Queensland Press, 1985.
———. *In Her Own Name: women in South Australian history*. Netley, Wakefield Press, 1986.
Joyce, Robin. 'Queensland'. In *The Emergence of the Australian Party System*, ed. P. Loveday, A. Martin and P. Weller, Sydney, Hale and Iremonger, 1977, pp. 119-71.
———. 'Labor women: political housekeepers or politicians?' In *Australian Women and the Political System*, ed. Marian Simms, Melbourne, Longman Cheshire, 1984, pp. 66-76.
Kelly, Farley. 'Mrs. Smyth and the body politic'. In *Worth Her Salt*, ed. M. Bevege, M. James and C. Shute, Sydney, Hale and Iremonger, 1982, pp. 213-29.
———. 'Feminism and the family: Brettena Smyth'. In *Rebels and Radicals*, ed. Eric Fry, Sydney, Allen and Unwin, 1983, pp. 134-47.
Kenway, H. 'The pastoral strikes of 1891 and 1894'. In *Prelude to Power*, ed. D. Murphy, R. Joyce and C. Hughes, Brisbane, Jacaranda Press, 1970, pp. 111-26.
Kiek, E. S. *An Apostle in Australia*, London, Independent Press, 1927.
Kingston, Beverley. *My Wife, My Daughter and Poor Mary Anne*, Melbourne, Nelson, 1975.
———. 'Yours very truly, Marion Phillips'. *Labour History*, no. 29 (1975), pp. 123-31.
———, ed. *The World Moves Slowly: a documentary history of Australian women*, Sydney, Cassell, 1977.
Kirkby, Diane. *Alice Henry: the power of pen and voice*. Melbourne, Cambridge University Press, 1991.
Klein, Viola. *The Feminine Character: history of an ideology*, London, Routledge and Kegan, Paul, 1946.
Kraditor, Aileen. *The Ideas of the Woman Suffrage Movement, 1890–1920*, Columbia University Press, 1967.
La Nauze, John. *The Making of the Australian Constitution*, Melbourne University Press, 1972.
Lake, Marilyn. 'The politics of respectability: identifying the masculine context'. *Historical Studies*, vol. 22, no. 86 (1986), pp. 116-31.
Lansbury, Coral. 'The feminine frontier: women's suffrage and economic reality'. *Meanjin*, vol. 31, no. 3 (1972), pp. 286-96.
Larmour, Constance. 'Women's wages and the web'. *Labour History*, no. 29 (1975), pp. 47-58.
Lather, A. E. *A Glorious Heritage: history of the Woman's Christian Temperance Union of Queensland, 1885–1965*. Brisbane, Abell and Co., 1965.
Lawson, Bertha. *My Henry Lawson*, Sydney, Frank Johnson, 1943.
Lawson, Sylvia. 'Edited, printed and published by women'. *Nation*, no. 3 (1958), pp. 15-18.
Loveday, P. 'The federal parties'. In *The Emergence of the Australian Party System*, ed. P. Loveday, A. Martin and P. Weller, Sydney, Hale and Iremonger, 1977. pp. 383-452.

——, Martin, A. and Weller, P., eds. *The Emergence of the Australian Party System*, Sydney, Hale and Iremonger, 1977.
Lyons, Enid. *Among the Carrion Crows*, Adelaide, Rigby, 1972.
——, and Cilento, Phyllis. 'The population problem in relation to the needs of mothers'. *National Health and Medical Research Council Report*, 1944, pp. 54-63.
McCorkindale, Isabel, ed. *Pioneer Pathways: sixty years of citizenship*, Melbourne, Woman's Christian Temperance Union of Australia, 1948.
——, ed. *Torch-Bearers: The Woman's Christian Temperance Union of South Australia, 1886–1948*, Adelaide, Woman's Christian Temperance Union of South Australia, 1949.
MacDonald, Louisa. *The Women's College within the University of Sydney*, Sydney, Halstead Press, 1949.
MacKenzie, Norman. 'Vida Goldstein: the Australian suffragette'. *Australian Journal of Politics and History*, vol. 6, no. 2 (1960), pp. 190-204.
——. *Women in Australia*, Melbourne, Cheshire, 1962.
McKinolty, Judy, and Radi, Heather, eds. *In Pursuit of Justice: Australian women and the law*, Sydney, Hale and Iremonger, 1979.
Margarey, Susan. *Unbridling the Tongues of Women: a biography of Catherine Helen Spence*, Sydney, Hale and Iremonger, 1985.
Magner, Teresa. 'Women's rights'. *Austral Light*, vol. 4, no. 9 (1903), pp. 639-41.
Makin, Norman J. *The Labor Party in South Australia 1882–1956*, no publisher cited, n.d.
Markey, Ray. 'Women and labour: 1880–1900'. *Women and Labour Conference Papers*, 1978, pp. 11-19.
Matthews, Brian. *Louisa*, Melbourne, McPhee Gribble, 1987.
Mercer, Jan, ed. *The Other Half: women in Australian society*, Ringwood, Victoria, Penguin, 1975.
Metcalfe, Agnes Edith. *Women's Effort*, London, Blackwell, 1917.
Métin, Albert. *Le Socialisme sans Doctrines*, Paris, Felix Alcan, 1901.
Mill, John Stuart. 'Considerations on Representative Government', 1859; *The Subjection of Women*, 1869. In *Liberty, Representative Government and the Subjection of Women*, Oxford University Press, 1975, pp. 144-423, 424-548.
Millet, Kate. *Sexual Politics*, London, Rupert Hart-Davis, 1969.
Mitchell, Juliet, and Oakley, Ann, eds. *What is Feminism?*, New York, Pantheon Books, 1986.
Mitchell, Winifred. 'Wives of the radical Labour movement'. *Labour History*, no. 29 (1975), pp. 1-14.
Montefiore, Dora. *From a Victorian to a Modern*, London, E. Archer, 1927.
Morgan, David. *Suffragists and Liberals: the politics of woman suffrage in England*, Oxford, Basil Blackwell, 1975.
Moss, Jim. *Sound of Trumpets: a history of the labour movement in South Australia*, Netley, Wakefield Press, 1985.
Murphy, D., Joyce, R., and Hughes, C., eds. *Prelude to Power*, Brisbane, Jacaranda Press, 1970.
Nance, Christopher. 'Paving the way: the women's suffrage movement in South Australia'. *Royal Australian Historical Society Journal*, vol. 65, no. 3 (1979), pp. 188-99.
Neale, R. S. 'Working class women and women's suffrage'. *Labour History*, no. 12 (1967), pp. 16-34.
Nicol, W. 'Women and the trade union movement in New South Wales, 1890–1900. *Labour History*, no. 36 (1979), pp. 18-30.
Norris, R. *The Emergent Commonwealth: Australian federation, expectations and fulfilment 1889–1910*, Melbourne University Press, 1975.
O'Farrell, Patrick. *The Catholic Church and Community in Australia*, Sydney, Nelson, 1977.
Olif, Lorna. *Louisa Lawson: Henry Lawson's crusading mother*, Adelaide, Rigby, 1978.
O'Neill, William. *Everyone was Brave*, Chicago, Quadrangle Books, 1979.
Owen, Mary. 'The political participation of women'. In *Labor Essays*, Richmond, Victoria, Drummond Publishing Company on behalf of the Australian Labor Party, 1980, pp. 132-154.
Parker, R. S . 'Australian federation: the influence of economic interests and political pressures'.

Historical Studies, Australia and New Zealand, vol. 4, no. 13 (1949), pp. 1-24.

Parkes, Hilma Molyneux. Woman's suffrage in New South Wales. *Red Funnel*, vol. 1, no. 1 (1905), pp. 77-9.

Paulson, Ross. *Women's Suffrage and Prohibition*, Glenview, Illinois, Scott Foresman and Co., 1973.

Pearce, Vicki. '"A few viragos on a stump"': the womanhood suffrage campaign in Tasmania 1889–1920'. *Tasmanian Historical Research Association, Papers and Proceedings*, vol. 32, no. 4 (1985), pp. 151-64.

Phillips, Jebby. 'How the vote was won'. *Women and Politics Conference*, Canberra, Australian Government Printing Service, 1977, vol. 1, pp. 81-93.

Phillips, Mary. *The Militant Suffrage Campaign in Perspective*, London, no publisher cited, 1957.

Popham, Daphne. *Reflections: profiles of 150 women who helped make Western Australia's history*, Perth, Carrol's, 1979.

Porter, Kirk H. A History of Suffrage in the United States, New York, Greenwood, 1969.

Powell, J. M. 'An Australian utopia'. *Australian Geographer*, vol. 12, no. 4 (1973), pp. 328-33.

Proud, Cornelius. 'How woman's suffrage was won in South Australia'. *Review of Reviews*, vol. 7, no. 1 (1895), pp. 28-30.

Pugh, Martin. *Electoral Reforms in War and Peace*, London, Routledge and Kegan Paul, 1978.

Radi, Heather. 'Whose child? Custody of children in New South Wales, 1854–1934'. In *In Pursuit of Justice: Australian women and the law*, ed. Judy McKinolty and Heather Radi, Sydney, Hale and Iremonger., 1979, pp. 119-31.

———. *Two Hundred Australian Women*, Sydney, Redress Press, 1989.

Rawson, D. W. 'Victoria'. In *The Emergence of the Australian Party System*, ed. P. Loveday, A. Martin and P. Weller, Sydney, Hale and Iremonger, 1977, pp. 44-116.

Rayner, S. 'Thomas Glassey, Queensland Labor leader'. *Royal Historical Society of Queensland Journal*, vol. 4, no. 2 (1949), pp. 231-52.

Reekie, Gail, 'With ready hands and new brooms: the women who campaigned for female suffrage in Western Australia, 1895–1899'. *Hecate*, vol. 7, no. 1 (1981), pp. 24-33.

Reeve, George G. 'Life and Louisa Lawson'. *Ross's*, vol. 6, no. 61 (1920), pp. 24-5.

———. 'The mother of Henry Lawson'. *Sydney Mail*, 2 November 1927.

Reeves, William Pember. *State Experiments in Australia and New Zealand*, vol. 1, London, Grant Richards, 1902.

Reid, R. L. 'The South Australian influence on the proposals for federation'. *Proceedings of the Royal Geographical Society of Australasia: South Australian branch*, vol. 58 (1957), pp. 97-110.

Reiger, Kerreen M. *The Disenchantment of the Home: modernizing the Australian family*, Melbourne, Oxford University Press, 1985.

Rigg, Julie, ed. *In Her Own Right*, Melbourne, Thomas Nelson, 1969.

Rischbieth, Bessie M. *March of Australian Women*, Perth, Paterson, 1964.

Robertson, J. A. *One Hundred Years of Responsible Government in Victoria, 1856–1956*, Melbourne, Government Printer, 1957.

Roderick, Colin. 'The formative years of Henry Lawson'. *Royal Australian Historical Society Journal*, vol. 45, no. 3 (1949), pp. 105-31.

Rosen, Andrew. *Rise Up, Women!: the militant campaign in perspective*, London, Routledge and Kegan Paul, 1974.

Ross, Williamina M. 'Votes for women in Western Australia'. *Western Australian Historical Society Journal*, vol. 5, no. 4 (1952), pp. 44-53.

Rover, Constance. *Women's Suffrage and Party Politics in Britain*, London, Routledge and Kegan Paul, 1967.

Ryan, Edna, and Conlon, Annie. *Australian Women at Work, 1788–1974*, Melbourne, Thomas Nelson, 1975.

———, and Prendergast, Helen. 'Unions are for women too!' In *Power, Conflict and Control in Australian Trade Unions*, ed. Kathryn Cole, Ringwood, Pelican Books, 1982, pp. 261-78.
Ryan, Penny, and Rowse, Tim. 'Women, arbitration and the family'. *Labour History*, vol. 29 (1975), pp. 15-30.
Sawer, Marian. 'Conditions of entry: women and politics in Australia'. In *Working it Out*, Women and Labour Publications Collective. Sydney, Hale and Iremonger, 1984, pp. 133-47.
———, and Simms, Marian. *A Woman's Place: women and politics in Australia*, Sydney, George Allen and Unwin, 1984.
Scharf, Lois, and Jensen, Joan, eds. *Decades of Discontent: the women's movement, 1920-1940*, Boston, Northeastern University Press, 1987.
Schneir, Miriam, ed. *Feminism: the essential historical writings*, New York, Vintage Books, 1972.
Scott, Dianne. 'Woman suffrage: the movement in Australia'. *Royal Australian Historical Society Journal*, vol. 53, no. 4 (1967), pp. 299-322.
Searle, Betty. *Silk and Calico: class, gender and the vote*, Sydney, Hale and Iremonger, 1988.
Shaw, George. '"Filched from us . . .", the loss of universal suffrage in Queensland, 1859-1863'. *Australian Journal of Politics and History*, vol. 26, no. 1 (1980), pp. 372-85.
Sherrard, Kathleen. 'The political history of women in Australia'. *Australian Quarterly*, vol. 15, no. 4 (1943), pp. 36-51.
Simms, Marian. 'Conservative feminism in Australia, a case study of feminist ideology'. *Women and Labour Conference Papers*, no. 3, (1978), pp. 7-17.
———. 'Writing the history of Australian women'. *Labour History*, no. 34 (1978), pp. 93-101.
———. 'Australia'. In *The Politics of the Second Electorate*, ed. J. Lovenduski and J. Hills, London. Routledge and Kegan Paul, 1981, pp. 83-111.
———. 'The Australian feminist experience'. In Australian Women: feminist perspectives, ed. Norma Grieve and Patricia Grimshaw, Melbourne, Oxford University Press, 1981, pp. 227-46.
———. 'Political science, women and feminism'. *Politics*, vol. 16, no. 2 (1981), pp. 315-25.
———, ed. *Australian Women and the Political System*, Melbourne, Longman Cheshire, 1984.
Sinclair, Keith. *A History of New Zealand*, 1959; reprinted Auckland, Penguin, 1976.
Smyth, Brettena. *Love, Courtship and Marriage*, Sydney, Austral Publishing Company, 1892.
———. *Limitation of Offspring*, Melbourne, Rae Brothers, 1893.
Spence, Catherine Helen. *A Plea for Pure Democracy*, Adelaide, Rigby, 1861.
———. *Catherine Helen Spence, an autobiography*, 1910; reprinted Adelaide, W. K. Thomas, 1975.
Spence, William Guthrie. *Australia's Awakening: thirty years in the life of an Australian agitator*, Sydney, Worker Trustees, 1909.
Spender, Dale. *Women of Ideas, and what men have done to them*, London, Routledge and Kegan Paul, 1982.
———, ed. *Feminist Theorists*, London, Women's Press, 1983.
———. *There's Always Been a Women's Movement this Century*, London, Routledge and Kegan, Paul, 1984.
Stannage, Charles, ed. *A New History of Western Australia*, University of Western Australia Press, 1981.
Stanton, Theodore, ed. *The Woman Question in Europe*, London, Sampson Low, 1884.
Stephenson, Rosalie. *Women in Australian Society*, Victoria, Heinemann, 1970.
Stout, Lady Anna. *Woman Suffrage in New Zealand*, London, Woman's Press, 1913.
Strachey, Ray. *The Cause: a short history of the women's movement in Great Britain*, 1928, reprinted London, Virago Press, 1978.
Street, Jessie. *Truth or Repose*, Sydney, Australasian Book Society, 1966.
Summers, Anne. *Damned Whores and God's Police*, Ringwood, Penguin, 1975.
———. 'The unwritten history of Adela Pankhurst Walsh'. In *Women, Class and History: feminist perspectives in Australia, 1788-1978*, ed. Elizabeth Windschuttle, Melbourne, Fontana Books, 1980.

Swinburne, Gwendolen. *Womanhood in the Life of Nations*, Melbourne, Australian Student Christian Movement Corporation, 1923.
Tomalin, Claire. *The Life and Death of Mary Wollstonecroft*, London, Weidenfeld and Nicolson, 1974.
Townley, W. A. *The Government of Tasmania*, University of Queensland Press, 1976.
    Tucker, Maya. 'Women in Australian history'. *Historical Studies*, vol. 17, no. 68 (1977), pp. 399-407.
Turner, Ian. 'Prisoners in petticoats: a shocking history of female emancipation in Australia'. In *In Her Own Right*, ed. Julie Rigg, Melbourne, Thomas Nelson, 1969, pp. 3-24.
Tyrrell, Ian. 'International aspects of the Woman's Christian Temperance Union in Australia: the influence of the American Woman's Christian Temperance Union, 1882–1914'. *Journal of Religious History*, vol. 12, no. 3 (1983), pp. 284-304.
van Tassell, G. L. 'Recruitment of women in Australian national politics: a research note'. *Australian Quarterly*, vol. 55, no. 3 (1981), pp. 334-42.
Walker, H. *Australasian Democracy*, London, Fisher Unwin, 1897.
Walker, R. B. 'Catherine Helen Spence and South Australian politics'. *Australian Journal of Politics and History*, vol. 15, no. 1 (1969), pp. 31-46.
———. 'Catherine Helen Spence, Unitarian utopian'. *Australian Literary Studies*, vol. 5, no. 1 (1971), pp. 31-41.
Ward, Elizabeth. *Out of Weakness Made Strong*, Sydney, Christian World Printing Press, 1903.
Watson, Thomas. *The First Fifty Years of Responsible Government in Victoria*, Melbourne, Government Printer, 1906.
Weeks, Jeffrey. *Sex, Politics and Society: the regulation of sexuality since 1800*, New York, Longman, 1981.
Weiner, Gaby. 'Vida Goldstein: the women's candidate'. In *Feminist Theorists*, ed. Dale Spender, London, Women's Press, 1983, pp. 245-55.
Weller, Patrick. 'Groups, parliament and elections'. *Tasmanian Historical Research Association, Papers and Proceedings*, vol. 21, no. 2 (1974), pp. 89-99.
———. 'Tasmania'. In *The Emergence of the Australian Party System*, ed. P. Loveday, A. Martin and P. Weller, Sydney, Hale and Iremonger, 1977, 355-82.
White, Kate. 'May Holman: Australian Labor's pioneer woman parliamentarian'. *Labour History*, no. 41 (1981), pp. 110-17.
———. 'Women and party politics in Australia'. *Australian Quarterly*, vol. 53, no. 1 (1981), pp. 29-39.
———. 'Bessie Rischbieth, Jessie Street, and the end of first-wave feminism in Australia'. In *Worth her Salt*, ed. M. Bevege, M. James, and C. Shute, Sydney, Hale and Iremonger, 1982, pp. 319-29.
———. 'Women and Unions in Australia'. In *All her Labours: women and labour conference papers*, Sydney, Hale and Iremonger, 1984, pp. 109-20.
———. *A Political Love Story: Joe and Enid Lyons*, Ringwood, Victoria, Penguin, 1987.
Whitlick, Arnold. *Woman into Citizen*, London, Athenaeum and Frederick Muller, 1979.
Whitney, W. Montague. 'Womanhood Suffrage'. *Sydney Quarterly Magazine*, vol. 8, no. 1 (1891), pp. 30-5.
Williams, Janice. 'Women in Queensland State Politics'. *Refractory Girl*, no. 4 (1973), pp. 13-17.
Williams, Mrs. M. J. and Holliday, Mrs M. I., eds. *Golden Records: Pathfinders of the Woman's Christian Temperance Union of New South Wales*, Sydney, John Sands, 1926.
Willis, Sabine. 'Homes are divine workshops'. In *Women, Class and History: feminist perspectives in Australia, 1788–1978*, ed. Elizabeth Windschuttle, Melbourne, Fontana Books, 1980, p. 173-91.
Windschuttle, Elizabeth. 'Women, class and temperance: moral reform in Eastern Australia, 1832–1857'. *Push from the Bush*, no. 3 (1979), pp. 5-25.
———., ed. *Women, Class and History: feminist perspectives in Australia, 1788–1978*, Melbourne, Fontana Books, 1980.
Wollstonecroft, Mary. *A Vindication of the Rights of Woman*, 1792; reprinted, New York, Norton, 1967.
Wood, Anne. 'Women's organizations in Queensland, 1859–1958'. *Royal Historical Society of Queensland*

Journal, Centenary Issue, vol. 6, no. 1 (1959), pp. 184-213.
Woods, Mary Tenison. 'Some reforms in law affecting women and children over the last hundred years'. In *A Book of South Australia: women in the first hundred years*, ed. Louise Brown, Adelaide, Rigby, 1936, pp. 127-38.
Woolf, Virginia. *A Room of One's Own*, London, Hogarth Press, 1929.
Wright, Andree (1975). 'Jessie Street, feminist'. *Labour History*, no. 29 (1975), pp. 59-68.
Young, Pam. 'Emma Miller, 1839–1917'. *Women and Labour Conference Papers*, 1978, pp. 1-4.
———. 'The struggle for woman's suffrage (Queensland)'. *Women and Labour Conference Papers*, 1980, vol. 1, pp. 1-8.
———. *Proud to be a Rebel: the life and times of Emma Miller*, St Lucia, University of Queensland Press, 1991.

Theses

Brownfoot, Janice. 'Women's Organizations and the Woman Movement in Victoria, 1890–1908', BA, (Hons) Department of History, Monash University, 1968.
Cobb, Joan. 'The Women's Movement in New South Wales 1880–1914', MA, Department of History, University of New England, 1966.
Cooper, R. G. 'The Women's Suffrage Movement in New South Wales', MA, Department of Government, University of Sydney, 1970.
Cotter, P. 'The Role of the Queensland Women's Electoral League in Politics and Social Legislation from 1903 till 1939', Penultimate Thesis, Department of History, University of Queensland, 1957.
Goring, Pam. 'The Political Development of the Women's Movement in Queensland', BA, (Hons), Department of Government, University of Queensland, 1987.
Reade, K. 'The Woman's Suffrage Movement in Victoria, 1902–1908', BA (Hons), Department of History, University of Melbourne, 1987.
Wadham, Elizabeth J. 'Women's Suffrage in South Australia 1883–1894', BA (Hons), Department of History, University of Adelaide, 1952.

Index

Aboriginal women, 15, 64-6, 119
Aborigines and the vote, 63-6
Ackerman, Jessie, 28-9, 45-6, 75, 84, 104, 117, 139, 199, 204, 212, 232
Adams, Abigail, 5
Adams, John, 4-5
Addams, Jane, 240
adult suffrage, 142, 149, 249-50, 252, 274-5, 281, 285, 288, 294-5
age of consent
   Annette Bear-Crawford, 142
   law in Australia (1902), 204-6
   New South Wales, 98
   Queensland, 116
   Rose Scott, 80
   South Australia, 26
Age of Reason, 4
age range of suffragists, 183-4
Age, Victoria, 133-4, 147, 154, 157, 160
America, *see* North America
American Declaration of Independence, 4-5, 7
American Woman Suffrage Association, 8
Anderson, Francis, 78, 218
Anderson, Maybanke, see Wolstenholme, Maybanke
Andrews, Mrs, 157
Anthony, Susan, 8-9, 239
anti-slavery campaign, 6-7, 11
Anti-Suffrage Leagues
   New South Wales, 92-3, 194-5
   Victoria, 147-8
arguments against woman suffrage
   esteem for the family would be lessened, 63
   husbands represent women, 24, 46-7
   intellectual inferiority, 23, 72, 189
   men will protect women's interests, 63, 194
   natural rights do not apply to women, 189
   not yet, 70
   prostitutes might gain the vote, 104, 137
   thin edge of the wedge, 63
   women are too emotional, 23-4
   women do not fight for their country, 189
   women do not want it, 23, 52, 107, 192
   women have indirect influence, 23, 113
   women need protection, 52
   women should be married and supported, 49, 198
   would cause discord in marriage, 24, 45, 199
   would double the vote of the husband, 48
   would not be good for the State, 50, 63, 64, 122, 216
   see also Biblical arguments; birth rate; contraception; defence; femininity; liquor interests, moral superiority of women; Parliamentary candidature for women; pedestal image; plural vote; property vote; ridicule; sentimentalism; woman's sphere
arguments for woman suffrage
   the family's interests should be represented, 46, 51, 52, 120, 139, 199
   for the benefit of the State, 19, 26, 49, 51, 68, 72, 122, 139, 189
   government must derive from the consent of the governed, 23, 24, 52, 69, 71, 114, 116, 123, 127, 139
   intellectual equality, 23, 69, 189
   men cannot represent women, 95, 114, 187, 194, 204
   natural rights of the individual, 9, 19, 26, 51, 52, 69-70, 72, 84, 106-7, 113, 116, 120-3, 150, 163, 172, 186-7
   to change discriminatory laws, 51, 74, 85, 113, 114, 121, 134, 184, 204, 216
   women pay taxes, 61, 69, 70, 89, 116, 120, 187
   women would elect the best men to Parliament, 215
   would improve Parliamentary proceedings, 215
   see also Biblical arguments; Contagious Diseases Acts; education, women; equal pay for women; guardianship of children; intuition; liquor interests; liquor reform; moral superiority of women; professions, women; prohibition; property vote; prostitution; symbolism of the vote;

university education, women; violence against women; wages and working conditions for women; woman's sphere
Argus, 131, 133, 147
Ashton, Lizzie, 78, 84-5
Asquith, Henry, 235-6, 237, 239
Astor, Lady Nancy, 239
Australian and New Zealand Women Voters' Association, 238
Australian Federation of Women Voters, 40
Australian Labor Federation, 117-18
Australian National League, 155
Australian Natives' Association, 60
Australian Socialist League of New South Wales, 82
Australian Woman, New South Wales, 86
Australian Woman's Sphere, 148, 153, 156, 232
Australian Women's National League
  Tasmania, 110
  Victoria, 155, 157, 159-60, 164, 220, 221
Australian Women's Suffrage Society, 137-8, 141
Australian Workers' Union, 61, 119

baby vote, 125
Bailey, Sarah, 118
basic wage, 219
Barton, Edmund, 61, 62, 63, 233
Bayles, Norman, 162
Bear-Crawford, Annette, 141-2, 145, 146, 183, 184, 204, 232
Becker, Lydia, 14
Bent, Sir Thomas, 155-64 *passim*, 177, 190, 221, 238
Bentham, Jeremy, 11
Berry, Graham, 132
Besant, Annie, 137
Bevan, Llewelyn, 161
Biblical arguments, 83, 92
biological determinism, 19, 218
Birks, Charles, 27
Birks, Rosetta, 26, 27, 182
birth-control, *see* contraception
birth-rate, concern about, 19, 125, 191, 200, 226
Black, George, 74
Blackstone, Sir William, 5-6
Bodichon, Barbara, 11
Boomerang, Queensland, 113-14, 116
Boyce, Francis, 75, 191
Bowes, Euphemia, 74, 75, 78
Braddon, Alice, 108
Braddon, Edward, 104-5, 106, 107, 108
Brentnall, Elizabeth, 117, 128, 232
Brentnall, Frederick, 117, 127
Brient, Lachlan John, 79
Bright, Jacob, 11

British woman suffrage movement, 4, 6, 10-14, 15, 213, 217, 233-9
  Australian women in, 233-8
  Commonwealth Parliament petitions British Parliament, 235-6
Bromby, John, 136
Brown, Olympia, 9
Bryce, James, 221
Burns, George, 154
Burt, Septimus, 48
Butler, Josephine, 207
Byrnes, Thomas, 121

Caldwell, Robert, 23, 25, 30-4 *passim*, 39, 40, 174
Campbell, James, 144
Campbell-Bannerman, Henry, 234, 235
candidature for women, *see* Parliamentary candidature for women
Catt, Alfred, 25, 30
Catt, Carrie Chapman 150, 154, 240, 241-2
Chaflin, Tennessee, 8
Champion, Henry, 192
Chapman, Henry, 146, 186
charity, 149
Charleston, David, 94
Chartism, 6, 10, 16, 134, 186
Chewings, Hannah, 26, 114
Christianity and women's oppression, 134
  see also Biblical arguments; *Woman's Bible*
churches
  attitudes to woman suffrage, 15, 26, 27, 29, 40, 123, 181-2
  women as participants, 6, 9, 181
Clark, Andrew Inglis, 59, 104, 105
Clark, Christine, 50, 51, 53, 55, 56, 187, 227
Clarke, J. A., 116
Clarke, Mrs J. A., 116
class background of suffragists, 98, 183
Cobden, Richard, 11
Cockburn, John, 30, 31, 35, 38, 143, 195, 237
Cockburn, Lady Sarah, 237
Coglin, Patrick, 25
Colton, John, 26
Colton, Mary, 26, 27
Commonwealth Constitutional Convention (1891), 32, 59, 106
Commonwealth Constitutional Convention (1897–8), 60-2, 143, 213
  Catherine Helen Spence as candidate, 41, 184
  South Australian influence on, 61-2, 213
Commonwealth Parliamentary election (1903)
  Vida Goldstein's campaign, 152-4

conditioning of women, 7, 12, 23, 148, 190
Congressional Union, North America, 242
conscription, 128, 221
Conservatism, 172-3, 175, 176-7, 181, 213
  New South Wales, 82
  Queensland, 112-13, 116, 120, 121, 122, 125-6
  South Australia, 22, 25, 35, 38, 40, 41
  Tasmania, 109
  Victoria, 133, 139, 147, 150-1, 154, 158-9, 160, 163-4
  Western Australia, 47
  see also property vote; plural vote
Constitutions, Parliamentary
  Australian, 16-17, 172
  Commonwealth, 15, 61-2, 65, 122-3, 149
  New South Wales, 68, 69
  Queensland, 112
  South Australia, 22-3, 25, 32, 172
  Tasmania, 69, 103, 172
  United States of America, 9, 239
  Victoria, 69, 131, 145, 159
  Western Australia, 45-6, 48
Contagious Diseases Acts, 104, 207-8
  see also Lock hospitals; prostitution
contraception, 10, 137-8, 141, 191, 200, 221
Cookworthy, J., 46-7, 173
Cooper, Leontine, 62, 113-14, 118-19, 120, 123-5, 128, 176
Cowan, Edith, 50-1, 55, 208, 223-4, 226, 227, 238
Curnow, Mrs Matilda, 78
Curzon, Lord George, 236

Dane, John, 132
Davidson, Emily, 238
Davidson, Eugenie, 157
Davies, John, 162
Dawn, 76-7, 79, 86, 93, 114, 148, 190, 204, 212, 232
Dawn Club, New South Wales, 77-8, 114, 191
Dawson, Anderson, 122, 123
De Gouge, Olympe, 5, 7
Deakin, Alfred, 150
Declaration of the Rights of Man and of the Citizen, 5, 7, 16, 186, 433
Declaration of the Rights of Woman, 5
defence, Australia, concern for, 19, 200
demonstrations, 88, 90
deputations
  New South Wales, 87, 88, 89, 90, 93
  Queensland, 125, 127
  South Australia, 33, 34, 36
  Victoria, 144
  Western Australia, 47

Derham, Freda, 147-8
deserted wives, 23
Dibbs, Robert, 72, 83, 84, 86, 87
Dickie, Miss, 84
Dickie, Mrs, 84, 92
Dickson, James, 122-3
Disraeli, Benjamin, 12
divorce laws,
 in nineteenth century, 6, 9, 10
 Louisa Lawson on, 77
 New South Wales, 85, 191
 post suffrage, 206
 South Australia, 23
 Western Australia, 49, 51, 206
Dobson, Emily, 108
domestic science, 218-19
domestic violence, *see* violence against women
Douglas, Adye, 179
Downer, John, 25, 34
dress for women, 77, 135, 192
Dugdale, Henrietta, 145, 152, 184, 228
 Annie Lowe, 135-8 *passim*, 145, 146, 163
 biography and character, 134-5
 dress reform, 192
 opinions, 134-5, 141
 Victorian Women's Suffrage Society, 135, 168-7, 141
Dugdale-Johnson, Henrietta, *see* Dugdale, Henrietta
Dwyer, Kate, 93-4

Early Closing Act, New South Wales, 94
Edgar, William, 160-1, 164
education, women, 6, 11, 12, 29, 189, 191
 see also university education, women; professions, women
Edwards, Mrs, 114, 116
Ellis, Havelock, 218
England, *see* Britain
Enlightenment, 4, 186
equal pay for women, 18, 50-1, 114, 126, 155, 163, 203-4, 217
 see also wages and working conditions for women
Equal Suffrage League of New South Wales, 86
eugenics, 218
Evans, Ada, 203
Evans, May, 62, 70

Factory Acts, 49, 94, 114
family wage, 49, 219
Fawcett, Millicent Garrett, 4, 14, 142, 232
Federal Constitutional Convention, *see* Commonwealth Constitutional Convention
federation, influence on woman suffrage, 15, 217
Fegan, John, 87, 89

feminine mystique, Australia, 218
femininity, 149-50, 153, 192
feminism, analysis of, 3-4, 5, 7-8, 9-10, 86, 98, 163-4, 190-1, 216-18, 221, 228
 see also New Woman, the
Ferguson, Mrs, 53
Fisher, Andrew, 236
Fisher, Margaret, 237
Forrest, Sir Alexander, 54
Forrest, Sir John, 18, 45, 46, 47-8, 49, 51-6, 117, 213, 215
Forrest, Lady Margaret, 50
Foulkes, Janetta, 46, 48, 50, 51, 55
Foxton, Justin, 123
Franklin, Miles (Stella), 81, 82, 240-1
Fraser, Simon, 63
French Revolution, 5, 16
Freud, Sigmund, 218
frontier theory, 214-16, 231
 see also gift theory

Gale, Susannah, 76
Gandon, P. J., 92-3
Gaunson, David, 198
Giblin, William, 103-4, 173
gift theory, 14, 15-16, 212-13
 see also frontier theory
Gladstone, William, 12-13
Glassey, Thomas, 120
Glyde, Mary, 183
goldfields
 Queensland, 112
 Western Australia, 46, 47-50, 51, 53, 54-6, 175, 176
Golding, Annie, 61, 84, 182
 biography and character, 93-4, 184, 238
 opinions, 195, 203
 sisters, 88, 93-4, 96, 98, 182, 183
 Womanhood Suffrage League, 88, 93, 96, 97, 98
 Women's Progressive Association, 96, 97
Golding, Belle, 88, 93-4, 96, 98, 183, 204
Golding, Kate, *see* Dwyer, Kate
Goldstein, Vida, 145-63, 240
 biography and character, 145-6, 184, 199
 Commonwealth Constitution, 62, 63
 debating skills, 93, 142, 153, 159, 237
 equal pay, 203, 228
 Labor party, 149, 223
 opinions, 16, 62, 63, 152, 155, 181, 194, 201, 221, 227-8, 237, 238
 religion, 181
 Senate candidacy, 152-4, 221, 223, 225, 227
 Victorian campaign, 136, 140, 147, 149, 156-63 *passim*, 238
 visits London, 237
 visits USA, 149-50, 231, 233

Goldstein, Isabella, 142, 145
Gordon, John, 39
Gormanston, Lady Georgina, 108
Gough, Evelyn, 153
governesses, 11
Grey, Sir George, 32
Grimke, Sarah, 6-7
guardianship of children, 6, 9, 206
 Annette Golding, 94
 Dora Montefiore, 78
 New South Wales, 98
 Western Australia, 49, 206
Gustafson, Axel, 138

Hall, Henry, 192
Hardy, Arthur, 187
Harney, Edward, 63
Harris, Mrs E., 127
Hart, Helen, 74
Harvester Judgment, 219
Harwood, Thomas, 162
Hay, Alexander, 23
Heagney, Muriel, 220
Henry, Alice, 240, 241
Hensman, Emily, 53, 55
Higgins, Henry, 64
Higinbotham, George, 131, 132-3, 135, 136
Hobbs, Eleanor, 157, 160
Holder, Frederick, 34, 35, 41, 61-2, 143, 214
Holman, Ada, 222, 241
Hopetoun, Lord John, 63
housework analogy, 198-9
Howe, James, 38-9
Hume, Joseph, 11
Hyne, Richard, 116-17

Illingworth, Frederick, 48, 50, 52, 54, 55, 175
Imperialism, 149, 155, 237
influence of woman suffrage on legislation affecting women, 227-8
Intercolonial Trades and Labor Congress, *see* Trades and Labor Congress of Australasia
International Council of Women Convention, 149
International Woman Suffrage Conference, 149, 150
international woman suffrage movement, 233
intuition of women, 195-6
Isaacs, John, 143
itinerant workers, 112-13, 120
Itinerants' Club, Tasmania, 108
Irvine, William, 151-2, 155

James, Annie, 117
James, Eleanora, 50, 53
James, Walter, 48-9, 52-6 *passim*, 195

Jersey, Lady Margaret, 85
Johnson, Eli, 74
Jordan, May, see O'Connell, May
Jull, Roberta, 51
juries, women on, 94

Karrakatta Club, Western Australia, 50-1, 53, 55, 182-3, 223, 238
Kelly, Dr Vandeleur, 85
Kendall, Henry, 76, 135
Kenny, Annie, 238
Kermode, Georgiana, 105, 110
Key, Ellen, 218
Kidston, William, 125
Kingsmill, Walter, 53
Kingston, Charles, 25, 26, 31, 35, 40, 60-3 passim, 214
Kirby, Joseph, 26
Kirkpatrick, Andrew, 34, 236

Labor Electoral League, New South Wales, 88
Labor Party, 17-18, 24, 88, 154, 156, 173-7, 213, 219-20
    New South Wales, 61, 71, 72-4, 76, 82, 87, 88, 89, 93-8 passim, 213
    Queensland, 17, 112-13, 114, 116, 118-27 passim, 174, 178, 213
    South Australia, 24, 25, 30-41 passim, 213
    Tasmania, 103, 109, 110, 213
    Victoria, 133, 138-9, 142, 147-64 passim, 213
    Western Australia, 47, 48-9, 53, 55-6, 175-6, 213
    see also plural vote
Labor Party, women in, 154, 183, 219-20
    New South Wales, 72-4, 93, 98, 176, 178
    Queensland, 17, 118-19, 126, 127, 128, 174, 177, 178
    South Australia, 30, 31, 32
    Tasmania, 110
    Victoria, 146, 147, 148, 149, 151, 152, 153-5, 157
    Western Australia, 56
    see also Woman's Equal Franchise Association, Queensland; Women's Progressive Association, New South Wales; Women's Progressive Leagues, Victoria
Labour Party, Britain, 13
Ladies' Social Purity Society, South Australia, see Society for the Promotion of Social Purity, South Australia
Lake, Octavius, 29
Lake, Serena, 29-30, 31, 36
Lane, William, 113, 114, 116, 204
Lawson, Henry, 76, 77

Lawson, Louisa, 228
    biography and character, 75-6
    Dawn, 65, 76-8, 79, 86, 89, 93, 96, 97, 114, 148, 190-1, 232
    maverick, 4, 74, 78
    opinions, 76-7, 84, 87, 89, 113, 187, 190-1, 192, 195, 196, 199
    Queensland Women's Suffrage League, 114, 116
    Rose Scott, 79, 83, 97
    Womanhood Suffrage League, 79, 81, 86, 97
    Women's Progressive Associations, 93, 97
Leavitt, Mary, 28, 45, 74, 104, 117, 139
Lee, Charles, 95
Lee, Mary, 40, 183, 232
    biography and character, 27
    criticised, 177
    Labor party, 35, 238
    opinions, 31, 35-6, 39, 41, 187, 194
    Robert Caldwell's bill, 33, 34
    Rose Scott, 39
    Women's Suffrage League of South Australia, 26-7, 184
    Working Women's Trade Union, 30
Lee, Mrs Harrison, 75
Lee-Cowie, Mrs Harrison, see Lee, Mrs Harrison
legislation affecting women, influence of woman suffrage, 227-8
Legislative Councils, 16-17, 172, 173-4, 176
    New South Wales, 69, 90-2, 95, 96
    Queensland, 112, 127-8
    South Australia, 22-3, 31, 36-8, 40, 176, 213
    Tasmania, 106, 107, 108, 109
    Victoria, 131, 132, 133, 140-5 passim, 148, 150-1, 156, 160, 162-4
    Western Australia, 46, 52, 176
Lewis, Lady Lina, 110
Lewis, Sir Neil, 109, 110
Liberalism, 11-16 passim, 173-4, 186, 213-17 passim
    New South Wales, 70-1, 87, 88, 95, 98, 213, 233
    Queensland, 113, 121-7 passim, 213
    South Australia, 22, 25, 30-7 passim, 40, 213
    Tasmania, 103, 104, 106, 109, 213
    Victoria, 133, 139, 141, 142, 148-60 passim, 163, 213
    Western Australia, 47-8, 56, 213
liquor interests
    in Australia, 92, 180-1
    in North America, 181
liquor reform, 15, 104, 191
Lilley, Charles, 118
Lloyd George, David, 160, 239
Lock hospitals, 207-8

    see also prostitution
Locke, Lilian, 183, 184
    as speaker, 97, 149, 151
    Labor movement, 110, 143, 149, 152, 154, 164, 238
    visits Tasmania, 110
Love, Mary, 139, 232
Lowe, Annie, 154, 184
    as speaker, 97, 135, 136, 144, 147, 150, 151, 156, 163, 194
    biography and character, 135-6
    Henrietta Dugdale, 135-8 passim, 145, 146, 163
    refuses Senate candidacy, 153
Lyne, William, 63, 64-5, 89, 90, 95, 96, 97, 153, 195, 198
Lyons, Enid, 225-6

McAuley, Ida, 108, 109
McCulloch, James, 182
Macdonald, Louisa, 72
McGowan, James, 89
McKenzie, Malcolm, 143
McKinnon, Donald, 152
McLean, Allan, 142
McLean, Mrs, 139, 163
McWilliams, William, 106, 107, 108
Magarey, Sylvanus, 34, 36, 38
Maloney, Dr William, 138-9, 146, 152, 161, 163, 175, 236
manhood suffrage, 17, 173, 194
    Commonwealth, 59, 60
    New South Wales, 69
    New Zealand, 32
    Queensland, 112, 113
    South Australia, 22
    Tasmania, 103, 106-7, 109
    Victoria, 131, 135, 172, 186
    Western Australia, 46, 47
    see also adult suffrage
Manning, May, 79
Manning, Sir William, 79
marriage, 19, 191, 196-9, 216-17
    laws, 5-6, 12, 134-5
    opinions of suffragists, 77, 84-5, 134-5
    post-suffrage, 218-19
    private-sphere feminism and, 8, 9-10, 200, 216-17
    wages for married women, 94, 224
    see also property vote
Married Women's Property Acts, 172, 173, 204
    South Australia, 23
    Victoria, 143-4
    Western Australia, 49
Martel, Nellie, 16, 93-8 passim, 228, 231-4 passim
Martineau, Harriet, 6
masculinity, 192
Mayo, Winifred, 238
Men's International Alliance for Woman

Suffrage, 237
Men's League for Woman Suffrage, Victoria, 160
Men's League for Women's Suffrage, Britain, 237
Michie, Sir Archibald, 143, 187
Michie, Janet, 143, 163
militancy
  Australia, 82, 160
  Britain, 85, 160, 234-5, 237, 238
  see also suffragettes
Mill, John Stuart, 11-12, 16, 23, 81, 104, 143, 144, 184, 186-7, 216-17, 232
Miller, Emma, 119-28 *passim*, 178, 183, 184, 219-20, 232, 238
Miller, Florence Fenwick, 150
mock elections, Victoria, 152
mock parliaments, Victoria, 155
Moginie, Mrs, 118
Montefiore, Dora, 16, 32, 78, 79, 85, 98, 184, 204, 206, 232, 233, 234-5
Montgomery, Mrs, 108
moral superiority of women, 30, 68, 70, 71, 83, 84, 107-8, 194-6, 200-1, 215-16, 217
  see also pedestal image; utopianism
Moran, Charles, 48, 49-50, 52, 191
Moran, Cardinal Patrick, 182
Morgan, Arthur, 127-8
Morgans, Alfred, 52-3
Moore, Mary Anne, 94
Morehead, Boyd, 116
Mott, Lucretia, 7, 8, 11
municipal candidature for women, 143, 224
municipal reform 94
municipal vote for women, 224
  Victoria, 131-2, 173
  Western Australia, 45
Munro, James, 59, 139, 140
Murcott, Ada, 104

National American Woman Suffrage Association, 8-9, 241
National Council of Women
  Edith Cowan, 224
  New South Wales, 81, 94, 149
  Queensland, 128
  Rose Scott, 232
  Tasmania, 108
  Victoria, 157, 161, 164
  Vida Goldstein, 149
  Western Australia, 224
National Defence League, 126
National Union of Women Suffrage Societies, Britain, 14, 233, 238-9
National Woman Suffrage Association, North America, 8-9
National Women's Trade Union League, North America, 240-1
nationalism, 19, 199-200, 216

Negro suffrage, North America, 8, 9
Nelson, Hugh, 121
New Woman, The, 134, 190-1
  see also feminism, analysis of
New Zealand
  attendance at Commonwealth Conventions, 32, 59
  frontier theory, 212, 214
  woman suffrage in, 14, 36, 40-1, 84, 95, 117, 194, 231-2
  women as parliamentary candidates, 96, 236, 237
  see also Australian and New Zealand Women Voters' Association; Stout, Lady Anna
Nicholls, Elizabeth, 31, 39, 125
  biography and character, 29-30
  opinions, 34, 153, 179, 201, 220
  visits Western Australia, 47, 50
  Women's Christian Temperance Union, 29, 34-5, 36, 40, 60, 104, 107, 121, 153
Nolan, Sara, 75, 179
non-party women, 177-8, 220-1
  New South Wales, 95, 98
  Queensland, 122, 126
  South Australia, 40, 41-2
  Tasmania, 109
  Victoria, 152, 155, 163
  see also Women's Federal Political Association, Victoria; Women's Political Association, Victoria
North American suffrage campaign, 6-10, 16, 213, 214, 239-42
  Australian women in, 240-1
Norton, Caroline, 10

Oakley-Fish, Mrs, 183
O'Connell, May, 117-18, 119
O'Connor, Edward, 63, 65
one-adult-one-vote, agitation for
  Commonwealth, 61, 64
  Tasmania, 106
  Queensland, 118, 120, 122, 126-7
one-man-one-vote, *see* plural vote
Onslow, Madeline, 50-1, 53, 55, 232, 233, 238
Our Federation, 153
O'Reilly, Dowell, 87
O'Sullivan, Edward, 89

pacifism, attitude of suffragists, 135, 201
Pankhurst, Adela, 212
Pankhurst, Christabel, 234
Pankhurst, Emmeline, 234
Pankhursts, 14, 234, 235, 237
Parke, Sir Henry, 69, 70-2, 83, 84, 89, 187
Parkes, Hilma Moluyneux, 98
Parliamentary candidature for women, 16, 178-80, 213, 222-7
  Commonwealth, 178

Edith Cowan, 223-4
Enid Lyons, 225-6
granting of the right to stand, 222-3
New South Wales, 69, 84, 87, 90, 95-6
Queensland, 116-17
South Australia, 24, 25, 26-7, 35, 38, 41
Tasmania, 107-8, 109
Victoria, 144-5, 155, 162, 163
Vida Goldstein, 153-4, 163
Western Australia, 55
Parliamentary procedure, notes on, 19-20
party politics, women, 219-21, 223-8
  see also conservatism; Labor Party, women; Liberalism; non-party women
Paul, Alice, 242
Paulson, Ross, 212
Payne, Mrs, 122
Peacock, Alexander, 159
Pearson, Karl, 218
pedestal image, 38, 76, 196, 218
  see also moral superiority
petitions, anti-suffrage, 92, 147-8, 162
petitions for woman suffrage
  Britain, 6, 11, 13
  Commonwealth Conventions 59, 61, 63, 106
  New South Wales, 81, 82, 88
  Queensland, 116, 119, 121
  South Australia, 38
  Tasmania, 106, 107
  Victoria, 140, 142, 157, 162
  Western Australia, 54
philanthropy, 9, 10, 108, 149, 196, 239
Philp, Robert, 123-5, 127
Piddington, William, 69-70
Piesse, Frederick, 50
Pilkington, Robert, 243
Pitt, William, 161
Playford, Thomas, 25, 33, 35, 64
plural vote, 17, 172-6
  Britain, 13, 17
  Commonwealth, 59
  New South Wales, 69, 71-2, 81-2, 86
  Queensland, 17, 113, 114, 116, 119, 121-6 *passim*, 174
  South Australia, 22-3
  Tasmania, 103, 109
  Victoria, 131, 137, 140, 142, 143, 147, 164
  Western Australia, 45, 55-6, 71-2
  see also baby vote; property vote
Political Labor League, New South Wales, 94
postal vote, South Australia, 39
Pottie, Eliza, 74, 75, 79, 85
Powell, Miss, 157
Power, Francis, 179
Powers, Charles, 120
Prendergast, George, 159, 160-1

press, attitudes
  New South Wales, 79, 82, 85, 86
  to Vida Goldstein's candidature, 133-4
  Western Australia, 52
Press, Mrs, 150
Preston, Annie, 201
prisons, women, 206
professions, women, 9, 12
  law, 203, 224
  medicine, 94, 103
  see also university education, women
prohibition, 15, 60, 140, 180-1
  in North America, 28, 181
  see also liquor interests; liquor reform
property vote, 17, 23-4, 30, 45, 46, 69, 103-5, 131-2, 172-4, 175
  see also plural vote
proportional representation, 32-3, 40, 41, 60
Propsting, William, 109
prostitution, 18, 104, 105, 137, 191, 207-8
  see also age of consent; Contagious Diseases Acts; Lock hospitals
Proud, Cornelius, 39-40
Pulsford, Edward, 64

Queen Victoria Hospital, 142, 146
Queensland Women's Electoral League, 126, 220
Quinlan, Timothy, 47

Rae, Arthur, 61, 82, 83, 84, 88, 175, 183, 195, 235-6
rape, 136
  see also violence against women
Reed, Carrie, 147
Reeves, William Pember, 212, 213, 214, 237
referenda, proposed for woman suffrage, 192-4
  New South Wales, 90
  South Australia, 35-7, 39, 41, 47
  Victoria, 143
referenda, Commonwealth Constitution, see Constitutions, Commonwealth
Reid, George, 87-9, 95
Rennick, Mrs, 136
Representative Government, 12, 186-7
  see also Mill, John Stuart
Richardson, John, 132
ridicule, 26, 47, 71, 78, 92, 107, 120, 132, 136, 179, 190-2
Rischbieth, Bessie, 208, 219, 228
Robertson, Dr Grace, 85-6
Robertson, John, 70
Rooke, Henry, 107, 178
Rooke, Jessie, 105-10 *passim*, 189-90
Roosevelt, President Theodore, 149
Rose, Thomas, 90
Rousseau, Jean Jacques, 5, 113-14
Ruffin, Josephine St Pierre, 9

rural interests, 176, 183
  Western Australia, 53

Salmon, Captain Charles, 192
Salvana, Miss, 155
Scherk, Johann, 31
School Boards of Advice, Victorian women on, 143
Scott, Rose, 39, 51, 61, 126, 181, 240
  biography and character, 80-1, 184, 204
  correspondence, 51, 62, 70, 74, 82-3, 87, 89, 92, 94, 96, 97, 114, 181, 183, 189, 227, 232
  Louisa Lawson, 79, 83, 97
  opinions, 80-1, 90, 95, 126, 184, 187, 192, 195, 200, 201, 204, 216, 220, 224, 228, 238
  surveys women, 204, 206
  Vida Goldstein, 148, 149, 153, 201, 225
  Womanhood Suffrage League, 79-89 *passim*, 93-8 *passim*, 141
Searle, Ethel, 104
secret ballot, 22
secularism, 133, 135, 141
See, John, 95-7
Selwyn, Dean Arthur, 83
Selwyn, Rose, 83
Seneca Falls Declaration, 7, 10
sentimentalism, 36, 52, 84
settlement movement, 9, 239
Sharpe, Lucinda, *see* Lane, William
Shepparton, Mrs, 159-60
Sholl, R., 46-7, 173
Simpson, J., 79, 81
Smith, Mary, 6
Smith, Colonel Thomas, 139
Smyth, Brettena, 137-8, 141, 145, 146, 163, 200
social Darwinism, 196
Socialism
  Britain, 14
  Dora Montefiore, 234
  New South Wales, 82, 93
  Victoria, 155, 164
  William Lane, 113
Society for the Promotion of Social Purity, South Australia, 26, 27
Soltau, Grace, 104
South Australian influence on woman suffrage, *see* Commonwealth Constitutional Convention (1897–8)
Spence, Catherine Helen
  as speaker, 89, 150
  biography and character, 32-3, 40, 199
  John Stuart Mill, 187, 217
  opinions, 34, 195
  political candidacy, 41, 60, 153, 184
  religion, 181
  visits USA and England, 35, 39, 187

Spence, William Guthrie, 61
Spruson, Wilfred, 20, 90
Stanbridge, William, 173
Stanton, Elizabeth Cady, 7, 8, 9, 11, 239
Star, Queensland, 114, 119
Staughton, Samuel, 176-7
Steel, Emily, 74
Stirling, Dr Edward, 23-7 *passim*, 173, 178, 187, 189, 215
Stone, Constance, 204, 233
Stone, Lucy, 7, 8, 189, 232
Stout, Lady Anna, 231-2
Street, Jessie, 226-7, 237-8
Strong, Dr Charles, 145, 146, 181
Subjection of Women, 12, 23, 187
  see also Mill, John Stuart
suffragettes, 4, 15-16, 234
  see also militancy
Suttor, Francis, 95, 96
Suttor, William, 79, 81
Swinburne, George, 159
Sydney Rescue Society, 56
Sydney University Women's College, 72, 81
Sydney Women's Literary Society, 78
symbolism of the vote, 30, 192, 215-16, 240

Taylor, Harriet, 12
Taylor, Dr William, 118, 120
Teachers' Federation, 94
temperance movement, 56, 60, 68-9, 75, 88, 104, 133, 139, 180
  see also Woman's Christian Temperance Union
terminology, 3-4
  see also suffragettes
Thompson, William, 10
Throssell, Ada, 51
Throssell, George, 47, 51
Tilley, Miss, 194, 233
Tozer, John, 121
trade unions, female, 217, 219, 203-4
  Britain, 13
  New South Wales, 94
  North America, 9, 241
  Queensland, 118, 119
  South Australia, 30-1
  Victoria, 133, 149, 154
trade unions, male, 18, 174-6, 203-4, 219
  Britain, 13
  New South Wales, 76
  Queensland, 116
  Victoria, 133, 138-9, 146
  Western Australia, 47, 49, 124
  see also Trades and Labor Councils
Trades and Labor Congress of Australasia, 82, 154, 175
Trades and Labor Congress of Western Australia, 53, 176
Trades and Labor Councils, 174-6

INDEX 263

New South Wales, 82
Queensland, 113
South Australia, 24, 25, 31-2, 33
Victoria, 138-9
Western Australia, 47, 49
Traylen, W., 47
Trenwith, William, 138-9, 161
Trundle, Eleanor, 118, 119, 121, 128, 187
Turner, George, 142, 143-4, 147

United Branches of the Womanhood Suffrage League, New South Wales, 96
United Council for Woman Suffrage, Victoria, 63, 142-5, 146, 148, 151, 156-7, 164
United Liberal Party, Victoria, 158-61 *passim*
university education, women, 11, 23, 79, 136, 114, 138, 162, 203
see also education, women; professions, women
Upper Houses, *see* Legislative Councils
Utah, 9, 204
see also frontier theory
Utopianism, 22, 135, 195
see also moral superiority of women

Vale, Mr, 122
Victoria, Queen, 12-13
Victorian Woman's Suffrage League, 141, 164
Victorian Women's Suffrage Society, 136-7, 138, 140-1, 187
vilification, *see* ridicule
Vindication of the Rights of Woman, 5, 6
see also Wollstonecraft, Mary
violence against women, 114, 135, 136, 142, 206
domestic, 7, 194
Voter's Right, Victoria, 161-2
voting patterns, women, 221-2

Waddell, Thomas, 71
wages and working conditions for women, 7, 9, 10-11, 13, 18, 24, 30-5 *passim*, 49, 72, 93, 98, 113, 114, 147-8, 176, 191, 194, 199, 201, 203-4
see also equal pay for women
Want, John, 95
Ward, Ebenezer, 38, 198
Ward, Elizabeth, 74-5, 84, 85, 92, 179-80
Warren, John, 31, 33-4
Watson, John, 156
Webb, Beatrice, 142
Webb, Sidney, 142
Webster, Ellen, 174
Webster, Mrs, 137
West, Rebecca, 218
Wheeler, Anna, 10
Whelan, Carrie, 240

Willard, Frances, 28
Williams, Agnes, 117, 126, 128, 178, 232
Windeyer, Margaret, 77, 79, 97
Windeyer, Lady Mary, 79, 82-3, 84, 85, 86, 183
Willis, William, 87
Wilson, Edward, 131
Wilson, President Thomas Woodrow, 242
Wise, Bernard, 92
Wollstonecraft, Mary, 5
Wolstoneholme, Maybanke, 78-9, 83-4, 85-6, 88, 192, 218, 232
Woman Suffrage Declaration Committee, Victoria, 157, 159, 160, 162
Womanhood Suffrage League, New South Wales, 60, 74-5, 79-89, 93-8 *passim*, 141, 144, 178, 183, 212, 218
Woman's Bible, 9
Woman's Christian Temperance Union, 3-4, 8, 15, 28-9, 177, 180-4, 207, 212, 232-3
Commonwealth vote, 60, 61, 63
New South Wales, 68, 74-5, 84, 88, 89, 90, 95, 97, 98, 197-8
Queensland, 117, 119, 120-3, 126, 128, 178, 179, 187
South Australia, 28, 30, 31, 34-5, 36, 39-40, 41-2
Tasmania, 104, 107-8, 110, 180
Victoria, 139-41, 152-3, 157, 163, 164
Western Australia, 45-6, 47, 48, 50, 51, 53, 55, 180
see also temperance movement
Woman's Electoral and Political Educational League, New South Wales, 97-8
Woman's Equal Franchise Association, Queensland, 62-3, 65, 117-19, 120, 121, 122, 126, 128, 175, 178, 183, 219-20
Woman's Franchise Association, New South Wales, *see* Dawn Club
Woman's Franchise League, Western Australia, 53-4, 55, 223
Woman's Sphere, *see* Australian Woman's Sphere
woman's sphere, 18
allowed her to vote, 29, 198-9, 200, 216
excluded her from the vote, 24, 25, 49, 50, 52, 182, 196-9, 215
Woman's Suffrage Journal, New South Wales, 81
Woman's Suffrage League, New South Wales, 75
Woman's Suffrage League, Queensland, 119, 120, 122, 123, 128
Woman's Suffrage League, Victoria, *see* Victorian Woman's Suffrage League
Woman's Voice, New South Wales, 86
Women Workers' Political Organisation, Queensland, 126
Women's Electoral League, Queensland, *see* Queensland Women's Electoral League
Women's Federal Political Association, Victoria, 152, 153, 155
Women's Freedom League, Britain, 236
Women's Liberal League, New South Wales, 98
Women's Political and Social Crusade, Victoria, 149
Women's Political Association, Tasmania, 110
Women's Political Association, Victoria, 155, 156, 157, 159
Women's Progressive Association, New South Wales, 93-5, 96, 97, 177
Women's Progressive Leagues, Victoria, 141, 143, 146, 148, 149, 152, 164
Women's Social and Political Reform League, Victoria, 144
Women's Social and Political Union, Britain, 234, 235, 237, 242
Women's Suffrage Association, Tasmania, 109-10
Women's Suffrage League, Queensland, 114-16
Women's Suffrage League, South Australia, 26-7, 30-6 *passim*, 39-40, 174, 181, 177-8
Women's Suffrage Society, Victoria, *see* Victorian Women's Suffrage Society
working conditions for women, *see* wages and working conditions for women
Working Women's Trade Union, South Australia, 30-1, 34-5
Workingmen's Political League, Victoria, 138
Woodhull, Victoria, 8
Wright, Frances, 6
Wrixon, Henry, 132, 144-5
Wyoming, 9, 214
see also frontier theory

Zadow, Augusta, 30-1, 35, 183
Zeal, Sir William, 144, 161